Professional Examinations

Managerial Level

Paper P2

Management Accounting Decision Management

CIMA Study Text

KAPLAN
PUBLISHING
FOULKS LYNCH

British Library Cataloguing-in-Publication Data

A catalogue record for this book is available from the British Library.

Kaplan Publishing Foulks Lynch
Unit 2 The Business Centre
Molly Millars Lane
Wokingham
RG41 2QZ

ISBN 1 84390 906 5

978 1 84390 906 4

Printed and bound in Great Britain.

Acknowledgements

We are grateful to the Chartered Institute of Management Accountants, the Association of Chartered Certified Accountants and the Institute of Chartered Accountants in England and Wales for permission to reproduce past examination questions. The answers have been prepared by Kaplan Publishing Foulks Lynch.

INTRODUCTION

This is the third edition of this Study Text. Our aim was to produce an even better, more syllabus-tailored, exam-focused and student-friendly range of publications. To achieve this we have worked closely with numerous CIMA tutors and experts, and we are confident that this Study Text forms the best resource for your exam preparation.

It covers all syllabus topics to the required depth, and contains a wealth of exam-style and practice questions. Throughout the text you will find plenty of relevant examples, activities, diagrams and charts. These will put the subject matter in context and help you absorb the material easily.

The following points explain some of the concepts we had in mind when developing the layout of this book.

DEFINITION

- **Definitions**. The text defines key words and concepts, placing them in the margin with a clear heading, as on the left. The purpose of including these definitions is to focus your attention on the point being covered.

KEY POINT

- **Key points**. Also in the margin, you will see key points at regular intervals. The purpose of these is to summarise concisely the key material being covered.
- **Activities**. The text involves you in the learning process with a series of activities designed to catch your attention and make you concentrate and respond. The feedback to activities is at the end of each chapter.
- **Self-test questions**. At the end of each chapter there is a series of self-test questions. The purpose of these is to help you revise some of the key elements of the chapter. All the answers to these questions can be found in the text.
- **End of chapter questions**. At the end of each chapter we include examination-type questions. These will give you a very good idea of the sort of thing the examiner will ask and will test your understanding of what has been covered.

Good luck with your studies!

CONTENTS

SYLLABUS AND LEARNING OUTCOMES

Syllabus outline

The syllabus comprises:

Topic and study weighting

A	Financial Information for Short-term Decision Making	30%
B	Financial Information for Long-term Decision Making	25%
C	The Treatment of Uncertainty in Decision Making	15%
D	Cost Planning and Analysis for Competitive Advantage	30%

Learning aims

Students should be able to:

- separate costs into their fixed and variable components and use these in break-even analysis and in decision-making under multiple constraints;
- establish relevant cash flows for decision making and apply these principles in a variety of contexts including process/product viability and pricing including evaluation of the tension between short-term, 'contribution based' pricing and long-term, 'return on investment' pricing;
- develop relevant cash flows for long-term projects taking account of inflation and taxation where appropriate, evaluate projects using discounting and traditional methods, critically assess alternative methods of evaluation and place evaluation techniques in the context of the whole process of investment decision making;
- apply learning curves in forecasting future costs and the techniques of activity-based management, target costing and value analysis in managing future costs and evaluate the actual and potential impacts of contemporary techniques such as JIT, TOC and TQM on efficiency, inventory and cost;
- undertake sensitivity analysis and assess the impact of risk in decision models using probability analysis, expected value tables and decision trees as appropriate;
- discuss externally oriented management accounting techniques and apply these techniques to the value chain, 'gain sharing' arrangements and customer/channel profitability analysis.

Below we reproduce the learning outcomes and syllabus content. The numbers in brackets denote the chapters in which each topic is covered.

Learning outcomes and syllabus content

A – Financial Information for Short-term Decision Making – 30%

Learning outcomes

On completion of their studies students should be able to:

(i) discuss the principles of decision making including the identification of relevant cash flows and their use alongside non-quantifiable factors in making rounded judgements; (2)

(ii) explain the particular issues that arise in pricing decisions and the conflict between 'marginal cost' principles and the need for full recovery of all costs incurred; (4)

(iii) apply an approach to pricing based on profit maximisation in imperfect markets and evaluate the financial consequences of alternative pricing strategies; (4)

(iv) explain the possible conflicts between cost accounting for profit reporting and stock valuation and the convenient availability of information for decision-making; (1)

(v) explain why joint costs must be allocated to final products for financial reporting purposes, but why this is unhelpful when decisions concerning process and product viability have to be taken; (1)

(vi) discuss the usefulness of dividing costs into variable and fixed components in the context of short-term decision making; (2)

(vii) apply variable/fixed cost analysis in multiple product contexts to break-even analysis and product mix decision making, including circumstances where there are multiple constraints and linear programming methods are needed to reach 'optimal' solutions; (1)

(viii) discuss the meaning of 'optimal' solutions and show how linear programming methods can be employed for profit maximising, revenue maximising and satisfying objectives. (3)

Syllabus content

- Relevant cash flows and their use in short-term decisions, typically concerning acceptance/rejection of contracts, pricing and cost/benefit comparisons. (2)
- The importance of strategic, intangible and non-financial judgements in decision-making. (2)

- Pricing decisions for profit maximising in imperfect markets. (Note: tabular methods of solution are acceptable). (4)
- Pricing strategies and the financial consequences of market skimming, premium pricing, penetration pricing, loss leaders, product bundling/optional extras and product differentiation to appeal to different market segments. (4)
- The allocation of joint costs and decisions concerning process and product viability based on relevant costs and revenues. (1)
- Multi-product break-even analysis, including break-even and profit/volume charts, contribution/sales ratio, margin of safety etc. (1)
- Simple product mix analysis in situations where there are limitations on product/service demand and one other production constraint. (3)
- Linear programming for more complex situations involving multiple constraints. Solution by graphical methods of two variable problems, together with understanding of the mechanics of simplex solution, shadow prices etc. (Note: questions requiring the full application of the simplex algorithm will not be set although candidates should be able to formulate an initial tableau, interpret a final simplex tableau and apply the information contained in a final tableau.) (3)

B – Financial Information for Long-term Decision Making – 25%

Learning outcomes

On completion of their studies students should be able to:

(i) explain the processes involved in making long-term decisions; (10)

(ii) apply the principles of relevant cash flow analysis to long-run projects that continue for several years; (10)

(iii) calculate project cash flows, accounting for tax and inflation, and apply perpetuities to derive 'end of project' value where appropriate; (10)

(iv) apply activity-based costing techniques to derive approximate 'long-run' product or service costs appropriate for use in strategic decision making; (10)

(v) explain the financial consequences of dealing with long-run projects, in particular the importance of accounting for the 'time value of money'; (9)

(vi) evaluate project proposals using the techniques of investment appraisal; (9)

(vii) compare, contrast and evaluate the alternative techniques of investment appraisal; (9)

(viii) evaluate and rank projects that might be mutually exclusive, involve unequal lives and/or be subject to capital rationing; (11)

(ix) apply sensitivity analysis to cash flow parameters to identify those to which net present value is particularly sensitive; (11)

(x) produce decision support information for management, integrating financial and non-financial considerations. (11)

Syllabus content

- The process of investment decision-making, including origination of proposals, creation of capital budgets, go/no go decisions on individual projects (where judgements on qualitative issues interact with financial analysis), and post audit of completed projects. (10)
- Generation of relevant project cash flows taking account of inflation, tax, and 'final' project value where appropriate. (10)
- Activity-based costing to derive approximate 'long-run' costs appropriate for use in strategic decision making. (10)
- The techniques of investment appraisal: payback, discounted payback, accounting rate of return, net present value and internal rate of return. (9)
- Application of the techniques of investment appraisal to project cash flows and evaluation of the strengths and weaknesses of the techniques. (9)
- Sensitivity analysis to identify the input variables that most affect the chosen measure of project worth (payback, ARR, NPV or IRR). (11)
- Methods of dealing with particular problems: the use of annuities in comparing projects with unequal lives and the profitability index in capital rationing situations. (11)

C – The Treatment of Uncertainty in Decision Making – 15%

Learning outcomes

On completion of their studies students should be able to:

(i) evaluate the impact of uncertainty and risk on decision models that may be based on CVP analysis, relevant cash flows, learning curves, discounting techniques etc.; (5)

(ii) apply sensitivity analysis on both short and long-run decision models to identify variables that might have significant impacts on project outcomes; (5)

(iii) analyse risk and uncertainty by calculating expected values and standard deviations together with probability tables and histograms; (5)

(iv) prepare expected value tables and ascertain the value of information; (5)

(v) prepare and apply decision trees. (5)

Syllabus content

- The nature of risk and uncertainty. (5)
- Sensitivity analysis in decision modelling and the use of computer software for 'what if' analysis. (5)
- Assignment of probabilities to key variables in decision models. (5)
- Analysis of probabilistic models and interpretation of distributions of project outcomes. (5)
- Expected value tables and the value of information. (5)
- Decision trees for multi-stage decision problems. (5)

D – Cost Planning and Analysis for Competitive Advantage – 30%

Learning outcomes

On completion of their studies students should be able to:

(i) compare and contrast value analysis and functional cost analysis; (6)

(ii) evaluate the impacts of just-in-time production, the theory of constraints and total quality management on efficiency, inventory and cost; (6)

(iii) explain the concepts of continuous improvement and Kaizen costing that are central to total quality management and prepare cost of quality reports; (6)

(iv) explain and apply learning and experience curves to estimate time and cost for new products and services; (6)

(v) apply the techniques of activity-based management in identifying cost drivers/activities and explain how process re-engineering can be used to eliminate non-value adding activities and reduce activity costs; (8)

(vi) explain how target costs can be derived from target prices and describe the relationship between target costs and standard costs; (7)

(vii) explain the concept of life cycle costing and how life cycle costs interact with marketing strategies at each stage of the life cycle; (7)

(viii) explain the concept of the value chain and discuss the management of contribution/profit generated throughout the chain; (7)

(ix) discuss gain-sharing arrangements whereby contractors and customers benefit if contract targets for cost, delivery etc. are beaten; (7)

(x) apply activity-based costing ideas to analyse 'direct customer profitability' and extend this analysis to distribution channel profitability; (8)

(xi) apply Pareto analysis as a convenient technique for identifying key elements of data and in presenting the results of other analyses, such as activity-based profitability calculations. (8)

Syllabus content

- Value analysis and quality function deployment. (6)
- The benefits of just-in-time production, total quality management and theory of constraints and the implications of these methods for decision-making in the 'new manufacturing environment'. (6)
- Kaizen costing, continuous improvement and cost of quality reporting. (6)
- Learning curves and their use in predicting product/service costs, including derivation of the learning rate and the learning index. (6)
- Activity-based management in the analysis of overhead and its use in improving the efficiency of repetitive overhead activities. (8)
- Target costing. (7)
- Life cycle costing and implications for marketing strategies. (7)
- The value chain and supply chain management, including the trend to outsource manufacturing operations to Eastern Europe and the Far East. (7)
- Gain sharing arrangements in situations where, because of the size of the project, a limited number of contractors or security issues (e.g. in defence work), normal competitive pressures do not apply. (7)
- The use of direct and activity-based cost methods in tracing costs to 'cost objects', such as customers or distribution channels, and the comparison of such costs with appropriate revenues to establish 'tiered' contribution levels, as in the activity-based cost hierarchy. (8)
- Pareto analysis. (8)

HELPING YOU WITH YOUR STUDIES

Take control

Create favourable conditions and a positive attitude

- Plan to study at specific times each week. Devise a schedule and set goals.
- Choose a location where you can concentrate.
- Ask questions to be an active learner and to generate interest.
- Continually challenge yourself.

Study

Develop good learning techniques

- Use the **SQR3** method – it works with reading accountancy and management subjects. **Survey** (get an overall picture before studying in detail), **Question** (important things to learn are usually answers to questions), **Read** actively (to answer your questions), **Recite** (recall what you have read and connect topics) and **Review** (what you have covered and accomplished).
- Use the **MURDER** method – **Mood** (set the right mood), **Understand** (issues covered and make note of any uncertain bits), **Recall** (stop and put what you have learned into your own words), **Digest** (go back and reconsider the information), **Expand** (read relevant articles and newspapers), **Review** (go over the material you covered to consolidate the knowledge).
- Create **associations** and analogies to relate new ideas to what you already know and to improve understanding.

Practise

Practise under exam conditions

- **Practise** as much as possible – go through exam style and standard questions under exam conditions.

Prepare for the exam

Develop exam technique

- Be familiar with the structure of your exam and know how to approach and answer the questions.

THE EXAMINATION

Format of the examination:

There will be a written examination paper of three hours, plus 20 minutes' reading time, with the following sections:

	Marks
Section A: a variety of compulsory objective test questions, each worth between 2 and 4 marks. Mini-scenarios may be given, to which a group of questions relate.	20
Section B: three compulsory medium answer questions, each worth 10 marks. Short scenarios may be given, to which some or all questions relate.	30
Section C: two questions, from a choice of three, each worth 25 marks. Short scenarios may be given, to which questions relate.	50
TOTAL	100

Note: The first 20 minutes of your exam is reading time. During reading time you can read, annotate and highlight the question paper, but you are not allowed to open the answer book, write in the answer book, add any loose sheets/supplements to your answer book or use a calculator. This change to the duration of the exams has been introduced by CIMA after we published our Exam Kits. Therefore you will notice that the exam length stated in this section will differ from the one stated in the Exam Kit. The length of the exam stated here is the correct one.

Before sitting the exam make sure that you are familiar with CIMA's *Exam Rules & Regulations*. You can find this document on the CIMA website (www.cimaglobal.com).

Examination tips

- Spend the first few minutes of the examination **reading the paper** and where you have a **choice of questions**, decide which ones you will do.
- **Divide the time** you spend on questions in proportion to the marks on offer. One suggestion is to allocate 1½ minutes to each mark available, so a 10-mark question should be completed in 15 minutes.
- Unless you know exactly how to answer the question, spend some time **planning** your answer. Stick to the question and **tailor your answer** to what you are asked.
- **Fully explain** all your points but be **concise**. Set out all workings **clearly and neatly**, and state briefly what you are doing. Don't write out the question.
- If you do not understand what a question is asking, **state your assumptions**.
- If you **get completely stuck** with a question, leave space in your answer book and **return to it later.**
- Towards the end of the examination spend the last **five minutes** reading through your answers and **making any additions or corrections**.

Answering the questions

- **Multiple-choice questions**: Read the questions carefully and work through any calculations required. If you don't know the answer, eliminate those options you know are incorrect and see if the answer becomes more obvious. Remember that only one answer to a multiple-choice question can be right!
- **Objective test questions**: These might ask for numerical answers, but could also involve paragraphs of text which require you to fill in a number of missing blanks, or for you to write a definition of a word or phrase, or to enter a formula. Others may give a definition followed by a list of possible key words relating to that description.
- **Essay questions**: Make a quick plan in your answer book and under each main point list all the relevant facts you can think of. Then write out your answer developing each point fully. Your essay should have a clear structure; it should contain a brief introduction, a main section and a conclusion. Be concise. It is better to write a little about a lot of different points than a great deal about one or two points.
- **Computations**: It is essential to include all your workings in your answers. Many computational questions require the use of a standard format: company profit and loss account, balance sheet and cash flow statement for example. Be sure you know these formats thoroughly before the examination and use the layouts that you see in the answers given in this book. If you are asked to comment or make recommendations on a computation, you must do so. There are important marks to be gained here. Even if your computation contains mistakes, you may still gain marks if your reasoning is correct.
- **Reports, memos and other documents**: Some questions ask you to present your answer in the form of a report or a memo or other document. Use the correct format – there could be easy marks to gain here.

MATHS TABLES AND FORMULAE

Present value table

Present value of £1 i.e. that is $(1+r)^{-n}$ where r = interest rate; n = number of periods until payment or receipt.

Periods (n)	Interest rates (r)									
	1%	2%	3%	4%	5%	6%	7%	8%	9%	10%
1	0.990	0.980	0.971	0.962	0.952	0.943	0.935	0.926	0.917	0.909
2	0.980	0.961	0.943	0.925	0.907	0.890	0.873	0.857	0.842	0.826
3	0.971	0.942	0.915	0.889	0.864	0.840	0.816	0.794	0.772	0.751
4	0.961	0.924	0.888	0.855	0.823	0.792	0.763	0.735	0.708	0.683
5	0.951	0.906	0.863	0.822	0.784	0.747	0.713	0.681	0.650	0.621
6	0.942	0.888	0.837	0.790	0.746	0705	0.666	0.630	0.596	0.564
7	0.933	0.871	0.813	0.760	0.711	0.665	0.623	0.583	0.547	0.513
8	0.923	0.853	0.789	0.731	0.677	0.627	0.582	0.540	0.502	0.467
9	0.914	0.837	0.766	0.703	0.645	0.592	0.544	0.500	0.460	0.424
10	0.905	0.820	0.744	0.676	0.614	0.558	0.508	0.463	0.422	0.386
11	0.896	0.804	0.722	0.650	0.585	0.527	0.475	0.429	0.388	0.350
12	0.887	0.788	0.701	0.625	0.557	0.497	0.444	0.397	0.356	0.319
13	0.879	0.773	0.681	0.601	0.530	0.469	0.415	0.368	0.326	0.290
14	0.870	0.758	0.661	0.577	0.505	0.442	0.388	0.340	0.299	0.263
15	0.861	0.743	0.642	0.555	0.481	0.417	0.362	0.315	0.275	0.239
16	0.853	0.728	0.623	0.534	0.458	0.394	0.339	0.292	0.252	0.218
17	0.844	0.714	0.605	0.513	0.436	0.371	0.317	0.270	0.231	0.198
18	0.836	0.700	0.587	0.494	0.416	0.350	0.296	0.250	0.212	0.180
19	0.828	0.686	0.570	0.475	0.396	0.331	0.277	0.232	0.194	0.164
20	0.820	0.673	0.554	0.456	0.377	0.312	0.258	0.215	0.178	0.149

Periods (n)	Interest rates (r)									
	11%	12%	13%	14%	15%	16%	17%	18%	19%	20%
1	0.901	0.893	0.885	0.877	0.870	0.862	0.855	0.847	0.840	0.833
2	0.812	0.797	0.783	0.769	0.756	0.743	0.731	0.718	0.706	0.694
3	0.731	0.712	0.693	0.675	0.658	0.641	0.624	0.609	0.593	0.579
4	0.659	0.636	0.613	0.592	0.572	0.552	0.534	0.516	0.499	0.482
5	0.593	0.567	0.543	0.519	0.497	0.476	0.456	0.437	0.419	0.402
6	0.535	0.507	0.480	0.456	0.432	0.410	0.390	0.370	0.352	0.335
7	0.482	0.452	0.425	0.400	0.376	0.354	0.333	0.314	0.296	0.279
8	0.434	0.404	0.376	0.351	0.327	0.305	0.285	0.266	0.249	0.233
9	0.391	0.361	0.333	0.308	0.284	0.263	0.243	0.225	0.209	0.194
10	0.352	0.322	0.295	0.270	0.247	0.227	0.208	0.191	0.176	0.162
11	0.317	0.287	0.261	0.237	0.215	0.195	0.178	0.162	0.148	0.135
12	0.286	0.257	0.231	0.208	0.187	0.168	0.152	0.137	0.124	0.112
13	0.258	0.229	0.204	0.182	0.163	0.145	0.130	0.116	0.104	0.093
14	0.232	0.205	0.181	0.160	0.141	0.125	0.111	0.099	0.088	0.078
15	0.209	0.183	0.160	0.140	0.123	0.108	0.095	0.084	0.079	0.065
16	0.188	0.163	0.141	0.123	0.107	0.093	0.081	0.071	0.062	0.054
17	0.170	0.146	0.125	0.108	0.093	0.080	0.069	0.060	0.052	0.045
18	0.153	0.130	0.111	0.095	0.081	0.069	0.059	0.051	0.044	0.038
19	0.138	0.116	0.098	0.083	0.070	0.060	0.051	0.043	0.037	0.031
20	0.124	0.104	0.087	0.073	0.061	0.051	0.043	0.037	0.031	0.026

Cumulative present value of £1

This table shows the Present Value of £1 per annum, Receivable or Payable at the end of each year for *n* years $\frac{1-(1+r)^{-n}}{r}$

Periods (*n*)	Interest rates (*r*)									
	1%	2%	3%	4%	5%	6%	7%	8%	9%	10%
1	0.990	0.980	0.971	0.962	0.952	0.943	0.935	0.926	0.917	0.909
2	1.970	1.942	1.913	1.886	1.859	1.833	1.808	1.783	1.759	1.736
3	2.941	2.884	2.829	2.775	2.723	2.673	2.624	2.577	2.531	2.487
4	3.902	3.808	3.717	3.630	3.546	3.465	3.387	3.312	3.240	3.170
5	4.853	4.713	4.580	4.452	4.329	4.212	4.100	3.993	3.890	3.791
6	5.795	5.601	5.417	5.242	5.076	4.917	4.767	4.623	4.486	4.355
7	6.728	6.472	6.230	6.002	5.786	5.582	5.389	5.206	5.033	4.868
8	7.652	7.325	7.020	6.733	6.463	6.210	5.971	5.747	5.535	5.335
9	8.566	8.162	7.786	7.435	7.108	6.802	6.515	6.247	5.995	5.759
10	9.471	8.983	8.530	8.111	7.722	7.360	7.024	6.710	6.418	6.145
11	10.368	9.787	9.253	8.760	8.306	7.887	7.499	7.139	6.805	6.495
12	11.255	10.575	9.954	9.385	8.863	8.384	7.943	7.536	7.161	6.814
13	12.134	11.348	10.635	9.986	9.394	8.853	8.358	7.904	7.487	7.103
14	13.004	12.106	11.296	10.563	9.899	9.295	8.745	8.244	7.786	7.367
15	13.865	12.849	11.938	11.118	10.380	9.712	9.108	8.559	8.061	7.606
16	14.718	13.578	12.561	11.652	10.838	10.106	9.447	8.851	8.313	7.824
17	15.562	14.292	13.166	12.166	11.274	10.477	9.763	9.122	8.544	8.022
18	16.398	14.992	13.754	12.659	11.690	10.828	10.059	9.372	8.756	8.201
19	17.226	15.679	14.324	13.134	12.085	11.158	10.336	9.604	8.950	8.365
20	18.046	16.351	14.878	13.590	12.462	11.470	10.594	9.818	9.129	8.514

Periods (*n*)	Interest rates (*r*)									
	11%	12%	13%	14%	15%	16%	17%	18%	19%	20%
1	0.901	0.893	0.885	0.877	0.870	0.862	0.855	0.847	0.840	0.833
2	1.713	1.690	1.668	1.647	1.626	1.605	1.585	1.566	1.547	1.528
3	2.444	2.402	2.361	2.322	2.283	2.246	2.210	2.174	2.140	2.106
4	3.102	3.037	2.974	2.914	2.855	2.798	2.743	2.690	2.639	2.589
5	3.696	3.605	3.517	3.433	3.352	3.274	3.199	3.127	3.058	2.991
6	4.231	4.111	3.998	3.889	3.784	3.685	3.589	3.498	3.410	3.326
7	4.712	4.564	4.423	4.288	4.160	4.039	3.922	3.812	3.706	3.605
8	5.146	4.968	4.799	4.639	4.487	4.344	4.207	4.078	3.954	3.837
9	5.537	5.328	5.132	4.946	4.772	4.607	4.451	4.303	4.163	4.031
10	5.889	5.650	5.426	5.216	5.019	4.833	4.659	4.494	4.339	4.192
11	6.207	5.938	5.687	5.453	5.234	5.029	4.836	4.656	4.486	4.327
12	6.492	6.194	5.918	5.660	5.421	5.197	4.988	7.793	4.611	4.439
13	6.750	6.424	6.122	5.842	5.583	5.342	5.118	4.910	4.715	4.533
14	6.982	6.628	6.302	6.002	5.724	5.468	5.229	5.008	4.802	4.611
15	7.191	6.811	6.462	6.142	5.847	5.575	5.324	5.092	4.876	4.675
16	7.379	6.974	6.604	6.265	5.954	5.668	5.405	5.162	4.938	4.730
17	7.549	7.120	6.729	6.373	6.047	5.749	5.475	5.222	4.990	4.775
18	7.702	7.250	6.840	6.467	6.128	5.818	5.534	5.273	5.033	4.812
19	7.839	7.366	6.938	6.550	6.198	5.877	5.584	5.316	5.070	4.843
20	7.963	7.469	7.025	6.623	6.259	5.929	5.628	5.353	5.101	4.870

Formulae

Time series

Additive model:

Series = Trend + Seasonal + Random

Multiplicative model:

Series = Trend*Seasonal*Random

Regression analysis

The linear regression equation of Y on X is given by:

$$Y = a + bX \text{ or } Y - \overline{Y} = b(X - \overline{X}),$$

where:

$$b = \frac{\text{Covariance}(XY)}{\text{Variance}(X)} = \frac{n\sum XY - (\sum X)(\sum Y)}{n\sum X^2 - (\sum X)^2}$$

and $a = \overline{Y} - b\overline{X}$

or solve

$$\sum Y = na + b\sum X$$

$$\sum XY = a\sum X + b\sum X^2$$

Exponential $Y = ab^x$

Geometric $Y = aX^b$

Learning curve

$$Y_x = aX^b$$

where:

Y_x = the cumulative average time per unit to produce X units;

a = the time required to produce the first unit of output;

X = the cumulative number of units;

b = the index of learning.

The exponent b is defined as the log of the learning curve improvement rate divided by log 2.

Chapter 1

ABSORPTION AND MARGINAL COSTING

Syllabus content

- This chapter provides underpinning knowledge to syllabus section A.

Contents

1 Absorption costing

1.1 Introduction

DEFINITION

Absorption costing is a method of costing that, in addition to direct costs, assigns all, or a proportion of, production overhead costs to cost units by means of one or a number of overhead absorption rates.

You should already be familiar with the methods of absorption costing from your earlier studies. Under absorption costing (also called full absorption costing or total absorption costing (TAC)) fixed overheads are absorbed into cost units on the basis of a predetermined absorption rate.

Absorption costing is a method of costing that, in addition to direct costs, assigns all, or a proportion of, production overhead costs to cost units by means of one or a number of overhead absorption rates.

1.2 Absorption costing reviewed

Indirect costs, by their nature, cannot be economically identified with cost units. Absorption costing is a technique which is used to calculate a fair share of overheads to be attributed to each cost unit. The technique follows five steps:

Step 1 *Establishing cost centres.*

Cost centres are identified as production or service cost centres. Production cost centres work directly on the cost unit while service cost centres support the production activities but do not work directly on the cost unit. Note that absorption costing focuses on *production* overheads.

Step 2 *Allocating overhead costs to cost centres.*

Some costs can be **allocated** immediately, e.g. the salary of a cost centre supervisor or indirect materials issued to a cost centre. Allocation means costing whole items of expenditure to a cost centre.

Step 3 *Apportioning overhead costs to cost centres.*

Some costs are shared over several cost centres e.g. factory rent and rates or the salary of the overall factory manager. The basis for apportioning a total amount will be selected so that the charge to a specific centre will reflect, with reasonable accuracy, the benefit obtained by that centre from the cost incurred.

Step 4 *Reapportioning service cost centre costs to production cost centres.*

Service cost centre costs must be reapportioned to production cost centres so that all overheads can be finally attributed to the cost unit.

Step 5 *Absorbing production cost centre costs into cost units.*

The overhead to be absorbed by a particular cost unit will be calculated by dividing the production cost centre overhead for a period by an appropriate measure of the volume of production in the period.

If a cost centre produces dissimilar units the volume of production must be expressed in a common measurement, e.g. direct labour hours: if product X takes workers twice as long to make as product Y, it is reasonable that it should bear twice the overhead. When a cost unit passes through several centres, the overhead absorbed should be calculated separately for each centre.

Activity 1

A business has the following production and fixed overhead budgets for the coming year:

Production department	*1*	*2*
Fixed overhead	£240,000	£200,000
Total direct labour cost	£2,400,000	£4,000,000
Total direct materials cost	£200,000	£400,000

Department 1 labour is paid £5 per hour and department 2 labour £4 per hour. The variable production cost of an IC is as follows:

		£
Direct labour		
Department 1 : 3 hours		15
Department 2 : 1 hour		8
Direct materials		
Department 1 : 1 kg	@ £4 per kg	4
Department 2 : 2 kgs	@ £5 per kg	10
Variable overheads		7
		44

If fixed overheads are absorbed on the basis of direct labour cost, what is the fixed overhead cost per unit of IC?

Feedback to this activity is at the end of the chapter.

1.3 Under- and over-absorption

A predetermined overhead absorption rate is used to smooth out seasonal fluctuations in overhead costs, and to enable unit costs to be calculated quickly throughout the year.

$$\text{Predetermined overhead absorption rate} = \frac{\text{Budgeted overhead}}{\text{Budgeted volume}}$$

'Budgeted volume' may relate to units, direct labour hours, machine hours, etc.

If either or both of the actual overhead cost or activity volume differ from budget, the use of this rate is likely to lead to what is known as **under-absorption or over-absorption of overheads**.

Example

In year 9 the budget for the machine shop shows:

Overhead £60,000 Volume of activity 12,000 machine hours

In January year 9 the machine shop incurred £5,400 of overhead and 1,050 machine hours were worked.

Calculate the pre-determined absorption rate and the overhead under- or over-absorbed in January.

Solution

$$\text{Absorption rate} = \frac{\text{Budgeted overhead}}{\text{Budgeted volume}} = \frac{£60,000}{12,000 \text{ machine hours}}$$

$$= £5.00 \text{ per machine hour.}$$

	£
Actual overhead incurred per question	5,400
Overhead absorbed (1,050 machine hours × £5.00)	5,250
Under-absorbed overhead	150

The under-absorption in this example arises from a combination of two factors:

- actual overhead costs were £400 higher than the budgeted amount of (£60,000 ÷ 12) = £5,000 for the month
- actual volume was 50 hours greater than the budgeted (12,000 hours ÷ 12) = 1,000 hours for the month.

Activity 2

A company budgeted to produce 3,000 units of a single product in a period at a budgeted cost per unit as follows:

	£/unit
Direct costs	17
Fixed overhead	9
	26

In the period covered by the budget:

(a) actual production was 3,200 units

(b) actual fixed overhead expenditure was 5% above that budgeted – all other costs were as budgeted.

What was the amount, if any, of over- or under-absorption of fixed overhead?

Feedback to this activity is at the end of the chapter.

The unit cost of production will include overhead at the predetermined rate and, generally, overhead under- or over-absorbed will be shown as a separate item in the costing profit and loss account.

Example

A company budgets to produce and sell 120 units of product at a price of £100. The direct cost of production is £30 per unit. Indirect costs are £4,800. Actual production and sales are 100 units and actual overhead cost is £5,000. Calculate the profit for the period.

Solution

The full cost per unit is	£
Direct cost	30
Indirect cost £4,800/120	40
	70
Absorbed overhead 100 × £40	4,000
Actual overhead cost	5,000
Under-absorbed overhead	1,000

Costing profit and loss account

	£000
Sales	100
Cost of sales (units sold × unit cost including absorbed overheads)	70
	30
(Under-)/over-absorption	(1)
Operating profit	29

Tutorial note: The examination questions on this syllabus are likely to focus on comparing an absorption costing profit statement with a marginal costing profit statement. When you are producing an absorption costing profit statement remember to check for any under- or over-absorption.

2 Marginal costing

2.1 Introduction

Under **marginal costing** only variable costs are charged to cost units; fixed costs for a period are fully written off in the profit and loss account of the period in which they are incurred. Its special value is in recognising cost behaviour, and hence assisting in short term decision-making.

DEFINITION

Marginal costing is the accounting system in which variable costs are charged to cost units and fixed costs of the period are written off in full against the aggregate contribution. Its special value is in recognising cost behaviour, and hence assisting in decision-making.

Marginal costing is particularly useful because it highlights the difference in the behaviour of costs in the short run; variable costs change with the volume of output whereas fixed costs stay the same. For short-run decisions attention should be focused on those costs which change as a result of the decision. Therefore contribution, sales price less variable cost, is a central concept and is highlighted in the profit statement.

2.2 Marginal costing as an alternative to absorption costing

The fundamental difference between marginal and absorption costing is one of timing. In marginal costing fixed costs are written off in the period incurred. In absorption costing fixed costs are absorbed into units and written off in the period in which the units are sold.

Example

Company A produces a single product with the following budget.

Selling price	£10
Direct materials	£3 per unit
Direct wages	£2 per unit
Variable overhead	£1 per unit
Fixed overhead	£10,000 per unit

The fixed overhead absorption rate is based on volume of 5,000 units per month. Show the operating statement for the month, when 4,800 units were produced and sold under:

(a) absorption costing

(b) marginal costing.

Assume that costs were as budgeted.

Solution

(a) **Absorption costing**

	£
Sales (4,800 units)	48,000
Cost of sales (4,800 × £8) (W1)	38,400
Operating margin	9,600
Under-absorbed overhead (W2)	(400)
Operating profit	9,200

Workings

(W1) **Unit cost**

	£
Materials	3
Wages	2
Variable overheads	1
Fixed overheads ($\frac{£10,000}{5,000}$)	2
Cost per unit	8

(W2)

	£
Fixed overhead incurred	10,000
Fixed overhead absorbed (4,800 × £2)	9,600
Under-absorption	400

(b) **Marginal costing**

	£
Sales (4,800 × £10)	48,000
Variable cost of sales (4,800 × £6)	28,800
Contribution	19,200
Fixed costs	10,000
Operating profit	9,200

Note that the marginal costing statement highlights total contribution. This is a particularly useful figure for decision making which will be used in conjunction with many techniques.

In this example operating profit is the same under both methods. This will always be the case when there are no movements of stock in the period.

3 Absorption and marginal costing compared

3.1 The impact of stock changes on profit

Stock valuation under marginal costing is based on variable production costs only. This is in contrast to absorption costing where fixed production overhead costs are included in stock valuations using the predetermined absorption rate.

This will have an impact on profit levels when stock levels are changing. If stock is increasing then, using absorption costing, an element of overhead cost will be carried forward in the stock valuation and set against sales in a future period. This will result in absorption costing profit being higher than marginal costing profit in the period.

If stock levels are falling then costs using absorption costing will be higher, as a portion of a previous period's overhead is being charged against sales. This will result in profit being lower using absorption costing compared to marginal costing in the period.

Example

Use the data from the example in the previous section but now assume that production was 6,000 units, with sales of 4,800 units, so the absorption costing statement would show:

	£	£
Sales (4,800 × £10)		48,000
Cost of sales:		
Production 6,000 × £8	48,000	
Less: Closing stock 1,200 × £8	9,600	
		38,400
Operating margin		9,600
Over-absorbed fixed overhead (see working)		2,000
Operating profit		11,600

Working

	£
Fixed overheads incurred	10,000
Fixed overheads absorbed (6,000 × £2)	12,000
Over-absorption	2,000

The marginal costing statement would show:

	£	£
Sales 4,800 × £10		48,000
Cost of sales		
Production 6,000 × £6	36,000	
Less: Closing stock 1,200 × £6	7,200	
		28,800
Contribution		19,200
Fixed costs		10,000
Operating profit		9,200

KEY POINT

The difference in profit is due to the different stock valuations.

There is a difference in the profit calculated: using absorption costing the profit is £11,600 and using marginal costing the profit is £9,200.

The difference in profit is due to the different stock valuations.

	£	£
Profit under MC		9,200
Stock valuation (TAC) (1,200 × £8)	9,600	
Stock valuation (MC) (1,200 × £6)	7,200	
Difference in stock valuation (1,200 × £2)		2,400
Profit under TAC		11,600

Example

A company sells a product for £10, and incurs £4 of variable costs in its manufacture. The fixed costs are £900 per year and are absorbed on the basis of the normal production volume of 250 units per year. The results for the last four years, when no expenditure variances arose (i.e. all costs were as budgeted), were as follows.

Item	*1st year units*	*2nd year units*	*3rd year units*	*4th year units*	*Total units*
Opening stock	–	200	300	300	–
Production	300	250	200	200	950
	300	450	500	500	950
Closing stock	200	300	300	200	200
Sales	100	150	200	300	750

Show the operating statements for each year under:

(a) absorption costing

(b) marginal costing.

Solution

(a) **Absorption costing**

	1st year	*2nd year*	*3rd year*	*4th year*	*Total*
	£	£	£	£	£
Sales value	1,000	1,500	2,000	3,000	7,500
Opening stock @ £7.60 (W1)	–	1,520	2,280	2,280	–
Costs of production @ £7.60	2,280	1,900	1,520	1,520	7,220
	2,280	3,420	3,800	3,800	7,220
Less: Closing stock @ £7.60	1,520	2,280	2,280	1,520	1,520
Cost of sales	(760)	(1,140)	(1,520)	(2,280)	(5,700)
(Under)/over absorption (W2)	180	Nil	(180)	(180)	(180)
Net profit	420	360	300	540	1,620

Workings

(W1) Unit cost is variable cost £4 + fixed overhead absorbed of £3.60 (i.e. £900/250), giving a cost per unit of £7.60.

(W2) Calculation of over/under-absorption.

Fixed cost control account

	£		£
Incurred:		Absorbed:	
Year 1	900	300 × £3.60	1,080
Over-absorption	180		
	1,080		1,080
Year 2	900	250 × £3.60	900
Year 3	900	200 × £3.60	720
		Under-absorption	180
	900		900
Year 4	900	200 × £3.60	720
		Under-absorption	180
	900		900

(b) **Marginal costing**

	1st year	*2nd year*	*3rd year*	*4th year*	*Total*
	£	£	£	£	£
Sales	1,000	1,500	2,000	3,000	7,500
Opening stock @ £4	–	800	1,200	1,200	–
Cost of production @ £4	1,200	1,000	800	800	3,800
	1,200	1,800	2,000	2,000	3,800
Less: Closing stock @ £4	800	1,200	1,200	800	800
Cost of sales	(400)	(600)	(800)	(1,200)	(3,000)
Contribution	600	900	1,200	1,800	4,500
Less: Fixed costs	900	900	900	900	3,600
Net profit/(loss)	(300)	–	300	900	900

The marginal costing presentation indicates clearly that the business must sell at least 150 units per year to break even, i.e. £900 ÷ (10 – 4), whereas it appeared, using absorption costing, that even at 100 units it was making a healthy profit. The total profit for the four years is less under the marginal principle because the closing stocks are valued at £800 (£4 × 200) instead of £1,520, i.e. £720 of the fixed costs are being carried forward under the absorption principle, but have been charged to profit under marginal costing.

The profit figures shown may be reconciled as follows.

	Year 1	*Year 2*	*Year 3*	*Year 4*	*Total*
	£	£	£	£	£
Profit/(loss) under marginal costing	(300)	Nil	300	900	900
Fixed overhead absorbed into stock					
(200 × £3.60) =	720				720
(100 × £3.60)		360			360
			-		-
(100 × £3.60)				(360)	(360)
Profit under absorption costing	420	360	300	540	1,620

Note: The under/over-absorption figures have nothing to do with the difference in the profit figures; they are caused by production not being at the budgeted level.

Activity 3

A company that manufactures one product has calculated its cost on a quarterly production budget of 10,000 units. The selling price was £5 per unit.

Sales in the four successive quarters of the last year were:

Quarter 1	10,000 units
Quarter 2	9,000 units
Quarter 3	7,000 units
Quarter 4	5,500 units

The level of stock at the beginning of the year was 1,000 units and the company maintained its stock of finished products at the same level at the end of each of the four quarters.

Based on its quarterly production budget, the cost per unit was:

	£
Prime cost	3.50
Production overhead (variable and fixed)	0.75
Selling and administration overhead	0.30
Total	4.55

Fixed production overhead, which has been taken into account in calculating the above figures, was £5,000 per quarter. Selling and administration overhead was treated as fixed, and was charged against sales in the period in which it was incurred.

You are required to present a tabular statement to show net profit of the four quarters:

(a) under absorption costing

(b) under marginal costing.

(Remember, only production costs can be absorbed into stock values; selling and administration fixed overheads must always be charged to profit in the period incurred.)

Feedback to this activity is at the end of the chapter.

3.2 Capacity considerations

Many questions in this area provide information based on 100% capacity and then state that the organisation expects to operate at a different capacity level.

This is simply a means of communicating an activity level. You must recognise which costs are variable and adjust them to the proposed activity level.

3.3 Criticisms of absorption costing

Preparation of routine operating statements using absorption costing is considered less informative because:

- profit per unit is a misleading figure – in the first example above, the operating margin of £2 per unit arises because fixed overhead per unit is based on 5,000 units; if another basis were used, margin per unit would differ even though fixed overhead was the same amount in total

- build-up or run-down of stocks of finished goods can distort comparison of period operating statements and obscure the effect of increasing or decreasing sales
- comparison between products can be misleading because of the effect of arbitrary apportionment of fixed costs.

3.4 Defence of absorption costing

Absorption costing is widely used and students should understand both principles. Defenders of the absorption principle point out that:

- it is necessary to include fixed overhead in stock values for financial statements; routine cost accounting using absorption costing produces stock values which include a share of fixed overhead
- for small businesses using job costing, overhead allotment is the only practicable way of obtaining job costs for estimating and profit analysis
- analysis of under/over-absorbed overhead is useful to identify inefficient utilisation of production resources.

Summary

- In marginal costing, fixed costs are treated as period costs and deducted in total from contribution to arrive at profit. In absorption costing, fixed costs are absorbed into the cost of stock items.
- Marginal costing is regarded as more useful for decision making because of its focus on variable costs. Because fixed costs are often unaffected by the decision taken, their inclusion in absorption costing makes this a less useful system for decision making.

Having completed your study of this chapter you should have achieved the following learning outcomes.

- Explain the possible conflicts between cost accounting for profit reporting and stock valuation and the convenient availability of information for decision-making.

Self-test questions

1. Define marginal costing. (2.1)
2. If stocks increase, will reported profit be greater under absorption costing or marginal costing? (3.1)
3. What are the disadvantages of absorption costing? (3.3)
4. What are the advantages of absorption costing? (3.4)

Objective test questions

Question 1

When comparing the profits reported using marginal costing with those reported using absorption costing in a period when closing stock was 1,400 units, opening stock was 2,000 units, and the actual production was 11,200 units at a total cost of £4.50 per unit compared to a target cost of £5.00 per unit, which of the following statements is correct?

A Absorption costing reports profits £2,700 lower

B Absorption costing reports profits £3,000 higher

C Absorption costing reports profits £3,000 lower

D There is insufficient data to calculate the difference between the reported profits

Question 2

A company made 17,500 units at a total cost of £16 each. Three quarters of the costs were variable and one quarter fixed. 15,000 units were sold at £25 each. There were no opening stocks.

By how much will the profit calculated using absorption costing principles differ from the profit if marginal costing principles had been used?

A The absorption costing profit would be £22,500 less

B The absorption costing profit would be £10,000 greater

C The absorption costing profit would be £135,000 greater

D The absorption costing profit would be £10,000 less

Question 3

Dundee makes cakes, for which the standard cost card is as follows:

	£ per cake
Materials and labour	5
Variable production overhead	3
Fixed production overhead	4
Variable selling cost	1
Fixed selling overhead	2
Profit	5
Sales price	20

Both types of fixed overheads were based on a budget of 10,000 cakes a year.

In the first year of production, the only difference from the budget was that Dundee produced 11,000 cakes and sold 9,000.

Calculate the profit using absorption costing and marginal costing. **(4 marks)**

For the answers to these questions, see the 'Answers' section at the end of the book.

Exam-type questions

Question 1: Rayners plc

Rayners plc manufactures and sells electric blankets. The selling price is £12 per blanket. Each blanket has the following unit cost:

	£
Direct material	2
Direct labour	1
Variable production overhead	2
Fixed production overhead	3
	8

Administration costs are incurred at the rate of £20,000 per annum.

The company achieved the following production and sales of blankets:

Year	*1*	*2*	*3*
Production (000 units)	100	110	90
Sales (000 units)	90	110	95

The following information is also relevant:

- The overhead costs of £2 and £3 per unit have been calculated on the basis of a budgeted production volume of 90,000 units.
- There was no inflation.
- There was no opening stock at the beginning of the year 1.

Required:

(a) Prepare an operating statement for each year using:

(i) marginal costing

(ii) absorption costing. **(8 marks)**

(b) Explain why the profit figures reported under the two techniques disagree. **(2 marks)**

(Total: 10 marks)

Question 2: Miozip Co

The Miozip Co operates an absorption costing system that incorporates a factory-wide overhead absorption rate per direct labour hour. For 20X0 and 20X1 this rate was £2.10 per hour. The fixed factory overhead for 20X1 was £600,000 and this would have been fully absorbed if the company had operated at full capacity, which is estimated at 400,000 direct labour hours. Unfortunately, only 200,000 hours were worked in that year so that the overhead was seriously under-absorbed. Fixed factory overheads are expected to be unchanged in 20X2 and 20X3.

The outcome for 20X1 was a loss of £70,000 and the management believed that a major cause of this loss was the low overhead absorption rate that had led the company to quote selling prices that were uneconomic.

For 20X2 the overhead absorption rate was increased to £3.60 per direct labour hour and selling prices were raised in line with the established pricing procedures which involve adding a profit mark-up of 50% onto the full factory cost of the company's products. The new selling prices were also charged on the stock of finished goods held at the beginning of 20X2. In December 20X2 the company's accountant prepared an estimated profit and loss account for 20X2 and a budgeted profit and loss account for 20X3. Although sales were considered to be depressed in 20X1, they were even lower in 20X2 but, nevertheless, it seems that the company will make a profit for that year. A worrying feature of the estimated accounts is the high level of finished goods stock held and the 20X3 budget provides for a reduction in the stock level at 31 December 20X3 to the (physical) level that obtained at 1 January 20X1. Budgeted sales for 20X3 are set at the 20X2 sales level.

The summarised profit statements for the three years to 31 December 20X3 are as follows.

Summarised profit and loss accounts

	Actual 20X1		*Estimated 20X2*		*Budgeted 20X3*	
	£	£	£	£	£	£
Sales revenue		1,350,000		1,316,250		1,316,250
Opening stock of finished goods	100,000		200,000		357,500	
Factory cost of production	1,000,000		975,000		650,000	
	1,100,000		1,175,000		1,007,500	
Less: Closing stock of finished goods	200,000		357,500		130,000	
Factory cost of goods sold		900,000		817,500		877,500
		450,000		498,750		438,750
Less: Factory overhead under-absorbed		300,000		150,000		300,000
		150,000		348,750		138,750
Administrative and financial costs		220,000		220,000		220,000
Profit/(loss)		(70,000)		128,750		(81,250)

Required:

(a) Write a short report to the board of Miozip explaining why the budgeted income for 20X3 is so different from that of 20X2 when the sales revenue is the same for both years. **(6 marks)**

(b) Restate the profit and loss account for 20X1, the estimated profit and loss account for 20X2 and the budgeted profit and loss account for 20X3 using marginal factory cost for stock valuation purposes. **(10 marks)**

(c) Comment on the problems that may follow from a decision to increase the overhead absorption rate in conditions when cost-plus pricing is used and overhead is currently under-absorbed. **(4 marks)**

(d) Explain why the majority of businesses use full costing systems whilst most management accounting theorists favour marginal costing. **(5 marks)**

Note: Assume in your answers to this question that the value of the £ and the efficiency of the company have been constant over the period under review.

(Total: 25 marks)

For the answers to these questions, see the 'Answers' section at the end of the book.

Feedback to activities

Activity 1

Department 1 absorption rate = £240,000 ÷ £2,400,000 =10% of direct labour cost

Department 2 absorption rate = £200,000 ÷ £4,000,000 = 5% of direct labour cost

Fixed overhead cost per unit of IC:

		£ per unit
Department 1	£15 × 10%	1.50
Department 2	£8 × 5%	0.40
Fixed overhead cost per unit		1.90

Activity 2

Over-/(under-) absorption = Absorbed overheads – Incurred overheads

Budgeted fixed overhead = 3,000 units × £9 = £27,000.

	£
Fixed overhead absorbed (3,200 units × £9)	28,800
Fixed overhead incurred (£27,000 × 1.05)	28,350
Over-absorbed fixed overheads	450

Activity 3

(a) **Net profit statement (absorption costing)**

Note: The company maintained its stock at the same level at the end of the four quarters. Therefore production = sales.

	1st quarter	2nd quarter	3rd quarter	4th quarter
Sales units	10,000	9,000	7,000	5,500
Production units	10,000	9,000	7,000	5,500
	£	£	£	£
Sales value (£5 per unit)	50,000	45,000	35,000	27,500
Cost of sales:				
Opening stock at £4.25	4,250	4,250	4,250	4,250
Production at £4.25	42,500	38,250	29,750	23,375
Less: Closing stock at £4.25	4,250	4,250	4,250	4,250
Cost of sales	42,500	38,250	29,750	23,375
Under-absorbed production overhead (W)	–	500	1,500	2,250
	42,500	38,750	31,250	25,625
Gross profit	7,500	6,250	3,750	1,875
Less: Selling and administration overhead (10,000 × 0.30)	3,000	3,000	3,000	3,000
Net profit/(loss)	4,500	3,250	750	(1,125)

Working

(W) Fixed production overhead absorption rate

$$\frac{\text{Fixed production overhead}}{\text{Budgeted production}} = \frac{£5,000}{10,000 \text{ units}} = £0.50 \text{ per unit}$$

	1st quarter	2nd quarter	3rd quarter	4th quarter
Overhead incurred	5,000	5,000	5,000	5,000
Overhead absorbed at 50p per unit				
10,000 × 50p	5,000			
9,000 × 50p		4,500		
7,000 × 50p			3,500	
5,500 × 50p				2,750
Under-absorption	-	500	1,500	2,250

(b) **Net profit statement (fixed overhead charged against period sales)**

	1st quarter	*2nd quarter*	*3rd quarter*	*4th quarter*
Sales units	10,000	9,000	7,000	5,500
	£	£	£	£
Sales value	50,000	45,000	35,000	27,500
Less: Variable cost of sales (£3.75 per unit)	37,500	33,750	26,250	20,625
Contribution	12,500	11,250	8,750	6,875
Less: Fixed production selling and administration overhead	8,000	8,000	8,000	8,000
Net profit/(loss)	4,500	3,250	750	(1,125)

Chapter 2

JOINT COSTS

Syllabus content

This chapter covers the following syllabus content.

- The allocation of joint costs and decisions concerning process and product viability based on relevant costs and revenues.

Contents

1 Accounting for joint costs

DEFINITION

A **joint cost** is the cost of a process that results in more than one main product. A **common cost** is a cost relating to more than one product or service.

1.1 Introduction

The term 'joint cost' refers to the cost of some common process before a split-off point after which various joint products and by-products can be identified.

'Common costs' is a wider term that need not relate to a process. For example, the absorption of fixed production overheads in total absorption costing described earlier in this chapter is an example of assigning common costs to cost units.

DEFINITION

Joint products are two or more products produced by the same process and separated in processing, each having a sufficiently high saleable value to merit recognition as a main product.
A **by-product** is output of some value produced incidentally in manufacturing something else (main product).

1.2 Joint products and by-products

The nature of process costing is that the process incurs joint costs and often produces more than one product. These additional products may be described as either joint products or by-products. Essentially joint products are all the main products, whereas by-products are incidental to the main products.

- Joint products are two or more products produced by the same process and separated in processing, each having a sufficiently high saleable value to merit recognition as a main product.
- A by-product is output of some value produced incidentally in manufacturing something else (main product).

These definitions still leave scope for subjective judgement, but they provide a basis for such judgement. The distinction is important because the accounting treatment of joint and by-products differs. Costs incurred in processing prior to the separation of the products are known as joint costs.

1.3 Relationship between processes, joint products and by-products

The following diagram illustrates the relationships:

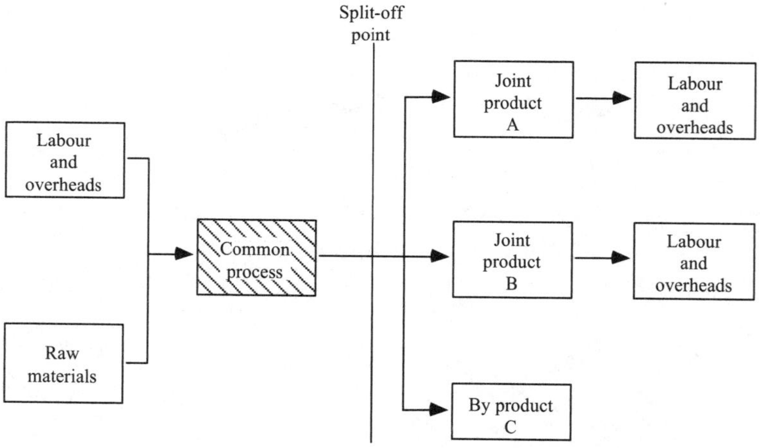

1.4 Accounting for by-products

Either of the following methods may be adopted:

(a) the proceeds from the sale of the by-product may be treated as pure profit

(b) the proceeds from the sale, less any handling and selling expenses, may be used to reduce the cost of the main products.

If a by-product needs further processing to improve its marketability, the cost will be deducted in arriving at net revenue, treated as in (a) or (b) above. Note that recorded profits will be affected by the method adopted if stocks of the main product are maintained.

Example

Output from a process was 1,300 kilos of the main product and 100 kilos of a by-product. Sales of the main product were 1,000 kilos realising £6,000; sales of the by-product realised £160 but incurred £30 distribution cost. Process costs were £5,200. Calculate the net profit under each of the two methods described above.

Solution

Method (a)

	£	£
Main product sales		6,000
Process costs	5,200	
Less: Closing stock $\frac{300}{1,300} \times £5,200$	1,200	
		4,000
		2,000
Add: Net profit of by-product sales (£160 – 30)		130
Net profit		2,130

Method (b)

	£	£
Main product sales		6,000
Process costs	5,200	
Less: By-product net revenue	130	
	5,070	
Less: Closing stock $\frac{300}{1,300} \times £5,070$		
	1,170	
Cost of sales		3,900
Net profit		2,100

Under method (b) a portion of by-product net revenue is deferred in the stock value of the main product (i.e. 300/1,300 × £130 = £30).

1.5 Accounting for joint products

Joint products are, by definition, subject to individual accounting procedures. Joint costs may require apportionment between products if only for joint valuation purposes.

The main bases for appointment are as follows:

- **Physical measurement of joint products** – Joint costs can be apportioned to the units of output of each joint product. When the unit of measurement is different, e.g. litres and kilos, some method should be found of expressing them in a common unit. Some joint costs are not incurred equally for all joint products: such costs can be separated and apportioned by introducing weighting factors.

- **Market value** – Joint costs can be apportioned on the basis of the market value of each joint product at the point of separation. The effect is to make each product appear to be equally profitable.
- **Net realisable value** – Where certain products are processed after the point of separation, further processing costs may be deducted from the market values before joint costs are apportioned.
- **Technical estimates of relative use of common resources** – A subjective apportionment based on technical estimates can be used.

KEY POINT

It is essential to realise that apportionment is, of necessity, an arbitrary calculation and product costs that include such an apportionment can be misleading if used as a basis for decision-making.

It is essential to realise that apportionment is, of necessity, an arbitrary calculation and product costs that include such an apportionment can be misleading if used as a basis for decision-making.

1.6 Valuation of joint product stocks

In the following example joint costs are apportioned on the following bases:

- physical measurement
- market value at point of separation
- net realisable value/net relative sales value
- technical estimates of relative usage.

The methods will result in different stock valuations and, therefore, different recorded profits.

Example

	Kgs produced	*Kgs sold*	*Selling price per kg*	*Joint cost*
Product A	100	80	£5	
				£750
Product B	200	150	£2	

Solution

(a) **Apportionment by physical measurement**

$$\frac{\text{Joint cost}}{\text{Kgs produced}} = \frac{£750}{300} = £2.50 \text{ per kg for A + B}$$

Trading results

	Product A		*Product B*		*Total*
		£		£	£
Sales	80 × £5.00	400	150 × £2.00	300	700
Cost of sales	80 × £2.50	200	150 × £2.50	375	575
Profit/(loss)		200		(75)	125
Value of closing stock	20 × £2.50	50	50 × £2.50	125	

The main point to emphasise about joint products is the production mix. In this case the production ratio is 100: 200 which means that, in order to obtain 1 kg of A, it is necessary also to produce 2 kgs of B. Although in the longer term it may be possible through research and development work to change the mix, in many processes this is not possible and for exam purposes you should assume that the ratio of output is fixed.

In attempting to assess the profitability of the common process it is necessary to assess the overall position as follows:

		£
Sales value of product A	100 × £5	500
Sales value of product B	200 × £2	400
		900
Joint cost		750
Profit		150

This profit figure should be used to evaluate the profitability of the common process.

Referring back to the trading results, it is important to appreciate that the 'loss' on B has been created by the joint cost apportionment, i.e.:

	£
Selling price	2.00
Share of joint cost	2.50
Loss	0.50

A decision not to produce and sell product B is not possible, because if product B were not produced, then neither could product A be produced.

A further point to note is that stock of B could not be valued in the financial statements at £2.50 bearing in mind that stock should be valued at the lower of cost and net realisable value.

(b) **Apportionment by market value at point of separation**

		Sales value of production	*Proportion*	*Joint cost apportionment*	*Per kg*
		£		£	£
A	100 × £5	500	$\frac{5}{9}$	417	4.17
B	200 × £2	400	$\frac{4}{9}$	333	1.67
				750	

Trading results:

	A	*B*	*Total*
Sales	400	300	700
Cost of sales	333.6	250.5	585.1
Profit	66.4	49.5	114.9
Profit/sales	16.6%	16.5%	
Closing stock	(20 × 4.17)	(50 × 1.67)	
	83	83	

Notes:

1 Apportionment is on the basis of proportionate sales value of production.

2 Profit per unit is the same (with a small rounding difference).

3 This approach provides a more realistic estimate of cost to use for valuing stock of B, i.e. £1.67.

(c) **Apportionment by net realisable value**

This approach should be used in situations where the sales value at the split-off point is not known – either because the product is not saleable, or if the examiner does not tell you – or if specifically asked for by the examiner.

Further information needed:

	Further processing costs	*Selling price after further processing*
Product A	£280 + £2.00 per kg	£8.40
Product B	£160 + £1.40 per kg	£4.50

Apportionment of joint costs:

	Product A £	*Product B* £
Final sales value of production (100 × £8.40; 200 × £4.50)	840	900
Further processing cost (280 + 100 × £2; 160 + 200 × £1.40)	480	440
Net realisable value	360	460
Joint cost apportionment (360: 460)	329	421
Joint cost per kg	£3.29	£2.10

Trading results (for common process only)

	£	£	£
Sales			700
Joint cost		750	
Less: Closing stock:			
A 20 × £3.29	66		
B 50 × £2.10	105		
		171	
Cost of sales			579
Profit			121

Notes:

1 As we know sales value of product B at the point of separation is £2, we can see that this method results in an unrealistic stock value of £2.10. Bear in mind that this approach should only be used where the sales value at the split-off point is not known, or if instructed to use it by the examiner.

2 The effect of further processing is considered in more detail below.

(d) **Using technical apportionment**

Suppose the technical apportionment ratios are:

A – 60%

B – 40%

	A	B	Total
	£	£	£
Sales	400	300	700
Joint costs (apportioned 60 : 40)	450	300	750
Less: Stock value:			
Joint costs A = $\frac{20}{100} \times £450$	90		90
B = $\frac{50}{200} \times £300$		75	75
Cost of sales	360	225	585
Net profit	40	75	115

Note that all the methods produce similar, but not identical results.

1.7 Problems of common costs and joint costs

Even if careful technical estimates are made of relative benefits, any apportionment of common costs or joint costs will inevitably be an arbitrary calculation. When providing information to assist decision-making, therefore, the cost accountant will emphasise cost and revenue differences arising from the decision.

Examples of decisions involving joint products are:

- withdrawing, or adding, a product
- special pricing
- economics of further processing.

Apportioned common costs are not relevant to any of the above decisions. Total joint costs are only relevant if they change as a result of the decision.

2 Joint costs and decision making

Decisions regarding joint process

The joint process should be evaluated by looking at the total revenue and total cost for that process. However, it is important also to note that further processing may well increase profits. This further processing is only possible if the joint process is carried out.

KEY POINT

To evaluate processing of the individual products it is necessary to identify the **incremental costs** and **incremental revenues** relating to that further processing, i.e. the **additional** costs and revenue brought about directly as a result of that further processing.

Decisions regarding further processing of individual products

For this purpose it is assumed that further processing of products is independent, i.e. a decision to process one joint product in no way affects the decision to process further the other joint products. It should also be noted that joint costs are not affected by whether individual products are further processed, and are therefore not relevant.

To evaluate processing of the individual products it is necessary to identify the **incremental costs** and **incremental revenues** relating to that further processing, i.e. the **additional** costs and revenue brought about directly as a result of that further processing.

Example

Reconsidering the data from the example in paragraph 1.6 above:

	Kgs produced	*Kgs sold*	*Selling price at split-off point*	*Further processing costs*	*Selling price after further processing*
Product A	100	80	£5	£280 + £2.00 per kg	£8.40
Product B	200	150	£2	£160 + £1.40 per kg	£4.50

Evaluation of further processing:

	Product A £	£		*Product B* £	£
Incremental revenue					
100 × £(8.40 – 5.00)		340	200 × £(4.50 – 2.00)		500
Incremental cost:					
Fixed	280			160	
Variable 100 × £2	200		200 × £1.40	280	
		480			440
Increase/(decrease) in profit		(140)			60

On the basis of these figures the decision to recommend would be:

Product A Sell at split-off point for £5.

Product B Sell after further processing for £4.50.

This would result in overall profits on this production volume of:

	£
Common process (as previously calculated)	150
Further processing of product B	60
Profit	210

Note: The timing of recognition of this profit is dependent on the basis used for valuation of stocks, as discussed above.

The recommendation to sell product A at the split-off point and product B after further processing is based on two assumptions:

(a) all relevant 'effects' of the decision have been included, i.e. quantified

(b) production volume achieved is A 100 kgs, B 200 kgs.

Before a final decision is made these assumptions must be considered in more detail.

(a) **All effects of decision quantified**

The course of action recommended could have other effects not included above, e.g.:

- products A and B in their final state may be in some way 'complementary', i.e. it may only be possible to sell B for £4.50 if A is also available in a further processed state at a price of £8.40
- the company may currently be carrying out further processing of A. The decision above could therefore result in having to reduce the workforce employed in this processing. The remaining workforce could, for example, go out on strike, causing a loss of production and sales of A and B. These factors should be carefully assessed before a final decision is made.

(b) **Production volume**

By looking in more detail at the further processing of A it is possible to see that further processing of 1 kg of A results in an incremental contribution of:

	£
Incremental revenue £(8.40 – 5.00)	3.40
Incremental variable cost	2.00
Incremental contribution	1.40

It is therefore possible to identify the level of activity at which further processing of A becomes worthwhile, i.e. the 'break-even volume':

$$\text{Break-even volume} = \frac{\text{Incremental fixed costs}}{\text{Incremental contribution per kg}}$$

$$= \frac{280}{1.40}$$

$$= 200 \text{ kgs}$$

Hence, if the volume of product A in the future is greater than 200 kgs, further processing becomes economically worthwhile.

Summary

- Joint products each have a sufficiently high saleable value to merit recognition as a main product. A by-product, as the name suggests, is merely an incidental output from a joint process.
- To account for a by-product we can either treat its sale proceeds as pure profit, or deduct them from the cost of the main (joint) products.
- There are three main methods of apportioning joint costs between products: physical measurement of outputs; market value of outputs; technical estimates of relative use of common resources.

Having completed your study of this chapter you should have achieved the following learning outcomes.

- Explain the possible conflicts between cost accounting for profit reporting and stock valuation and the convenient availability of information for decision-making.
- Explain why joint costs must be allocated to final products for financial reporting purposes, but why this is unhelpful when decisions concerning process and product viability have to be taken.

Self-test questions

1 What is a joint cost? (1.1)

2 State two possible methods for accounting for by-products. (1.4)

3 State three possible methods of apportioning joint costs to joint products. (1.5)

Objective test questions

Question 1

Two types of plastic piping are produced in a joint production process. UB-1 may be sold immediately after split off. UB-2 requires further processing before it is ready for sale. There is no opening stock. The following production data are available.

Total joint cost	£80,000
Additional cost of processing UB-2	£38,400

	Sales quantity (metres)	*Sales price (per metre)*	*Closing stock (metres)*
UB-1	200,000	£0.30	8,000
UB-2	180,000	£0.40	12,000

What is the cost of closing stock using the final sales revenue method of joint cost allocation (to the nearest £100)?

A £4,000

B £6,400

C £6,500

D £7,200

Questions 2 and 3 are based on the following data:

Joint products	*Output (kg)*	*Selling price per kg*
X	5,000	£10
Y	10,000	£4
Z	10,000	£3

Joint costs of the process are £100,000.

Question 2

If the joint costs of the process are apportioned to each product on the basis of physical quantity, the profit per unit of product X is:

A £4

B £6

C £8

D £10

Question 3

If the joint costs of the process are apportioned to each product on the basis of sales value, the total profit of product Y is:

A £20,000

B £16,667

C £6,667

D £2,000

Question 4

Which of the following statements is correct?

A When joint costs are apportioned on the basis of physical quantity the percentage profit margin is the same for all joint products.

B There will be a higher total profit if joint costs are apportioned on the basis of sales value rather than on the basis of physical quantity.

C By-products are separate products produced from a joint process which have a significant sales value.

D The normal accounting treatment for by-products is to deduct the sales value from common costs.

For the answers to these questions, see the 'Answers' section at the end of the book.

Exam-type questions

Question 1: Mineral Separators Ltd

Mineral Separators Ltd operates a process which produces four unrefined minerals known as W, X, Y and Z. The joint costs for operating the process for Period 5 were as below.

Process overhead is absorbed by adding 25% of the labour cost.

The output for Period 5 was as shown below.

There were no stocks of unrefined materials at the beginning of Period 5, and no work-in-progress, but the stocks shown below were on hand at the end of the period, although there was no work-in-progress at that date.

The price received per tonne of unrefined mineral sold is shown below and it is confidently expected that these prices will be maintained.

Required:

(a) Calculate the profit earned by each joint product using sales value as the basis for allocating joint costs. **(5 marks)**

(b) Comment on the value of the information calculated in (a) for decision making purposes.

(5 marks)

(Total: 10 marks)

Joint costs for Period 5

	£
Raw material	75,000
Labour	24,000

Output for Period 5

	Tonnes
W	700
X	600
Y	400
Z	100

Stocks at end of Period 5

	Tonnes
W	30
X	20
Y	80
Z	5

Price per tonne

	£
W	40
X	90
Y	120
Z	200

Question 2: XY Ltd

XY Ltd operates a chemical process that jointly produces four products, A, B, C and D. Product B is sold without further processing, but additional work is necessary on the other three before they can be sold. Budgeted data for the year were as follows:

	Production kg	*Closing stock* kg	*Sales* kg
Production:			
Product A	150,000	10,000	140,000
Product B	110,000	15,000	95,000
Product C	60,000	5,000	55,000
Product D	180,000	Nil	180,000

There were no opening stocks of the four products. Closing stocks were ready for sale.

	Selling prices per kg	*Cost of additional work to make product saleable per kg*
	£	
Product A	0.70	0.10
Product B	0.60	–
Product C	0.60	0.20
Product D	1.35	0.35

	£
Production cost of the joint process	180,000
Other costs:	
Administration (fixed)	45,000
Selling:	
Fixed	35,000
Variable (£0.01 per lb sold)	4,700

An overseas customer has expressed interest in buying from existing production 50,000 kg each in one year of any or all of Products A, C and D before they have been further processed by XY Ltd. The customer has offered to pay the following prices.

	Price per kg
	£
Product A	0.65
Product C	0.52
Product D	0.90

On such sales, variable selling costs would be only £0.006 per kg. Fixed administration and selling costs would remain as stated above.

Required:

(a) Calculate gross profit per product and total net profit if joint costs are apportioned on the basis of weight of products produced. **(6 marks)**

(b) Calculate gross profit per product and total net profit if joint costs are apportioned on the basis of the net realisable value of the products produced. **(6 marks)**

(c) State which products you would recommend XY Ltd to sell to the overseas customer before further processing at the prices quoted in order to increase net profit. **(8 marks)**

(d) Calculate the increase in the annual net profit of XY Ltd if your advice in (c) above was followed. **(5 marks)**

(Total: 25 marks)

For the answers to these questions, see the 'Answers' section at the end of the book.

Chapter 3

COST-VOLUME-PROFIT ANALYSIS

Syllabus content

This chapter covers the following syllabus content.

- Multi-product breakeven analysis including breakeven and profit/volume charts, contribution/sales ratio, margin of safety, etc.

Contents

1 Cost-volume-profit (CVP) analysis

1.1 Introduction

DEFINITION

CVP analysis is the study of the effects on future profit of changes in fixed cost, variable cost, sales price, quantity and mix.

CVP analysis is the study of the effects on future profit of changes in fixed cost, variable cost, sales price, quantity and mix.

CVP analysis is a particular example of 'what if?' analysis. A business sets a budget based upon various assumptions about revenues, costs, product mixes and overall volumes. CVP analysis considers the impact on the budgeted profit of changes in these various factors.

Where changes in volume/mix are involved, the essential measure required is **contribution**.

1.2 What is contribution?

Contribution is the term used to describe the difference between sales revenues and variable costs. This may be calculated in total, or on a per unit basis using selling prices and variable costs per unit.

The difference between contribution and fixed costs is profit (or loss). A target profit can be converted into a target contribution to use to calculate the number of units required to achieve the desired target profit.

In particular, at **breakeven**, the target profit is **zero** and contribution = fixed costs.

KEY POINT

Profit per unit should never be used to assess profit or profit changes except at the budgeted level of activity.

It is very difficult to use profit in the calculations because if total fixed costs are assumed to be constant, fixed cost per unit, and thus profit per unit, is changing every time the activity level changes; whereas contribution per unit is constant.

The following example illustrates the basic principles, terminology and techniques of CVP analysis – work through it carefully.

Example

Company	:	Widgets Ltd
Product	:	Widgets
Selling price	:	£3 per unit
Variable costs	:	Raw materials, £1 per unit
Fixed costs	:	Factory rent, £500 pa.

(a) How many widgets must be sold per annum to **break even**?

$$\text{Volume target} = \frac{\text{Contribution target}}{\text{Selling price - variable costs per unit}}$$

$$= \frac{£500 + £0}{£3 - £1} = 250 \text{ widgets.}$$

At sales volume of 250 units per annum, Widgets Ltd will make nil profit or loss:

	£
Sales 250 × £3	750
Variable costs 250 × £1	250
Contribution	500
Fixed costs	500
Profit/(loss)	Nil

(b) If rent goes up by 10% and Widgets Ltd aims to make £200 pa profit, what annual output is needed?

$$\text{Volume target} = \frac{\text{Contribution target}}{\text{Unit contribution}} = \frac{£500 + £50 + £200}{£3 - £1} = 375 \text{ widgets}$$

(c) Assuming the maximum possible output of Widgets Ltd is 250 widgets pa, what selling price (SP) would achieve the required profit target of £200 (assuming the increased rent)?

Contribution target = Fixed costs + Profit target

= £550 + £200 = £750

and

Total contribution = Volume × (Selling price per unit – Variable costs per unit)

$\therefore$ 750 = 250 × (SP – 1)

750 = 250 SP – 250

1,000 = 250 SP

The required selling price is therefore, £4 per unit, giving:

		£
Sales	: 250 widgets × £4 =	1,000
Variable costs	: 250 × £1	250
Contribution		750
Fixed costs:		550
Profit		200

The simple example above illustrates that, given the cost/selling price structure, a range of alternative predictions can be easily calculated. Any change in selling price or variable costs will alter unit contribution; changes in fixed costs or profit required will affect the contribution target.

1.3 Contribution to sales (C/S) ratio

The C/S ratio measures contribution **per pound sales value** instead of **per physical unit**. It can therefore be used to deduce break-even sales value, sales revenue targets, etc. in a similar manner to the above analyses. Its particular use, though is in a multiple product situation.

DEFINITION

Contribution to sales ratio (C/S ratio)

$= \frac{\text{Contribution in £}}{\text{Sales in £}}$

Contribution to sales ratio (C/S ratio) $= \frac{\text{Contribution in £}}{\text{Sales in £}}$

Note: you will also encounter the term profit to volume (or P/V) ratio, which is synonymous with the contribution to sales ratio. (For instance, the CIMA syllabus for this subject refers to a 'profit/volume chart'.)

The C/S ratio is conveniently written as a percentage.

1.4 Multiple products analysis

In the above illustration, it was assumed that Widgets Ltd had sold only one product. If it had produced three products, say widgets, gidgets and shmidgets, and the unit contribution of each product was different, then it would be uninformative to assess total volume in terms of units.

If, however, the relative proportion of each product sold could be assumed to remain similar or if each product has the same ratio of contribution to sales value, then similar calculations could be made for the business as a whole. Output would be expressed in terms of sales revenue rather than numbers of units.

Example

Widgets Ltd operating statement for year 3 shows:

	Widgets	*Gidgets*	*Shmidgets*	*Total*
Sales units	100	40	60	200
	£	£	£	£
Sales value	450	270	180	900
Variable costs	261	162	99	522
Contribution	189	108	81	378
Fixed costs				350
Profit				28
C/S ratio	42%	40%	45%	42 %

Break-even volume in sales value $= \frac{\text{Fixed costs}}{\text{C/S ratio}}$

$= \frac{£350}{42\%} = £833.33$

Thus, the business must sell about £835 of a mixture of widgets, gidgets and shmidgets before it starts to make a profit. Use of the total C/S ratio would only be valid if the proportions of widgets, gidgets and shmidgets to total sales remained the same over the range of output considered.

1.5 Calculating a missing C/S ratio in a multi-product scenario

Using the above example it can be shown that, if the sales mix is given, problems can be set which involve finding a 'missing' C/S ratio. The information in the above example could be restated as follows:

	Widgets	*Gidgets*	*Schmidgets*	*Total*
Proportion of sales by value	50%	30%	20%	100%
C/S ratio	42%	40%	?	42%

The problem is to find the missing C/S ratio for Schmidgets.

Solution

The overall ratio is given by:

Widgets	$50\% \times 42\%$	21%
Gidgets	$30\% \times 40\%$	12%
Schmidgets	$20\% \times ?$	9% (balancing figure)
Total		42%

Therefore the C/S ratio for Schmidgets is 9%/20% = 45%

Activity 1

Using the example of Widgets Ltd above calculate the total C/S ratio if the proportion of total sales changes to 30% Widgets, 20% Gidgets and 50% Schmidgets. Assume that the C/S ratios and fixed costs are unchanged. What is the new breakeven point?

Feedback to this activity is at the end of the chapter.

1.6 Margin of safety

DEFINITION

The difference between budgeted sales volume and break-even sales volume is known as the **margin of safety.**

The difference between budgeted sales volume and break-even sales volume is known as the margin of safety. The margin of safety indicates the vulnerability of a business to a fall in demand. It is often expressed as a percentage of budgeted sales.

Example

Budgeted sales	:	80,000 units
Selling price	:	£8
Variable costs	:	£4 per unit
Fixed costs	:	£200,000 pa
Break even volume	=	$\frac{200,000}{8-4}$
	=	50,000 units
∴ Margin of safety	=	80,000 – 50,000
	=	30,000 units or 37½% of budget

The margin of safety may also be expressed as a percentage of actual sales or of maximum capacity.

Students should note the relationship between the margin of safety when expressed as a percentage of actual sales and the C/S and profit to sales (P/S) ratio.

P/S ratio = Margin of safety × C/S ratio

Example

	£
Sales	10,000
Variable costs	6,000
	4,000
Fixed costs	2,500
Net profit	1,500

(a) P/S ratio $= \frac{1,500}{10,000}$

$= 15\%$

(b) C/S ratio $= \frac{4,000}{10,000}$

$= 40\%$

(c) Break-even sales $= \frac{2,500}{0.4}$

$=$ £6,250

Excess sales $= 3,750$

Margin of safety $= \frac{3,750}{10,000}$

$= 37.5\%$

∴ P/S ratio $= 37.5\% \times 40\%$

$= 15\%$

2 Breakeven charts

2.1 CVP assumptions

CVP analysis is based on the following assumptions:

- selling price is constant per unit irrespective of the number of units to be sold
- fixed costs are constant in total
- variable costs are constant per unit irrespective of the number of units produced.

There is also an assumption that if there is any difference between sales and production volumes such stocks are valued at their variable cost.

2.2 The conventional breakeven chart

The conventional breakeven chart plots total costs and total revenues at different output levels, and under the above assumptions appears as follows:

Conventional breakeven chart

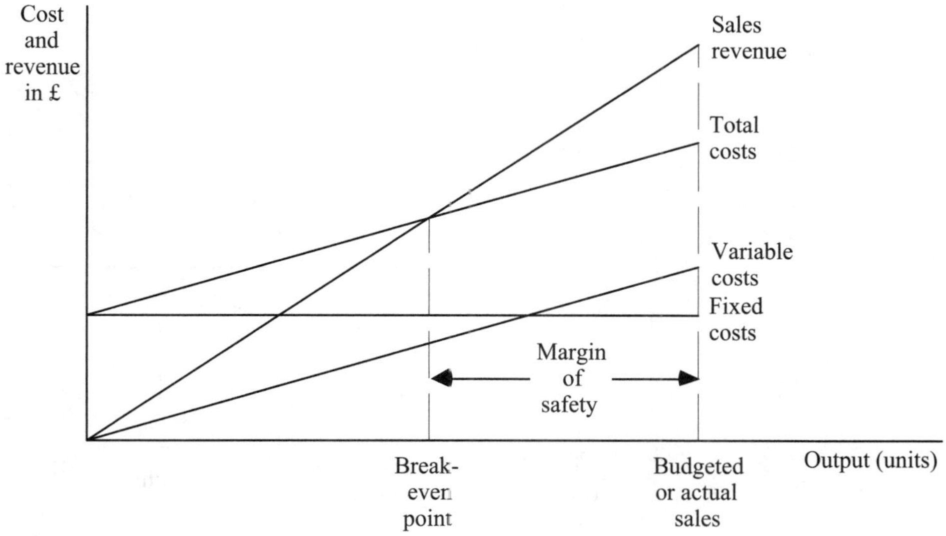

The chart or graph is constructed by:

- plotting fixed costs as a straight line parallel to the horizontal axis
- plotting sales revenue and variable costs from the origin
- total costs represent fixed plus variable costs.

The point at which the sales revenue and total cost lines intersect indicates the **break even** level of output. The amount of profit or loss at any given output can be read off the chart.

The chart is normally drawn up to the budgeted sales volume.

2.3 Usefulness of charts

The conventional form of breakeven charts was described above. Many variations of such charts exist to illustrate the main relationships of costs, volume and profit. Unclear or complex charts should, however, be avoided as a chart which is not easily understood defeats its own object.

Generally, breakeven charts are most useful to:

- compare products, time periods or actual versus plan
- show the effect of changes in circumstances or in plans
- give a broad picture of events.

KEY POINT

Breakeven charts allow costs and revenues at varying activity levels to be read off. PV charts show profit/loss values at various activity levels.

2.4 Profit-volume chart

Breakeven charts usually show both costs and revenues over a given range of activity and they do not highlight directly the amounts of profits or losses at the various levels. A chart that does simply depict the net profit and loss at any given level of activity is called a profit-volume chart (or graph).

Breakeven charts allow costs and revenues at varying activity levels to be read off. PV charts show profit/loss values at various activity levels.

Profit-volume chart (1)

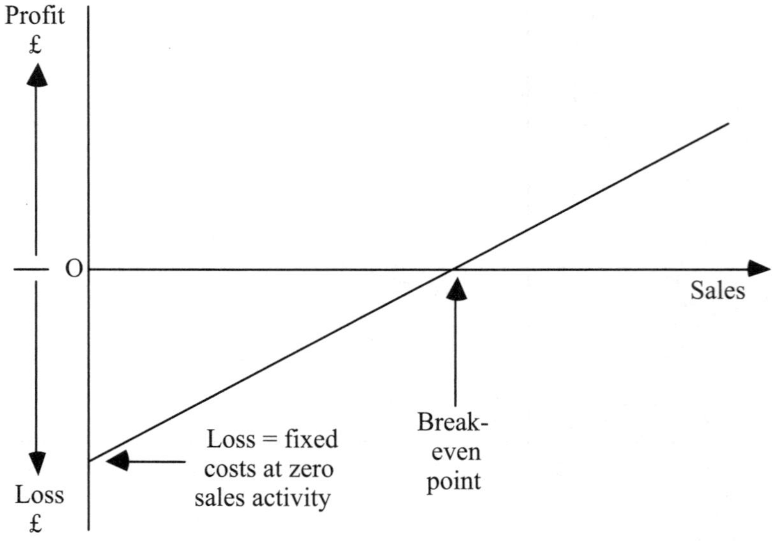

From the above chart the amount of net profit or loss can be read off for any given level of sales activity.

The points to note in the construction of a profit-volume chart are:

(a) The horizontal axis represents sales (in units or sales value, as appropriate). This is the same as for a breakeven chart.

(b) The vertical axis shows net profit above the horizontal sales axis and net loss below.

(c) When sales are zero, the net loss equals the fixed costs and one extreme of the 'profit volume' line is determined – therefore this is one point on the graph or chart.

(d) If variable cost per unit and fixed costs in total are both constant throughout the relevant range of activity under consideration, the profit-volume chart is depicted by a straight line (as illustrated above). Therefore, to draw that line it is only necessary to know the profit (or loss) at one level of sales. The 'profit-volume' line is then drawn between this point and that determined in (c) and extended as necessary.

(e) If there are changes in the variable cost per unit or total fixed costs at various activity levels, it would be necessary to calculate the profit (or loss) at each point where the cost structure changes and to plot these on the chart. The 'profit-volume' line will then be a series of straight lines joining these points together, as simply illustrated below:

Profit-volume chart (2)

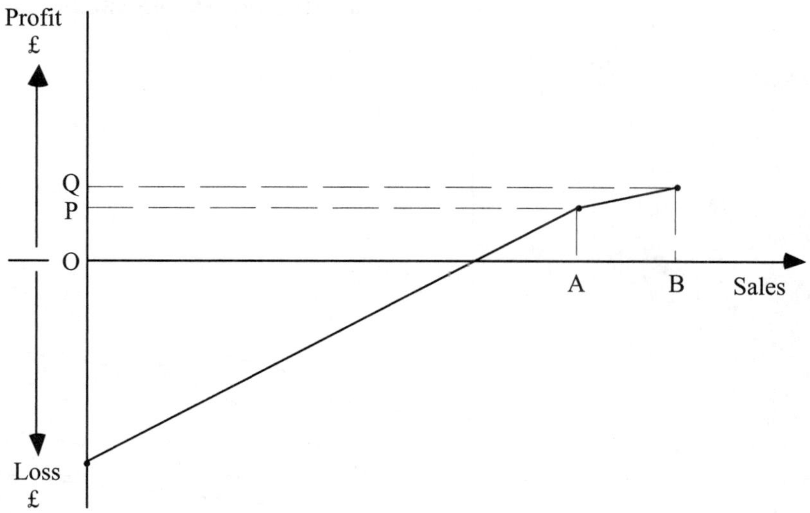

This illustration depicts the situation where the variable cost per unit increases after a certain level of activity (OA), e.g. because of overtime premiums that are incurred when production (and sales) exceed a particular level.

Points to note:

- the profit (OP) at sales level OA would be determined and plotted
- similarly the profit (OQ) at sales level of OB would be determined and plotted
- the loss at zero sales activity (= fixed costs) can be plotted
- the 'profit-volume' line is then drawn by joining these points, as illustrated.

2.5 Changes to variables

Breakeven charts can also be used to illustrate the effects of changes to variables:

Conventional breakeven chart showing increasing selling price

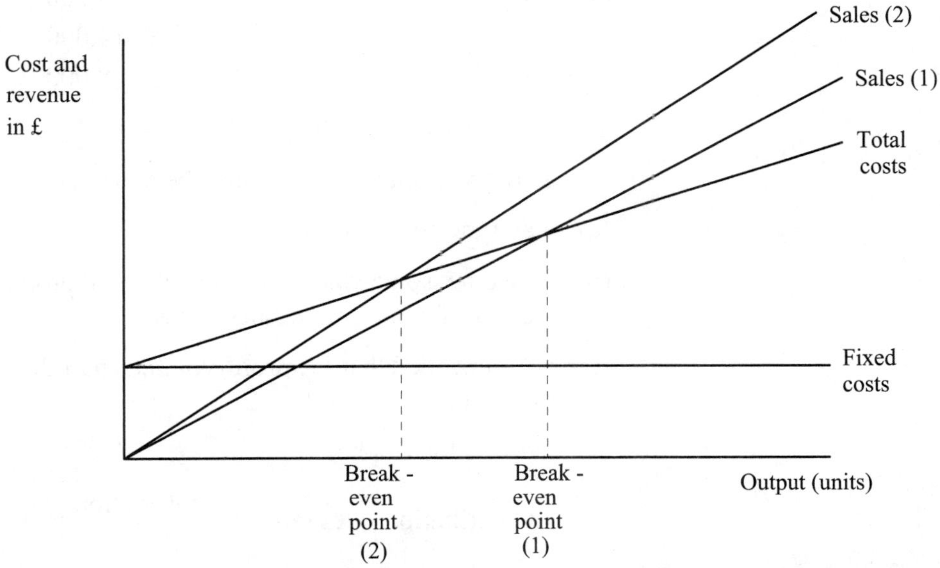

The diagram above shows the effect on the breakeven point of a change in the selling price.

Contribution breakeven chart showing increasing variable costs/unit

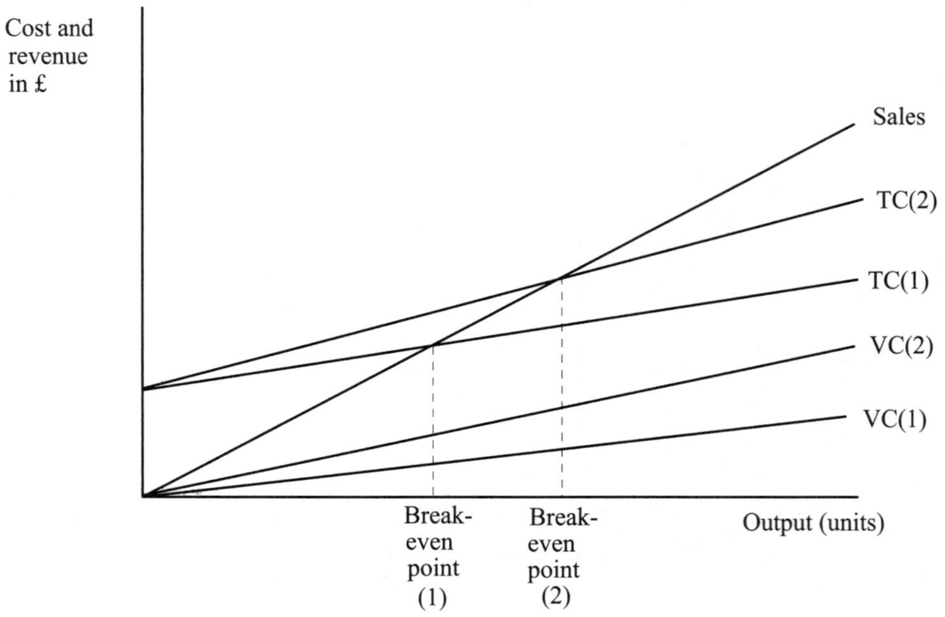

KEY POINT

A multiple product PV chart can be drawn using an **average contribution per unit** of **C/S ratio** assuming constant sales mix for all total quantities.

Note how a change in a variable cost automatically changes the total cost.

2.6 Multi-product profit-volume chart

A further complication that could be encountered is in situations where there is more than one product.

A multiple product PV chart can be drawn using an **average contribution per unit** of **C/S ratio** assuming constant sales mix for all total quantities.

Example

Budgeted data:

	Sales	*Contribution*
	£	£
Product A	10,000	2,000
Product B	14,000	7,000
Product C	8,000	2,400

Total fixed costs £8,000 pa.

There are two approaches that may be adopted:

(a) assume constant sales mix

(b) assume, somewhat unrealistically, that products are sold in descending order of contribution sales ratios.

It is recommended that the profit-volume chart drawn in this context should incorporate both (a) and (b).

Data needed for graph:

Contribution sales ratios $\left(\frac{\text{Contribution}}{\text{Sales}} \times 100\right)$

Product A $\frac{2,000}{10,000} \times 100 = 20\%$ 3rd

Product B $\frac{7,000}{14,000} \times 100 = 50\%$ 1st

Product C $\frac{2,400}{8,000} \times 100 = 30\%$ 2nd

The order of sale and cumulative profit figures will be assumed to be as follows:

	Total sales	*Total contribution*	*Fixed costs*	*Profit/(loss)*
	£	£	£	£
1 Product B	14,000	7,000	8,000	(1,000)
2 Product C	8,000	2,400		
	22,000	9,400	8,000	1,400
3 Product A	10,000	2,000		
	32,000	11,400	8,000	3,400

The multi-product profit-volume chart would appear as follows:

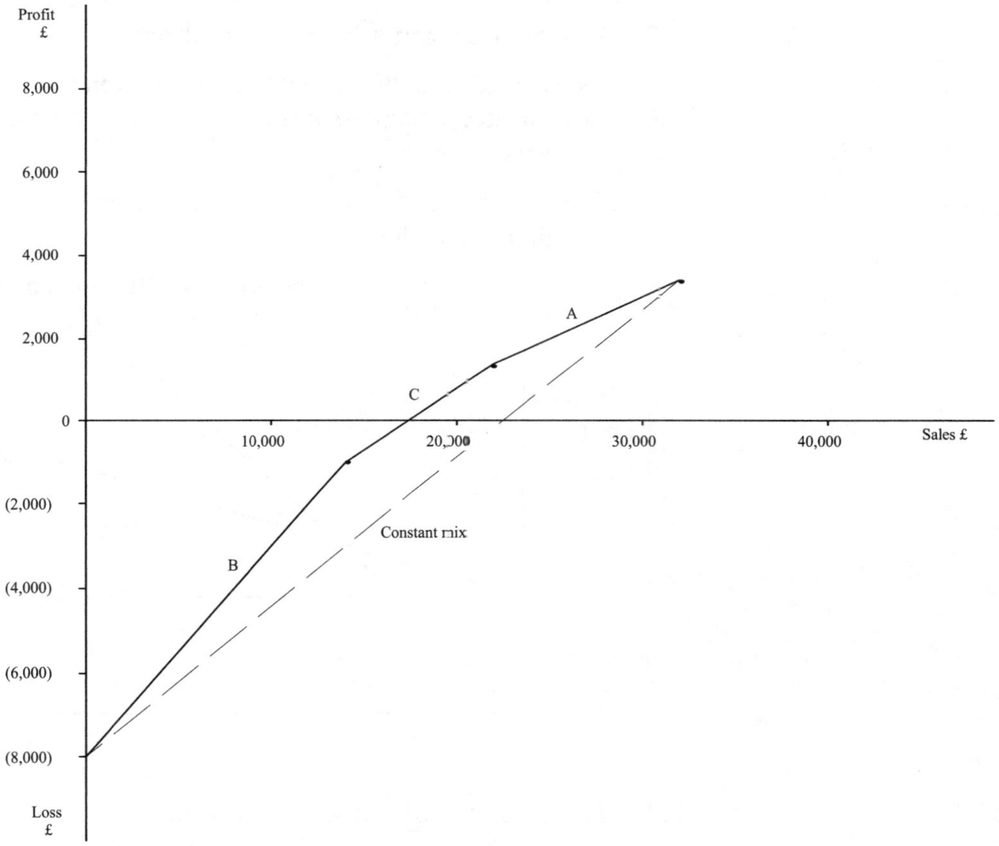

Activity 2

From the following data **you are required** to:

(a) Construct a profit-volume chart showing:

(i) budget contribution of each product to the total budget profit

(ii) actual contribution each product achieved in the overall profit earned in the month.

(b) Comment briefly on useful management points which could be read from the chart.

Data for the month of April was as follows:

	Product	Sales volume in units	Selling price each, £	Contribution/ sales ratio %
Budget:	W	8,000	30	25
	X	12,000	20	15
	Y	6,000	10	30
	Z	4,000	25	10
Fixed overhead for month, £40,000.				
Actuals:	W	6,000	34	30
	X	14,000	15	Negative 10
	Y	8,000	15	40
	Z	3,000	24	8
Fixed overhead for month, £35,000.				

Feedback to this activity is at the end of the chapter.

2.7 The accountant's breakeven chart

As we have seen, the accountant's breakeven chart upon which CVP analysis is based makes certain **assumptions** concerning the linearity of costs and revenues.

The accountant's breakeven chart is thus depicted with costs and revenues as straight lines as shown below.

Accountant's breakeven chart

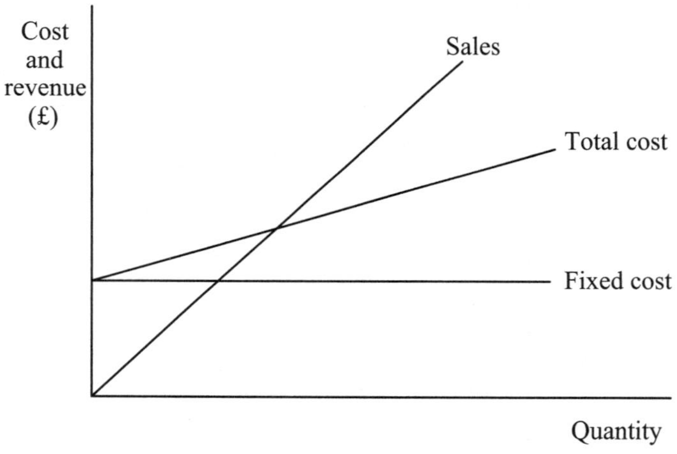

2.8 The economist's breakeven chart

However, most firms would ultimately encounter the conditions generally postulated by the economist:

- it is unlikely the last unit could be sold for the same price as the first
- material costs and labour costs rise as output tends upward. The effect of quantity discounts is offset by less efficient production and overtime rates or less skilled labour force.

The economist's breakeven chart has two break-even points thus:

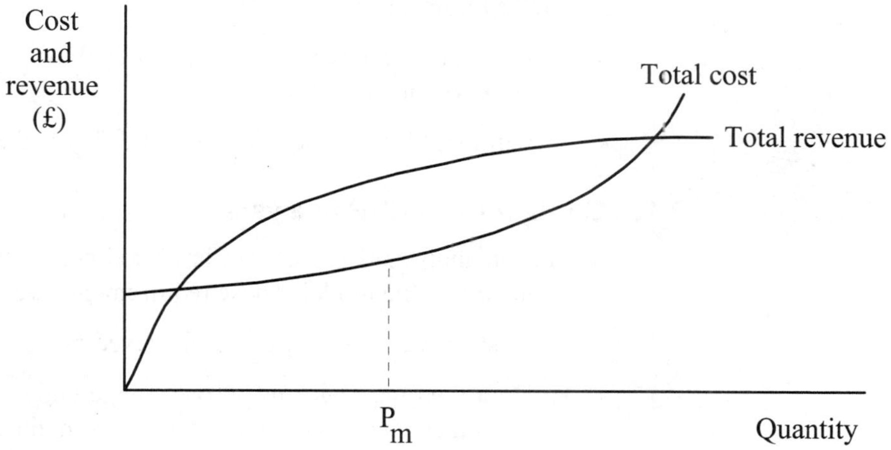

Profit is maximised at the level of output P_m where there is the greatest vertical difference between the total cost and total revenue curves.

2.9 The economist's revenue curves

To sell more units demand must be increased, and to do this the price must be reduced. Thus sales revenue may be depicted:

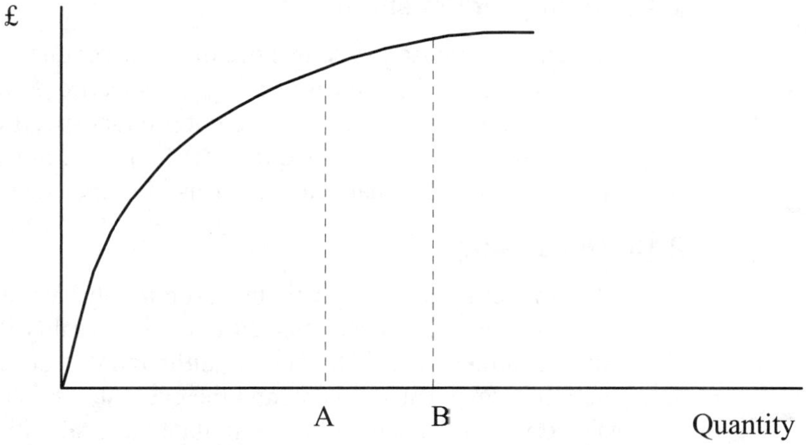

However, in such a chart the range of activity levels depicted is from zero to maximum and this is unlikely to occur in reality. It is more likely that the range of activity will lie between points A and B. It can be seen that between these points the revenue curve is virtually a straight line.

2.10 Curvi-linear variable costs

A similar principle applies to variable costs where it could be argued that the effects of quantity discounts on materials, and overtime/inefficiencies on labour costs, cause these to be depicted as curves:

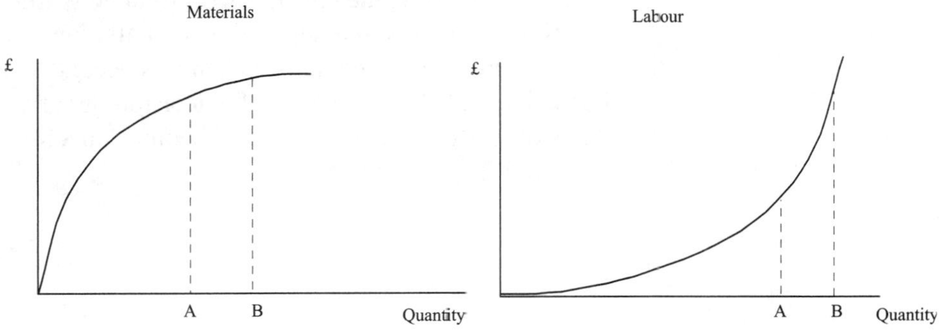

However, two arguments exist to support the accountant's linear model in respect of these costs:

- if each of these types of cost are added together, their total will approximate to a straight-line
- within a likely range of activity the curves themselves are virtually linear.

2.11 Limitations of CVP analysis

Breakeven analysis is useful insofar as it either meets or approximates to the requirements of the model. These requirements are:

- Costs can be classified as either fixed or variable.
- Over the time scale and activity range under review, unit variable costs remain constant and total fixed costs remain constant.
- Unit sales price remains constant.
- The costs and relationships are known.

These requirements limit the usefulness of CVP analysis for planning and decision-making. In particular its usefulness is limited in multi-product situations and where uncertainty of input values exists.

2.12 Multi-product situations

When an organisation sells more than one product there is always difficulty in identifying the fixed costs relating to a specific product, and inevitably there will be some fixed costs that are not product specific. Consequently a particular sales mix has to be assumed in order to use the model, and then the break-even point can only be quantified in terms of sales values.

2.13 Uncertainty

The model is over-simplistic by assuming that variable costs are constant per unit and fixed costs are constant in total. In reality there will be economies and diseconomies of scale that occur, although it is uncertain as to the level of activity which causes them, and the extent to which the costs will be affected. The CVP model cannot be manipulated to deal with these and other forms of uncertainty.

2.14 Fixed costs and time

A fixed cost is a cost that is assumed in CVP analysis to remain constant irrespective of the level of activity. Such costs are often considered to be uncontrollable, but this is not usually true within the longer term.

The controllability of costs must be considered in connection with the powers of the managers concerned. In the context of fixed costs it is common for costs to be uncontrollable because of a contractual agreement or similar long-term arrangement. Thus the cost is uncontrollable within the short-term but outside this timescale the agreement will eventually lapse, or significant changes can be made to production methods. When this occurs costs that were uncontrollable become controllable because of a decision opportunity. However, once the decision has been made, the cost becomes uncontrollable at its new level and therefore fixed once again.

Summary

- CVP analysis is the study of the effects on future profits of changes in fixed cost, variable cost, sales price, quantity and mix.
- Contribution is the difference between sales revenue and marginal costs.
- Margin of safety is the difference between budgeted sales volume and break-even sales volume.
- Charts used in CVP analysis include breakeven charts and profit volume charts.

Having completed your study of this chapter you should have achieved the following learning outcomes.

- Apply variable/fixed cost analysis in multiple product contexts to break-even analysis and product mix decision-making, including circumstances where there are multiple constraints and linear programming methods are needed to reach 'optimal' solutions.

Self-test questions

1 What is CVP analysis? (1.1)

2 Why does CVP use contribution, and not profit, per unit? (1.2)

3 What is the contribution to sales ratio? (1.3)

4 Explain the term 'margin of safety'. (1.6)

5 Distinguish between the accountant's and economist's breakeven chart. (2.7, 2.8)

6 Explain the limitations of CVP analysis. (2.11)

Objective test questions

Question 1

Raith sells three products, X, Y and Z

	Selling price	*Maximum demand*	*Variable cost of production*
X	£10	30,000	£8
Y	£15	10,000	£10
Z	£5	20,000	£4

Fixed costs are £26,000.

If Raith always sells its products in the same proportions as the maximum demand for each, the amount made and sold of X when the company breaks even is:

A 6,000

B 6,545

C 12,000

D 13,000

Question 2

If both the selling price per unit and variable cost per unit of a company rise by 10%, the breakeven point will:

A remain constant

B increase

C fall

D be impossible to determine.

Question 3

A company manufactures and sells a single product. The following data have been extracted from this year's budget:

Sales and production	1,000 units
Variable cost per unit	£60
Fixed cost per unit	£25
Contribution margin ratio	52%

The selling price per unit for the next year is budgeted to increase by 8% whereas both the variable cost per unit and the total fixed costs are expected to increase by only 5%.

The objective for next year is that the total budgeted profit should remain the same as that budgeted for this year.

Calculate the minimum number of whole units that should be produced and sold next year in order to achieve the objective.

A 650

B 883

C 903

D 921

Question 4

ABC Ltd sells three products in the proportion 25% K, 35% L, 40% M. The contribution to sales ratios of the products are:

K 35%

L 20%

M 30%

If fixed costs for the period are expected to be £350,000, the revenue (to the nearest £1,000) needed to earn a marginal costing profit of £75,000 is:

A £1,532,000

B £1,531,000

C £1,275,000

D £1,274,000

Question 5

M plc manufactures and sells two products, A and B, in the proportion 30% A and 70% B. Total annual sales are planned to be £1,300,000. Product A has a contribution to sales ratio of 50% whereas that of product B is 28%. Annual fixed costs are estimated to be £350,000.

The budgeted breakeven sales value is:

A £686,912

B £700,000

C £897,436

D £1,011,561

The following data is relevant to questions 8 and 9.

M plc currently sells products A, B and C in equal quantities and at the same selling price per unit. The contribution to sales ratio for product A is 40%; for product B it is 35%; the total is 42%. Fixed costs are unaffected by mix and are currently 25% of sales.

Question 6

Calculate the C/S ratio of Product C.

Question 7

Calculate the total contribution/total sales ratio if the product mix changed to:

A 50% **B** 35% **C** 15%

For the answers to these questions, see the 'Answers' section at the end of the book.

Exam-type question

JK Ltd

JK Ltd has prepared a budget for the next 12 months when it intends to make and sell four products, details of which are shown below:

Product	*Sales in units (thousands)*	*Selling price per unit* £	*Variable cost per unit* £
J	10	20	14.00
K	10	40	8.00
L	50	4	4.20
M	20	10	7.00

Budgeted fixed costs are £240,000 per annum and total assets employed are £570,000.

You are required:

(a) produce a profit-volume graph of the above data **(6 marks)**

(b) comment on useful management points which can be read from the graph. **(4 marks)**

(Total: 10 marks)

For the answers to these questions, see the 'Answers' section at the end of the book.

Feedback to activities

Activity 1

The new total C/S ratio is:

Widgets	30% × 42%	12.6%
Gidgets	20% × 40%	8.0%
Schmidgets	50% × 45%	22.5%
Total		43.1%

The new BEP = 350/0.431 = £812

Activity 2

(a) **Profit-volume chart**

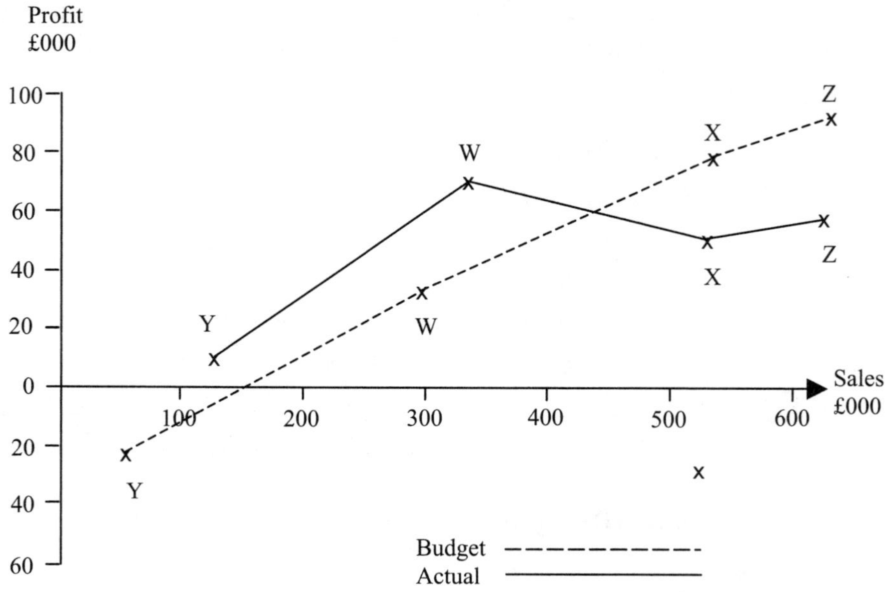

(b) **Useful management points:**

- expectations of profitability were mainly centred on products W and X
- overall profit fell appreciably short of expectation, mainly due to the bad result shown by product X
- the position was retrieved to some extent by an excellent result on product Y
- a saving was effected on fixed overhead
- actual profit was well below budgeted profit
- overall sales were less than the budgeted level
- the steeper climbing lines of products W and Y indicate that their actual contributions to sales ratios were better than expected.

Workings

Budget:

Plotting in descending order of budgeted c/s ratios

	Product	*Sales value* £000	*Cumulative* £000	*Contribution ratio* %	*Contribution* £000	*Cumulative* £000
Y	6 × 10	60	60	30	18	18
W	8 × 30	240	300	25	60	78
X	12 × 20	240	540	15	36	114
Z	4 × 25	100	640	10	10	124

At zero sales loss = £40,000

Therefore plot:	18 – 40	=	–22,000 Y
	78 – 40	=	38,000 W
	114 – 40	=	74,000 X
	124 – 40	=	84,000 Z

Similarly for 'Actual'.

	Product	*Sales value* £000	*Cumulative* £000	*Contribution ratio* %	*Contribution* £000	*Cumulative* £000
Y	8 × 15	120	120	40	48	48
W	6 × 34	204	324	30	61	109
X	14 × 15	210	534	–10	–21	88
Z	3 × 24	72	606	8	6	94

At zero sales loss = £35,000

Therefore plot:	48 – 35	=	13,000 Y
	109 – 35	=	74,000 W
	88 – 35	=	53,000 X
	94 – 35	=	59,000 Z

Chapter 4

RELEVANT COSTS

Syllabus content

This chapter covers the following syllabus content.

- Relevant cash flows and their use in short-term decisions typically concerning acceptance/rejection of contracts, pricing and cost-benefit comparisons.
- The importance of strategic, intangible and non-financial judgements in decision-making.

This chapter starts by considering the process and methods of decision making under conditions of certainty. It revises material that should be familiar from your earlier studies before moving on to the topics of shut down and divestment.

Contents

1 Decision making under conditions of certainty

1.1 Introduction

There are basically two types of decision facing managers.

(a) **Accept or reject decisions**

These arise when a particular opportunity is under consideration that, if accepted, will not prejudice any other opportunities which might arise. An example of this type of decision might be whether or not to undertake a special order that does not conform to normal trading arrangements. In this situation a decision may be taken with regard to the worthiness of the opportunity without having to compare it with others.

(b) **Ranking decisions**

These involve a choice between two or more competing opportunities. A ranking of opportunities is necessary where the organisation is prevented from accepting all of those being considered, either because of limited resources or because the projects are mutually exclusive. A situation of mutual exclusivity arises when different ways of meeting the same objective are being considered as, for example, in choosing between a number of locations for the siting of a new factory.

A number of decision situations will be examined in this chapter, but it is important first to establish the accounting principles that should be adopted if efficient decisions are to be made and to consider briefly the nature of the decision-making process itself.

1.2 The decision-making process

Decisions are always concerned with choices made between alternative courses of action; if no alternatives exist, there is no decision to be taken.

The decision-making process may be summarised by the following steps.

Step 1

Become aware of the need for a decision.

Step 2

Identify all available alternative courses of action.

Step 3

Evaluate each alternative.

Step 4

Select a course of action.

1.3 The accountant's role in decision making

Within the area of decision making, the primary task of the management accountant is to collect and present valid information. Although it is possible for the accountant to be involved in all four steps in decision making, the main concern will be with the evaluation process. The accountant's role is essentially that of a technical expert on cost analysis, with responsibility for ensuring that the operating manager or executive is guided towards making the best decision via the use of accurate and relevant information.

KEY POINT

The process is essentially forward looking and dynamic. Therefore, the information must satisfy the criteria of being applicable and appropriate.

The concept of relevance is central to management accounting. Relevance requires that management accountants must ensure that flexibility is maintained in assembling and interpreting information. This facilitates the exploration and presentation, in a clear, understandable and timely manner, of as many alternatives as are necessary for impartial and confident decisions to be taken.

The process is essentially forward looking and dynamic. Therefore, the information must satisfy the criteria of being applicable and appropriate.

1.4 Quantitative and qualitative factors

DEFINITION

Quantitative factors – factors which are relevant to a decision and that are expressed numerically.

Qualitative factors – factors which are relevant to a decision, but which are not expressed numerically. (CIMA *Official Terminology*)

The decision-making process will be influenced by quantitative and qualitative factors.

- **Quantitative factors** – factors that are relevant to a decision and that are expressed numerically.
- **Qualitative factors** – factors that are relevant to a decision, but which are not expressed numerically.

For example, the cost of a packet of cigarettes may be stated as £5. However, there may be an implicit cost attached to using the cigarettes, namely the effect on health. Such an implicit cost can only be a subjective estimate, but its identification may well influence the eventual decision outcome, i.e. to smoke or not to smoke, and is an example of a qualitative factor.

Thus qualitative factors are those which are difficult to measure because subjectivity comes into the analysis and different appraisers are likely to assign different values to them. Nevertheless, qualitative factors are important and the decision-maker should be aware of them. In practice the accountant will attempt to express as many decision factors as possible in quantitative terms, thus reducing the subjective element inherent in the decision-making process.

1.5 Relevant costs and benefits

DEFINITION

A **relevant cost** may be defined as a cost appropriate to a specific management decision, i.e. it is expected to occur and it differs from other costs in the process of evaluating possible alternative courses of action.

A relevant cost may be defined as a cost appropriate to a specific management decision, i.e. it is expected to occur and it differs from other costs in the process of evaluating possible alternative courses of action.

Information used by the decision-maker primarily relates to the future and should therefore be relevant to the decision situation under consideration.

This principle of relevance applies also to revenues. In order to illustrate the concept of relevant costs and revenues, consider the following.

Example

Brian has an old car on which he has spent £150 in the last three months for repairs. He now discovers that a further £100 needs to be spent on it in order to obtain a new MOT certificate. If an MOT certificate is obtained, the car could be sold to a friend for £150. The scrap value of the car is £25. Assuming that Brian does not wish to keep the car, should he scrap it or sell it to his friend?

Solution

The relevant costs and revenues in this decision situation will be as follows.

	Scrap	*Sell*
	£	£
Revenue	25	150
Cost	-	100
Net income	25	50

In determining relevance, the important consideration is – to what extent will present circumstances be altered as a result of following a particular course of action?

It is clear from the example that, from a financial standpoint, selling the car will generate £25 more income than if the car were scrapped, and on this basis the car should be sold.

Note that in reaching the decision, the changes relative to present circumstances have been evaluated. The amount of £150 already spent on repairs is disregarded since it has been paid out in the past and cannot be recovered. This is an example of a sunk cost or historic cost which is deemed to be irrelevant for the purpose of reaching a decision. What have been considered are the additional costs and revenues relating to those factors which are expected to arise in the future as a result of following a particular course of action.

KEY POINT

In the decision-making process, what has happened in the past is considered only to the extent that it might provide an indication as to what might happen in the future.

In the decision-making process, what has happened in the past is considered only to the extent that it might provide an indication as to what might happen in the future.

1.6 Opportunity cost

DEFINITION

Opportunity cost is the value of the benefit sacrificed when one course of action is chosen, in preference to an alternative. The opportunity cost is represented by the forgone potential benefit from the best rejected course of action. (CIMA *Official Terminology*)

Opportunity cost is the value of the benefit sacrificed when one course of action is chosen, in preference to an alternative. The opportunity cost is represented by the forgone potential benefit from the best rejected course of action. (CIMA *Official Terminology*)

Opportunity cost can be measured in terms of the maximum benefit that could have arisen by selecting the next best alternative.

Using the above example of the car, if it had been decided to obtain an MOT certificate and use the car for another year, then the real cost of implementing the decision would be £150, i.e. £100 actual repair cost plus £50 opportunity cost representing the maximum net income that has been surrendered in order to have the car available for personal use.

Activity 1

Leopard Ltd has 600 units of raw material X that it is considering using in the manufacture of a new product. The raw material X cost £3 per unit when purchased three months ago. The current purchase price is now £5 per unit. If X is not used in manufacturing the new product it can be sold for £2 per unit. Alternatively it could be used to replace material Y currently costing £6 per unit and used to manufacture an existing product.

(a) What is the relevant value of the 600 units of X if they are to be used in producing the new product?

(b) What is the relevant value per unit of X when the existing stock runs out, assuming there is plenty of material X available?

Feedback to this activity is at the end of the chapter.

1.7 The contribution approach to decision making

Since the function of the decision-making process is the selection of a future course of action from a number of available alternatives, it follows that in the evaluation process those costs that are common to every alternative will have no direct bearing on the eventual ranking of alternatives. Therefore in most decision-making situations fixed costs may be disregarded, since by definition such costs will be insensitive to any proposed changes in activity. Note, however, that if an element of fixed cost is identified as being specifically related to a particular course of action, then it will be brought into the evaluation as a relevant cost.

It is because fixed costs tend to be irrelevant for decision-making purposes that marginal costing techniques should be applied. The overriding objective in business management should be to select those courses of action which will obtain, from given resources, the maximum amount of contribution to the business.

The contribution approach is a more flexible approach than an absorption costing approach for the purpose of assessing decision situations, possessing the following distinct advantages:

- more detailed information is offered, based on cost behaviour patterns
- sensitivity to cost-volume-profit relationships
- comprehensive build-up of cost can be used to determine 'normal' or 'target' selling prices on a full cost basis.

In the following sections the contribution approach will be used to assess different decision situations. In each situation, a consideration of all relevant incremental costs and revenues will lead to the identification of incremental or marginal contribution which, together with a consideration of qualitative factors, will allow the optimum decision to be reached.

It is never possible to know future costs and revenues with certainty, and estimates will have varying degrees of confidence attached to them. However, in the examples of decision situations that follow, the problem of uncertainty is ignored, and there will be a single figure estimate of costs and revenues.

2 Examples of decision situations

2.1 Introduction

In this section the principle of relevance is applied to a number of simple decision-making problems of a common type. Qualitative factors are taken into account as appropriate.

You are advised to attempt to find a solution to each example before reading the printed answers.

2.2 Utilisation of spare capacity

Where production is below capacity, opportunities may arise for sales at a special below normal price, for example:

(a) export orders

(b) manufacturing under another brand name.

Such opportunities are worthwhile if the answer to two key questions is 'yes'.

- Is spare capacity available?
- Does additional revenue (units × price) exceed additional costs (units × variable cost)? Or, more simply, is contribution (revenue – variable cost) positive?

However, the evaluation should also consider the following three questions.

- Is there an alternative more profitable way of utilising spare capacity (e.g. sales promotion, making an alternative product)?
- Will fixed costs be unchanged if the order is accepted?
- Will accepting one order at below normal selling price lead other customers to ask for price cuts?

The longer the time period in question, the more important are these other factors.

Example

At production level of 8,000 units per month, which is 80% of capacity, the budget of Export Ltd is as follows.

Sales	*Per unit*	*8,000 units*
	£	£
Price	5.00	40,000
Direct labour	1.00	8,000
Raw materials	1.50	12,000
Variable overheads	0.50	4,000
	3.00	24,000
Fixed costs	1.50	12,000
Total	4.50	36,000
Budgeted profit	0.50	4,000

An opportunity arises to export 1,000 units per month at a price of £4.00 per unit. Should the contract be accepted?

Solution

- Is spare capacity available? Yes.
- Is contribution positive?

	£ per unit
Additional revenue	4.00
Additional/variable costs	3.00
Additional contribution	1.00

Since each unit sold results in an additional contribution, the contract should be accepted.

Total additional contribution = 1,000 × £1.00 = £1,000.

Note that fixed costs remain unchanged and are therefore ignored: the additional contribution of £1,000 means additional profit of £1,000.

Activity 2

(a) If Export Ltd (from the above example) accepts the contract for 1,000 units, what is the remaining unused production capacity?

(b) If the same customer requires to increase the contract to 1,600 units but at a price of £3.60, would it be worth accepting the new contract instead of the first contract?

Feedback to this activity is at the end of the chapter.

3 'Accept or reject' decisions

A common type of exam question is the 'accept or reject' decision. We illustrate this in the example below.

Example

Spartan plc manufactures a wide range of soft toys. The managers of the business are considering whether to add a new type of toy animal, the Wimble, to the product range. A recent market research survey, undertaken at a cost of £2,000, has indicated that demand for the Wimble would last for only one year, during which time 100,000 of these could be sold at £6 each.

It is assumed that production and sales of the Wimble would take place evenly throughout the year. Manufacturing cost data is available below.

Raw materials

Each Wimble would require three types of raw material – A, B and C. Material A is used regularly in the business and stocks are replaced as necessary. Material B is currently being held as surplus stock as a result of over-ordering on an earlier contract. This material is not used regularly by Spartan plc and would be sold if not required for the manufacture of the Wimble. Material C would have to be bought in specially for the Wimble, since stocks of this item are not normally held.

Current stock levels and costs of each raw material are shown below.

Raw material	*Amount required per Wimble*	*Current stock level*	*Original cost*	*Replacement cost*	*Realisable value*
	(m)	(m)	(£/m)	(£/m)	(£/m)
A	0.8	200,000	1.05	1.25	0.90
B	0.4	30,000	1.65	1.20	0.55
C	0.1	0	-	2.75	2.50

Labour

In producing one Wimble, half an hour of skilled labour and a quarter of an hour of unskilled labour would be required, at wage rates of £3 per hour and £2 per hour respectively. One supervisor would be required full-time at an annual salary of £7,000.

Skilled labour for the production of Wimbles would have to be recruited specially, whilst 25,000 surplus unskilled labour hours are expected to be available during the coming year if Wimbles are not manufactured. However, company policy dictates that no unskilled worker will be made redundant in the foreseeable future.

The supervisor has agreed to delay immediate retirement for one year, and to waive an annual pension of £4,000 in return for the annual salary during this period.

Machinery

Two machines, X and Y, would be required to manufacture Wimbles, details of which are below.

	X	*Y*
Original cost	£35,000	£25,000
Accumulated depreciation	£24,000	£18,000
Written down value	£11,000	£7,000
Age	4 years	6 years
Estimated remaining useful life	1 year	2 years
Estimated value at end of useful life	£5,000	£1,000

Details are also available of cash values relating to the two machines at the start and end of the year during which Wimbles would be produced.

		Start of year	*End of year*
		£	£
Machine X:	Replacement cost	40,000	45,000
	Resale value	7,000	5,000
Machine Y:	Replacement cost	30,000	33,000
	Resale value	4,000	3,000

If machine X were not used for the manufacture of Wimbles then it would be used to manufacture existing products, the sale of which would result in an estimated £30,000 net receipts.

Machine X is one of a number of identical machine types used regularly on various products by Spartan plc. Each of this type of machine is replaced as soon as it reaches the end of its useful life.

Machine Y is the only one of its type within the firm and, if not used in the manufacture of Wimbles, would be sold immediately.

Overheads

Variable overhead costs attributable to Wimbles are estimated at £1.50 per item produced. Production fixed overheads are allocated by Spartan plc to products on the basis of labour hours, and the rate for the coming year has been established at £2.50 per labour hour. The manufacture of Wimbles will not result in any additional fixed costs being incurred.

Solution

We can now turn our attention to assessing whether, on the basis of the information given, the manufacture and sale of Wimbles represents a profitable opportunity to Spartan plc. In doing so, the relevant cost of using each resource required to produce Wimbles must be identified. For each resource a comparison is required showing the cash flows associated with manufacture and those associated with non-manufacture.

The difference between the two represents the incremental cost of applying each resource to the production of Wimbles.

Cash flows

	Manufacture	*Non-manufacture*	*Incremental cost*
	£	£	£
Raw materials:			
A	(100,000)	0	(100,000)
B	(12,000)	16,500	(28,500)
C	(27,500)	0	(27,500)
			(156,000)

	Manufacture	*Non-manufacture*	*Incremental cost*
	£	£	£
Labour:			
Skilled	(150,000)	0	(150,000)
Unskilled	(50,000)	(50,000)	0
Supervisor	(7,000)	(4,000)	(3,000)
			(153,000)
Machinery:			
X	0	30,000	(30,000)
Y	3,000	4,000	(1,000)
			(31,000)
Overheads:			
Variable	(150,000)	0	(150,000)
Fixed	-	-	-
			(150,000)
Total incremental cost			(490,000)
Total sales revenue			600,000
Net cash inflow (contribution)			110,000

Thus £490,000 is the relevant cost to Spartan plc for producing 100,000 Wimbles during the forthcoming year. Taking the cash generated from sales into consideration, a net cash inflow of £110,000 would result from this trading opportunity.

The basis for establishing the relevant cost of each resource is examined below.

Raw materials

A: Since this material is used regularly within the business and stocks are replaced as used, the 80,000 metres required would be replaced for subsequent use on other jobs at the current replacement cost of £1.25 per metre.

B: If Wimbles are manufactured a further 10,000 metres would have to be purchased at £1.20 per metre. The historic cost of 30,000 metres already in stock is a sunk cost and is therefore not relevant. If Wimbles were not manufactured, the existing stock would be sold off at the realisable value of £0.55 per metre.

C: The only cash flow arising here is that relating to the special purchase of 10,000 metres at £2.75 per metre if Wimbles are produced.

To summarise, the relevant cost of raw materials is identified as being their current replacement cost, unless the material in question is not to be replaced, in which case the relevant cost becomes the higher of current resale value or the value if applied to another product (economic value).

Labour

Skilled: In manufacturing Wimbles additional wage payments of £150,000 would be made, i.e. 50,000 hours at £3 per hour. These payments relate to specifically recruited labour.

Unskilled: The cost of 25,000 hours of unskilled labour will be incurred by Spartan plc regardless of whether Wimbles are produced. Company policy has effectively turned this unskilled labour wages element into a fixed cost that cannot be adjusted in the short term and is therefore not relevant to the decision at hand.

Supervisor: The relevant cost of the supervisor is the difference between the wages paid if Wimbles are produced, and the pension cost that would be avoided in this situation.

In assessing the relevant cost of labour the avoidable costs of production have been identified, i.e. those that will not be incurred unless Wimbles are produced. If any element of the labour resource could be used for some other profitable purpose, then the opportunity cost representing the income forgone would have to be included in the analysis.

Machinery

X: It would cost Spartan plc £30,000 if the company were to lose the use of machine X, being the annual net receipts associated with the existing use of the machine. Note that it may be economically better to replace the machine to avoid this loss, but we would need to know the net cost of replacement (cost now (£40,000) less 'value' in one year's time – unknown). If this net cost were less than £30,000, it would be worthwhile, and would be the relevant cost to include. In the absence of this information, £30,000 is used.

Y: The manufacture of Wimbles would delay the sale of machine Y by one year, during which time the resale value of the machine would have been reduced by £1,000 as shown in the table of machine values.

In determining the relevant costs associated with the use of plant and machinery, similar considerations apply as to those identified in respect of raw materials. If plant and equipment is to be replaced at the end of its useful life, or would be immediately replaced should the business be deprived of the use of an asset, then current replacement cost is the relevant cost. If the asset is not to be replaced, then the relevant cost becomes the higher of resale value or associated net receipts arising from use of the asset (economic value).

In this analysis of relevant cost, the assumption is made that the use of machine X is profitable for the company. If a situation arises in which an asset is not generating sufficient net receipts to meet a target rate of return, the replacement of the asset would presumably not be encouraged since its use is uneconomic, and thus replacement cost is not relevant since it would not represent a viable option.

You should note, however, that correctly identifying the true cost of using a particular asset might be difficult in practice, since economic values are not easily identified.

Overheads

Variable costs of £1.50 per Wimble are avoidable, being incurred only if Wimbles are produced. In contrast, fixed overhead may be assumed to be fixed regardless of the product being produced and the level of activity over a given range. Since fixed overhead is unaffected by the opportunity being considered, any apportionment of fixed cost is meaningless and would serve only to distort the profitability of the project.

For decision purposes, only those costs that will vary as a result of the decision taken are relevant.

A form of statement similar to that shown above for the analysis of differential cash flows could be used for presentation to management. In addition, supplementary information should be provided in order to disclose the principles adopted in evaluating the cost of use of each resource. Attention should be drawn to the fact that the surplus cash figure of £110,000 is the anticipated increase in Spartan plc's cash reserves arising from the manufacture of Wimbles rather than applying the required resources to their best alternative use.

Thus from a purely financial viewpoint the production and sale of Wimbles appears to be worthwhile. However, as was noted earlier, there may be other factors of interest to the decision-maker. Non-quantifiable qualitative factors such as the effect on longer-term marketing strategy, customer reaction, competitor reaction, etc. should be identified and incorporated into the analysis so that a balanced judgement may be made.

KEY POINT

In the above analysis the principle of relevance was applied in the evaluation of the financial factors surrounding the manufacture of Wimbles.

In the above analysis the principle of relevance was applied in the evaluation of the financial factors surrounding the manufacture of Wimbles. At no time was historic cost suggested as being an appropriate measure of the relevant cost of a resource.

4 Shut down and divestment

4.1 Introduction

A company may have to drop existing product-market areas as well as develop new ones. For instance, a product might be nearing the end of its life cycle and it might be better to 'kill it off' once sales have fallen below a certain level rather than let it decline to zero. Advertising expenditure to boost the sale of a declining product is often not worthwhile in terms of the return achieved.

The timing of a decision to drop a certain line is difficult, and most companies probably leave it too late. Here are some of the reasons for reluctance to drop products.

- The company might have invested large sums of money in the project and does not want to abandon it. Management accountants will recognise that this is a quite erroneous standpoint – the money already spent is a sunk cost and it is the future not the past that is important. Companies should be prepared to 'cut their losses'.

- Perhaps the person who designed the product is still with the firm and, probably along with many others, is 'attached' to the product and wants to keep it going. In addition, the marketing director might be an optimist who thinks that sales of the product will suddenly turn up again. This can happen, but is unlikely unless the cause of the fall in demand is the general economic climate – but we are really talking about products that have a history of continuously falling demand.
- Attention is directed towards new products and no one thinks what should happen to the old ones (until resources are scarce and there is a search for economies).
- There is a feeling that customers should be kept happy and a fear that they will be lost to the firm if the particular product is withdrawn. This fear need have no foundation if a new product is launched as the old one is withdrawn. Anyway, does it matter if some old customers are lost, as long as more new ones are gained?
- A very real problem exists of what to do with the work force who have been running an existing production line if it is suddenly shut down. It may be easier to absorb the work force into other areas if production is run down gradually.

However, there are arguments against this last point.

- Morale among those remaining on the product may fall if they know that their job is eventually going to go and they do not know when or where they will be moved. If this loss of morale is reflected in their work, the product may become even more uneconomic.
- A sensible programme of retraining can ensure that workers released from an old line will be available for a new process.
- It may prove more costly to keep the workers employed on the old process than to pay them for doing nothing until their services are again required elsewhere.

KEY POINT

The detailed programming of divestment is, of course, a matter for the administrative and operating plans but at the strategic level it is important to emphasise that this is one area for examination.

The detailed programming of divestment is, of course, a matter for the administrative and operating plans, but at the strategic level it is important to emphasise that this is one area for examination.

Activity 3

The annual flexible budget of a company is as follows:

Production capacity	*40%*	*60%*	*80%*	*100%*
Costs:	£	£	£	£
Direct labour	16,000	24,000	32,000	40,000
Direct material	12,000	18,000	24,000	30,000
Production overhead	11,400	12,600	13,800	15,000
Administration overhead	5,800	6,200	6,600	7,000
Selling and distribution overhead	6,200	6,800	7,400	8,000
	51,400	67,600	83,800	100,000

Owing to trading difficulties the company is operating at 50% capacity. Selling prices have had to be lowered to what the directors maintain is an uneconomic level and they are considering whether or not their single factory should be closed down until the trade recession has passed.

A market research consultant has advised that in about 12 months' time there is every indication that sales will increase to about 75% of normal capacity and that the revenue to be produced in the second year will amount to £90,000. The present revenue from sales at 50% capacity would amount to only £49,500 for a complete year.

If the directors decide to close down the factory for a year it is estimated that:

(a) the present fixed costs would be reduced to £11,000 per annum

(b) closing down costs (redundancy payments, etc.) would amount to £7,500

(c) necessary maintenance of plant would cost £1,000 per annum

(d) on re-opening the factory, the cost of overhauling plant, training and engagement of new personnel would amount to £4,000.

Prepare a statement for the directors, presenting the information in such a way as to indicate whether or not it is desirable to close the factory.

Feedback to this activity is at the end of the chapter.

Summary

- Most decisions faced by managers can be classified as either 'accept or reject' decisions, or ranking decisions.
- To arrive at a correct decision managers must consider only relevant costs (often opportunity costs) and benefits.
- A common type of exam question relates to shut down or divestment. To tackle such questions it is important to focus on contribution earned, i.e. to ignore apportioned fixed costs which will not be eliminated as a result of the decision to close down.

Having completed your study of this chapter you should have achieved the following learning outcomes.

- Discuss the principles of decision making including the identification of relevant cash flows and their use alongside non-quantifiable factors is making rounded judgements.
- Discuss the usefulness of dividing costs into variable and fixed components in the context of short-term decision making.

Self-test questions

1 What is the contribution approach to decision making? (1.7)

2 In what circumstances may a company divest some of its activities? (4.1)

Objective test questions

Question 1

A firm has some material that originally cost £45,000. It has a scrap value of £12,500 but, if reworked at a cost of £7,500, it could be sold for £17,500.

What would be the incremental effect of reworking and selling the material?

A A loss of £27,500

B A loss of £2,500

C A profit of £5,000

D A profit of £10,000

Question 2

In order to utilise some spare capacity, Z Ltd is preparing a quotation for a special order that requires 1,000 kg of material R.

Z Ltd has 600 kg of material R in stock (original cost £5.00 per kg). Material R is used in the company's main product Q.

The resale value of material R is £4.00 per kg. The present replacement price of material R is £6.00 per kg. Material R is readily available in the market.

Calculate the relevant cost of the 1,000 kg of material R to be included in the quotation.

Question 3

A company is considering accepting a one-year contract that will require four skilled employees. The four skilled employees could be recruited on a one-year contract at a cost of £40,000 per employee. The employees would be supervised by an existing manager who earns £60,000 per annum. It is expected that supervision of the contract would take 10% of the manager's time.

Instead of recruiting new employees, the company could retrain some existing employees who currently earn £30,000 per year. The training would cost £15,000 in total. If these employees were used they would need to be replaced at a total cost of £100,000.

Calculate the relevant labour cost of the contract.

For the answers to these questions, see the 'Answers' section at the end of the book.

Exam-type questions

Question 1: Mike Limited

Mike Limited has been asked to quote a price for a one-off contract. Management has drawn up the following schedule:

		£
Contract price	(Cost plus 20%)	60,780
Costs:		
Materials:	V (300 kg at £10/kg)	3,000
	I (1,000 litres at £7/litre)	7,000
	C (550 kg at £3/kg)	1,650
Labour:	Department 1 (1,500 hours at £8/hour)	12,000
	Department 2 (2,000 hours at £10/hour)	20,000
Overheads:	Absorbed on a budgeted labour hour basis 3,500 hours at £2/labour hour)	7,000
Total costs		50,650

The following is also relevant:

Material V. The cost of £10 is the original purchase cost incurred some years ago. This material is no longer in use by the company and if not used in the contract then it would be sold for scrap at £3/kg.

Material I. This is in continuous use by the business. £7 is the historic cost of the material although current supplies are being purchased at £6.50.

Material C. Mike Limited has 300 kg of this material in stock and new supplies would cost £4/kg. If current stocks are not used for the contract then they would be used as a substitute for material Y in another production process costing £7/kg. 2 kg of C replaces 1 kg of Y.

Department 1. This department has spare labour capacity sufficient for the contract and labour would be retained.

Department 2. This department is currently working at full capacity. Mike Limited could get the men to work overtime to complete the contract paid at time and a half, or they could divert labour hours from the production of other units that currently average £3 contribution per labour hour.

Overheads. These are arbitrarily absorbed at a pre-determined rate. There will be no incremental costs incurred.

Required:

Calculate the minimum contract price that Mike Limited could accept to break even using relevant costing techniques. **(10 marks)**

Question 2: Fiona Ltd

The management of Fiona Ltd is considering the closure of one of its operations and the financial accountant has submitted the following report.

Department	*1*	*2*	*3*	*Total*
Sales (units)	5,000	6,000	2,000	13,000
Sales (£)	150,000	240,000	24,000	414,000
Cost of sales				
Direct material	75,000	150,000	10,000	235,000
Direct labour	25,000	30,000	8,000	63,000
Conversion overhead	5,769	6,923	2,308	15,000
Gross profit	44,231	53,077	3,692	101,000
Expenses	(15,384)	(18,461)	(6,155)	(40,000)
Net profit (£)	28,847	34,616	(2,463)	61,000

In addition to the information supplied above, you are told that:

- production overheads of £15,000 are apportioned to the three departments on the basis of unit sales volume
- expenses are head office overhead, again apportioned to departments on sales volume.

As management accountant, you further ascertain that, on a cost driver basis, 50% of the production overheads can be allocated on the basis 2:2:1 and 60% of the expenses can be allocated 3:3:2. In addition, 80% of the so-called direct labour is fixed and cannot be readily allocated. The remaining 20% can be allocated on the basis of sales volume.

You are required to prepare a report for management including a restatement of the financial position in terms of contribution made by each department and making a clear recommendation. **(10 marks)**

For the answer to this question, see the 'Answers' section at the end of the book.

Feedback to activities

Activity 1

(a) Relevant cost = £6 × 600 = £3,600 (an opportunity cost as, if not used for the new product, it would be used for the existing product saving £6 per item).

(b) Relevant cost/unit = £5 (replacement cost).

Activity 2

(a) Remaining production capacity = (8,000 ÷ 80%) – 8,000 – 1,000 = 1,000 units

(b) Additional contribution/unit = £3.6 – 3.0 = £0.6

Additional contribution = 1,600 × £0.6 = £960

This is less than the £1,000 of extra contribution for the first contract. Reject the new contract or negotiate for a better price.

Activity 3

To: The board of directors

From: The management accountant

Date: X–X–20XX

Subject: Desirability of closing the factory for a year

In the forthcoming year (20X1) our alternatives are:

(1) Continuing operating

	£
Sales	49,500
Total cost	59,500
Loss	10,000

(2) Close down for 20X1 and re-open in 20X2

		£
(a)	Unavoidable fixed cost	11,000
(b)	Redundancy payment	7,500
(c)	Necessary maintenance	1,000
(d)	Re-opening cost	4,000
Loss		23,500

This is more than twice the loss incurred if we continue at 50% capacity and I would suggest continuing production.

(3) The anticipated result for 20X2 would be

	£
Sales	90,000
Total cost	79,750
Profit	10,250

Finally assuming the consultant's forecast is correct and we carry on producing, the cumulative position at the end of year 20X2 would be a small profit of £250 without the trauma of closing down.

Workings

(W1) Since direct labour and direct material increase from zero by equal increments of cost for each 20% change in volume, they must be entirely variable. The increments for activity changes on production, administration and selling overhead do not account for all the cost and these must therefore include a fixed proportion.

Production capacity	*40%*	*60%*	*Increment for 20%*	*Fixed*
	£	£	£	£
Direct labour	16,000	24,000	8,000	-
Direct material	12,000	18,000	6,000	-
Production overhead	11,400	12,600	1,200	9,000
Administration	5,800	6,200	400	5,000
Selling and distribution	6,200	6,800	600	5,000
Total			16,200	19,000

Allowance for 50% $= \frac{50}{20} \times 16{,}200 + 19{,}000 = £59{,}500$

or

				£
Direct labour	=	$\frac{50}{20} \times 8{,}000$	=	20,000
Direct material	=	$\frac{50}{20} \times 6{,}000$	=	15,000
Production overhead	=	$\left[\frac{50}{20} \times 1{,}200\right] + 9{,}000$	=	12,000
Administration	=	$\left[\frac{50}{20} \times 400\right] + 5{,}000$	=	6,000
Selling	=	$\left[\frac{50}{20} \times 600\right] + 5{,}000$	=	6,500
Total cost				59,500
Revenue at 50%				
Loss at 50% activity				(10,000)

Second year

Total cost	=	$\left[\frac{75}{20} \times 16{,}200\right] + 19{,}000$	=	79,750
Revenue at 75% activity				90,000
Profit at 75% activity				10,250

Chapter 5

THE PROBLEM OF SCARCE RESOURCES

Syllabus content

This chapter covers the following syllabus content.

- Simple product mix analysis in situations where there are limitations on product/service demand and one other production constraint.
- Linear programming for more complex situations involving multiple constraints. Solution by graphical methods of two-variable problems together with understanding of the mechanics of the simplex solution, shadow prices etc. (***Note:*** Questions requiring the full application of the simplex algorithm will not be set although candidates should be able to formulate an initial tableau, interpret a final simplex tableau and apply the information contained in a final tableau.)

Contents

1 Single scarce resource problems

1.1 Production scheduling with one limiting factor

KEY POINT

In most business situations only a limited number of business opportunities may be undertaken. Some factor will limit the ability to undertake all the alternatives. This factor is referred to as the **limiting factor**.

In most business situations only a limited number of business opportunities may be undertaken. Some factor will limit the ability to undertake all the alternatives. This factor is referred to as the **limiting factor**.

A limiting factor is 'anything which limits the activity of an entity. An entity seeks to optimise the benefit it obtains from the limiting factor' (CIMA, *Official Terminology*).

Consider the situation where there is one factor limiting operations and two or more possible products. The management accountant must advise management on how to schedule production so as to maximise profits subject to the constraint. The essential elements of the problem are as follows.

- The object is to maximise profits. Therefore only costs and revenues that vary according to the decision are considered; since fixed costs do not, they are irrelevant and may be ignored.
- This leaves revenue and variable costs, which together specify the contribution of each product line. The aim is to maximise the total contribution.
- The real cost of producing Product 1 rather than Product 2 is the contribution of Product 2 forgone – the opportunity cost. It must be ensured that the total contribution of Product 1 gained exceeds that of Product 2 lost.
- Total contribution is given by units multiplied by contribution per unit. The number of units is limited by the limiting factor. In the evaluation of alternative products, consideration must be given not only to contribution per unit, but also to the number of units that can be produced, subject to the limiting factor.
- To take both of these factors together, total contribution is maximised by concentrating on that product which yields the highest contribution per unit of limiting factor.

Example

X Ltd makes a single product that requires £5 of materials and two hours of labour. There are only 80 hours labour available each week and the maximum amount of material available each week is £500.

Which of these two factors is a limiting factor on production?

Solution

It can be said that the supply of both labour hours and materials is limited and that therefore they are both scarce resources. However, there is more to this problem than meets the eye. The maximum production within these constraints can be shown to be:

Materials:	£500/£5	=	100 units
Labour hours:	80 hours/2 hours	=	40 units

Thus the shortage of labour hours is the significant factor – the scarcity of the materials does not limit production.

In the context of the decision in this example the materials are not a scarce resource.

1.2 Single limiting factor analysis

When more than one product or service is provided from the same pool of resources, profit is maximised by making the best use of the resources available.

KEY POINT

Profit maximisation (possibly via cost minimisation) is the assured objective in scarce resource problems.

Profit maximisation (possible via cost minimisation) is the assured objective in scarce resource problems.

Example

A company makes and sells two products – X and Y. It has a shortage of labour, which is limited to 200,000 hours per year. This is insufficient to satisfy the full demand for both products. The unit costs, contributions and labour hours used are as follows.

	Product X	*Product Y*
Labour hours per unit of output	5	10
	£	£
Selling price	80	100
Variable cost	50	50
Contribution per unit	30	50

How should the company schedule its production activities so as to maximise profit?

Solution

There are two ways in which the production-scheduling problem can be solved.

(a) Calculate total contribution if each is produced in turn.

	Total contribution
Product X units = $\frac{200,000}{5}$ = 40,000	
Contribution × units = £30 × 40,000	£1,200,000
Product Y units = $\frac{200,000}{10}$ = 20,000	
Contribution × units = £50 × 20,000	£1,000,000

(b) The quicker alternative is to find which product has the higher contribution per unit of limiting factor, i.e. per labour hour:

	Contribution per labour hour
Product X = $\frac{£30}{5}$ =	£6
Product Y = $\frac{£50}{10}$ =	£5

This is of course merely a way of shortcutting the calculations in (a) above, and exactly the same conclusion is reached: production should concentrate on Product X.

Example

Z Ltd makes two products which both use the same type of materials and grades of labour, but in different quantities as shown by the table below:

	Product A	*Product B*
Labour hours/unit	3	4
Material/unit	£20	£15

During each week the maximum number of labour hours available is limited to 600, and the value of material available is limited to £6,000.

Each unit of product A made and sold earns Z Ltd a contribution of £5 and each unit of product B earns £6 per unit. The demand for these products is unlimited.

Advise Z Ltd which product they should make.

Solution

Step 1

Determine the scarce resource.

Each resource restricts production as follows:

Labour hours	600/3	=	200 units of A, or
	600/4	=	150 units of B
Materials	£6,000/£20	=	300 units of A, or
	£6,000/£15	=	400 units of B

It can be seen that whichever product is chosen the production is limited by the shortage of labour hours, therefore this is the limiting factor or scarce resource.

Step 2

Calculate each product's contribution per unit of the scarce resource consumed by its manufacture.

Product A contribution per labour hour

= £5/3 hours = £1.66 per hour

Product B contribution per labour hour

= £6/4 hours = £1.50 per hour

KEY POINT

In general, the rule to follow in questions involving a single limiting factor is to concentrate production on the product which earns the highest contribution per unit of the limiting factor.

Thus Z Ltd maximises its earnings by making and selling product A. In general, the rule to follow in questions involving a single limiting factor is to concentrate production on the product which earns the highest contribution per unit of the limiting factor.

Activity 1

A Ltd makes two products, X and Y. Both products use the same machine and the same raw material that are limited to 200 hours and £500 per week respectively. Individual product details are as follows:

	Product X	*Product Y*
Machine hours/unit	5	2.5
Materials/unit	£10	£5
Contribution/unit	£20	£15

Recommend which product A Ltd should make and sell (assuming that demand is unlimited).

Feedback to this activity is at the end of the chapter.

1.3 Other considerations in the limiting factor situation

- In the long run management must seek to remove the limiting factor. In the above example management should be recruiting and training additional labour. Thus, any one limiting factor should only be a short-term problem. However, as soon as it is removed it will be replaced by another limiting factor.
- Even in the short-run management may be able to find ways round the constraint. For example, overtime working, temporary staff and subcontracting might all be solutions to the situation described.
- Nor may it always be easy to identify the limiting factor. In practice several limiting factors may operate simultaneously. However, even in examination questions, where there is only one limiting factor, it may be necessary to distinguish between several possible limiting factors.
- It is also possible that there may be other parameters setting minimum production levels, e.g. there may be a contract to supply Y so that certain minimum quantities must be produced.

Example

X Ltd makes three products, A, B and C, of which unit costs, machine hours and selling prices are as follows:

	Product A	*Product B*	*Product C*
Machine hours	10	12	14
	£	£	£
Direct materials @ 50p per kg	7 (14 kg)	6 (12 kg)	5 (10 kg)
Direct wages @ 75p per hour	9 (12 hours)	6 (8 hours)	3 (4 hours)
Variable overheads	3	3	3
Marginal cost	19	15	11
Selling price	25	20	15
Contribution	6	5	4

Sales demand for the period is limited as follows.

Product A	4,000
Product B	6,000
Product C	6,000

As a matter of company policy, it is decided to produce a minimum of 1,000 units of Product A. The supply of materials in the period is unlimited, but machine hours are limited to 200,000 and direct labour hours to 50,000.

Indicate the production levels that should be adopted for the three products in order to maximise profitability, and state the maximum contribution.

Solution

First determine which is the limiting factor. At potential sales level:

	Sales potential units	*Total machine hours*	*Total labour hours*
Product A	4,000	40,000	48,000
Product B	6,000	72,000	48,000
Product C	6,000	84,000	24,000
		196,000	120,000

Thus, labour hours is the limiting factor. The next stage is to calculate contribution per labour hour.

Product A $\frac{£6}{12} = £0.500$

Product B $\frac{£5}{8} = £0.625$

Product C $\frac{£4}{4} = £1.000$

Thus, production should be concentrated on C, up to the maximum available sales, then B, and finally A.

However, a minimum of 1,000 units of A must be produced. Taking these factors into account, the production schedule becomes:

	Units produced	*Labour hours*	*Cumulative labour hours*	*Limiting factor*
Product A	1,000	12,000	12,000	Policy to produce 1,000 units
Product C	6,000	24,000	36,000	Sales
Product B	1,750	14,000	50,000	Labour hours

The maximum contribution is therefore as follows.

	£
A (1,000 × £6)	6,000
B (1,750 × £5)	8,750
C (6,000 × £4)	24,000
	38,750

KEY POINT

Where there is only one scarce resource the method above can be used to solve the problem. However where there are two or more resources in short supply which limit the organisation's activities then linear programming is required to find the solution.

1.4 Conclusion

Where there is only one scarce resource the method above (key factor analysis) can be used to solve the problem. However where there are two or more resources in short supply which limit the organisation's activities (for example if materials had been limited to £3,000 per week in the example above), then linear programming is required to find the solution.

2 Linear programming

2.1 Introduction

Linear programming is one of the most important post-war developments in **operations research**. It is in fact the most widely used of a group of mathematical programming techniques.

Linear programming can be thought of as a method of balancing many factors (e.g. distance, time, production capacity) to obtain a predetermined objective (e.g. minimum cost). Some of the factors are variable, while others are fixed.

In order to apply linear programming there must be, as its title suggests, a linear relationship between the factors. For example, the cost of shipping five extra units should be five times the cost of shipping one extra unit.

2.2 Field of application of linear programming

- **Mixing problems** – A product is composed of several ingredients, and what is required is the least costly mix of the ingredients that will give a product of predetermined specification.
- **Job assignment problems** – A number of jobs or products must be handled by various people and/or machines, and the least costly arrangement of assignments is required.
- **Capacity allocation problems** – Limited capacity is allocated to products so as to yield maximum profits. This is the most common application in exam questions.
- **Production scheduling** – An uneven sales demand is met by a production schedule over a period of time, with given penalties for storage, overtime, and short-time working.
- **Transportation problems** – Various suppliers (or one company with several plants) throughout the country make the same products, which must be shipped to many outlets that are also widely distributed. This may involve different transportation costs and varying manufacturing costs. Linear programming can determine the best way to ship; it denotes which plant shall service any particular outlet. It can also evaluate whether it pays to open a new plant.
- **Purchasing** – Multiple and complex bids can be evaluated, in order to ensure that the orders placed with suppliers comply with the lowest cost arrangement.
- **Investment problems** – The results of alternative capital investments can be evaluated when finance is in short supply.
- **Location problems** – Linear programming can help to select an optimum plant or warehouse location where a wide choice is possible.

2.3 Method of linear programming

Linear programming reduces the kind of problems outlined above to a series of linear expressions and then uses those expressions to discover the best solution to achieve a given objective. The student should appreciate that not all situations can be reduced to a linear form. Nevertheless, a surprising number of problems can be solved using this relatively straightforward technique.

KEY POINT

Linear programming:

Step 1

- Define the unknown, i.e. the variables (that need to be determined).

Step 2

- Define the objective function (that needs to be maximised or minimised).

Step 3

- Formulate the constraints, i.e. the limitations that must be placed on the variables.

Step 4

- Graph the constraints.

Step 5

- Find the optimal solution.

The steps involved are as follows:

Step 1

- Define the unknowns, i.e. the variables (that need to be determined).

Step 2

- Define the objective function (that needs to be maximised or minimised).

Step 3

- Formulate the constraints, i.e. the limitations that must be placed on the variables.

Step 4

- Graph the constraints.

Step 5

- Find the optimal solution.

2.4 Linear programming – graphical method

We will now look at each of the steps involved in a linear programming problem in more detail by working through a comprehensive example.

Example

Hebrus Ltd manufactures summerhouses and garden sheds. Each product passes through a cutting process and an assembly process. One summerhouse, which makes a contribution of £50, takes six hours cutting time and four hours assembly time; while one shed makes a contribution of £40, takes three hours cutting time and eight hours assembly time. There is a maximum of 36 cutting hours available each week and 48 assembly hours.

2.5 Step 1 – defining the unknowns

The variables that need to be determined in this example are the number of summerhouses and garden sheds to be produced each week.

Let x = number of summerhouses produced each week

and y = number of garden sheds produced each week.

Activity 2

Alfred Ltd is preparing its plan for the coming month. It manufactures two products, the flak trap and the sap trap. Details are as follows.

	Product		
	Flak trap	*Sap trap*	*Price/wage rate*
Amount/unit:			
Selling price (£)	125	165	
Raw material (kg)	6	4	£5/kg
Labour hours:			
Skilled	10	10	£3/hour
Semi-skilled	5	25	£3/hour

The company's overhead absorption rate is £1/labour hour (for both skilled and semi-skilled labour). The supply of skilled labour is limited to 2,000 hours/month and the supply of semi-skilled labour is limited to 2,500 hours/month. At the selling prices indicated, maximum demand for flak traps is expected to be 150 units/month and the maximum demand for sap traps is expected to be 80 units/month.

You are required to define the decision variables.

Feedback to this activity is at the end of the chapter.

DEFINITION

The **objective function** is a quantified statement of what is trying to be achieved, for instance the minimisation of costs or maximisation of profit. The objective function is always expressed in terms of the unknown variables.

2.6 Step 2 – define the objective function

The **objective function** is a quantified statement of what is trying to be achieved, for instance the minimisation of costs or maximisation of profit. The objective function is always expressed in terms of the unknown variables.

In the Hebrus example, the objective function is in terms of x and y. Hence, continuing this example:

The objective is to maximise contribution C, given by:

$$C = 50x + 40y$$

The company undoubtedly wishes to maximise profit. However, given the usual assumptions of linear programming (stated later), this is achieved by maximising contribution. Take care that the coefficients of x and y (i.e. 50 and 40 respectively) represent the amount by which contribution (and hence profit) increases per unit of each item produced and sold.

2.7 Step 3 – define the constraints

As we saw earlier in the chapter most resources are scarce to a certain degree and that usually puts some limitation on what can be achieved. When formulating a linear programming problem those limitations are included as a set of conditions that any solution to the problem must satisfy and they are referred to as constraints.

The constraints (limitations) in our Hebrus example are the amounts of cutting and assembly time available.

If 1 summerhouse requires 6 hours cutting time,
x summerhouses require $6x$ hours cutting time.

If 1 shed requires 3 hours cutting time,
y sheds require $3y$ hours cutting time.

Hence total cutting time required = $6x + 3y$ hours.

Similarly, if one summerhouse and one shed require 4 and 8 hours assembly time respectively, the total assembly time for x summerhouses and y sheds will be $4x + 8y$.

The conventional way of setting out the constraints is to place the units **utilised** on the left, and those **available** on the right; the inequality sign is the link.

Constraint		*Utilised*		*Available*
Cutting time	(i)	$6x + 3y$	$\leq$	36
Assembly time	(ii)	$4x + 8y$	$\leq$	48

In addition, two other logical constraints must be stated, i.e.

$x \geq 0$

$y \geq 0$

These simply state that negative amounts of garden sheds or summerhouses cannot be made.

Activity 3

Using the information in the previous activity (Alfred Ltd), formulate the constraints.

Feedback to this activity is at the end of the chapter.

2.8 Graphing a straight line

Step 4 of the linear programming model is to represent the constraints as straight lines on a graph. We do this in paragraph 2.9 below. In the meantime, this paragraph contains basic revision for students who are not familiar with the process of graphing a straight line.

To begin with, we must have a linear relationship between two measurements, in other words if we know the value for x we can work out the value for y.

Examples $y = 3x + 1$

$y = 2x + 42$ etc.

Note:

1. To recognise a linear relationship the equation must have only 'x' not 'x' to the power of anything, e.g. x^2.
2. A straight line has two characteristics:
   (i) a slope or gradient – which measures the 'steepness' of the line
   (ii) a point at which it cuts the y axis – this is called the intercept:

   $y = (\text{slope} \times x) + \text{intercept}$

   e.g. $y = 2x + 3$

   $\therefore$ the gradient is 2 and the point at which the line cuts the y axis is 3.

To draw a straight line graph we only need to know two points that can then be joined.

Consider the following two equations:

(i) $y = 2x + 3$

(ii) $y = 2x - 2$

In order to draw the graphs of these equations it is necessary to decide on two values for x and then to calculate the corresponding values for y. Let us use x = 0 and 3. These calculations are best displayed in tabular form.

x	0	3
1. y = 2x + 3	3	9
2. y = 2x – 2	-2	4

So to draw the first line we plot the points (0, 3) and (3, 9) and simply join them up. Similarly, for the second line we plot the points (0, -2) and (3, 4) and join them up.

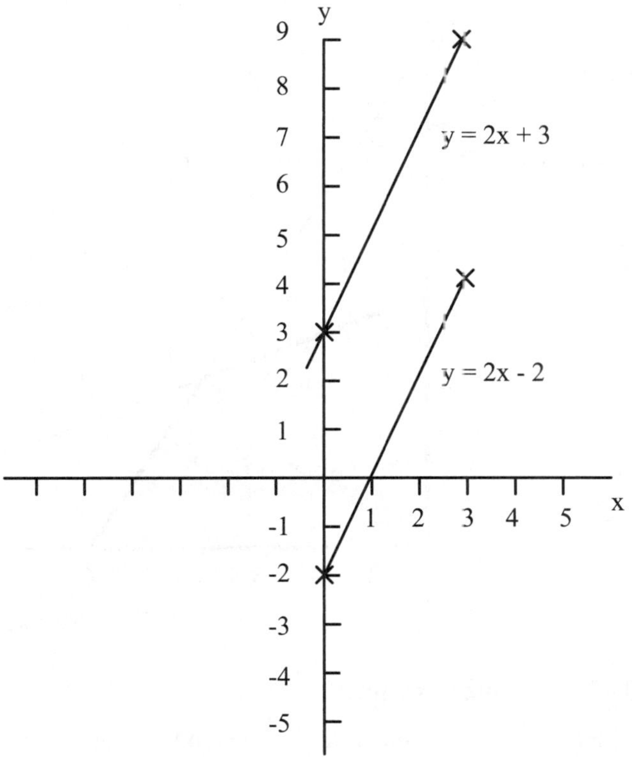

Note: The lines are parallel because the equations have the same gradient of 2.

2.9 Step 4 – graph the constraints

KEY POINT

LP constraints are generally of the form ax + by = c which can be rearranged to y = c/b – ax/b.

Having revised how to plot a straight line on a graph, we can now move on to graphing the constraints that are simply linear equations of the type we have just looked at.

In order to plot the constraints it is normally best to compute the intercepts of the equalities on the horizontal and vertical axes. Thus, x and y are each set equal to zero in turn and the value of y and x computed in these circumstances.

Returning to the Hebrus example.

For the equation $6x + 3y = 36$ – cutting time constraint

when x = 0, $y = \frac{36}{3} = 12$

when y = 0, $x = \frac{36}{6} = 6$

To graph this constraint, we draw a straight line between the points (0, 12) and (6, 0).

For the equation $4x + 8y = 48$ – assembly time constraint

when x = 0, $y = \frac{48}{8} = 6$

when y = 0, $x = \frac{48}{4} = 12$

To graph this constraint, we draw a straight line between the points (0, 6) and 12, 0).

The constraints can now be represented graphically:

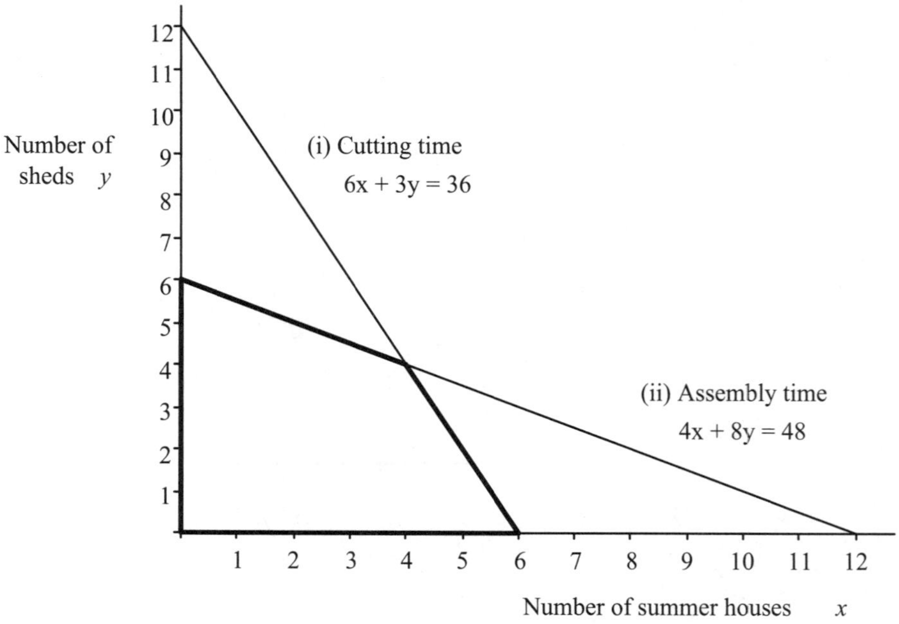

2.10 The feasible region

Having inserted the straight lines in the graph, we are then ready to work out what is called the **feasible region**.

Each line inserted on the graph represents a constraint. In the Hebrus example, there can only be 36 hours of cutting time and no more, and only 48 hours of assembly time and no more. Therefore the area on the graph above these lines is 'out of bounds' or more technically 'not feasible'. The area below these lines is therefore called the feasible region; it is possible for total cutting time and total assembly time to be any of these values up to and on the constraint line but not above.

Hence, the feasible region for Hebrus is as shown below.

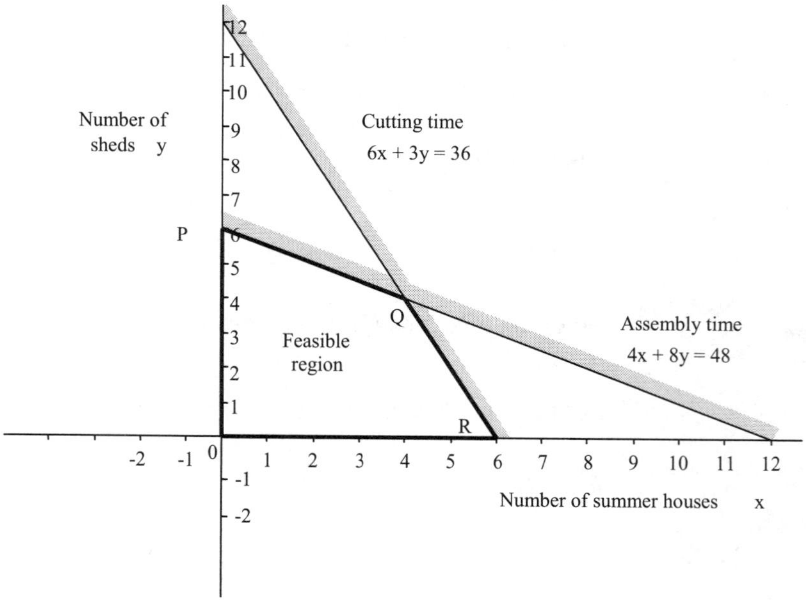

The area 0PQR that is outlined in bold represents all feasible solutions, i.e. combinations of the two products that are achievable given the constraints. It is therefore called the feasible region.

To recognise that feasible solutions are, as in this case, all below the constraint lines, it is normal practice to add shading or hatch marks above the line indicating that anything above is outside the feasible region.

Some questions can be minimising problems, e.g. the objective function will be to minimise costs subject to minimum output levels. The constraints will be minimum output levels, therefore the feasible region will be on or above the line and will be shaded or hatched underneath.

Activity 4

Using the Alfred Ltd example again you are required to plot the constraints on a graph and indicate on the graph the feasible region.

Feedback to this activity is at the end of the chapter.

2.11 Step 5 – find the optimal solution

Having found the feasible region the problem now is to **find the optimal solution within this feasible region**.

KEY POINT

It can be shown that the optimum solution will lie on the boundaries of the feasible region. To find it:

- try each corner to see which gives highest contribution (or lowest cost)
- draw an iso-contribution line.

There are two approaches to this final stage.

(a) By inspection it is clear that the maximum contribution will lie on one of the corners of the feasible region. In the Hebrus example the corners are P, Q, R (it could lie on the line PQ or the line QR) – the optimal solution can be reached simply by calculating the contributions at each corner.

(b) By drawing an **iso-contribution** line (an objective function for a particular value of C), which is a line where all points represent an equal contribution. This is the recommended approach, particularly for more complex problems.

Using the Hebrus example, consider a contribution of £200. This would give the contribution line 50x + 40y = 200 and could be achieved by producing four summerhouses, or five sheds, or any combination on a straight line between the two.

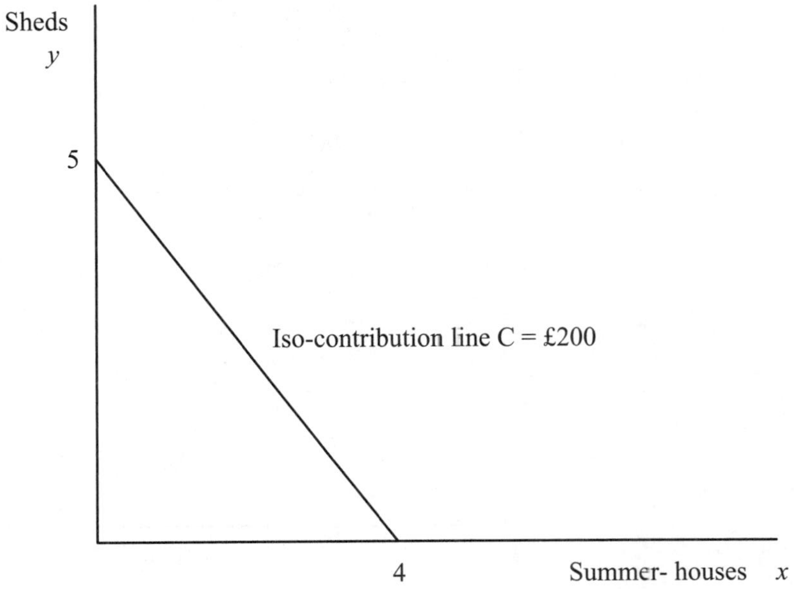

Another iso-contribution line could be drawn at £240, i.e. 50x + 40y = 240:

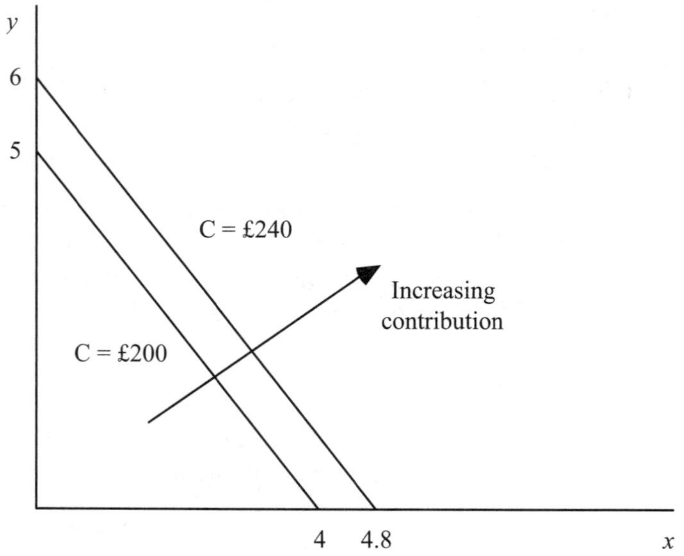

Clearly, iso-contribution lines move to and from the origin in parallel; the arrow indicates increasing contribution. The object is to get on the highest contribution line within (just touching) the binding constraints.

The optimum point is found by drawing an example of an iso-contribution line on the diagram (any convenient value of C will do), and then placing a ruler against it. Then, by moving the ruler away from the origin (in the case of a maximisation problem) or towards the origin (in the case of a minimising problem) but keeping it parallel to the iso-contribution line, the last corner of the feasible solution space which is met represents the optimum solution.

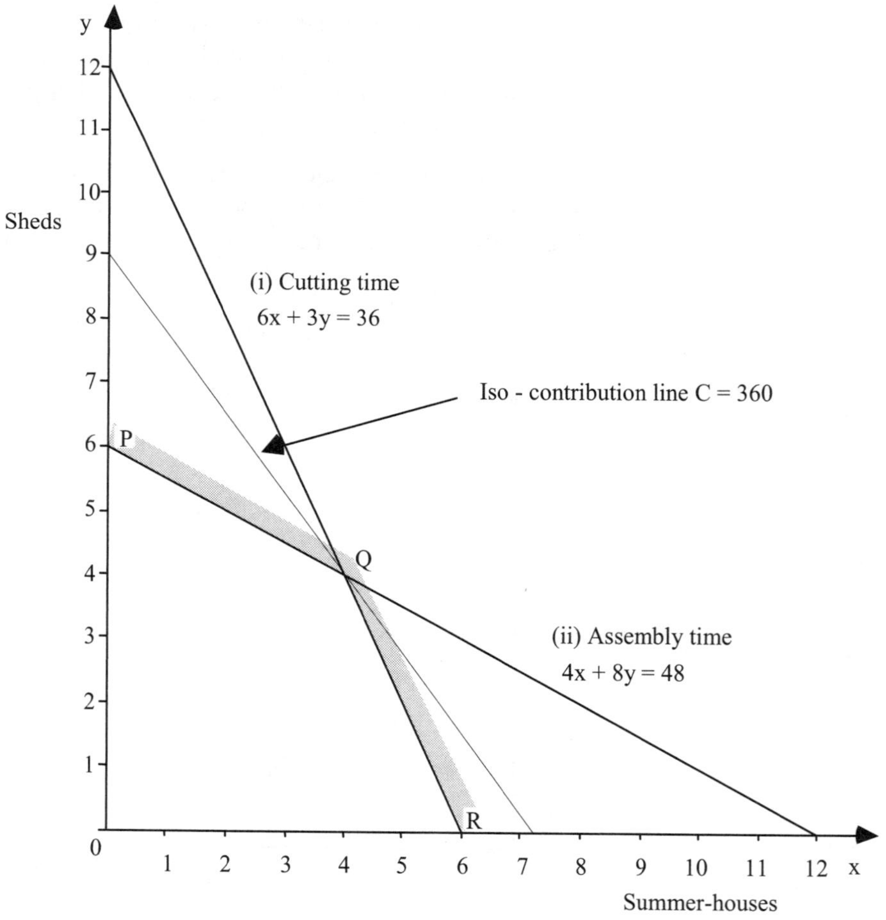

The highest available iso-contribution line occurs at C = 360, at point Q, where, reading from the graph, x = 4 and y = 4.

2.12 Evaluating the optimal solution using simultaneous equations

You may consider that the whole process would be easier by solving the constraints as sets of simultaneous equations and not bothering with a graph. This is possible and you may get the right answer, but such a technique should be used with caution and is not recommended until you have determined graphically which constraints are effective in determining the optimal solution. Furthermore if the question asks for a graphical solution, then a graph must be used.

The technique can, however, be used as a check. For example using the Hebrus example the optimal solution can be checked by solving the two simultaneous equations for the two constraint boundaries.

Point Q is the intersection of the lines:

			Constraint
6x + 3y	=	36	(i)
4x + 8y	=	48	(ii)

3 × (ii) – 2 × (i) gives:

18y	=	72
y	=	4

Substituting into (i)

x	=	4

Thus, the maximum contribution is obtained when four summerhouses and four sheds per week are produced, and the maximum contribution is 4 × £50 + 4 × £40 = £360.

2.13 Limitations of linear programming

There are a number of limitations to this technique.

- Single value estimates are used for the uncertain variables.
- Linear relationships must exist.
- Only suitable when there is one clearly defined objective function.
- When there are a number of variables, it becomes too complex to solve manually and a computer is required.
- It is assumed that the variables are completely divisible.
- It is assumed that the situation remains static in all other respects.

2.14 Cost minimisation problems

The main differences in tackling such problems are:

- constraints are in the form $ax+by \geq c$
- objective is to **minimise** cost
- an **iso-cost** line is moved towards the origin to determine the optimum point.

This type of problem is illustrated by the following activity.

Activity 5

J Farms Ltd can buy two types of fertiliser which contain the following percentage of chemicals:

	Nitrates	*Phosphates*	*Potash*
Type X	18	5	2
Type Y	3	2	5

For a certain crop the following minimum quantities (kg) are required:

Nitrates 100 Phosphates 50 Potash 40

Type X costs £10 per kg and type Y costs £5 per kg. J Farms Ltd currently buys 1,000 kg of each type and wishes to minimise its expenditure on fertilisers.

You are required:

(a) to write down the objective function and the constraints for J Farms Ltd

(b) to draw a graph to illustrate all the constraints (equations/inequalities), shading the feasible region

(c) to recommend the quantity of each type of fertiliser which should be bought and the cost of these amounts

(d) to find the saving J Farms Ltd can make by switching from its current policy to your recommendation

(e) to state briefly any limitations of using this approach to problem-solving in practice.

Feedback to this activity is at the end of the chapter.

3 Explaining the solution

3.1 Slack

KEY POINT

Slack is important because unused resources can be put to another use, e.g. hired out to another manufacturer.

Slack is the amount by which a resource is under utilised. It will occur when the optimum point does not fall on the given resource line.

Slack is important because unused resources can be put to another use, e.g. hired out to another manufacturer.

In the above example, the optimum point Q lies on both the cutting and assembly time lines; therefore both resources are fully utilised. This can be checked from the constraint inequalities.

When $x = 4$, $y = 4$,

Cutting time:	available = 36,	utilised	=	$6x + 3y$
			=	$(6 \times 4) + (3 \times 4)$
			=	36
Assembly time:	available = 48,	utilised	=	$4x + 8y$
			=	$(4 \times 4) + (8 \times 4)$
			=	48

Hence all available time in both departments is utilised.

If, however, the optimum had been at P (x = 0, y = 6) then, because P does not lie on the cutting time line, there would be slack cutting time.

Cutting time utilised	=	$6 \times 0 + 3 \times 6$	=	18
Slack	=	36 – 18		
	=	18 hours		

3.2 Shadow (or dual) prices

DEFINITION

The **shadow price** of a resource is an increase in value which would be created by having available one additional unit of a limiting resource at its original cost. (CIMA *Official Terminology*)

The **shadow price** of a resource is an increase in value which would be created by having available one additional unit of a limiting resource at its original cost. (CIMA, *Official Terminology*, 2000).

Shadow prices (also known as opportunity costs or dual prices) are one of the most important aspects of linear programming.

Example

Refer back to the earlier example concerning Hebrus Ltd.

Suppose one extra hour was available for the cutting process each week.

By how much would contribution (and profit) be increased?

The extra hour would alter the constraints to:

Cutting	(i)	$6x + 3y \leq$	37, and
Assembly	(ii)	$4x + 8y \leq$	48

To solve simultaneously multiply (ii) by 1.5.

(iii) $6x + 12y \leq$ 72

Solving as before:

Subtracting (i) from (iii) gives:

$9y = 35$

and thus:

$y = 35/9 = 3.8889$

Inserting this value in (i) gives:

$6x + (3 \times 3.8889)$	=	37	
$6x + 11.6667$	=	37	
6x	=	25.3333	
x	=	4.2222	
C	=	(£50 × 4.2222) + (£40 × 3.8889) =	366.6666
Original contribution			360
Increase			6.666

Thus, £6.67 is the shadow price of one hour in the cutting process.

Similarly the shadow price of assembly time may be found by keeping the cutting time constraint unchanged, but relaxing the assembly constraint by one unit so that it becomes:

Assembly $4x + 8y \leq$ 49 (ii)

Whilst (i) remains as:

Cutting $6x + 3y \leq 36$ (i)

Solving as before:

$3 \times \text{(ii)} - 2 \times \text{(i)} \Rightarrow \quad 18y = 75$

$y = 4.1667$

Substituting into (i) gives x = 3.9166

		£
Contribution C = (£50 × 3.9166) + (£40 × 4.1667)	=	362.498
Original contribution	=	360.000
Increase		2.498

Thus, the shadow price of one hour of assembly time = £2.50.

Note: In view of these calculations it is important that no attempt is made to simplify the original constraints by cancelling, otherwise you will not be able to calculate correct values for the shadow prices.

Activity 6

Using the following data, calculate the shadow price for machining time.

(i) $20x + 25y \leq 500$ (machining time)

(ii) $40x + 25y \leq 800$ (finishing time)

$C = 80x + 75y$ (contribution)

Solution: x = 15, y = 8

Feedback to this activity is at the end of the chapter.

3.3 Usefulness of shadow prices – conclusion

KEY POINT

The shadow price indicates the maximum premium (above normal cost) it is worth paying to obtain an extra unit of the resource.

Shadow prices have the following relevance:

- The shadow price is the extra profit that may be earned by relaxing each of the constraints by one unit.
- It therefore represents the maximum **premium** that the firm should be willing to pay for one extra unit of each constraint.
- Since shadow prices indicate the effect of a one unit change in each of the constraints, they provide a measure of the sensitivity of the result.

The shadow price for any constraint that is not binding at the optimum solution is zero. In the above example suppose production of summerhouses and sheds was also limited by the amount of painting time available – each product took 4 hours to paint and only 40 hours a week were available.

Since the optimum plan involved production of four sheds and four summerhouses the painting time would only be 32 hours a week – consequently it would make no difference to the optimum solution if painting time availability either increased to 41 hours or decreased to 39. Under these circumstances the dual price of painting time is zero.

However, if the painting time was reduced to only 32 hours this too would become a binding constraint, and a reduction by one further hour, to 31, might affect the optimum solution. It should be noted that shadow prices are valid for only a small range of changes before, eventually, they become non-binding or make different resources critical.

3.4 Further sensitivity analysis

Shadow prices provide an approach to measuring the sensitivity of a solution to changes in a binding constraint. The sensitivity of other aspects of the solution can also be measured. For instance, what would happen to the optimal solution if:

- the contribution from product X were £1 higher than expected?
- the sales price of product Y was reduced by 15%?

Example

Returning once again to the Hebrus example.

Suppose the contributions from summerhouses and sheds turned out to be slightly different from £50 and £40 respectively, perhaps due to an error in estimating costs. Would the optimal solution change?

This question is best answered by looking again at the graphical solution:

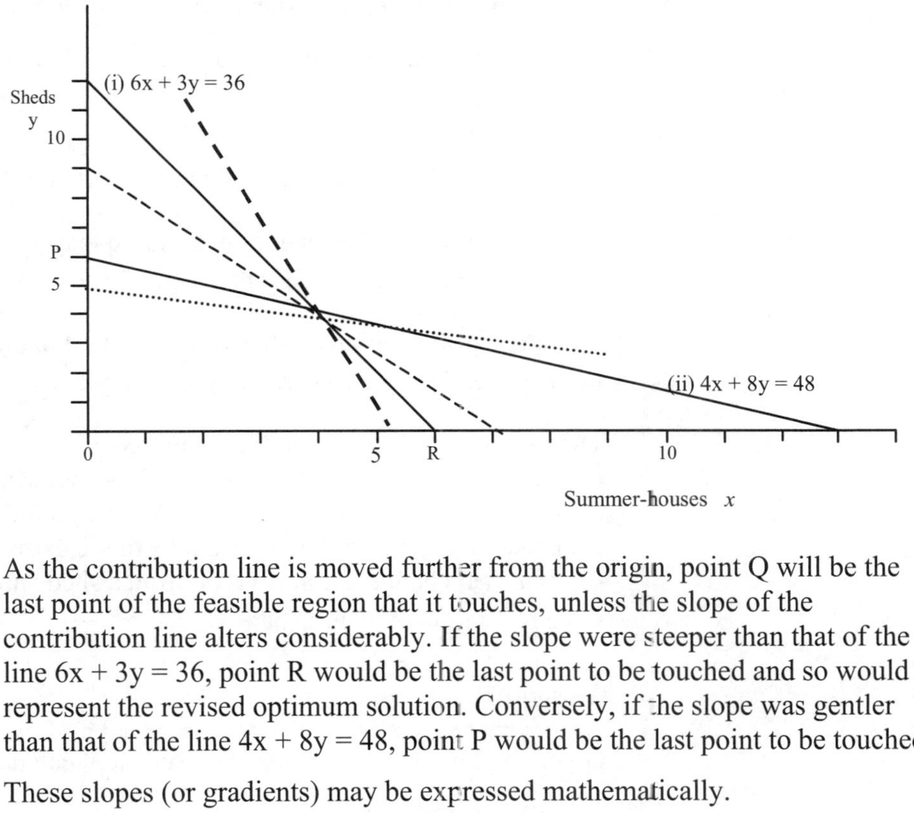

As the contribution line is moved further from the origin, point Q will be the last point of the feasible region that it touches, unless the slope of the contribution line alters considerably. If the slope were steeper than that of the line 6x + 3y = 36, point R would be the last point to be touched and so would represent the revised optimum solution. Conversely, if the slope was gentler than that of the line 4x + 8y = 48, point P would be the last point to be touched.

These slopes (or gradients) may be expressed mathematically.

(a) **Cutting constraint line**

$6x + 3y = 36$

This may be rewritten, in standard form, $3y = 36 - 6x$ or $y = 12 - 2x$

This is of the form $y = a + bx$ where a represents the intercept of the line with the y axis and b represents the gradient.

Thus, in the case of the cutting constraint line, the gradient is –2.

(b) **Assembly constraint line**

$4x + 8y = 48$

$8y = 48 - 4x$

$y = 6 - \frac{1}{2}x$

The gradient is therefore $-\frac{1}{2}$

(c) **Contribution line**

In general terms $C = px + qy$, where p = contribution from a summerhouse

and q = contribution from a shed

Re-arranging: $qy = C - px$

$$y = \frac{C}{q} - \frac{px}{q}$$

The gradient is ∴ $\frac{-p}{q}$ (The coefficient of × ÷ the coefficient of y.)

The optimal solution will not alter if the gradient of the contribution line lies between the gradients of the constraint lines.

∴ Optimal solution will not alter provided that:

– p/q lies between –2 and $-\frac{1}{2}$

In other words, p/q must lie between 2 and $\frac{1}{2}$.

Initially p was £50. If this does not alter, q may vary so that 50/q lies between 2 and $\frac{1}{2}$. Therefore, q can vary between 25 and 100.

Similarly, q was initially £40 and if this does not alter, p may vary so that p/40 lies between 2 and $\frac{1}{2}$. Therefore p can vary between 20 and 80.

The optimal product mix is, therefore, remarkably insensitive to changes in the original data. Note, however, that the above contribution ranges are valid only if the contributions of the two products are varied independently. For instance, if contribution from a summerhouse falls to the extreme value of £20, the optimal solution will change if contribution from a shed simultaneously rises above £40, since p/q will then be less than $\frac{1}{2}$.

Activity 7

Given the following machine time constraint calculate the gradient of the line:

$20x + 25y = 500$

Feedback to this activity is at the end of the chapter.

Activity 8

Given the answer to the previous activity and the following finishing time constraint calculate the range of contribution gradients that will not cause the optimal solution to alter.

$40x + 25y = 800$

Feedback to this activity is at the end of the chapter.

4 The simplex method

In a problem with just two constraints (e.g. the limited cutting time and assembly time in the example of Hebrus) a graphical solution is possible, as we have already seen. However, if there are three or more variables the graphical method will not work, because it is not feasible to draw a graph in more than two dimensions. In such a case we can use an advanced form of linear programming called the simplex method.

The simplex method, which readily lends itself to computer solution, is invaluable in problems with three or more variables, which cannot be solved graphically.

A further feature of the simplex method is that shadow prices emerge automatically as part of the solution.

For the purposes of the examination you will need to be able to formulate an initial simplex tableau and interpret the final solution.

For simplicity, this will be demonstrated with a two-variable problem, namely Hebrus. For convenience, we repeat the data for this problem below.

Example

Hebrus Ltd manufactures summer houses and garden sheds. Each product passes through a cutting process and an assembly process. One summer house, which makes a contribution of £50, takes 6 hours cutting time and 4 hours assembly time, while one shed, which makes a contribution of £40, takes 3 hours cutting time and 8 hours assembly time. There is a maximum of 36 cutting hours available each week and 48 assembly hours.

What quantities of summer houses and garden sheds should be made in order to maximise the weekly contribution and profit?

Solution

Let x = number of summer houses produced per week

and y = number of sheds produced per week,

The objective is to maximise contribution, £C, where:

$$C = 50x + 40y$$

subject to the following constraints

$6x + 3y \leq 36$ (cutting hours)

$4x + 8y \leq 48$ (assembly hours)

$x \geq 0$ (non-negative constraint)

$y \geq 0$ (non-negative constraint)

4.1 Slack variables

Inequalities are difficult to deal with algebraically and for the simplex method the inequalities must be converted into equations. If an unknown quantity, z say, is less than 36, then another quantity can be added to z to make it equal to 36. Similarly, if $z \geq 36$, then another quantity can be subtracted from z to make it equal to 36. A variable that is added is called a **slack variable**, and a variable that is subtracted is called a **surplus variable**.

As both inequalities in our model are '≤', a slack variable is added to each inequality to make an equation. The slack variable for cutting hours will be called S_1 and the slack variable for assembly hours will be called S_2.

The equations are therefore:

$$6x + 3y + S_1 = 36$$

$$4x + 8y + S_2 = 48$$

S_1 represents the amount by which the utilised cutting time $(6x + 3y)$ falls short of the available cutting time (36) and is therefore the amount of unused cutting time. Similarly, S_2 is the amount of unused assembly time.

4.2 The initial simplex tableau

The initial simplex method puts a feasible solution into a table or 'tableau'. To construct the initial tableau for solving a problem, the procedure is as follows.

The constraint equations and objective function are first set out so that the variables are aligned in columns. This necessitates re-arranging the objective function to bring the x and y terms to the left-hand side, giving:

$$\begin{array}{lllllll} & 6x & + 3y & + S_1 & & = & 36 \\ & 4x & + 8y & & + S_2 & = & 48 \\ C & - 50x & - 40y & & & = & 0 \end{array}$$

The coefficients of each equation are then tabulated, putting zeros in the blank spaces.

C is placed in a separate column called the **basic variable** or **basis** column (or 'variables in the solution' column). The other entries in this column are the slack variables associated with each constraint, S_1 for the first constraint and S_2 for the second constraint. The basic variable column shows the variables in the feasible solution we are testing.

Basic variable	*x*	*y*	*S_1*	*S_2*	*Solution*
S_1	6	3	1	0	36
S_2	4	8	0	1	48
C	-50	-40	0	0	0

Note that the non-negativity constraints are not included. The simplex method implicitly assumes that all variables are greater than or equal to zero.

4.3 Interpretation of initial tableau

The basic variable column is not essential, but it makes the interpretation of the simplex tableau much easier. It contains those variables whose values are listed in the solution column. In our initial tableau, we have:

$$S_1 = 36$$

$$S_2 = 48$$

$$C = 0$$

KEY POINT

The starting point for solving a problem by the simplex method is to construct a tableau where the value of the objective function is 0.

The starting point for solving a problem by the simplex method is to construct a tableau where the value of the objective function is 0.

The solution being tested is the contribution that will be £0 if $S_1 = 36$, $S_2 = 48$, x = 0 and y = 0.

This means that if all the variable time is slack, i.e. no work is being done, then the contribution will be zero. If no work is being done, x and y are both = 0. This is readily inferred from the tableau; any variables not listed in the basic variable column always have a value of zero in the solution.

The initial tableau therefore represents the feasible but trivial solution that if no items are produced, there will be no contribution.

Note: The basic variables can be identified from those columns having one cell, and one only, equal to 1, and all the other cells in that column equal to zero. The position of the 1 gives the row to which the basic variable relates. Thus, in the above tableau, the S_1 column has a 1 in the first row and all other values in this column are zero. Hence S_1 is the basic variable for the row in which the 1 occurs, i.e. row 1.

The figures in the x and y columns and the contribution row are – 50 for x and – 40 for y. *A minus sign shows that the value of the objective function (contribution) can be increased.* Here, contribution can be increased by £50 for each additional unit of x that is made and sold, and can be increased by £40 for every unit of y that is made and sold.

4.4 Interpretation of the final simplex tableau

The initial simplex tableau is the starting point for an algorithm, which is easily computerised, which generates an optimal solution. The final tableau for this example is as follows:

Basic variable	*x*	*y*	*S_1*	*S_2*	*Solution*
x	1	0	$\frac{2}{9}$	$-\frac{1}{12}$	4
y	0	1	$-\frac{1}{9}$	$\frac{1}{6}$	4
C	0	0	$6\frac{2}{3}$	$\frac{15}{6}$	360

The solution is:

- x = 4: make and sell 4 summer houses each week
- y = 4: make and sell 4 garden sheds each week
- C = 360: the contribution would be £360 per week

S_1 and S_2 = 0. All the available cutting hours and assembly hours are fully used up.

KEY POINT

In the objective function row, the values for the variables not in the solution are their shadow price.

The values in the objective function line show the shadow prices.

- The shadow price of S_1 (cutting hours) is £6⅔, which means that for every additional cutting hour that could be made available, the achievable contribution would be increased by £6⅔. (Similarly, if there were less each week of cutting time, the optimal solution would be reduced by £6⅔ for each one hour reduction in the available time.)
- The shadow price of S_2 (assembly time) is £15/6 = £2.50.This shows that for every additional assembly hour that could be made available, the achievable contribution would be increased by £2.50.

The other values in the tableau are also significant, and have a meaning. The figures in the columns for the variables that are 0 in the solution (here, the slack variables) show how the shadow prices for those variables are made up. Take the column in the final tableau for S_1 (cutting time).

- If one extra hour of cutting time could be made available, the contribution per week could be increased by £6⅔.
- This would be achieved by making an additional 2/9 of a unit of x and making 1/9 of a unit less of y. The change in contribution would be:

  + (2/9 × £50) – (1/9 × £40) = + £60/9 = + £6⅔.

  (A linear programming model assumes that fractions of units in the optimal solution is possible.)
- Similarly, if one extra hour of assembly time could be made available (variable S_2), the company would make 1/12 of a unit less of x and 1/6 of a unit more of y, so that the change in contribution would be – (1/12 × £50) + (1/6 × £40) = +£30/12 = +£2.50. This is the shadow price of assembly hours.

5 Problems with the linear programming model and the simplex method

5.1 Limitations

There are some limitations to the linear programming model and the simplex method of finding a solution.

- The model assumes linearity in values. For example, if the model is used to identify a profit-maximising volume of production and sales, an assumption would have to be constant unit variable costs and unit sales prices, regardless of volume. Similarly, an assumption would be that fixed costs are unchanged regardless of production activity. In reality, these assumptions could be too simplistic.
- The optimum solution could be in fractions of units. For example, in the example above of the company making summer houses and garden sheds, the optimum solution might have been to make a fraction of a number of summer houses and sheds so as to maximise contribution (for example, 4.1429 summer houses and 3.8174 garden sheds). When large quantities are involved, it is a simple matter to round down the figures in the optimal solution to the nearest whole number. However, when the numbers in the optimal solution are quite small, fractions in the solution might make it difficult to identify the best practical solution with the model.
- In the simplex method, there will always be as many variables in the solution as there are constraints in the model. For example, suppose that a company makes 10 products and is facing shortages of certain resources. A linear programming model might be constructed with six constraints. There would be 10 variables for the products and six slack variables, making 16 variables in total. The optimal solution produced by the model would have six variables, one for each constraint, which means that 10 of the variables (products or slack variables) would have a zero value in the optimal solution.

Summary

- This chapter has considered decision problems where activity is limited by the existence of one or more scarce resources.
- Companies often assume that sales demand is the limiting factor when preparing a budget or plan for production and sales. However, scarce resources might sometimes be a limiting factor on production and sales.
- When an organisation makes and sells more than one product, and is faced with more than one limiting factor, a profit maximising (= contribution-maximising) budget, or sales revenue-maximising budget, can be derived by formulating and solving a linear programming model.
- When there are more than two variables in the problem (e.g. more than two products), the linear programming model can be solved by the simplex method.
- A linear programming model consists of an objective function, which is something for which a maximum (or possibly a minimum) value is sought, and a number of constraints. A constraint is formulated initially as an inequality, ≤ or ≥.
- To solve the problem by the simplex method, each constraint is converted into an equation by introducing a slack variable (or surplus variable, in the case of 'greater than or equal to' inequalities). It is also assumed that all variables have a value equal to or greater than 0.
- The values in the final tableau can be interpreted. In particular, there is a solution column, showing the value of each variable in the solution. The objective function row shows the shadow price of all the variables with a 0 value on the solution. If a shadow price has a negative value, the optimal solution has not yet been found.

Having completed your study of this chapter you should have achieved the following learning outcome.

- Discuss the meaning of optimal solutions and show how linear programming methods can be employed for profit maximising, revenue maximising and satisfying objectives.

Self-test questions

1 What is a scarce resource? (1.2)

2 What is linear programming? (2.1)

3 List some common applications of linear programming. (2.2)

4 What is the feasible region? (2.10)

5 What is an iso-contribution line? (2.11)

6 What are the limitations of linear programming? (2.13)

7 What is slack in the context of linear programming? (3.1)

8 What is a shadow price? (3.2)

9 How is an inequality converted into an equation for the simplex method? (4.1)

10 What is the meaning of all the values in the objective function row in a simplex tableau? (5.4)

11 State three limitations of the simplex method. (5.1)

Objective test questions

Question 1

A company's existing production plan is as follows:

	A	*B*
Units	1,000	750
	£	£
Unit selling price	13.00	21.00
Unit variable costs		
Direct material	1.00	1.00
Direct labour at £2 per hour	5.00	12.00
Overhead	0.50	1.20
	£6.50	£14.20

This represents the maximum demand for each product. The company is limited to 7,000 labour hours availability. A contract to produce 200 units of product C is under review. These are required by a customer who will provide his own materials. Net proceeds from the contract after deducting labour and overhead costs amount to £3,000 and will utilise 1,500 labour hours.

Assuming that the company wishes to maximise profit, which is the optimum production plan?

	A	**B**	**C**
A	400	750	200
B	1,000	750	0
C	1,000	500	200
D	0	750	200

Question 2

A company makes three products as follows:

	Kilts	*Skirts*	*Dresses*
	£	£	£
Material @ £5/square metre	5	2.50	10
Labour @ £2/hour	6	2.00	2
Fixed costs absorbed	6	2.00	2
Profit	6	3.50	5
Selling price	£23	£10.00	£19

Maximum demand is 1,000 for each product, but supplies of material are limited to 4,000 square metres while the labour force will only work 1,000 hours.

To maximise its profits the company should produce:

A 1,000 kilts

B 1,000 skirts

C 1,000 dresses

D 333 kilts

Question 3

Z Ltd manufactures three products, the selling price and cost details of which are given below:

	Product X	*Product Y*	*Product Z*
	£	£	£
Selling price per unit	75	95	95
Costs per unit:			
Direct materials (£5/kg)	10	5	15
Direct labour (£4/hour)	16	24	20
Variable overhead	8	12	10
Fixed overhead	24	36	30

In a period when direct materials are restricted in supply, the most and the least profitable uses of direct materials are:

	Most profitable	*Least profitable*
A	X	Z
B	Y	Z
C	X	Y
D	Z	Y

Question 4

In linear programming, the amount by which a resource is used less than the limit is called:

A slack

B shadow price

C feasible region

D sensitivity

The following information is relevant to questions 5 and 6.

A company makes three products A, B and C subject to the constraints represented by the slack variables S1, S2 and S3. It has assessed the profit-maximising budget using the simplex method of linear programming, and the final tableau for the simplex calculation is as follows.

	A	B	C	S1	S2	S3	
B	0	1	– 0.5	0.4	0	0.8	167
S2	0	0	0.8	– 0.3	1	– 1.67	233
A	1	0	0	0	0	– 0.2	250.0
	0	0	15	12	0	20	10,010

Question 5

How many of each product should the company produce to maximise contribution? What is the maximum contribution that can be achieved?

Question 6

Explain the meaning of the term 'shadow price' illustrating your answer from the data given.

For the answers to these questions, see the 'Answers' section at the end of the book.

Exam-type questions

Question 1: Flintstones

The Flintstones are involved in the manufacture of two products, Chip and Dale. Due to an industrial dispute, which is expected to go on for some time, material B, which is required in the production of Dale, is expected to be limited to 300 units per week. Material A, required for both products, is freely available.

Flintstones are experiencing labour shortages and it is expected that only 800 hours of unskilled labour and 1,000 hours of skilled labour will be available in any week, in the short run.

Due to a transport problem, the Flintstones will be able to import only 400 Dinos into the country each week. This item is required in the manufacture of both Chip and Dale.

It is the company's policy to limit the production of Dale to not more than three times the production of Chip.

The following information is available:

	Chip	*Dale*
	£	£
Material B (2 units for Dale only)	-	10
Material A 15	10	
Labour – unskilled £3 per hour	12	15
– skilled £5 per hour	50	20
Dinos (£10 each)	20	20
Total cost	97	75
Selling price	127	100

Fixed costs each week amount to £3,000.

Required:

(a) Calculate the optimal plan for Flintstones together with the weekly profit that may be earned. **(15 marks)**

(b) Explain and illustrate the meaning of a shadow price in the specific scenario facing Flintstones. **(10 marks)**

(Total: 25 marks)

Question 2: Electronic component mix

In a machine shop a company manufactures two types of electronic component, X and Y, on which it aims to maximise the contribution to profit. The company wishes to know the ideal combination of X and Y to make. All the electronic components are produced in three main stages: Assembly, Inspection and Packing.

In Assembly each X takes 1 hour and each Y takes 2 hours.

Inspection takes 7.5 minutes for each X and 30 minutes for each Y, on the average, which includes the time required for any faults to be rectified.

In total there are 600 hours available for assembly and 100 hours for inspection each week. At all stages both components can be processed at the same time.

At the final stage the components require careful packing prior to delivery. Each X takes 3 minutes and each Y takes 20 minutes on average to pack properly. There is a total of 60 packing hours available each week.

The contribution on X is £10 per unit and on Y is £15 per unit. For engineering reasons not more than 500 of X can be made each week. All production can be sold.

Required:

Using a linear programming approach advise the company on the optimum production plan.

(Total: 10 marks)

For the answers to these questions, see the 'Answers' section at the end of the book.

Feedback to activities

Activity 1

Production is restricted as follows:

Machine hours	200/5	=	40 units of X, or
	200/2.5	=	80 units of Y
Materials	£500/£10	=	50 units of X, or
	£500/£5	=	100 units of Y

Therefore machine hours is the limiting factor since X's and Y's production are most severely limited by machine hours.

Contribution per machine hour:

Product X	£20/5 hours	=	£4/hour
Product Y	£15/2.5 hours	=	£6/hour

Product Y should be made.

Activity 2

The variables are:

1 The quantity of flak traps to produce per month.

2 The quantity of sap traps to produce per month.

Let x = number of flak traps produced per month.

Let y = number of sap traps produced per month.

Activity 3

Skilled labour	10x	+	10y	≤	2,000
Semi-skilled labour	5x	+	25y	≤	2,500
Flak trap demand	x			≤	150
Sap trap demand			y	≤	80
Non-negative constraints	x			≥	0
			y	≥	0

Activity 4

Skilled labour: x = 0, y = 2,000/10 = 200

y = 0, x = 2,000/10 = 200

We simply join up the points (0, 200) and (200, 0).

Semi-skilled labour: x = 0, y = 2,500/25 = 100

y = 0, x = 2,500/5 = 500

We join up the points (0, 100) and (500, 0).

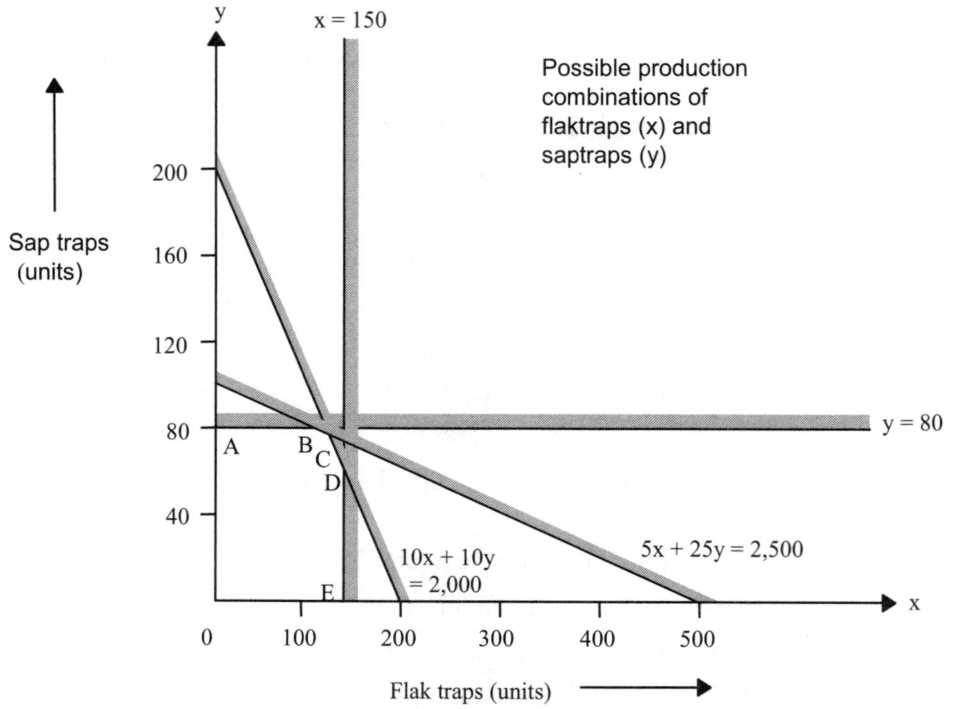

This give a feasibility region of 0ABCDE.

Activity 5

(a) ***Tutorial note:*** The chemicals are given in percentage terms that are converted to decimals.

Let x = number of kg of X, cost = 10x

Let y = number of kg of Y, cost = 5y

Total cost: z = 10x + 5y, the objective function which has to be minimised.

The constraints exist on the chemical composition of the fertilisers:

Nitrates:	0.18x + 0.03y	≥	100… 1
Phosphates:	0.05x + 0.02y	≥	50… 2
Potash:	0.02x + 0.05y	≥	40… 3
Logic:	x ≥ 0, y ≥ 0		

(b) In this example, all the points where the lines cut the axes are required, so that the easiest way to draw the constraints is to calculate these points.

$0.18x + 0.03y = 100$

$x = 0 \quad \therefore \quad y = \frac{100}{0.03} = 3{,}333.3$

$y = 0 \quad \therefore \quad x = \frac{100}{0.18} = 555.5$

$0.05x + 0.02y = 50$

$x = 0 \quad \therefore \quad y = \frac{50}{0.02} = 2{,}500$

$y = 0 \quad \therefore \quad x = \frac{50}{0.05} = 1{,}000$

$0.02x + 0.05y = 40$

$x = 0 \quad \therefore \quad y = \frac{40}{0.05} = 800$

$y = 0 \quad \therefore \quad x = \frac{40}{0.02} = 2{,}000$

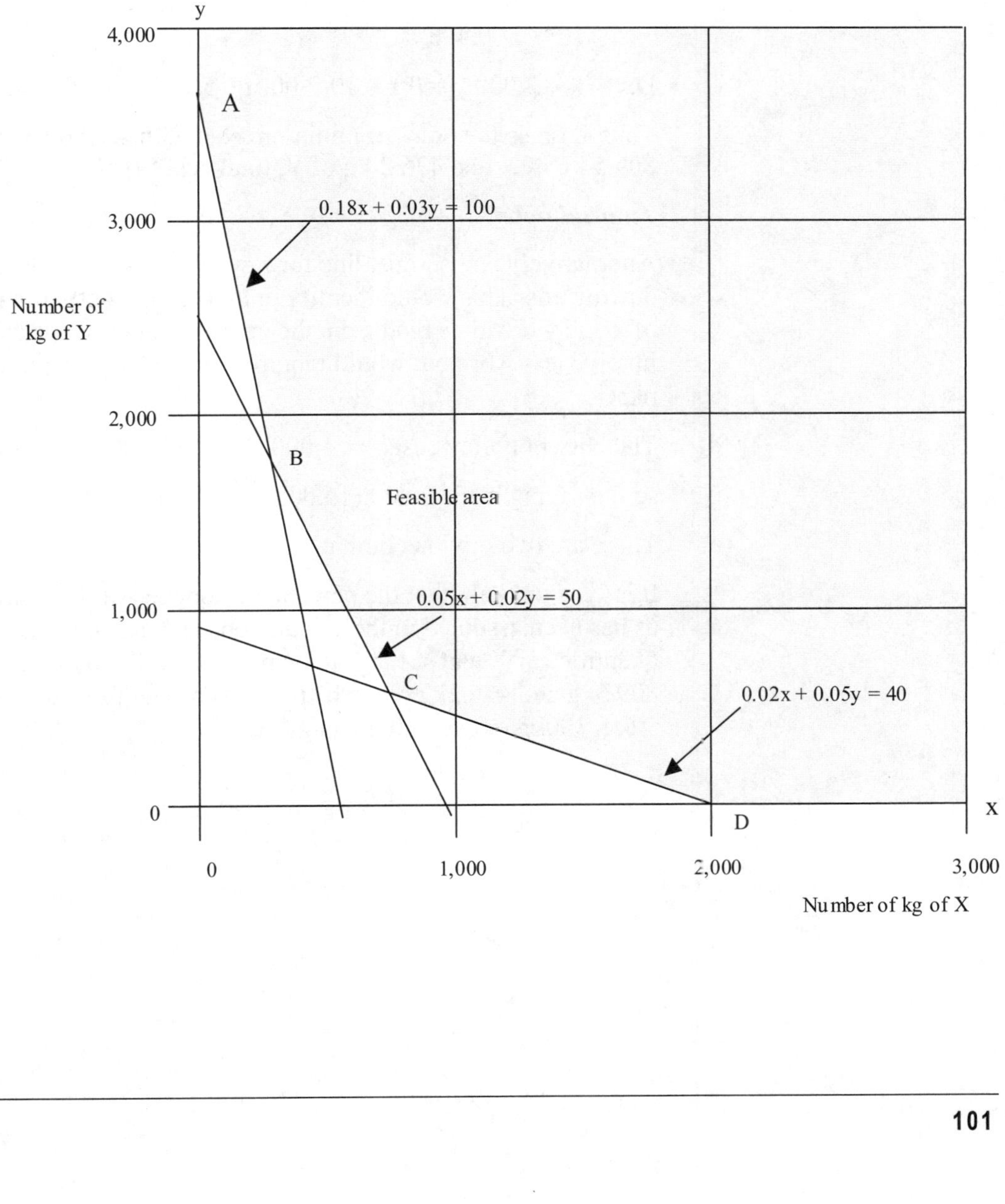

(c) Considering the vertices of the feasible area.

A: $x = 0$ $y = 3{,}333.3$ $z = 10x + 5y$

$z = 10(0) + 5(3{,}333.3) = £16{,}666.5$

B: Solving $(0.18x + 0.03y = 100) \times 2$ $0.36x + 0.06y = 200$

and $(0.05x + 0.02y = 50) \times 3$ $0.15x + 0.06y = 150$

$\therefore 0.21x = 50$

$\therefore x = 238.1$

replacing gives $y = 1{,}904.8$

$z = 10(238.1) + 5(1{,}904.8)$
$= £11{,}905$

C: Solving $(0.05x + 0.02y = 50) \times 5$ $0.25x + 0.1y = 250$

and $(0.02x + 0.05y = 40) \times 2$ $0.04x + 0.1y = 80$

$\therefore 0.21x = 170$

$\therefore x = 809.5$

replacing gives $y = 476.2$

$z = 10(809.5) + 5(476.2)$

$= £10{,}476$

D: $x = 2{,}000$ $y = 0$ $z = 10(2{,}000) + 5(0) = £20{,}000$

Thus C gives the point of minimum cost with x = 809.5 and y = 476.2, i.e. 809.5 kg of X and 476.2 kg of Y, total cost £10,476.

Tutorial note:

Alternatively, an iso-cost line for z = 20,000 (say) could be plotted and moved downwards. This would identify point C as the optimum point, and the values of x and y could be read from the graph, as in previous examples. This would involve less work but would require the graphs to be plotted accurately on graph paper.

(d) The current policy costs: 1,000 (£10) + 1,000 (£5) = £15,000

so the saving made is of £(15,000 – 10,476) = £4,524

(e) There are two obvious limitations:

It is very unlikely that the percentage contents of the fertilisers will be as exact as has been assumed in the calculations. No account has been taken of the actual quantities of X and Y that can be purchased. It would seem highly unlikely that 809.5kg and 476.2kg could be purchased. The fertilisers may only be sold in 50kg, 100kg or even 500kg bags.

Activity 6

Machining time – the constraints become:

(i) $20x + 25y \leq 501$

(ii) $40x + 25y \leq 800$

Subtracting (i) from (ii) gives

$20x = 299$

and thus $x = 14.95$

Inserting into (i) gives

$(20 \times 14.95) + 25y = 501$

$25y = 202$

$y = 8.08$

Original contribution:

		£
(15 × £80) + (8 × £75)	=	1,800
Amended contribution		
(14.95 × £80) + (8.08 × £75)	=	1,802
Increased contribution		2

The shadow price per machine hour is £2.

Activity 7

Rearranging gives: $25y = 500 - 20x$

Dividing by 25 gives: $y = 20 - 0.8x$

The gradient is therefore –0.8.

Activity 8

Re-arranging gives: $25y = 800 - 40x$

Dividing by 25 gives: $y = 32 - 1.6x$

The gradient is therefore –1.6.

The gradient of the objective function = $\frac{p}{q} = \frac{-\text{contribution from X}}{\text{contribution from Y}}$

which must lie between –0.8 and –1.6

Thus $\frac{p}{q}$ must lie between 0.8 and 1.6 for the optimal solution not to alter.

Chapter 6

PRICING

Syllabus content

This chapter covers the following syllabus content.

- Pricing decisions for profit maximising in imperfect markets. (Note tabular methods of solution are acceptable).
- Pricing strategies and the financial consequences of market skimming, premium pricing, penetration pricing, loss leaders, product bundling/optional extras and product differentiation to appeal to different market segments.

Contents

1 Cost-plus pricing

1.1 Introduction

Any discussion of pricing usually focuses on two approaches to the pricing decision:

- a cost-based approach
  - using a 'full cost-plus' method
  - marginal cost may be used in the short term
  - aims to recover costs
- a demand-based approach
  - aims to maximise profits using marginal cost and marginal revenue considerations.
  - takes into consideration the type of market and product.

1.2 Factors in pricing decisions

Several factors underlie all pricing decisions and effective decisions will be based on a careful consideration of the following factors.

- **Organisational goals** – If a goal of profit or cash maximisation is assumed, then the setting of selling prices must be seen as a means of achieving this end.
- **Product mix** – If the organisation produces a range of different products, it is faced with the problem of setting selling prices for each individual product in such a manner as to obtain the optimum product mix, i.e. that mix which will maximise profit or cash inflows generated from the sale of all products.
- **Price/demand relationships (demand curves)** – For most products, there exists a relationship between selling price and the quantity demanded at that price. Customers will usually have an alternative source of supply and will be driven away by a selling price that is set too high. Product quality will also tend to influence the price and demand relationship.
- **A knowledge of the price elasticity of demand** (i.e. the responsiveness of changes in demand to changes in price) is therefore vital in the selling price decision.
- **Competitors and markets** – An organisation's competitors will usually react in some way to changes made to the selling price structure. In practice, therefore, price adjustments may be heavily influenced by expectations of competitor reaction.
- **A discussion of the type of market** within which the firm may operate, and the effect that this may have on pricing policy, is found later in this chapter.
- **Product life cycle** – During the life of an individual product, several stages are apparent – introduction, growth, maturity, saturation and decline. The duration of each stage of the life cycle varies according to the type of product, but the concept is nevertheless important as each stage is likely to influence the firm's pricing policy. The sales pricing mechanism is sometimes used to 'control' the life cycle of a product.

- **Marketing strategy** – Selling prices should be set with reference to overall marketing strategy. Product design and quality, advertising and promotion, distribution methods, etc. are likely to influence the sales pricing decision. For example, by concentrating on advertising or packaging, a firm may be able to set higher prices for its product or, conversely, lower prices might be necessary in order to distribute the product through a supermarket chain.
- **Cost** – In the long run, all operating costs must be fully covered by sales revenue. However, as will be seen later, over-emphasis on cost in the short run may result in suboptimal decisions.

1.3 Full cost pricing

A number of studies, most notably an old American study by Hall and Hitch in 1939 and a more recent UK study by Hankinson in the early 1980s, showed that the major determinant for the selling price of a product or service was its cost. This may go against the 'demand-based' approaches discussed later in this chapter, but firms may not adopt 'profit-maximising' pricing policies because the necessary information may not always be available.

The principle of cost-plus pricing is to estimate the likely direct costs for a product, then add a percentage to that to cover overheads then a further percentage to provide a profit. Clearly there is a heavy reliance on the correct estimation of costs for a new product; under-estimate and an item will be sold at a loss, over-estimate and a price will be set that is too high to attract demand. However the 'marginalist' approach to pricing is just as dependent on accurate costs information. There are several variations on this basic approach that are discussed later.

When a comparison is made between a cost-plus approach and a demand based approach, it is assumed that the pricing process stops there – this is not the case and it would be disastrous if it were. Any pricing policy will require figures to be reviewed to assess the likely effect on customer demand and also the prices that competitors currently charge or are expected to charge. However a review of the advantages and disadvantages are set out below.

1.4 Advantages and disadvantages of cost-plus pricing

These comments are based on an approach that takes no notice of other influences.

Advantages

- Inability of organisations to get a complete picture of how selling price affects demand.
- Cost of getting any market information may be prohibitive.
- Easy to produce prices, relies on a formula, so pricing decisions can be delegated.
- Gives justification for price rises.
- Said to produce stable prices.

Disadvantages

- Said to ignore demand.
- Thought to ignore competitors.

- Ignores distinction between incremental costs and fixed costs.
- The selling price depends on how fixed costs are apportioned to products (which may depend on estimates of demand which, in turn, will depend on selling price).

1.5 Short-term pricing

In the short term, a business may accept orders at any price above marginal cost in order to utilise spare capacity, provided that:

- fixed costs are unchanged by the decision
- more profitable work is not displaced
- other customers will not be encouraged to seek price reductions.

Occasionally, businesses will accept work at a price below marginal cost in order to keep the workforce employed.

Note that marginal cost pricing is widely employed in practice: British Telecom is able to offer cheap rate telephone calls at evenings and weekends because it is using equipment provided to meet the heavy demand for calls during business hours. In the off-peak period, it need only cover marginal cost and perhaps obtain some contribution towards fixed costs. Similar considerations apply to the off-peak fares available from the rail operators.

The Hankinson survey mentioned earlier showed that firms did use an opportunity cost approach to short-term pricing decisions involving disposal of otherwise obsolete stock or using spare capacity. The big danger is that the low selling prices that might be charged under these circumstances must not be allowed to affect the demand for other products or services that the firm produces. This is achieved by some form of product differentiation, e.g. marking products as 'special reduction' or even 'damaged stock'.

Example

The Snipe Company is an electronics company having eight product lines. Income data for one of the products for the year just ended is as follows.

	£m	£m
Sales – 200,000 units @ average price of £100		20
Variable costs:		
Direct materials @ £35	7	
Direct labour @ £10	2	
Variable factory overhead @ £5	1	
Sales commission = 15% of selling price (£15)	3	
Other variable costs @ £5	1	
Total variable costs @ £70		14
Contribution		6
Fixed costs:		
Discretionary	3	
Committed	2	
		5
Operating income		1

Consider the following situations.

(a) The electronics industry had severe price competition throughout the year. Near the end of the year, Albacone Co, which was experimenting with various components in its regular product line, offered £80 each for 3,000 units. The latter would have been in addition to the 200,000 units actually sold. Acceptance of the special order by Snipe would not affect regular sales. The salesman hoped that the order might provide entrance into a new application so he told Jean Hooper, the product manager, that he would accept half his regular commission rate if the order were accepted. Hooper pondered for a day, but was afraid of the precedent that might be set by cutting the price. She said 'the price is below our full costs of £95 per unit. I think we should quote a full price, or Albacone Co will expect favoured treatment again and again if we continue to do business with them.' If Hooper had accepted the offer, what would operating income have been?

(b) The Gall Company had offered to supply a key part (MIA) for £20 each. One MIA is used in every finished unit. The Snipe Company had made these parts for variable costs of £18 plus some additional fixed costs of £200,000 for supervision and other items. What would operating income have been if Snipe purchased rather than made the parts? Assume that discretionary costs for supervision and other items would have been avoided if the parts were purchased.

(c) The company could have purchased the MIA parts for £20 each and used the vacated space for the manufacture of a different electronics component on a subcontracting basis for Hewlett-Packard, a much larger company. Assume that 40,000 special components could have been made for Hewlett-Packard (and sold in addition to the 200,000 units sold through regular channels) at a unit variable cost of £150, exclusive of parts. MIA parts would be needed for these components as well as for the regular production. No sales commission would have to be paid. All the fixed costs pertaining to the MIA parts would have continued, including the supervisory costs, because they related mainly to the facilities used. What would operating income have been if Snipe had made and sold the components to Hewlett-Packard for £170 per unit and bought the MIA parts?

Solution

(a) **Analysis of special order**

	Per unit	*3,000 units*	*3,000 units*
	£	£000	£000
Additional sales	80		240
Variable costs (excluding commission)	55	165	
Commission ($15\% \times \frac{1}{2} \times 240$)		18	
			183
Contribution			57

Note that variable costs, except for commission, are affected by physical units of volume, not pounds revenue.

Operating income would have been £1,000,000 plus £57,000, or £1,057,000, if the order had been accepted. In a sense, the decision to reject the offer means that Snipe is willing to invest £57,000 in immediate gains forgone (an opportunity cost) to preserve the long run selling price structure.

(b) **Making or purchasing**

	Make £000	*Purchase* £000
Purchase cost @ £20		4,000
Variable costs @ £18	3,600	
Avoidable discretionary costs	200	
Total relevant costs	3,800	4,000

Operating income would have fallen by £200,000, or from £1,000,000 to £800,000, if Snipe had purchased the parts.

(c) **Operating income**

	£000	£000	£000
Sales would increase by 40,000 units @ £170			6,800
Additional costs to the company as a whole:			
Variable costs exclusive of MIA parts would increase by 40,000 units @ £150		6,000	
Effects on overall costs of MIA parts: Cost of 240,000 parts purchased @ £20	4,800		
Less: Savings from not making 20,000 parts @ £18 (only the variable costs are relevant because fixed costs continue)	3,600		
Additional cost of parts		1,200	7,200
Disadvantage of making components for Hewlett-Packard			(400)

Operating income would decline by £400,000 from £1,000,000 to £600,000.

1.6 Pricing in limiting factor situations

When there is a factor limiting production, opportunity cost (contribution per key factor) may be taken into account in price fixing. Consider the following example.

Example

A company has the following budget based on orders from the domestic market:

	£	£
Sales (2,000 units)		10,000
Cost of sales:		
Direct material	1,000	
Direct labour	4,000	

	£	£
Variable overhead	1,000	
Fixed overhead	3,000	
		9,000
		1,000

At this level of output, the company has spare capacity and it is therefore planning to develop export markets. It believes that it will be able to sell an additional 750 units of its standard model – the limit of its production due to a shortage of raw materials. No additional fixed costs would be incurred and selling prices and variable costs per unit would be the same as for the home market.

Before launching its export campaign, however, the company is approached by a domestic buyer who wishes to purchase 200 deluxe models which use twice as much material as the standard model. What is the minimum price which should be charged if this order is accepted?

Solution

If the company accepts the deluxe order, it will lose export sales due to the shortage of materials. On export sales the contribution per unit would be as follows:

	£	£
Selling price		5
Direct material	0.50	
Direct labour	2.00	
Variable overhead	0.50	
		3
Contribution		2
Contribution per £1 of raw material (£2.00 ÷ £0.50)		£4

Each deluxe model uses £1 worth of raw material. In order to be no worse off by accepting this order, therefore, the company must obtain a contribution of at least £4 per unit – the opportunity cost of the raw material.

The minimum price to be charged is therefore:

	£
Direct material	1.00
Direct labour	2.00
Variable overhead	0.50
	3.50
Required contribution	4.00
Selling price per unit	7.50

If 200 deluxe models are made sales in the export market will fall by 400 to 350.

Check	*Deluxe order rejected*		*Deluxe order accepted*			
	Export sales		*Export sales*		*Deluxe sales*	
	£	£	£	£	£	£
Sales:						
Standard model (750 @ £5)		3,750				
Deluxe model (200 @ 7.50)						1,500
Standard model (350 @ £5)				1,750		
Direct material (£0.50/£1)	375		175		200	
Direct labour (£2)	1,500		700		400	
Variable overhead (£0.50)	375		175		100	
		2,250		1,050		700
Contribution		1,500		700		800

Therefore, if it charges the minimum price recommended for the deluxe model, the company will obtain the same contribution as if it rejected the order and concentrated on the export market.

In practice, of course, the company will take other considerations into account, e.g. the deluxe order is definite, export sales are speculative; more labour is required if the company concentrates on exports; there may be additional selling costs or other fixed costs associated with exporting.

KEY POINT

In practice, of course, the company will take other considerations into account, e.g. the deluxe order is definite, export sales are speculative; more labour is required if the company concentrates on exports; there may be additional selling costs or other fixed costs associated with exporting.

1.7 Pricing policy in inflationary conditions

Inflation presents problems for those responsible for fixing prices, particularly if there is legislation limiting the frequency and extent of price rises. It is desirable to have a system whereby review of a firm's price and cost structure is automatically triggered each time one of its inputs increases in price. However, there will also have to be some anticipation of cost increases, since it will not be practical to raise selling prices each time an input price increases. The Hankinson survey showed evidence of delays between cost increases and increases in selling price.

Price increases should not, of course, be made without considering the effect on demand. Taken over a period, people's wages may rise at least in line with inflation, and, therefore, price increases which are no more than the general level of inflation may have no permanent effect on demand. However, there will almost inevitably be a 'timing difference', with demand being reduced immediately after a price rise but then picking up again. The effect of this on cash flow must be considered. If demand can be stimulated, it might be possible to absorb the effects of input price rises by producing greater output and thereby achieving economies of scale.

Firms undertaking long-term contract work usually insert a clause in the contract governing price escalation. For instance, the contract might specify that 20% of the price is considered fixed and that, of the remaining 80%, half will be inflated in line with an index of wage rates and half in line with a price index (e.g. the retail price index or a more specific index related to the type of contract).

Activity 1

Capel plc is carrying out a long-term contract in connection with maintenance of the Channel Tunnel. The contract specifies that, of the total £8m price, 30% is considered fixed, 25% should be inflated in line with the retail prices index, while the balance should be inflated in line with an index of industrial wage rates.

Relevant values for the indices are as follows:

	RPI	*Wage rate index*
Capel starts work	130	215
Capel finishes work	150	240

What is the total final value of the contract to the company?

Feedback to this activity is at the end of the chapter.

1.8 Value analysis

DEFINITION

Value analysis is a systematic interdisciplinary examination of factors affecting the cost of a product of service, in order to devise means of achieving the specified purpose most economically at the required standard of quality and reliability. (CIMA *Official Terminology*)

Value analysis is a systematic interdisciplinary examination of factors affecting the cost of a product or service, in order to devise means of achieving the specified purpose most economically at the required standard of quality and reliability. (CIMA, *Official Terminology*)

Value analysis is basically a form of cost reduction, i.e. a method of improving profitability by reducing costs without necessarily increasing prices; it is thus particularly useful to manufacturers or suppliers who are unable to fix their own price because of, for example, a competitive market. However, the use of value analysis in all circumstances should be considered as any failure to reduce costs will result in suboptimisation of profitability.

Value analysis resulted from a realisation by manufacturers that they were incorporating features into their product which the user of the product did not require and was not prepared to pay for. For instance, few manufacturers of bath taps are prepared to produce taps in solid gold, as the demand for such expensive taps is very limited – most people are quite satisfied with brass. In the same way, other not so obvious but equally useless, features can be incorporated into products. Value analysis takes a critical look at each feature of a product, questioning its need and its use, and eliminating any unjustifiable features.

DEFINITION

Utility value is the value an item has because of the uses to which it can be put. **Esteem value** is the value put on an item because of its beauty, craftsmanship, etc.

It is useful to distinguish two types of value – utility value and esteem value. The difference may be illustrated by reference to furniture. An individual who requires something to sit on may be satisfied with a crudely made three-legged stool or even a tree stump, and will be prepared to pay a very low sum of money for this. This individual may be prepared, however, to pay a great deal more money for a well-made fashionable leather reclining chair. Both serve the same basic purposes – a seat – but while a tree stump only has utility value, the leather reclining chair has esteem value as well.

- Utility value is the value an item has because of the uses to which it can be put.
- Esteem value is the value put on an item because of its beauty, craftsmanship, etc.

Value analysis is concerned with those products for which no esteem value is paid. In these circumstances there is little need for craftsmanship and beauty, and it may be possible to reduce costs by excluding such unnecessary features.

KEY POINT

Value analysis is concerned with those products for which no esteem value is paid. In these circumstances there is little need for craftsmanship and beauty, and it may be possible to reduce costs by excluding such unnecessary features.

1.9 The value analysis method

Value analysis is concerned with five basic steps.

Step 1

Establish the precise requirements of the customer. It should be possible to discover precisely why customers want an item, whether the item has any esteem value, etc. Only in this way can the manufacturer be certain that each function incorporated into the product contributes some value to it.

Step 2

Establish and evaluate alternative ways of achieving the requirements of the customers. There may be methods of producing the item which have not been considered, e.g. replacing metal panels with plastic. Each alternative method must be costed out in units of:

(i) **materials** – amount required, acceptable level of wastage (can it be improved?), alternative, cheaper materials.

(ii) **labour** – can the cost be reduced by eliminating operations or changing production methods?

(iii) **other factors** – can new, cheaper processes be found? Would a cheaper finish be acceptable?

Step 3

Authorise any proposals put forward as a result of Step 2. The assessment in Step 2 may be carried out by middle management and, if so, it will require ratification by top management before implementation.

Step 4

Implementation of proposals.

Step 5

Evaluate feedback from new proposals to establish the benefits from the change.

Several benefits will result from value analysis. In the first place, many customers will be impressed by the interest shown in their requirements and this will lead to increased sales. In addition, a firm that adopts this approach is likely to attract better staff, due both to the prospects for an outlet for their ideas and the higher morale resulting from the team approach. Of course, there are the economic and financial benefits arising from the elimination of unnecessary complexity and the better use of resources.

1.10 Target costing

DEFINITION

Target cost – a product cost estimate derived by subtracting a desired profit margin from a competitive market price. This may be less than the planned initial product cost, but will be expected to be achieved by the time the product reaches the mature production stage. (CIMA *Official Terminology*)

A target cost is a product cost estimate derived by subtracting a desired profit margin from a competitive market price. This may be less than the planned initial product cost, but will be expected to be achieved by the time the product reaches the mature production stage. (CIMA, *Official Terminology*)

Target costing, as with several other developments in management accounting, has come from Japan where manufacturers such as Sony and Toyota feel that it is responsible for those firms improving their market share. The main theme behind target costing is not finding what a new product does cost but what it should cost.

The starting point for target costing is an estimate of a selling price for a new product that will enable a firm to capture a required share of the market. The next step is to reduce this figure by the firm's required level of profit. This will take into account the return required on any new investment and on working capital requirements. This will produce a target cost figure for product designers to meet. The cost-reduction process, usually described as value analysis, then tries to provide a product which meets that target cost.

2 Pricing and marketing policies

2.1 Introduction

Pricing decisions are not made in a vacuum and there are very few completely new products. Most new products are simply developments of older ones or substitutes for something that already exists.

There is, therefore, a background, or an expected price range, within which a new product will fit. This can sometimes give a completely new product development an enormous opportunity for profit.

For example, when the ballpoint pen first appeared, it was offered to the public as a competitor to good quality fountain pens, which were then selling for around £1.50. The ballpoint pen sold at around this price until competitors discovered that it cost only a few pence to make, whereupon the price tumbled. For some time, however, the ballpoint continued with its fountain pen image being sold as a long-lasting holder for which refills were supplied. Later the cheap throw-away ballpoint became more general.

Occasionally, there are completely new products that create new markets. In this case price tends to follow supply costs. These costs can be expected to fall as mass markets develop, as production becomes more reliable and as initial research, development and fixed equipment costs are recovered. One such product has been the small electronic calculator. Until the development of microprocessors, a calculator was a piece of office equipment outside the price range of most individuals. Early electronic calculators were unreliable and prone to breakdown; initially they were expensive.

The microprocessor made possible a cheap, efficient and reliable piece of equipment of value to any individual. There was no price background for such an item because nothing like this had previously existed. Prices were established by a combination of competition and falling supply costs – a good example of the working of a free market economy.

For more normal products the supplier is operating in a known market with a price history. Decisions may be taken with some knowledge of the likely demand within a given possible price range.

2.2 Charging the 'going rate'

There are situations where producers are satisfied that they can sell a satisfactory quantity at a satisfactory profit at a price which is in line with prices of similar goods or services. The existence of such a situation depends on the nature and strength of competition, especially price competition in the market. The Hall & Hitch survey produced strong evidence for people charging what they felt was 'the fair price'.

Firms are more likely to charge the 'going rate' under the following conditions.

- When the quality or some other feature of a product or a service is more important than price and the price elasticity of demand at the ruling price is elastic. Examples include local hairdressing services, daily and local newspapers, beer and cigarettes.
- When it is believed that a fixed price has become established for a particular product and identified with that product in the market. Inflation, metrication and the economic upheavals of the 1970s and 1980s have upset most of these identities, of which one of the best known examples was probably that of the 6d (2½p) bar of chocolate which lasted for a long period in the 1950s and early 1960s. Fixed prices of this type tend to be associated with 'oligopolies' (see later).

- When price competition will simply reduce revenue for all suppliers without giving additional profits or any other significant market advantage to any individual supplier. This position is associated with oligopolies and with what may be called, perhaps, local oligopolies where local supply is dominated by a small number of traders who are content to retain their local market share. Formal market-sharing agreements or collusive behaviour are not necessary under these conditions. Self-interest builds up a form of custom and practice which all established suppliers observe as long as there is no internal or external threat to market stability. It is also likely that all suppliers will share similar cost conditions and will act together to avoid competing for factors and to preserve stable factor costs, including wages.

2.3 The price strategy

The price strategy to be adopted for any particular product is part of the total marketing strategy for the product. This, in turn, is part of the firm's total production strategy. Firms will adopt very different behaviour patterns for different products and markets.

For example, breaking into a market requires different tactics from those needed when defending an established market position from new entrants or possible new entrants to the market.

KEY POINT

It is desirable for business managers to keep an open mind in their approach to the place of prices in the total marketing strategy, but at the same time to recognise clearly the economic forces operating in the market area.

Similarly, the approach to a new market area in which there has been substantial recent investment and which, it is hoped, will expand, will be very different from one to an old area expected to be in decline and where a decision has already been made not to renew investment.

Failure to recognise a change in market demand and in supply conditions such as the arrival of new and more attractive substitutes can lead to expensive errors involving more than just mistakes in pricing.

It is desirable for business managers to keep an open mind in their approach to the place of prices in the total marketing strategy, but at the same time to recognise clearly the economic forces operating in the market area.

DEFINITION

The setting of an initial low price to achieve a desired level of market acceptance is known as **penetration pricing**.

2.4 Market penetration

This relates to the attempt to break into a market and to establish that market share which, it has been calculated, will enable the firm to achieve its revenue and profit targets. The setting of an initial low price to achieve a desired level of market acceptance is known as **penetration pricing**.

Whether the market is an established one which the firm hopes to break open or a new and developing one, the most likely price strategy is to set price as low as possible and substantially below the ruling price of competitors without being so low that the product is thought to be inferior. To achieve this in an established market, the firm is likely to need the benefit of a production or marketing innovation thought to give a special advantage.

Once the target market share has been achieved the next stage in the total strategy is likely to be to build up distributor and customer loyalty, i.e. to reduce the product's price elasticity of demand (make the demand curve steeper). By reducing the relative attraction of substitutes it will also influence the cross elasticity of demand with rival products. This is unlikely to be achieved solely through price changes. There will also have to be changes in advertising, in policies over distribution margins and services and possibly over the availability of services and even of packaging. At this stage there may be a greater emphasis on price stability and stress on quality and availability. This, of course, assumes that successful penetration is now leading to consolidation of the market share and probably an improvement in profitability.

2.5 Market skimming

This is also associated with the launching of a new product but represents a rather different approach. If the product is new and innovative and likely to be the first in the market, there will be a window of opportunity in which monopoly prices can effectively be set.

The skimming approach involves setting a relatively high price stressing the attractions of new features likely to appeal to those with a genuine interest in the product or its associated attractions. Reaction and support is thus solicited from the 'top end' of the particular market. If the launch is successful in this 'cream skimming' exercise, and when the decision has been taken to invest in the necessary new production resources so that larger scale production becomes possible, then the appeal of the new product can be enlarged through a shift in advertising and a reduction in price. The price reduction can be made in stages to coincide with supply-side increases as new resources come into use.

One of the conditions necessary for market skimming is the existence of technical barriers to entry into the market – it must be difficult for competitors to come up with a similar product quickly with which they can undercut the price. There is often high research and development costs which can be recovered more quickly using a skimming approach. Such conditions are common in 'high-tech' fields which is why calculators, personal computers, domestic stereo sets and videos initially sold at a high price but now those same products are sold for a fraction of their launch price. The same can be said of computer software, although in all of these cases the product life cycle has an influence on longer-term pricing policy.

2.6 Other pricing strategies

- **Premium pricing** – This is the deliberate uplifting of the price charged to more than the equilibrium long-term price. For example, when new faster processors are introduced by chip-makers such as Intel and AMD, they are launched at a very high price. Those purchasers who feel they have to have the fastest available processor may be indifferent to the price charged and will pay whatever they have to. The large majority of purchasers will find better value in processors which, although they are not the very fastest, are priced much more reasonably.

- **Optional extras** – These can be offered to the purchaser at the time of sale as a means of generating extra profits. In the field of computers it is still normal practice in the UK for printers to be sold without a printer cable being provided in the box. The printer might be cheap, but the seller would expect to make profits by selling a (necessary) cable as well as spare cartridges of inks and toner. Alternatively a computer could be sold with a baseline specification (e.g. with a 14" monitor) and the seller would hope to persuade all purchasers to upgrade to a larger more usable monitor.

- **Product bundling** – This refers to the offer of further products provided 'free' with the main product that is being bought. Staying with the field of computers, a computer package of £1,000 + VAT may have a cheap printer or scanner thrown in as part of the package, simply so that the manufacturer can keep the same price point in the minds of consumers.

As prices continue to fall, the manufacturer may have to throw in a cheap digital camera, MP3 player, etc. if the £1,000 + VAT price is to be maintained. There is the additional opportunity to persuade the purchaser to pay more to upgrade from the cheap provided item up to a more expensive better item, which will add to the profits earned by the seller.

- **Loss leaders** – These are products that are deliberately sold at below marginal cost (i.e. at a loss) in order to attract customers to the seller. The hope is that, once the customers have been captured by the lure of the loss leader, they will purchase sufficient other goods at normal prices to offset the losses on the loss leaders. For example, in recent years supermarkets have been known to offer tins of baked beans at 1p a tin, and to advertise this fact widely. The supermarket hopes that it will make profits on all other groceries bought by a customer to offset the losses suffered on selling baked beans at below cost.

2.7 Product differentiation

Differentiating your company's products or services means creating an offering that is perceived to be unique in the market. It is an obvious defensive competitive response for a company faced by a strong low-cost competitor. The strategy is to gain advantage through differentiating the product from lower priced ones on the basis of some non-price factor such as:

- quality (Marks and Spencer in clothing and other products)
- features (Sony in domestic, 'brown furniture' items)
- style (Jaguar in motor cars)
- brand image (Mars in chocolate, drink and ice cream)
- dealer network (Caterpillar tractor in construction equipment)
- customer service (Littlewoods in mail-order shopping)
- technology and performance (IBM in computers of all sizes)
- packaging (After Eight in mint chocolates)
- uniqueness (Coca Cola in taste).

A highly differentiated market position will protect the company against the competitive forces in its industry. Its 'uniqueness', brand loyalty and resulting lower sensitivity to price, will protect it against new entrants, the power of buyers, the power of suppliers, the effects of new substitutes entering the market and rivalry within its markets. However differentiation does have its downside. The customer perception 'exclusivity' is often incompatible with high market share. Also a lowering of price sensitivity will only be achieved within a price range. Although customers perceive the superiority of the company's offerings, they might not be willing to pay prices significantly higher than the industrial average.

2.8 Product line promotion

A decision may be taken to promote a particular product line. There may be a number of possible reasons for this, e.g. it is thought that demand is likely to expand; or profit on this line is found to be greater than others; or the firm attaches particular importance to market leadership in this line thinking that such leadership gives advantages in the marketing of other products. Whatever the reasons for the promotion, pricing will be part of the total promotional package and the price is likely to be set below that of competing brands. A price may also be chosen for its psychological appeal, e.g. manufacturers of early mass-produced small cars in the 1930s made great efforts to achieve a price as near as possible to £100; this is now seen in the need to set the prices of personal computers below £1,000 or advanced multimedia packages below £2,000.

2.9 The product life cycle

Reference was made earlier to the fact that there are various stages in the life of a product. This idea has been formalised in the concept of the product life cycle.

DEFINITION

The **product life cycle** is the period which begins with the initial product specification, and ends with the withdrawal from the market of both the product and its support. It is characterised by defined stages including research, development, introduction, maturity, decline and abandonment. (CIMA *Official Terminology*)

The product life cycle is the period which begins with the initial product specification, and ends with the withdrawal from the market of both the product and its support. It is characterised by defined stages including research, development, introduction, maturity, decline and abandonment. (CIMA, *Official Terminology*)

The figure below depicts the pattern of demand (in terms of volume of sales) over the life cycle.

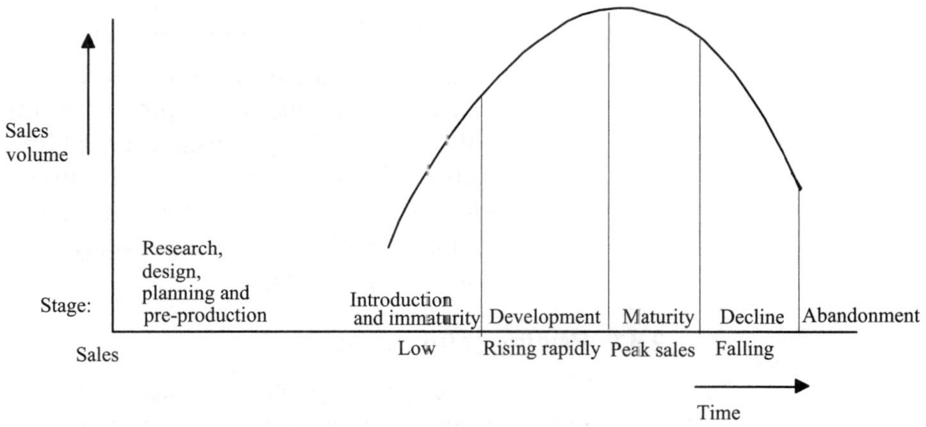

Each stage of the product life cycle possesses different characteristics, as described below.

- **Introduction and market development** – This is the most risky stage, when the product is launched. Some people will try it because it is new; their reaction is crucial. If they do not take to it then the product will 'die' very quickly. If they like it, others follow and the product will move into the next stage.
- **Growth** – This stage is marked by rapid increases in sales volume but a relatively low level of profit because the fixed costs of introduction and development have still to be met and there are still heavy promotional and marketing costs.
- **Maturity** – Growth continues but at a slower rate. Nevertheless, profits now increase as initial fixed costs are recovered and economies in marketing and distribution are achieved.

- **Saturation** – Growth ceases and starts to go into reverse. Profits may still be high as running costs are low. This is the stage when profits need to be used for preparing further products and for finding ways, perhaps, of prolonging the life of the product, e.g. by developing new foreign markets where improvements in living standards lag a little behind those in the home market.
- **Decline and abandonment** – Sooner or later this stage must appear as no product lasts forever. The firm will abandon the product when profits decline towards an unacceptable level or where capacity has to be renewed. The firm will not direct investment into declining areas of activity but towards those where future growth can be anticipated.

The timescale represented by the cycle varies with different products from a matter of months with fashion wear, to many years with some food lines, e.g. the well known sauces and many breakfast cereals. Decline may also be postponed and a new life cycle started if the product can be 'renewed' by modification or by a new marketing twist.

2.10 Implications of the life cycle for pricing policy

During the introduction and growth stages of the product life cycle, the selling price may be adjusted downwards, away from the short-term optimum price for profit maximisation. This might be done in order to sustain growth and therefore stimulate demand for the future. In this situation, the firm would be forgoing short-term product profitability in order to secure longer-term gain. This policy would only be sensible if the product involved were expected to have a life cycle which spanned a number of years. Once a position of market strength has been secured, progressive price increases may be possible.

At the maturity stage, the firm will be less concerned with the future effect of selling price on the demand for the product. Short-term profit maximisation will now probably be the pricing objective, as the firm seeks to 'harvest' the profit arising from sales of the product. Once the product enters the decline stage, selling price will be set at the level which keeps demand as buoyant as possible in a deteriorating market. The pricing policy of models of Japanese cars can be seen following this scheme.

2.11 Pricing joint products

The aim of pricing decisions is to maximise profit, i.e. the difference between total costs and total revenue. Increasing price is likely to reduce unit sales and thereby, possibly, total revenue. Such a price increase is still worthwhile if cost savings at the reduced production level are greater than lost revenue.

Joint products, which are produced from a common process, may be apportioned joint costs on an arbitrary basis. These will only be relevant for pricing decisions if they change in total as a result of the decision. Analysis of pricing decisions should be carried out by comparing the incremental revenue and costs of all of the joint products together.

> KEY POINT
>
> Joint products may be apportioned joint costs on an arbitrary basis. These will only be relevant for pricing decisions if they change in total as a result of the decision. Analysis of pricing decisions should be carried out by comparing the incremental revenue and costs of all of the joint products together.

3 Profit maximisation

3.1 Introduction

By determining cost and revenue functions for its range of products, a firm will be in a position to derive both optimal selling price and optimal output level for each product.

The demand schedule will relate selling prices to quantities demanded by customers. It should be noted, however, that the precise quantification of this relationship is often very difficult to derive in practice, particularly as the relationship is likely to be volatile. The supply schedule relates to the costs incurred in producing and selling a given level of output, measured in terms of units of product sold.

If cost and revenue functions can be determined, optimal selling prices and output levels can be found using an algebraic or tabular approach. These methods are considered below.

3.2 Demand curves

The nature of revenue functions (the way sales revenue varies with price) depends upon the degree of competition in the market. Four types of market are usually described:

- perfect competition
- imperfect (monopolistic) competition
- monopoly
- oligopoly.

The nature of the market is usually described in terms of a demand curve that shows how selling price influences demand. At this stage only a very brief outline of the theory behind these demand curves is required; what is important is to know their shape, the shape of marginal revenue functions and the effect of pricing policy.

Perfect competition

The characteristic of this market is a large number of firms operating, all too small to influence the market price. As a consequence there is a prevailing market price which all operators in the market should follow. The result is shown graphically below.

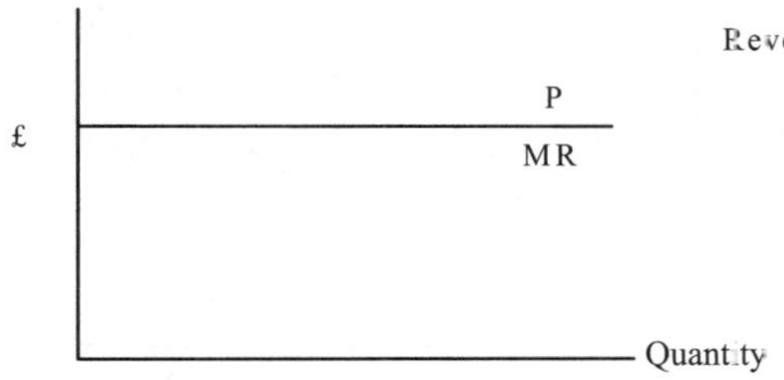

Demand function

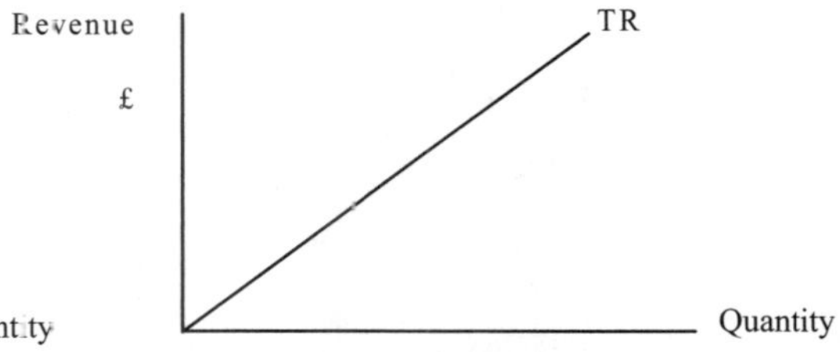

Total revenue function

MR = marginal revenue, the additional revenue gained (i.e. the amount added to total revenue (TR)) from the sale of one extra good/service.

For each individual product the demand curve is horizontal and marginal revenue is constant. Demand is perfectly elastic because any attempt to change price from the prevailing market price will result in losses (if price is reduced) or loss of all demand (if price is increased and consumers switch to other suppliers). The total revenue function is therefore a straight line given by a constant price multiplied by quantity.

Imperfect (monopolistic) competition

Individual firms are in a position to control price and quantity; they face a downward-sloping demand curve. Marginal revenue falls as sales are increased and the total revenue function will have the typical curvilinear shape. Although there is no evidence to suggest that demand curves are any more or less likely to be straight lines, examiners tend to concentrate on linear relationships in order to keep the maths simple.

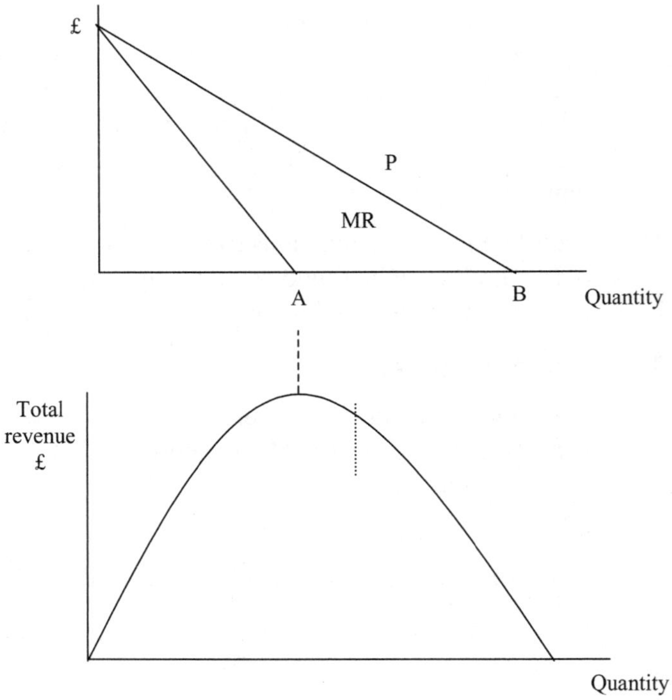

Revenue is maximised where marginal revenue (the slope of the revenue function) is zero – at A. However profit is maximised where MR = MC, MC being marginal cost, the addition to total cost from the production of an extra good/service.

A typical marginal cost curve is shown as follows.

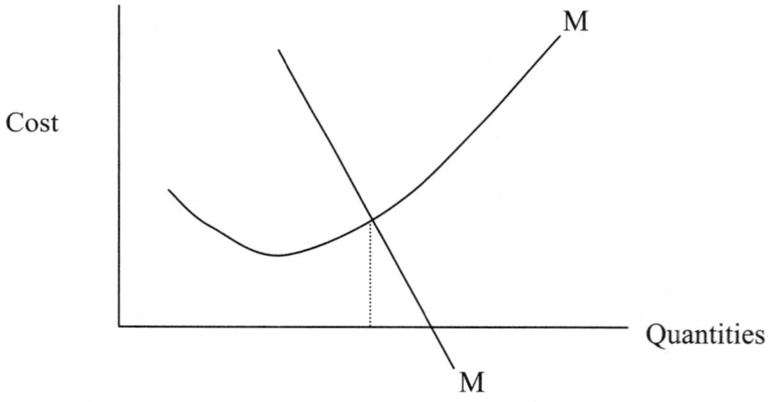

The interaction between MR and MC indicates the profit maximising output, which can then be used to determine a selling price, in order to sell this stated quantity of goods/service.

The profit maximising price depends on the market structure being either perfect competition, imperfect (monopolistic) competition, monopoly or oligopoly (the latter two structures are discussed below).

Activity 2

Firms in monopolistic competition will often try to avoid competing with each other on price, but carry out non-price competition instead. Can you think of examples of such non-price competition?

Feedback to this activity is at the end of the chapter.

Monopoly

Monopoly exists where one supplier dominates the market. Such a situation can operate against the public interest and so attempts are often made to reduce the chance of firms achieving monopoly status. In the UK the main examples of monopolies used to be in state-run industries. With the gradual sell-off of these organisations there are fewer examples of monopolies, but some major companies still have a sufficiently large share of their market to be treated as such.

The shape of demand curves, marginal revenue lines and revenue functions is similar to that for monopolistic competition – the downward-sloping demand curve.

Oligopoly

DEFINITION

Oligopoly is that market structure in which supply is in the hands of, or is dominated by, relatively few large producers.

Oligopoly is that market structure in which supply is in the hands of, or is dominated by, relatively few large producers. It is thought that the way in which these oligopolistic producers behave is that, if one of their number tries to increase selling price then the rest do not attempt to match the increases. As a consequence the share of the market of the firm raising prices falls rapidly. If, on the other hand, an oligopolist tries to cut prices then the rest follow suit, the price-cutter's share of the market stays the same and demand increases only gradually. The consequence of this is the so-called 'kinked demand curve' and its consequential marginal revenue line with a discontinuity.

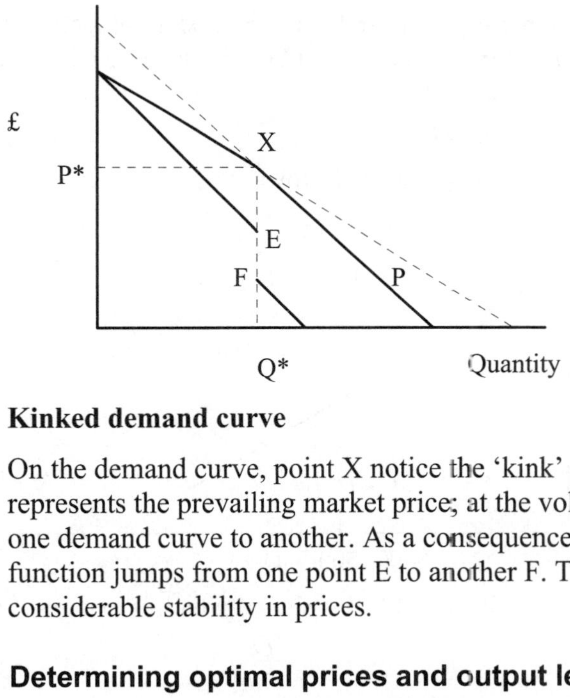

Kinked demand curve

On the demand curve, point X notice the 'kink' (price P*, quantity Q*) represents the prevailing market price; at the volume Q* the market moves from one demand curve to another. As a consequence at Q* the marginal revenue function jumps from one point E to another F. The result of this is thought to be considerable stability in prices.

3.3 Determining optimal prices and output levels

As mentioned earlier, if information about cost and revenue functions exists then optimal prices and output levels can be found algebraically or using tabulation. You will be expected to produce pricing and output decisions and so each method will be looked at using the illustration below.

Example

Spout Ltd manufactures and sells one product. The present selling price for the product is £50, at which price 500 units are demanded annually. The sales manager of Spout Ltd estimates that annual demand will fall by 100 units for each successive £10 increase in price. Similarly, each successive £10 decrease in price will cause an increase in demand of 100 units. The company's total fixed costs are £10,000 pa and a variable cost of £20 is incurred for each unit produced.

3.4 Revenue and cost function

If production and sales per annum is denoted by Q, then the total annual cost, (in £s) C, is given by:

$$C = 10{,}000 + 20Q$$

The expression for total annual revenue requires a little more thought. At present, unit selling price is £50 and output is 500 units. Each increase or decrease of £10 in the selling price results in a corresponding decrease or increase of 100 units in the level of demand. If the selling price were increased by £50 (i.e. to £100), then demand would be zero. From this point, if demand is to be increased by one unit, selling price must be reduced by £10/100, or 10p. Therefore, for a given level of output, the maximum selling price attainable for this level will be found using the formula:

$$P = £100 - £0.1Q$$

This formula represents the company's demand (or average revenue) function.

The same formula can be determined graphically, where there is a linear relationship between P and Q as in the case of Spout Ltd. The demand line is of the general form:

$$P = a - bQ$$

and can be depicted as follows:

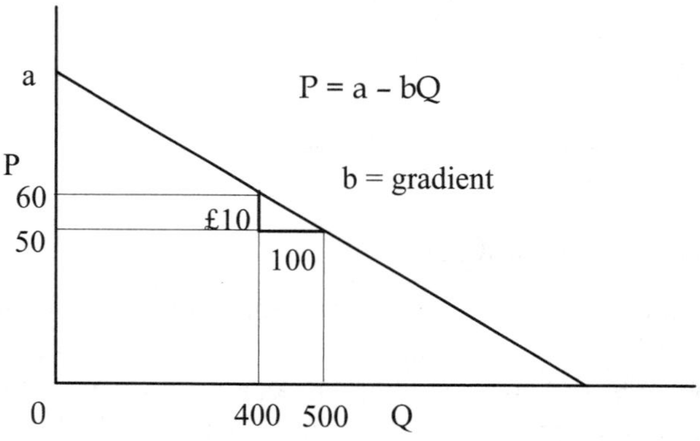

The data for Spout Ltd is shown which is expanded upon in the next table.

P	*Q*
£	*units*
50	500
60	400
40	600
0	1,000
100	0

When Q = 0, P = 100 and therefore a = 100.

$$b = \text{gradient} = \frac{\text{vertical change}}{\text{horizontal change}} = \frac{£10}{100} = 0.1$$

and P = a – bQ becomes P = 100 – 0.1Q as before.

Since total revenue is given by unit selling price multiplied by the number of units sold, the formula for total revenue is:

$$R = P \times Q$$

Where $P = 100 - 0.1Q$

$$\therefore R = (100 - 0.1Q) \times Q$$

$$\text{or } R = 100Q - 0.1Q^2$$

The optimum selling price and output level can now be calculated using each of the methods referred to above.

3.5 Algebraic approach

If algebraic expressions are available describing cost and revenue functions, then an approach based on differential calculus would provide the quickest and most effective way of finding an optimal pricing and output policy. While calculus is outside the scope of the syllabus, the approach is still commonly examined and should be studied carefully.

The algebraic approach is based on the economic principle that a profit maximising price will be set at the volume of output where:

Marginal cost = Marginal revenue.

Using the example of Spout the following functions have already been derived:

Demand function	$P = £100 - £0.1Q$
Total cost function	$C = 10{,}000 + 20Q$
Total revenue function	$R = 100Q - 0.1Q^2$

These functions can now be used to find the profit maximising price.

Mathematically, marginal cost and revenue functions can be found by differentiating (using calculus) the total cost and revenue functions respectively. As calculus is outside of the scope of your syllabus you may be given the marginal cost and revenue functions or told how to derive them from the total functions.

For example, you could be given an instruction:

If total revenue is of the form $R = aQ - bQ^2$

Then marginal revenue will be given by $MR = a - 2bQ$

For the example of Spout as total revenue is $R = 100Q - 0.1Q^2$

Then marginal revenue is $MR = 100 - 0.2Q$

Similarly you may be told that:

If total cost is of the form $C = a + bQ$

Then marginal cost will be given by $MC = b$

For the example of Spout as total cost is $c = £10{,}000 + £20Q$

Then marginal cost is $MC = £20$

(This should be inherently logical as you will know from your previous studies that, if costs are assumed to have a linear relationship with output, then they can be expressed in the form $y = a + bx$ where a represents fixed costs and b represents variable costs.)

Once you have the expressions for marginal cost and marginal revenue you can equate them to find the profit-maximising output.

For Spout Ltd:

MC = MR

20 = 100-0.2Q

0.2Q = 80 So Q = 400

Once you have found the profit-maximising output the price can be found from the demand function.

P= 100 – 0.1 Q

Therefore P = 100 – 0.1 × 400 = £60

3.6 Tabular approach

In the case of Spout Ltd a tabular approach is the least efficient method of solution with continuous cost and revenue functions available. However, in different circumstances such continuous functions may not be available. It may be that only a table of a few prices and estimates of the likely demand that they will generate is available. These tables may indicate non-linear demand functions in which a method based on calculus would be difficult. Even if the tabular information suggested a straight-line demand function, it would be unwise to assume a continuous function in view of opinions about the effect on demand of raising a price from £4.99 to £5 or £99 to £100.

For Spout Ltd:

Total annual cost, C = 10,000 + 20Q

Total revenue, R = $100Q - 0.1Q^2$

The relationship between selling price, demand and output, total revenue and total costs can be tabulated as shown below:

Price £	*Demand (units)*	*Revenue* £	*Variable cost* £	*Fixed cost* £	*Total cost* £	*Profit/(Loss)* £
100	0	0	0	10,000	10,000	(10,000)
90	100	9,000	2,000	10,000	12,000	(3,000)
80	200	16,000	4,000	10,000	14,000	2,000
70	300	21,000	6,000	10,000	16,000	5,000
60	400	24,000	8,000	10,000	18,000	6,000
50	500	25,000	10,000	10,000	20,000	5,000
40	600	24,000	12,000	10,000	22,000	2,000
30	700	21,000	14,000	10,000	24,000	(3,000)
20	800	16,000	16,000	10,000	26,000	(10,000)
10	900	9,000	18,000	10,000	28,000	(19,000)

From the table, profit appears to be maximised at an output level of 400 units and the optimal selling price to be £60. It might be worth checking that a greater profit is not achieved at an output level of 390 or 410 units. Sometimes in exams data is presented in a tabular fashion such as this; if so it is dangerous to interpolate (e.g. to find cost, revenue and profit at 390 or 410) unless you are specifically told that the demand curve and cost functions are linear.

Summary

- The factors affecting a pricing decision are:
  - organisational goals
  - costs
  - customers
  - competitors
  - product mix
  - product life cycle
  - marketing strategies.
- The advantages of cost-plus pricing are:
  - no need to obtain demand curves
  - cost of getting market information
  - easy, formula, delegating pricing
  - justification for price rises
  - produces stable prices.
- Target pricing involves adjustment of the 'plus' in cost-plus pricing to achieve some objective or 'target', typically a given return on the capital investment in a new product or service.
- Particular policies practised (often with new products) are market skimming (setting a high price initially then reducing it) and penetration pricing (starting at a low price to achieve a large market share).
- A marginalist approach to pricing requires perfect information about cost and revenue functions.
- The way price influences demand depends upon the degree of competition in the market and is described by 'demand curves':
- **Profit is maximised** where marginal cost (MC) and marginal revenue (MR) are equal.
- The profit maximising price and output can be found using an algebraic approach if demand and cost have linear relationships or by using a tabular approach.

Having completed your study of this chapter you should have achieved the following learning outcomes.

- Explain the particular issues that arise in pricing decisions and the conflict between marginal cost principles and the need for full recovery of all costs incurred.
- Apply an approach to pricing based on profit maximisation in imperfect markets and evaluate the financial consequences of alternative pricing strategies.

Self-test questions

1 What are said to be the disadvantages of cost-plus pricing? (1.4)

2 How should pricing decisions be reached if a single factor needed for production is in short supply? (1.6)

3 What is product line promotion? (2.8)

4 What effect does the product life cycle have on pricing decisions? (2.10)

5 How is the total revenue function derived from the demand function? (3.5)

6 How is the profit-maximising price found once the profit-maximising output has been established? (3.5)

Objective test questions

Question 1

Which of the following costs could be used in cost-plus pricing?

A Marginal cost only

B Full cost only

C ABC cost only

D All three of the above

Question 2

A product cost estimate derived from subtracting a desired profit margin from a competitive market price is called a:

A shadow cost

B target cost

C marginal cost

D joint cost

Question 3

The setting of an initial high price followed by subsequent reductions is known as:

A Penetration pricing

B Profit maximising pricing

C Premium pricing

D Market skimming

The following data is relevant to questions 4 and 5.

A product has a demand curve

$P = 175 - 0.2Q$

And a cost function

$C = 12{,}500 + 7Q$

Question 4

Explain the meaning of each variable in the demand and cost functions.

Question 5

If total revenue = a Q + b Q^2, marginal revenue = a + bQ. Calculate the profit maximising price and quantity of output.

For the answers to these questions, see the 'Answers' section at the end of the book.

Exam-type question

Scenic Snaps Ltd

Scenic Snaps Ltd provides a number of products, with cameras being produced in Department C. The company draws up budgets for each department based upon the fullest practical capacity. For the year commencing 1 January 20X9, the following budget has been formulated for Department C:

	£000
Direct costs:	
Materials	120
Labour	80
	200
Production overheads	200
Factory cost	400
Administrative and marketing overheads	100
Full cost	500
Profit	100
Revenue*	600

* from budgeted sales of 40,000 units.

Production overheads are absorbed on the basis of 100% of direct costs. However, half are fixed, while the remainder are related to the machining of the materials. The administration and marketing overheads are based on 25% of factory costs and do not vary within wide ranges of activity. For each department, a profit margin of 20% is applied to the 'full costs', as this is felt to give both a fair return on assets employed as well as providing a fair reward to entrepreneurial effort. This also results in a price which appears to be fair to consumers.

Halfway through the budget period, it became obvious to the management of Scenic Snaps Ltd that there was going to be a shortfall on sales which could be expected to be 25% below those forecast. At about the time that this shortfall in sales became evident, a chain of photographic shops became interested in purchasing 10,000 units of a special camera which would be stripped down to bare essentials and sold under the chain's brand name 'Aremac'. If Scenic Snaps produced such a model, there would obviously be a saving on the usual material and labour unit costs. The management accountant of Scenic Snaps estimated that materials costing £24,000 and labour of £16,000 would be required to produce the 10,000 cameras. As the production could take place within the firm's existing capacity, fixed costs would not be affected.

Required:

(a) Produce computations showing the price that should be quoted for the order, based on:

(i) full costs plus pricing, on the current basis

(ii) a price that would enable the original budgeted profit to be attained

(iii) overheads being absorbed on a unit basis, with profit applied on the current basis. **(12 marks)**

(b) Advise the management of Scenic Snaps Ltd on a pricing policy for this quotation. Discuss any factors that you feel should be brought to the management's attention when they consider the pricing strategy for this special order. **(8 marks)**

(Total: 20 marks)

For the answer to this question, see the 'Answers' section at the end of the book.

Feedback to activities

Activity 1

		£000
Fixed value	30% × £8m	2,400
In line with RPI	$25\% \times £8m \times \frac{150}{130}$	2,308
In line with wages	$45\% \times £8m \times \frac{240}{215}$	4,019
		8,727

The total final value of the contract is £8.727m.

Activity 2

(1) Smarter packaging.

(2) Better after-sales service.

(3) Branding, i.e. advertising and promotional expenditure to promote the product.

(4) Special limited editions with unique features.

Chapter 7

UNCERTAINTY IN DECISION MAKING

Syllabus content

This chapter covers the following syllabus content.

- The nature of risk and uncertainty.
- Sensitivity analysis in decision modelling and the use of computer software for 'what if' analysis.
- Assignment of probabilities to key variables in decision models.
- Analysis of probabilistic models and interpretation of distributions of project outcomes.
- Expected value tables and the value of information.
- Decision trees for multi-stage decision problems.

Contents

1 Single decisions made in uncertainty

1.1 Introduction

Most decisions that a company's management has to make can be described as decisions made under uncertainty. The essential features of making a decision under uncertain conditions are:

- the decision-maker is faced with a choice between several alternative courses of action
- each course of action may have several possible outcomes, dependent on a number of uncertain factors, i.e. even when a decision has been made, the outcome is by no means certain
- which choice is made will depend upon the criteria used by the decision-maker in judging between the outcomes of the possible courses of action.

We begin by defining the terms risk and uncertainty. Although the terms are often used interchangeably, a distinction can be identified.

Risk is a condition in which the possible outcomes from any activity are known and can be quantified.

KEY POINT

The term 'risk' is used when numerical values can be placed on the probabilities of the various outcomes.

Uncertainty is the inability to predict the outcome from an activity due to a lack of information about the required input/output relationships or about the environment within which the activity takes place.

Thus the term 'risk' is used when numerical values can be placed on the probabilities of the various outcomes. For example, the tossing of a coin involves risk, since one can say that p (heads) = p (tails) = 0.5. But the weather tomorrow is uncertain, since no mathematical relationship can be drawn up to explain what will happen. Most decisions are made under conditions of uncertainty but managers use their judgement to define outcomes and assign probabilities so that risk can be managed.

1.2 The pay-off table

KEY POINT

The **pay-off table** is a tabular layout specifying the result (pay-off) of each combination of decision and the 'state of the world', over which the decision-maker has no control.

The **pay-off table** is a tabular layout specifying the result (pay-off) of each combination of decision and the 'state of the world', over which the decision-maker has no control.

Example

Clynes Ltd has three new products – A, B and C – of which it can introduce only one. The level of demand for each product might be low, medium or high. If the company decides to introduce product A, the net income that would result from the levels of demand possible are estimated at £20, £40 and £50 respectively. Similarly, if product B is chosen, net income is estimated at £80, £70 and –£10, and for product C, £10, £100 and £40 respectively.

Construct a pay-off table to present this information concisely.

Solution

Level of demand	*Decision (action to introduce)*		
	A	*B*	*C*
	£	£	£
Low	20	80	10
Medium	40	70	100
High	50	(10)	40

Tutorial note: A realistic assumption might be that the company is obliged to meet whatever level of demand arises for fear of losing customer goodwill, and thus fewer sales of its other products. This would justify the fall in net income at higher levels of demand in the case of product B in particular, where it appears that there are considerable diseconomies of scale.

Activity 1

The Zeta company has estimated that the demand for one of its products is either 100, 200 or 300 units in a month. The product is sold for £15 per unit and total variable costs amount to £7 per unit. If demand is less than supply the product may be sold off cheaply for £5 per unit. There is no penalty cost if demand is not met.

Considering only production levels of 100, 200 and 300, draw up a pay-off table for this situation.

Feedback to this activity is at the end of the chapter.

1.3 Decision-making criteria

In the example of Clynes Ltd, it is by no means clear which decision is going to produce the most satisfactory result, since each product gives the most desirable outcome at one level of demand.

KEY POINT

A company's choice of actions is influenced by:

- attitude to risk/losses
- whether the decision is long-term.

The choice of product may depend upon:

- **The company's attitude to risk/losses** – If the company is not willing to face the possibility of loss at all, it will not choose Product B, even though it offers relatively good returns for two of the three possible levels of demand. Of the remaining two, Product C offers the greatest potential return (£100), but also the lowest (£10) – so it has greatest risk. Different criteria can be used to make choices depending on a manager's attitude to risk
- **Whether the decision is to be long-term** – If the net incomes given are 'one-offs' then it may be appropriate to look at the nature and range of actual possible outcomes as discussed above. If the net incomes will be repeated year after year, where the levels of demand will repeatedly be subject to chance, an expected value approach may be taken, which looks at the average net income in the long term. In order to do this, the probabilities attached to each level of demand will be needed.
- The spread of data will be another factor that will influence the degree of risk assigned to a particular outcome. The greater the spread the greater the potential impact of different 'states of the world'. Spread may be measured using the range, standard deviation or by producing a histogram of grouped data.

2 Decision models

2.1 Introduction

When it is assumed that all possible actions and outcomes are known, but that there is no information available concerning the probabilities of the different outcomes, then pay-off tables can be used to identify and record all the possible outcomes (or pay-offs) and a decision rule must be used to make a choice. The decision rule chosen will depend on the organisation's or manager's attitude to risk.

2.2 Attitude to risk

There are three common classifications of managers' attitudes to risk.

- **Risk-seeking**

Managers seek the highest return and are prepared to accept a high level of risk to achieve this. For example, faced with alternative investment projects, one of which has potentially very high returns but with a high level of risk and another with lower but safer returns, the organisation would choose the more risky project in the hope of achieving the high returns.

- **Risk-averse**

Managers seek to avoid risk and are prepared to accept lower returns as a consequence. They may, for example, wish to avoid any chance of losses occurring.

- **Risk-neutral**

Managers do not consider the range of outcomes but focus their decision on a single point estimate. The most common measure used is expected value but the most likely outcome could also be used.

2.3 Illustration

A fruiterer has to decide how many pounds of apples he needs to buy from the market, and has assessed the possible daily demand levels as being either 60, 100, 125 or 175 kg.

He can buy quantities of 50,100, 150, or 200 kg at a price of £4 per 10 kg.

The selling price is £1 per kg and unsold apples have to be thrown away.

How many should he buy?

Here, the number of apples sold (and therefore the contribution made) depends partly on the level of demand, but also on the number that the fruiterer decides to buy.

All possible contributions are shown in the following pay-off table (and some of the contribution calculations are explained). Make sure that you can calculate all the figures in the table. Note in particular:

(i) If he buys 200 kg, demands of 250 kg or 350 kg will still only result in sales of 200 kg.

(ii) Contribution per kg bought and sold is 60p per kg.

Qty demanded (kg) \ *Qty purchased* (kg)	50	100	150	200
60	30 (note 1)	20 (note 2)	0	(20)
100	30	60	40	20
125	30	60 (note 3)	65	45
175	30	60	90	95

For the various criteria we need to extract:

Minimum contribution for each action	30	20	Nil	(20)
Maximum contribution for each action	30	60	90	95

(Look down each 'action' column and find lowest/ highest contribution.)

Explanations of contributions in contingency table

(1) If the fruiterer purchases 50 kg, they are certain to be sold (since the lowest demand level is 60 kg).

		£
∴ Revenue at all possible levels of demand (50 × £1)		50
Cost	(50 × 40p)	20
		30

(2) If the fruiterer purchases 100 kg and demand is 60 kg.

		£
Revenue	(60 × £1)	60
Cost	(100 × 40p)	(40)
		20

(3) If the fruiterer purchases 100 kg and demand is 125 kg, he will sell 100 kg (remember that he cannot sell more than he has bought).

		£
Revenue	(100 × £1)	100
Cost	(100 × 40p)	(40)
		60

Having identified all possible actions (amount of apples bought) and all possible outcomes (levels of contribution), we must rank the actions according to the criterion selected by the manager.

KEY POINT

Maximin criterion: choose the action which maximises the smallest possible pay-off.

2.4 Maximin (or the pessimist's) criterion

The action taken is that which maximises the smallest possible pay-off for each action.

The manager who employs this criterion is assuming that whatever action he takes, the worst will happen (pessimist) – a very risk-averting approach (see minimum contribution row).

So for the fruiterer: the highest minimum contribution arises from buying 50 kg (£30).

KEY POINT

Maximax criterion: choose the action which maximises the largest possible pay-off.

2.5 Maximax (or the optimist's) criterion

The action taken is that which has the highest maximum possible pay-off.

The manager who employs this criterion is assuming that, whatever action he takes, the best will happen (risk-seeker).

For the fruiterer, the highest maximum contribution arises from buying 200 kg (£95).

He will, of course, be running the risk of lower returns up to a loss of £20 if he takes this action.

KEY POINT

Minimax regret criterion: choose the action which minimises the maximum possible regret.

2.6 Minimax regret (or the bad loser's criterion)

The action taken is that which minimises the maximum possible 'regret'.

Regret is the amount of pay-off lost by not having taken the optimal action for a particular outcome (level of demand).

It is the difference between:

(i) the maximum possible value under the particular outcome; and

(ii) the value which results from a particular action under that outcome.

The manager who employs this criterion is trying to limit the potential 'opportunity loss'.

The maximum contributions that can be earned under each outcome are:

Outcome (quantity demanded)	*Maximum contribution*
60	30
100	60
125	65
175	95

The regret values (maximum – actual) are set out in the matrix below.

Qty purchased (kg) / *Qty demanded* (kg)	50	100	150	200
60	0	10	30	50
100	30	0	20	40
125	35	5	0	20
175	65	35	5	0

The values are the amounts by which the manager regrets selection of the particular action (with hindsight of outcome). So, for each action, we can now state the maximum possible regret:

Amount purchased	50 kg	100 kg	150 kg	200 kg
Maximum 'regret'	65	35	30	50

The lowest maximum regret is £30, so a manager employing the minimax regret criterion would buy 150 kg of apples.

Activity 2

Using the pay-off table calculated in Activity 1 determine the production level that would be chosen using each of the following criteria:

(a) maximin

(b) maximax

(c) minimax regret.

Feedback to this activity is at the end of the chapter.

3 Expected values

DEFINITION

Expected value – the financial forecast of the outcome of a course of action multiplied by the probability of achieving that outcome. (CIMA *Official Terminology*)

3.1 Introduction

Expected value is the financial forecast of the outcome of a course of action multiplied by the probability of achieving that outcome. (CIMA *Official Terminology*) Expected values are used to determine the course of action when the decision being made is either repeated regularly or where it is a small, isolated decision in a large organisation. The principle of 'maximisation of expected value' ensures that the product with the highest expected value will be chosen.

Example

Using the data from the Clynes example (reproduced below), apply the criteria of **maximisation of expected value** to decide the best course of action for the company, assuming the following probabilities:

P (low demand)	0.1
P (medium demand)	0.6
P (high demand)	0.3
	1.0

Clynes Ltd has three new products – A, B and C – of which it can introduce only one. The level of demand for each course of action might be low, medium or high. If the company decides to introduce product A, the net income that would result from the levels of demand possible are estimated at £20, £40 and £50 respectively. Similarly, if product B is chosen, net income is estimated at £80, £70 and –£10, and for product C, £10, £100 and £40 respectively.

Solution

The expected value of the decision to introduce product A is given by the following summation:

$$0.1 \times 20 + 0.6 \times 40 + 0.3 \times 50 = £41$$

(i.e. on 10% of all occasions demand will be low and net income £20; on 60% of all occasions demand will be medium and net income £40; and on 30% of all occasions demand will be high and net income £50. Thus, on average, net income will be the average of all three net incomes, weighted by their respective probabilities.)

The expected value of all the products may be calculated by a table of expected values.

		Product					
		A		*B*		*C*	
Level of demand	*Probability of demand*	*Income* £	*Income ×prob.* £	*Income* £	*Income ×prob.* £	*Income* £	*Income ×prob.* £
Low	0.1	20	2	80	8	10	1
Medium	0.6	40	24	70	42	100	60
High	0.3	50	15	(10)	(3)	40	12
Total	1.0		**41**		**47**		**73**

Thus, if the criterion is to maximise the expected value, it means that the product with the highest expected value will be chosen – in this case product C, unless, of course, all products have negative expected value, in which case none should be chosen.

Activity 3

If the probabilities of demands for Zeta company in Activity 1 are as follows:

Demand	100	200	300
Probability	0.3	0.6	0.1

determine the optimal solution using expected values.

Feedback to this activity is at the end of the chapter.

3.2 Applicability of expected values

The criterion of expected value is only valid where the decision being made is either:

- one that is repeated regularly over a period of time, or
- a one-off decision, but where its size is fairly small in relation to the total assets of the firm and it is one of many, in terms of the sums of money involved, that face the firm over a period of time.

In other words, the law of averages will apply in the long run, but clearly the result of any single action must, by definition, be one of the specified outcomes. Thus, while the expected value of introducing product C is £73 in the example here, each actual outcome will result in either £10, £100 or £40 net income, and it is only if a whole series of product introductions were involved that the average over a period of time would approach £73, so long as the expected value criterion were applied consistently to all the decisions.

Therefore, it is quite acceptable to adopt the expected value as the decision-making criterion for the company, as long as it has several other products and the same sort of marketing decision arises fairly regularly.

To illustrate the distinction being made, consider a person insuring their house against fire damage for a year. Suppose the house is worth £50,000 and the probability of the house being burnt down is 0.0001 (the only other outcome being that the house is not burnt down with a probability of 0.9999). The person would be quite prepared to pay, say, £15 pa to insure the house even though the expected value (or expected cost in this case) is only 0.0001 × £50,000 + 0.9999 × 0 = £5. The person cannot afford to pay £50,000 out more than once in their lifetime and therefore cannot afford to play the averages by using expected value as their decision criterion (if so, the person would refuse to pay a premium greater than £5). However, to the insurance company, £50,000 is not a large sum, most of their transactions being for similar or greater amounts, and therefore expected value would be appropriate as a decision criterion for them. In fact, the expected value of the insurance company's decision to insure the house at £15 pa is:

$$0.0001 \times (-\,£49{,}985) + 0.9999 \times £15$$

or $$-\,£4.9985 + £14.9985 = £10$$

and any positive expected value would, in theory, have made it worth their while to insure.

4 Measures of spread

4.1 Measuring dispersion

The expected value provides a measure of the statistical average of a distribution but is limited in that it does not directly consider the spread of the data. There are several statistical measures which may be used to measure spread or dispersion.

The **range** is by far the simplest measure of dispersion, being the difference between the extreme values of the distribution:

Range = Highest value – lowest value

Example

Using the pay-off table produced for the Clynes'example:

Level of demand	*Decision (action to introduce)*		
	A £	*B* £	*C* £
Low	20	80	10
Medium	40	70	100
High	50	(10)	40
Range	30	90	90

It can be seen that the range of data is much greater for products B and C than for product A and could therefore be considered to be more risky. A decision would have to be made as to whether the higher expected returns for products B and C were adequate to offset the increased risk and may depend on the manager's attitude to risk.

The range is a very crude statistical measure of spread as it does not take into account the dispersion of data between the highest and lowest values. Standard deviation overcomes this limitation.

DEFINITION

The **standard deviation** is a measure of the amount by which the values in a set of numbers differ from the arithmetic mean. It is defined as the square root of the mean square deviations of the values from the mean. The defining formula is therefore:

Standard deviation = $\sqrt{\frac{\Sigma(x-\bar{x})^2}{n}}$ where n is the number of x values. The standard deviation is usually denoted by σ (the Greek lower case sigma) or by the abbreviation SD.

4.2 Standard deviation

Standard deviation is the most valuable and widely used measure of dispersion. However, it is also the most complex to calculate and the most difficult to understand.

The standard deviation is a measure of the amount by which the values in a set of numbers differ from the arithmetic mean.

It is defined as **the square root of the mean square deviations of the values from the mean**. The defining formula is therefore:

$$\text{Standard deviation} = \sqrt{\frac{\Sigma(x-\bar{x})^2}{n}}$$

where n is the number of x values. The standard deviation is denoted by σ (the Greek lower case sigma) or by the abbreviation SD.

While the formula above defines the standard deviation, it is rarely used for calculations, as there is an alternative formula which is algebraically equivalent, but is easier and quicker for computation. This formula is:

$$\sigma = \sqrt{\frac{\Sigma x^2}{n} - \left(\frac{\Sigma x}{n}\right)^2}$$

Example

Using the pay-off table for the Clynes' example calculate the standard deviation of the pay-offs from each product.

Solution

The pay-off table previously calculated is as follows:

Level of demand	*Decision (action to introduce)*		
	A	*B*	*C*
	£	£	£
Low	20	80	10
Medium	40	70	100
High	50	(10)	40

In order to calculate the standard deviation of a set of data it is best to lay out your workings in a table:

Demand	*Product A (x)*	x^2	*Product B (x)*	x^2	*Product C (x)*	x^2
Low	20	400	80	6,400	10	100
Medium	40	1,600	70	4,900	100	10,000
High	50	2,500	(10)	100	40	1,600
	$\Sigma x = 110$	$\Sigma x^2 = 4{,}500$	$\Sigma x = 140$	$\Sigma x^2 = 11{,}400$	$\Sigma x = 150$	$\Sigma x^2 = 11{,}700$

$$\text{Hence } \sigma \text{ (product A)} = \sqrt{\frac{4{,}500}{3} - \left(\frac{110}{3}\right)^2}$$

$$= \sqrt{1{,}500 - 1{,}344.44}$$

$$= 12.5$$

$$\sigma \text{ (product B)} = \sqrt{\frac{11{,}400}{3} - \left(\frac{140}{3}\right)^2}$$

$$= \sqrt{3{,}800 - 2{,}177.77}$$

$$= 40.3$$

$$\sigma \text{ (product C)} = \sqrt{\frac{11{,}700}{3} - \left(\frac{150}{3}\right)^2}$$

$$= \sqrt{3{,}900 - 2{,}500}$$

$$= \mathbf{37.4}$$

The standard deviation is highest for Product B, indicating that the pay-offs for this product carry the greatest risk.

Activity 4

Using the pay-off table calculated in Activity 1, calculate the standard deviation for the pay-offs from each level of production.

Feedback to this activity is at the end of the chapter.

4.3 Coefficient of variation

DEFINITION

Coefficient of variation is a measure expressing the standard deviation as a percentage of the mean. It is a way of comparing variability between data sets.

When comparing the dispersion in two or more sets of data, for example for each product in the above example, the **mean** of each set of data can be taken into account. For example, a variation of 2 units in a set of data with a mean of 5 is of much greater significance than a variation of 2 units in a set of data with a mean of 50. To compare the amount of variation, or dispersion, between sets of data, the coefficient of variation is often used, which expresses the standard deviation as a percentage of the mean.

$$\text{Coefficient of variation} = \frac{\text{Standard deviation} \times 100}{\text{Arithmetic mean}}$$

Example

Using a simple average of the pay-offs and the standard deviations calculated for the Clynes' example, we have the following data available:

Level of demand	*Decision (action to introduce)*		
	A	*B*	*C*
	£	£	£
Low	20	80	10
Medium	40	70	100
High	50	(10)	40
Average (mean)	36.7	46.7	50
Standard deviation	12.5	40.3	37.4

Product A Coefficient of variation $= \frac{0.062 \times 100}{1.05}$ 12.5/36.7= 34.1%

Product B: Coefficient of variation $= \frac{0.384 \times 100}{7.13}$ 40.3/46.7= 86.3%

Product C: Coefficient of variation $= \frac{0.384 \times 100}{7.13}$ 37.4/50= 74.8%

Therefore product B has the greatest variation in pay-off relatively speaking.

Activity 5

Using the pay-off table calculated in Activity 1, calculate the coefficient of variation for the pay-offs from each level of production.

Feedback to this activity is at the end of the chapter.

DEFINITION

A **histogram** is a special form of column or bar chart that is used to represent data given in the form of a grouped frequency distribution. The area of each rectangle rather than the height represents the frequency of a particular class interval.

KEY POINT

If the class intervals are all equal then the heights of the rectangles in the histogram are proportional to the frequencies.

4.4 Histograms

A **histogram** is a special form of column or bar chart that is used to represent data given in the form of a grouped frequency distribution. The **area** of each rectangle rather than the height represents the frequency of a particular class interval.

Histograms may be useful for assessing the dispersion of a grouped frequency distribution visually.

There are various types of histogram described below. It is unlikely that you will be expected to construct a histogram but you may be required to interpret the information given in the form of a histogram and you should work through the following examples carefully which review the principles previously covered in the certificate level Business Maths syllabus.

If all the class intervals are of the same size (as in the example below) then the rectangles have the same length of base (or width) and the heights will be proportional to the frequencies (just as in a bar chart).

Example

Class interval	*Range of class*	*Frequency (f)*
Age (years)		*No. of people*
11 and less than 16	5	9
16 and less than 21	5	17
21 and less than 26	5	22
26 and less than 31	5	18
31 and less than 36	5	10

The standard width of a class interval is five years.

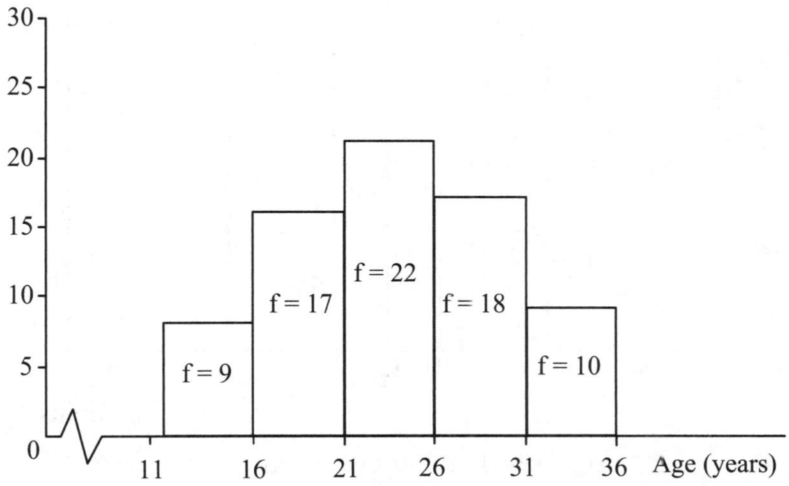

Part of the horizontal axis has been omitted for clarity. The omission is shown by a jagged line.

Note: The vertical lines are always drawn at the mathematical class limits, so there are no gaps as in a bar chart. If class intervals are equal, as here, there is no need to put the frequency in each bar (except for additional accuracy reading the diagram). It is a useful technique if class intervals are unequal.

4.5 Unequal class intervals

If the distribution has unequal class intervals (e.g. in the example below, the third and fourth class intervals have twice the range of the others), it is necessary to adjust the heights of the bars to compensate for the fact that the rectangles do not all have the same length of base. Only by doing this will the area of the rectangle represent the frequency.

Example

The following data refers to the weights (in kg) of 42 crates of frozen fish landed at Grimsby:

Class interval	*Range of class*	*Frequency (f)*
Weights (kgs)		*N.o of crates*
10 and less than 15	5	2
15 and less than 20	5	5
20 and less than 30	10	12
30 and less than 40	10	16
40 and less than 45	5	7

The standard width of a class interval is 5 kg. Therefore, since the third and fourth intervals are twice as wide, it is necessary to halve the frequencies of these two classes to find the actual heights of the rectangles.

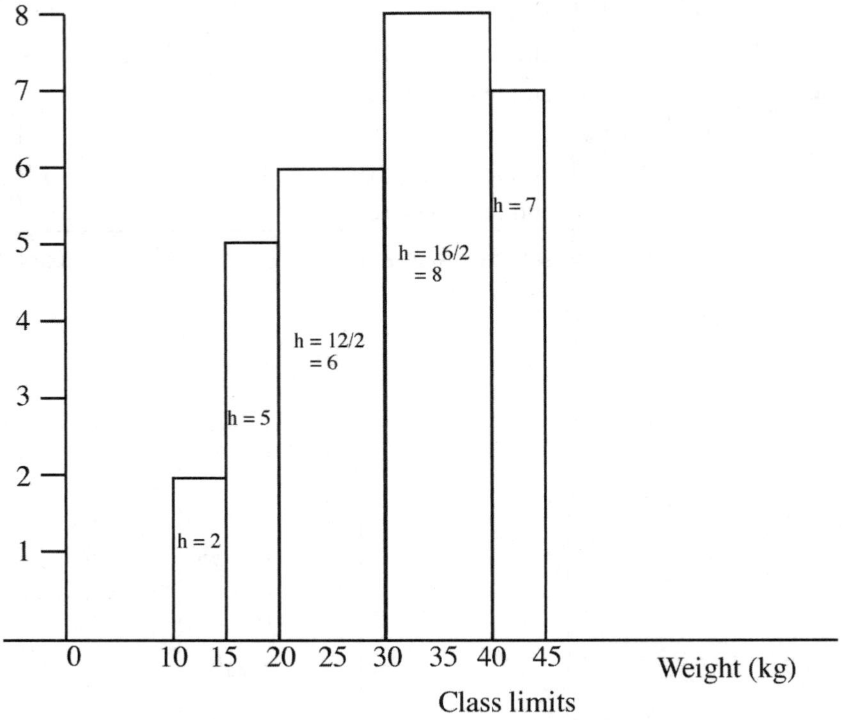

Similarly, if a distribution has a class interval that is three times the width of the standard class interval, the frequency of that class must be divided by three to find the height of the rectangle.

In the above example it was the central classes which were wider than standard. Usually it will be the tail-end classes which are wider, in order to avoid classes with no members if possible.

Interpretation must always be in terms of the standard width of class interval. For example, the height of the third rectangle is 6 units. This does not mean that there are 6 items in the class 20 to 30 kg, but that there is an average of 6 in each of the classes 20 to 25 kg and 25 to 30 kg. The vertical axis no longer represents frequency, but 'frequency density'.

Activity 6

A frequency distribution of a sample of incomes is as follows:

£	*Frequency*
40 and less than 80	7
80 and less than 100	16
100 and less than 120	28
120 and less than 130	21
130 and less than 140	8
	80

In the histogram of this data, the rectangle for the £80 – £100 class has a height of 8 cm.

What should be the height of the rectangles for the following classes:

(a) £100 to 120?

(b) £130 to 140?

Feedback to this activity is at the end of the chapter.

5 Joint decisions

5.1 Introduction

The techniques considered so far have been suitable for situations when there is only one uncertain variable. In reality any decision will have numerous uncertain variables and expected values can be calculated using joint probabilities which take into account potential variations in more than one variable.

5.2 Joint probabilities

If it can be assumed that two values are independent, i.e. the value of one variable is not influenced by the value of the other variable, then the probabilities of each outcome can be multiplied together to find a joint probability which is the probability of both outcomes occurring.

Example

If the probability that the weather is fine tomorrow is 0.5 and the probability that the train arrives on time is 0.9, then the probability of both events occurring is $0.5 \times 0.9 = 0.45$.

This assumes that the two events are independent. This may not strictly be the case as the state of the weather may influence the ability for the train to arrive on time but in management accounting problems this assumption is made to enable the probability distribution of the outcomes to be modelled.

If the probabilities of all of the outcomes are known, then the sum of the joint probabilities must equal 1.

Example

A new product is to be launched and there is uncertainty surrounding the level of demand and the level of unit contribution. The following information is estimated:

Demand (units)	*Probability*	*Contribution (£ per unit)*	*Probability*
1,000	0.2	2.25	0.4
1,500	0.5	2.10	0.4
1,800	0.3	1.80	0.2

Produce a table showing all of the outcomes possible and their joint probabilities.

Solution

Demand (units)	*Prob*	*Contribution per unit (£)*	*Prob*	*Total contribution (£)*	*Joint probability*
1,000	0.2	2.25	0.4	2,250	0.08
1,500	0.5	2.25	0.4	3,375	0.2
1,800	0.3	2.25	0.4	4,050	0.12
1,000	0.2	2.10	0.4	2,100	0.08
1,500	0.5	2.10	0.4	3,150	0.2
1,800	0.3	2.10	0.4	3,780	0.12
1,000	0.2	1.80	0.2	1,800	0.04
1,500	0.5	1.80	0.2	2,700	0.1
1,800	0.3	1.80	0.2	3,240	0.06
				Total	1.00

The joint probabilities add to 1 which indicates that these are all of the possible outcomes. This is known as a joint probability distribution. It is assumed that the values for demand and unit contribution are independent.

5.3 Using joint probabilities in decision making

Once a joint probability distribution is known then the information can be used to aid decision making in two ways:

- an expected value can be calculated and used as a decision criterion
- the distribution of the data can be analysed and measured against targets.

Example

Using the joint probability distribution calculated previously, recommend whether the product should be launched if it is known that the estimated fixed costs are £3,000 and management is risk neutral.

Solution

Calculate the expected value by multiplying each total contribution by the joint probability then sum.

Total contribution (£)	*Joint probability*	*Expected value*
2,250	0.08	180
3,375	0.2	675
4,050	0.12	486
2,100	0.08	168
3,150	0.2	630
3,780	0.12	453.6
1,800	0.04	72
2,700	0.1	270
3,240	0.06	194.4
Total	1.00	3,129

The total expected value is £3,129 deducting fixed cost of £3,000 results in an expected profit of £129. Therefore, taking a risk neutral approach, the project would be worthwhile.

Strictly, the expected value criterion is only suitable for decisions which are carried out many times as it is a long-run average. For a one-off decision there are many possible outcomes, none of which will be a profit of £129. It may be argued that the company carries out many decisions of this type and therefore this approach is valid.

The information produced can be used in conjunction with other decision criteria to help management arrive at a decision.

Example

Using the joint probability distribution calculated previously, what would be the decision if:

(a) the company is risk averse

(b) the company is a risk seeker

(c) the company will accept the project if the probability of a profit is greater than 75%.

Solution

Demand (units)	*Prob*	*Contribution per unit* (£)	*Prob*	*Total contribution* (£)	*Profit* (£)	*Joint probability*
1,000	0.2	2.25	0.4	2,250	(750)	0.08
1,500	0.5	2.25	0.4	3,375	375	0.2
1,800	0.3	2.25	0.4	4,050	1,050	0.12
1,000	0.2	2.10	0.4	2,100	(900)	0.08
1,500	0.5	2.10	0.4	3,150	150	0.2
1,800	0.3	2.10	0.4	3,780	780	0.12
1,000	0.2	1.80	0.2	1,800	(1,200)	0.04
1,500	0.5	1.80	0.2	2,700	(300)	0.1
1,800	0.3	1.80	0.2	3,240	240	0.06
						1.00

(a) The information shows that there are three options for which a loss will be made. The probability of this occurring is 0.08 + 0.08 + 0.04 = 0.2. If the company is risk averse this level of risk is likely to be unacceptable and the project would be rejected.

(b) There is an 80% chance of making a profit and a probability of 0.12 of making a profit of 1,050 which represents a return of 35% on the fixed costs invested. A risk seeker may accept the project if there are no better alternatives.

(c) The company would accept the project as the total chance of making a profit is 80%.

6 Decision trees

6.1 Introduction

DEFINITION

A **decision tree** is a way of applying the expected value criterion to situations where a number of decisions are made sequentially. It is so called because the decision alternatives are represented as branches in a tree diagram.

So far only a single decision has had to be made. However, many managerial problems consist of a rather long, drawn-out structure involving a whole sequence of actions and outcomes. Where a number of decisions have to be made sequentially, the complexity of the decision-making process increases considerably. By using decision trees, however, highly complex problems can be broken down into a series of simpler ones while providing, at the same time, opportunity for the decision-maker to obtain specialist advice in relation to each stage of the problem.

A decision tree is a way of applying the expected value criterion to situations where a number of decisions are made sequentially. It is so called because the decision alternatives are represented as branches in a tree diagram.

Example

A retailer must decide whether to sell a product loose or packaged. In either case, the product may sell or not sell. The decision facing the retailer can be represented by a tree diagram.

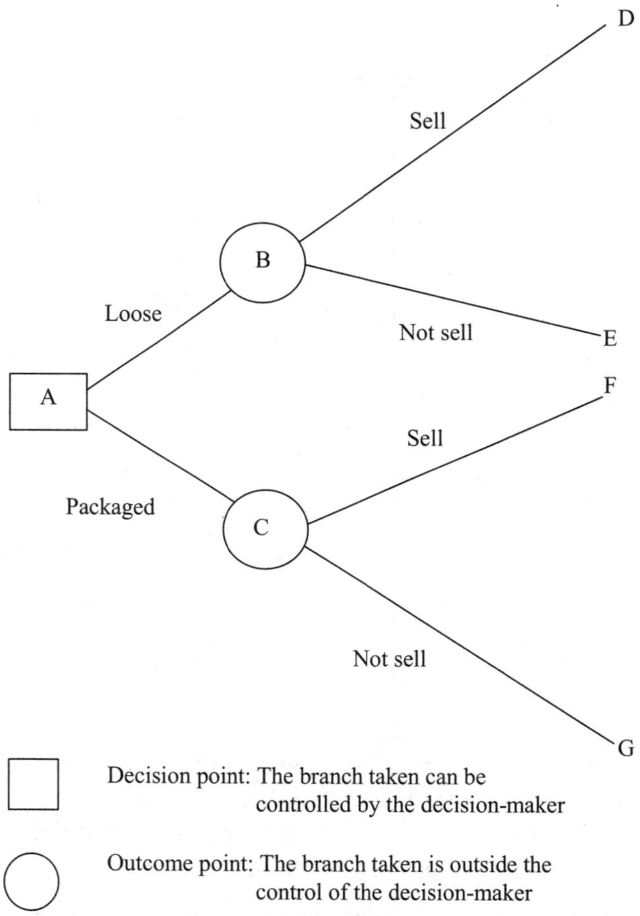

In this example, say the profitability of selling packaged products is £10, loose products £15. The loss through not selling is £5 in either case. The probability of the product being sold is 0.7 for packaged products, 0.5 for loose products.

You are required to evaluate the expected values of each decision alternative.

Solution

The decision tree is evaluated working back from right to left. At each outcome point the expected value (EV) of the possible outcomes is computed. At each decision point it is assumed, initially, that the decision-maker will choose the route with the highest EV. All other branches from such a point are therefore eliminated.

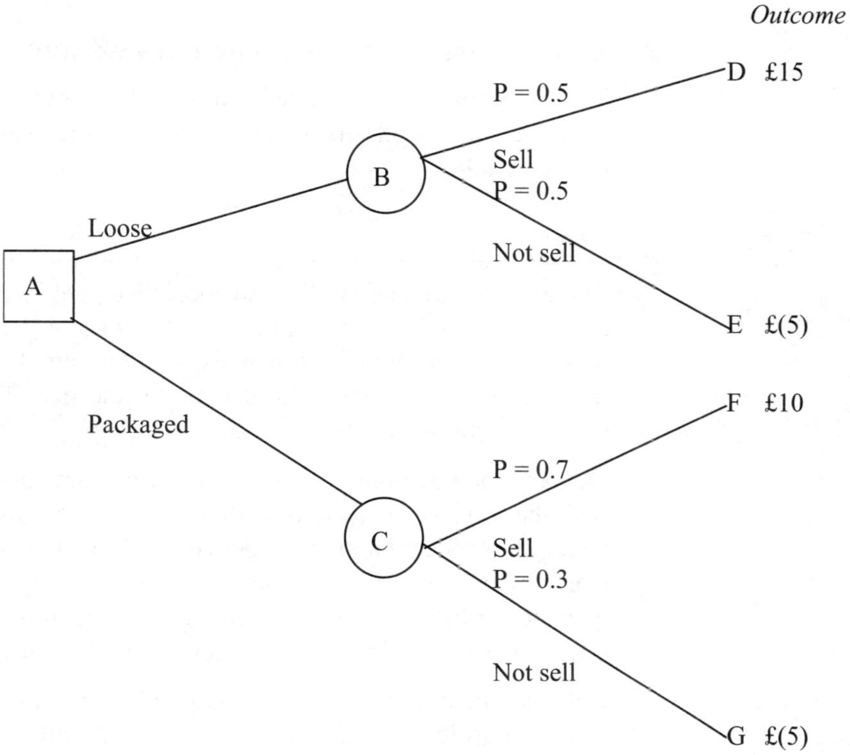

The diagram is then evaluated as follows (using obvious notation):

$EV_B \quad = (0.5 \times EV_D) + (0.5 \times EV_E)$

$\quad\quad = (0.5 \times 15) + (0.5 \times (-5)) = 5$

$EV_C \quad = (0.7 \times EV_F) + (0.3 \times EV_G)$

$\quad\quad = (0.7 \times 10) + (0.3 \times (-5)) = 5.5$

∴ at point A the retailer will choose to go towards point C as this has the higher EV. The discarded routes are sometimes indicated by drawing two short parallel lines across that particular path.

Therefore the decision to sell a packaged product has the higher expected value.

Activity 7

The Janus company is considering expanding its activities either in the UK, or in Europe or in Asia. It can, at this time, only expand in one region.

If it expands in the UK, there is a probability of 0.3 that contribution will increase by £200,000 or a probability of 0.7 that it will increase by £800,000.

If it expands in Europe, there is a probability of 0.4 that contribution will increase by £100,000 or a probability of 0.6 that it will increase by £1,000,000.

If it expands in Asia, there is a probability of 0.6 that contribution will decrease by £1,000,000 or a probability of 0.4 that it will increase by £2,500,000.

(a) Draw a decision tree and determine whether the company should expand and, if so, where?

(b) What important aspect does this analysis ignore?

Feedback to this activity is at the end of the chapter.

6.2 Decision trees – a comprehensive example

The last problem could have been solved without a tree diagram, but the technique comes into its own in a more complex situation, as illustrated by the next example.

Example

The manager of a newly formed specialist machinery manufacturing subsidiary has to decide whether to build a small plant or a large plant for manufacturing a new piece of machinery with an expected market life of ten years. One of the major factors influencing this decision is the size of the market that the company can obtain for its product.

Demand may be high during the first two years but, if initial users are unhappy with the product, demand may then fall to a low level for the remaining eight years. If users are happy then demand will be maintained at its high level. Conversely, caution by prospective buyers may mean only a low level of demand for the first two years but again, depending on how satisfied these few buyers are, demand may then either remain low or rise to a high level.

If the company initially builds a large plant, it must live with it for the whole ten years, regardless of the market demand. If it builds a small plant, it also has the option after two years of expanding the plant but this expansion would cost more overall, when taken with the initial cost of building small, than starting by building a large plant.

Various pieces of information have been collected or estimated by the marketing manager, the production manager and the finance department.

(a) **Marketing information**

The probabilities of the outcomes have been assessed as follows:

Outcome	*First two years*	*Next eight years given first two years were:* *High*	*Low*
High	0.8	0.75	0.25
Low	0.2	0.25	0.75

(b) **Annual income estimate**

(i) A large plant with high market demand would yield £1m pa, for each of ten years.

(ii) A large plant with low market demand would yield only £0.1m pa because of high fixed costs and inefficiencies.

(iii) A small plant with low demand would yield £0.4m pa.

(iv) If demand were high, a small plant during an initial period of high demand would yield £0.45m pa for the first two years, but this would drop to £0.25m pa for the next eight years because of increasing competition from other manufacturers.

(v) If the initially small plant were expanded after two years and demand were high in the last eight years, it would yield £0.7m pa, i.e. being less efficient than one that was initially large.

(vi) If the small plant were expanded after two years but demand was low for the eight-year period, then it would yield £0.05m pa.

(c) **Capital costs**

(i)	Initial cost of building a large plant	£3m
(ii)	Initial cost of building a small plant	£1.3m
(iii)	Additional cost of expanding a small plant	£2.2m

Using expected value as the decision criterion, advise the manager on what choice of plant to make.

Ignore the time value of money and taxation.

Solution

The first stage in solving a problem of this nature, which involves more than one decision being made over a period of time, is to construct a decision tree to demonstrate the structure of the decisions that have to be made.

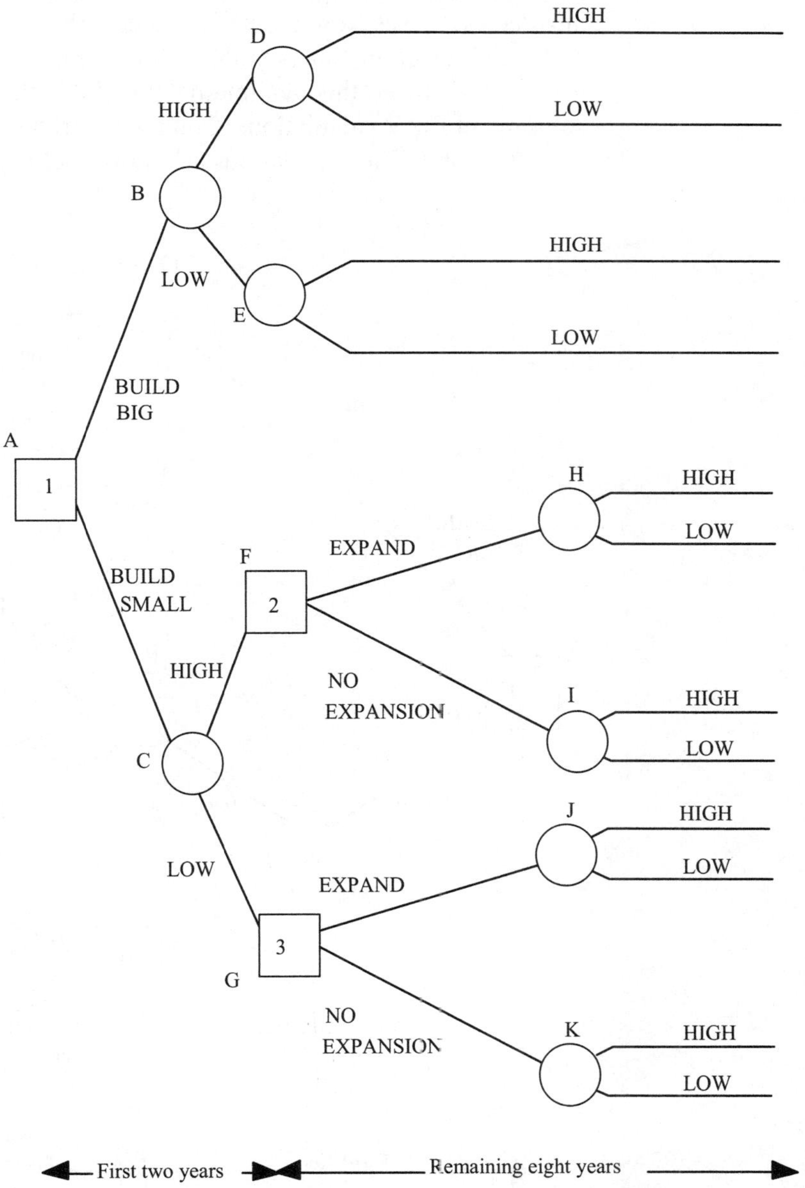

Each path represents a different series of events and outcomes; for example path ACFH Low represents:

- an initial decision to build a small plant
- demand for the first two years turns out be high
- whereupon a further decision is taken to expand the plant
- but unfortunately demand for the next eight years falls to a low level.

Each of the 12 possible monetary outcomes has a certain chance of occurring, depending on which decisions are made and, since expected value is the criterion to be used in making the decisions, the expected value of building the large plant must be compared with the expected value of building the small plant (whichever gives the higher value being chosen). This is done by a process known as roll-back.

Method

Insert relevant cash flows and probabilities on each branch. Starting from the right-hand side, work back towards the left-hand side. At each outcome point, calculate the expected monetary value (EMV) for events leading out from the node, and insert this value in the circle. At each decision point, after subtracting any decision costs from the EMVs, accept the decision with the highest net EMV and reject the others at that point by placing a barrier (a double line) across them. Insert this maximum net EMV in the triangle and use this value in subsequent EMV calculations. Continue working back in this way to the initial decision point. The calculations are shown below, where cash flows are in £m.

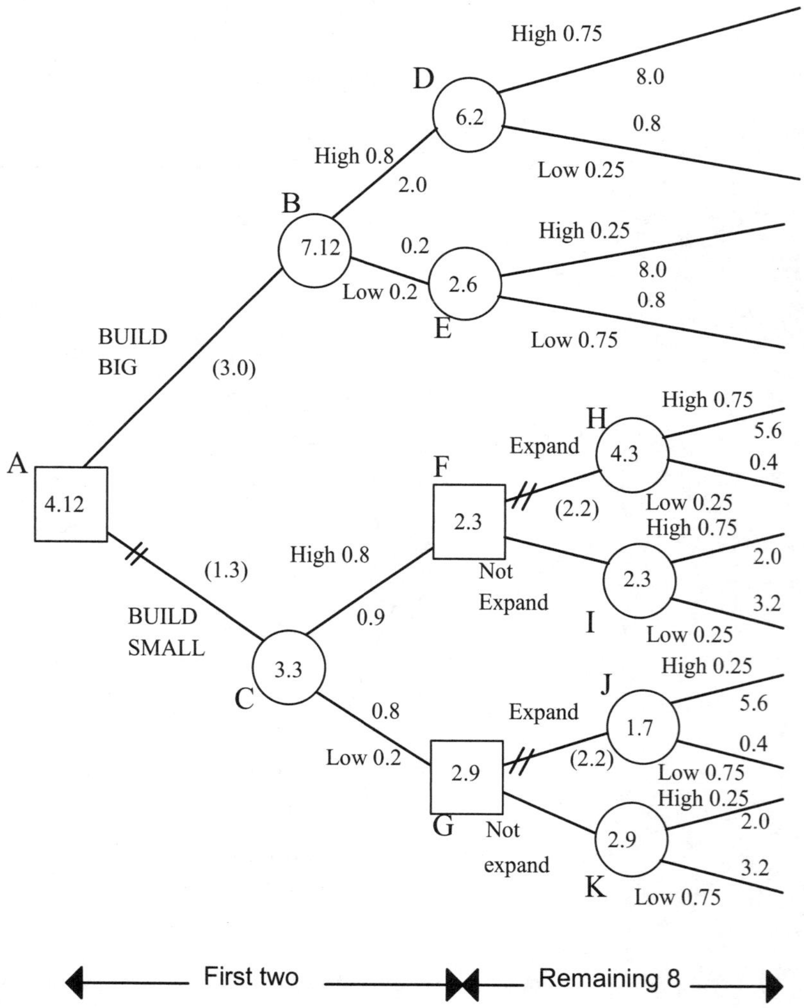

Calculations

The cash inflows are the yields per annum multiplied by the number of years. These are inserted on each line. The cash outflows are put in brackets and treated as negative inflows. The probabilities are also inserted on each line where appropriate.

At node D, EMV = $(8.0 \times 0.75) + (0.8 \times 0.25)$ = 6.2

At node E, EMV = $(8.0 \times 0.25) + (0.8 \times 0.75)$ = 2.6

The total cash inflows from B are: 6.2 + 2.0 = 8.2 (high) and

2.6 + 0.2 = 2.8 (low)

At node B, EMV = $(8.2 \times 0.8) + (2.8 \times 0.2)$ = 7.12

At node H, EMV = $(5.6 \times 0.75) + (0.4 \times 0.25)$ = 4.3

At node I, EMV = $(2.0 \times 0.75) + (3.2 \times 0.25)$ = 2.3

From F, expanding will yield an EMV of 4.3 – 2.2 = 2.1

not expanding will yield an EMV of 2.3

It is better not to expand, so a barrier is put across the expansion line and the EMV at F is then 2.3.

At node J, EMV = $(5.6 \times 0.25) + (0.4 \times 0.75)$ = 1.7

At node K, EMV = $(2.0 \times 0.25) + (3.2 \times 0.75)$ = 2.9

From G, expanding will yield an EMV of 1.7 – 2.2 = 0.5 (a loss)

not expanding will yield an EMV of 2.9

It is better not to expand, so a barrier is put across the expansion line from G and the EMV at G is then 2.9.

The total cash inflows from C are: 2.3 + 0.9 = 3.2 (high) and

2.9 + 0.8 = 3.7 (low)

At node C, EMV = $(3.2 \times 0.8) + (3.7 \times 0.2)$ = 3.3

At node A, building big has a net EMV of 7.12 – 3.0 = 4.12

building small has a net EMV of 3.3 – 1.3 = 2.0

Hence, it is better to build big, and the EMV of the optimum policy of building big is inserted in the triangle.

Tutorial notes:

1. For the purpose of clarity in this book, cash flows and probabilities have been inserted in a separate diagram. In practice, of course, only one diagram is used and all data and results are inserted on the one tree.

2. Do not eliminate branches from an outcome point. The decision-maker has no control over which of these branches will be taken and all outcomes must therefore be considered. In particular include a "do nothing" option if this is a viable alternative.

3. When stating the optimum policy, the route to be taken at each decision node must be specified. For example, if building small had been the best initial policy, the decision whether or not to expand at F and G should also have been stated.

4 No account has been taken in this example of the timing of cash flows, i.e. discounting has not taken place. This was omitted deliberately to keep the example simple. In practice, however, cash flows must not be added or subtracted unless they have been discounted to the same point in time. The simplest method of doing this is to discount all cash flows to their present values.

However, it should be borne in mind that decisions are often based on the cash flow occurring at the time when the decision is made. If, for example, an investor is considering aborting an investment after one year if it yields less than a specified amount of £x in the first year, then this decision would depend on the value of the cash flow at the end of the first year, not on its present value. In such cases, cash flows should be discounted to the point in time when the decision is to be made.

7 Sensitivity analysis

It is possible to assess how sensitive a decision is to changes in the various probabilities that have been used. If probabilities have been estimated, they may not be entirely accurate and it is important to check what the decision would have been if the probabilities had been different. If only a very slight change in the probability of one of the outcomes causes a different decision to be made, the situation is very sensitive, but where it requires a very large change in probability to alter the decision made, then the decision-maker can feel far more confident that the correct choice has been made.

Example

Using the data of the decision tree example above, the manager has doubts as to the probability forecasts and, on closer questioning of the marketing director, ascertains that:

- if demand in the first two years is low, there is very little chance at all of the product catching on; thus, a more accurate probability of 'high demand in the last eight years given low demand in the first two years' is zero
- if demand is high in the first two years, there is almost as much chance of customers disliking as liking the product; therefore, the manager estimates the following probabilities:

  P (high last eight years/first two years high) = 0.55

  P (low last eight years/first two years high) = 0.45
- the probability of high demand in the first two years may have been optimistic and a more cautious estimate would be 0.7.

You are required:

(a) to state what the manager's decision will be if these new probabilities are used

(b) to discuss whether the original decision is sensitive.

Solution

The optimal decision is ascertained under these conditions by the means just explained.

(a) The manager's decision should now be to build small and not to expand even if initial demand is high, since this policy has a net expected value of (3.61 – 1.3) = 2.31 (£m) compared with (5.032 – 3.0) = 2.032 (£m).

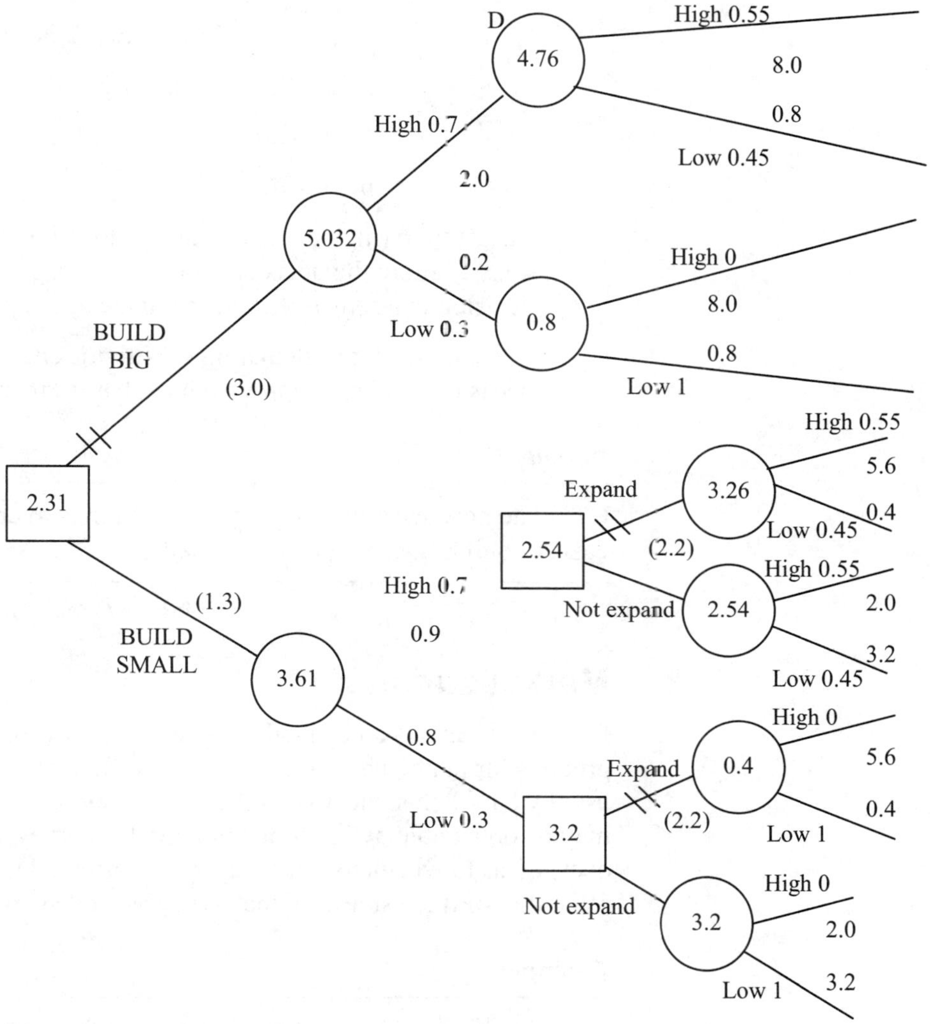

(b) The extent to which the original estimate is sensitive to a change in the various probabilities can only be established by varying each probability in turn and continuing to vary it until the decision changes.

For example, if the probability of the demand in the first two years is varied and all other probabilities are held constant, the probability that high demand would have to be before the decision changed to choosing the build small option could be calculated.

From the original diagram the values at D=6.2, E=2.6, F=2.3 and G=2.9

If p=the probability of high demand then (1-p) = probability of low demand.

The EMV of Build big can now be expressed as:

$$[6.2p + 2.6(1-p)] - 3.0$$

The EMV of Build small can be expressed as:

$$[2.3p + 2.9(1-p)] - 1.3$$

The point where the manager becomes indifferent between the two alternatives is where:

EMV of Build big = EMV of build small

$$[6.2p + 2.6(1-p)] - 3.0 = [2.3p + 2.9(1-p)] - 1.3$$

Solving this equation for p:

$$6.2p + 2.6 - 2.6p - 3.0 = 2.3p + 2.9 - 2.9p - 1.3$$

$$3.6p - 0.4 = -0.6p + 1.6$$

$$4.2p = 2.0$$

$$p = 0.476$$

Therefore p (high demand) can fall to 0.476, a fall of (0.8-0.476)/0.8 = 40.5% before the decision would change. This is a high percentage so the decision is insensitive to the estimate of the probability of high demand.

This approach to calculating sensitivities has been examined on several occasions and may apply both to short term and long term decisions.

Activity 8

Calculate how sensitive the original decision is to changes in the initial capital costs of building big or building small.

Feedback to this activity is at the end of the chapter.

8 Market surveys

Before a decision can be made to launch a new product, there must be some grounds for believing that there will be sufficient demand for the product, usually based on subjective probability. A more accurate assessment of demand may be obtainable by carrying out a market survey. This introduces a further decision as to whether such a survey is worthwhile, which depends on the reliability of the result from the survey as well as its cost.

Example

The probabilities of a good and bad market for a new product overall are assessed at 0.6 and 0.4 respectively. A survey can be carried out to give a better idea of the state of the potential market prior to the decision whether or not to launch the product.

However, the surveys do not always predict the market correctly. In previous launches of other products, when the market was good, market surveys had predicted that it would be good 75% of the time, but when the market was poor surveys had predicted a poor market in seven cases out of every eight. The net present value of the yield will be £5m if the market is good, and –£3m (i.e. a loss of £3m) if the market is poor. Should market research be undertaken and, if so, what is the maximum that should be paid for it?

Solution

Decision tree

Symbols used:

MS = Carry out market survey

MSIG = Market survey indicates a good market

MSIB = Market survey indicates a bad market

G = Market is good

B = Market is bad

L = Launch product

NL = Do not launch product

The initial structure of the tree is:

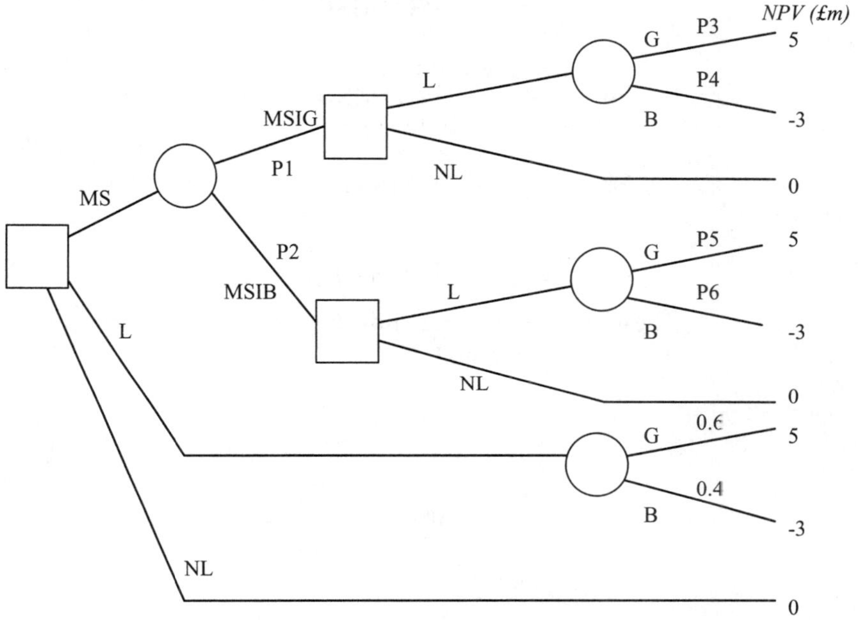

Tutorial note: The third branch (NL or do nothing) should always be included in decision trees as, if the other branches prove to have negative EMVs, this would be the preferred option.

Calculation of probabilities

The branches from the top right-hand outcome point represent the events 'Good market' and 'Bad market' respectively, given that the market survey indicated a good market; the probabilities P3 and P4 are therefore P(G | MSIG) and P(B | MSIG) respectively.

The probabilities given in the question, however, are the probabilities of a given survey result conditional on a given state of the market, i.e. P(MSIG | G) and P (MSIB | B).

A similar situation applies to probabilities P5 (P(G | MSIB)) and P6 (P(B | MSIB)).

Although you can use formal probability laws (Bayes' Theorem) to find the appropriate conditional probabilities, they are not necessary. An alternative approach is to draw up a two-way table assuming (say) 100 trials as follows (sometimes referred to as a 'joint probability table').

		Market survey indication					
Market condition		*Good*		*Bad*	*Total*		
Good	(75% × 60)	45	(balance)	15	60	} Overall market probs given in question
Bad	(balance)	5	(7/8 × 40)	35	40	
Total		50		50	100	

The probabilities needed can now be calculated as:

$$P3 = P(G \mid MSIG) = \frac{45}{50} = 0.9$$

$$P4 = P(B \mid MSIG) = \frac{5}{50} = 0.1$$

$$P5 = P(G \mid MSIB) = \frac{15}{50} = 0.3$$

$$P6 = P(B \mid MSIB) = \frac{35}{50} = 0.7$$

$$P1 = P(MSIG) = \frac{45+5}{100} = \frac{50}{100} = 0.5$$

$$P2 = P(MSIB) = \frac{15+35}{100} = \frac{50}{100} = 0.5$$

These probabilities can now be inserted on the tree, and the tree evaluated by the roll-back method.

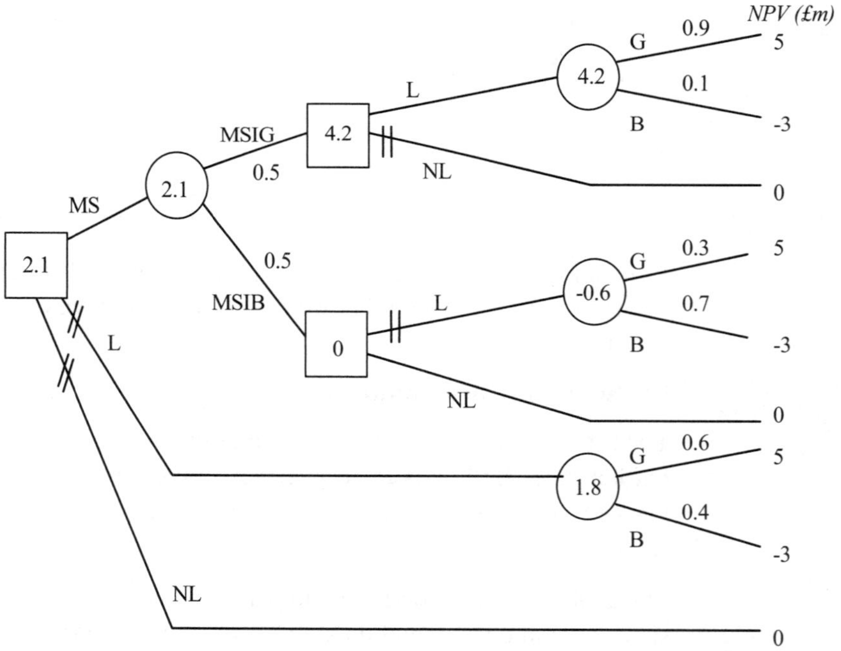

The double parallel lines indicate routes that are 'blocked off', i.e. would not be chosen on the basis of expected values. (NPV = net present value.)

The optimum strategy, without taking into account the cost of the survey (but see below), is to carry out the survey and, if it indicates a good market, launch the product, but if it indicates a poor market, do not launch. This strategy has an EMV of £2.1m.

Activity 9

A survey is being carried out to determine in which of two areas a company should start to sell a new product. There is a 0.3 probability that area A will be recommended and 0.7 that area B will be recommended.

If the company goes into area A the probability of getting good sales is 0.6 and of poor sales is 0.4. If the company goes into area B the probability of good sales is 0.2 and of poor sales 0.8.

(a) Draw a probability tree for this situation and hence obtain the joint probability table.

(b) Using the table obtained in (a) calculate the following probabilities:

(i) P (Going into area A and getting good sales)

(ii) P (Getting good sales)

(iii) P (That the company went into A given that they achieved good sales).

Feedback to this activity is at the end of the chapter.

9 The value of information

9.1 Introduction

The expected value of information (EVI) is defined as:

EVI = EMV of best strategy when the information is possessed minus EMV of best strategy when the information is not possessed.

Thus in the above example, if the survey is not carried out, the best strategy would be to launch without survey, which has an EMV of £1.8m. The expected value of the information from the survey is therefore:

EVI = £(2.1 – 1.8)m

= £0.3m

This is the maximum that management should be prepared to pay for the information from the survey.

It should be noted that the risks associated with the survey cost and the expected value of the outcome are not comparable – one is certain, fixed; the other is an average, and the actual outcome may vary from this.

9.2 Perfect/imperfect information

The information given by the market survey in the previous example was ‘imperfect’ – if the survey said the market was good, there was a 25% chance that this information would be incorrect.

Perfect information will predict exactly what the outcome will be. This will allow the business to choose the best action based upon known values, rather than expected ones.

For example, had the survey in the example above been perfect, then if it indicated the market was good, the company could launch the product knowing that they would benefit by the full £5m NPV, with no chance of making a loss.

Clearly this type of information would be of greater value than imperfect information, and the maximum payable could be determined in a similar way as in the previous example, with a simplified decision tree.

This is a problem that occurs in stock control when dealing with goods that are perishable or rapidly become obsolete. One example is the decision of the newspaper seller as to how many newspapers should be stocked at the start of each day. Too few will result in stock-out with lost sales and goodwill, while too many will result in surplus stock that becomes valueless once the day is out.

Example

A confectioner has the following daily demand for cakes.

Demand (number of cakes)	*Probability*
100	0.1
200	0.2
300	0.3
400	0.3
500	0.1
	1.0

Each cake costs £0.10 to make and sells for £0.20. Any left over at the end of the day are sold off cheaply for £0.05 each.

(a) What is the optimum number of cakes to produce each day?

(b) How much would advance perfect information as to the demand be worth? (This could be achieved, perhaps, by asking customers to e-mail him their cake requirements the previous evening.)

Solution

(a) The pay-off table is (£):

Market demand / *Strategy*		*Demand per day*				
		100	*200*	*300*	*400*	*500*
Production per day	100	10	10	10	10	10
	200	5	20	20	20	20
	300	0	15	30	30	30
	400	(5)	10	25	40	40
	500	(10)	5	20	35	50

How are the monetary outcomes in the table calculated? We illustrate the procedure below, focusing on the strategy of producing 400 units.

Demand	*100*	*200*	*300*	*400*	*500*
Revenue @ £0.20	£20	£40	£60	£80	£80*
Surplus cakes	300	200	100	0	0
Revenue from surplus @ £0.05	£15	£10	£5	0	0
Total revenue	£35	£50	£65	£80	£80
Less: Production cost @ £0.10	£40	£40	£40	£40	£40
Net gain (£)	(5)	10	25	40	40

* If only 400 are produced, only 400 can be sold.

To find the expected value of each strategy, multiply each outcome by its probability.

Strategy	*EMV (£)*
100	$(10\times0.1) + (10\times0.2) + (10\times0.3) + (10\times0.3) + (10\times0.1) = 10.0$
200	$(5\times0.1) + (20\times0.2) + (20\times0.3) + (20\times0.3) + (20\times0.1) = 18.5$
300	$(0\times0.1) + (15\times0.2) + (30\times0.3) + (30\times0.3) + (30\times0.1) = 24.0$
400	$(-5\times0.1) + (10\times0.2) + (25\times0.3) + (40\times0.3) + (40\times0.1) = 25.0$
500	$(-10\times0.1) + (5\times0.2) + (20\times0.3) + (35\times0.3) + (50\times0.1) = 21.5$

The optimum strategy is to produce 400 per day as this has the highest EMV of £25.

Students with a knowledge of matrices will recognise this as a matrix multiplication thus:

$$\begin{bmatrix} 10 & 10 & 10 & 10 & 10 \\ 5 & 20 & 20 & 20 & 20 \\ 0 & 15 & 30 & 30 & 30 \\ -5 & 10 & 25 & 40 & 40 \\ -10 & 5 & 20 & 35 & 50 \end{bmatrix} \times \begin{bmatrix} 0.1 \\ 0.2 \\ 0.3 \\ 0.3 \\ 0.1 \end{bmatrix} = \begin{bmatrix} 10.0 \\ 18.5 \\ 24.0 \\ 25.0 \\ 21.5 \end{bmatrix}$$

(b) With advance knowledge of the demand each day, the best strategy would be to make just sufficient to meet that demand. Hence:

Demand	*Number produced*	*Pay-off**	*Prob.*	*Expectation = Pay-off × Prob.*
100	100	10	0.1	1.0
200	200	20	0.2	4.0
300	300	30	0.3	9.0
400	400	40	0.3	12.0
500	500	50	0.1	5.0
				31.0

* Obtained as the maximum value of each row of the pay-off table. The expected value of this strategy is £31.0, and the expected value of the best strategy without the information is £25.0.

Hence, the expected value of the information is £(31.0 – 25.0) = £6 per day.

Thus, a daily survey amongst customers would only be worthwhile if it cost no more than £6 per day.

Summary

- In this chapter decision making under conditions of uncertainty was considered. Several methods were examined, the most important being the criterion of maximising the expected value of potential outcomes.

- Pay-off tables and decision trees are very useful tools which can be applied in decision analysis as they readily incorporate the laws of probability thereby making their application relatively easy.

- Any difficulties with probabilities on a decision tree are best dealt with by initially determining the joint probability table. From the table any decision tree probability can be obtained.

- Of all the measures of dispersion used in business, the standard deviation is by far the most important, its main uses and applications being in the field of more advanced statistics.

Having completed your study of this chapter you should have achieved the following learning outcomes.

- Evaluate the impact of uncertainty and risk on decision models that may be based on CVP analysis, relevant cash flows, learning curves, discounting techniques, etc.
- Apply sensitivity analysis on both short and long-run decision models to identify variables that might have significant impacts on project outcomes.
- Analyse risk and uncertainty by calculating expected values and standard deviations together with probability tables and histograms.
- Prepare expected value tables and ascertain the value of information.
- Prepare and apply decision trees.

Self-test questions

1 Distinguish between risk and uncertainty. (1.1)

2 Explain the maximax criterion. (2.4)

3 What is the standard deviation? (4.2)

4 What is the coefficient of variation? (4.3)

5 What is a histogram? (4.4)

6 Do the probabilities on a decision tree occur immediately after a decision point or an outcome point? (6.1)

7 What is sensitivity analysis? (7)

8 What is the expected value of information? (9.1)

Objective test questions

Question 1

Quality control of four independent production processes reveals the length of certain parts (in mm) to be as follows:

Process	*Mean*	*Standard deviation*
W	100	10
X	40	5
Y	80	8
Z	150	12

The process(es) with the largest relative variation, as measured by the coefficient of variation, is/are:

A X only

B Z only

C X and Y

D W and Y

Question 2

Several groups of invoices are being analysed. For each group the coefficient of variation has been calculated.

The coefficient of variation measures:

A the range of values of the invoices

B the correlation between the invoice values

C the relative dispersion of the invoice values

D the variation between the sample mean and the true mean

Question 3

In a histogram in which one class interval is one and a half times as wide as the remaining classes, the height to be plotted in relation to the frequency for that class is:

A × 0.67

B × 0.75

C × 1.00

D × 1.50

Question 4

Hannah estimates that her salary next year will be:

Salary £000	*Probability*
25	0.2
28	0.6
30	0.15
32	0.05

What is the expected value of her salary next year?

A £27,900

B £28,300

C £28,750

D £32,000

Question 5

A decision tree is drawn for a possible new product launch:

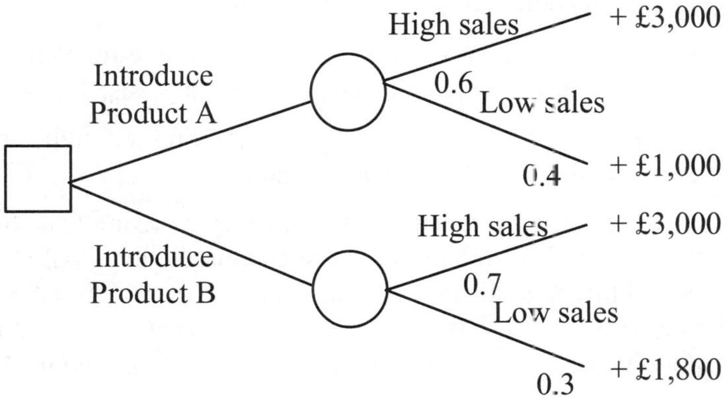

Either product A or product B can be introduced into the market.

(i) Which product should be launched?

A A

B B

C Neither

D Both A and B

(ii) The EV of the optimum decision is:

A £2,200

B £2,480

C £2,640

D £4,840

Question 6

A fish salesman calculates his expected profits next week to be £120. A survey company offers to sell him for £20 information that he could use to increase his profits to £200 next week. The value of the information is:

A £60

B £80

C £180

D £200

For the answers to these questions, see the 'Answers' section at the end of the book.

Exam-type questions

Question 1: Tripe

The Animal Products Co is considering whether to produce a new pet food 'Tripe'. Tripe production would require the purchase of new capital equipment costing £25,000, and would displace an existing product earning an annual contribution of £30,000. The variable costs of Tripe production would be 25 pence per unit. Expected sales volumes are uncertain. The marketing manager estimates it to be equally likely that, at the market selling price of 35 pence per unit, the annual sales volume would be 600,000 units or 200,000 units.

It is possible to carry out test-marketing at a fixed one-time cost of £7,000 before committing further costs. Previous experience suggests:

- that there is a 75% chance that test-marketing will indicate that the higher sales estimate of 600,000 units applies; and
- that, owing to improvements to the product arising from the test marketing, there is an 80% probability that such a prediction would be correct, and a 20% probability that, given the prediction of sales of 600,000 units, sales would be only 200,000 units. (In this eventuality it is assumed that it would not be possible to change back to current production, giving up Tripe.)

However, almost certainly the fact (but not the results) of the test-marketing will come to the attention of competitors. It is estimated that, in that case, there is a 20% probability that a competitor would then enter the market, causing a reduction in the market price of Tripe to 30 pence per unit. The Animal Products Co would then have to reduce its price to 30 pence per unit of Tripe. At this price the two likely sales volumes would not be affected.

The Animal Products Co would not proceed with preparations to market Tripe if the test-marketing indicated the lower sales volume of 200,000 units.

The Animal Products Co's cost of capital and its planning horizon are such that the present value of an annual sum, whether costs or revenues, is four times that annual sum.

Required:

(a) Draw a decision tree of the problem facing the Animal Products Co. **(8 marks)**

(b) Calculate the expected net present value of each possible course of action. **(4 marks)**

(c) Calculate the maximum price which the company would be willing to pay for the test-marketing. **(3 marks)**

(d) Comment on the limitations of using expected net present values in decision making. **(5 marks)**

(e) Outline the advantages to a company of undertaking market research to determine the level of demand for a product. **(5 marks)**

(Total: 25 marks)

Question 2: Butterfield Ltd

Butterfield Ltd manufactures a single brand of dog-food called 'Lots O' Grissle' (LOG). Sales have stabilised for several years at a level of £20 million per annum at current prices. This level is not expected to change in the foreseeable future (except as indicated below). It is well below the capacity of the plant. The managing director, Mr Rover, is considering how to stimulate growth in the company's turnover and profits. After rejecting all of the alternative possibilities that he can imagine, or that have been suggested to him, he is reviewing a proposal to introduce a new luxury dog-food product. It would be called 'Before Eight Mince' (BEM), and would have a recommended retail price of 50p per tin. It would require no new investment, and would incur no additional fixed costs.

Mr Rover has decided that he will undertake this new development only if he can anticipate that it will at least break even in the first year of operation.

(a) Mr Rover estimates that BEM has a 75% chance of gaining acceptance in the market-place. His best estimate is that if the product gains acceptance it will have sales in 20X0 of £3.2 million at retail prices, giving a contribution of £1 million after meeting the variable costs of manufacture and distribution. If, on the other hand, the product fails to gain acceptance, sales in 20X0 will, he thinks, only be £800,000 at retail prices, and for various reasons there would be a negative contribution of £400,000 in that year.

You are required to show whether, on the basis of these preliminary estimates, Mr Rover should give the BEM project further consideration. **(2 marks)**

(b) Mr Rover discusses the new project informally with his sales director, Mr Khoo Chee Khoo, who suggests that some of the sales achieved for the new product would cause lost sales of LOG. In terms of retail values he estimates the likelihood of this as follows:

(1) There is a 50% chance that sales of LOG will fall by half of the sales (by value) of BEM.

(2) There is a 25% chance that sales of LOG will fall by one-quarter of the sales (by value) of BEM.

(3) There is a 25% chance that sales of LOG will fall by three-quarters of the sales (by value) of BEM.

The contribution margin ratio of LOG is 25% at all relevant levels of sales and output.

You are required to show whether, after accepting these further estimates, Mr Rover should give the BEM project further consideration. **(6 marks)**

(c) Mr Rover also wonders whether, before attempting to proceed any further, he should have some market research undertaken. He approaches Delphi Associates, a firm of market research consultants for whom he has a high regard. On previous occasions he has found them always to be right in their forecasts, and he considers that their advice will give him as near perfect information as it is possible to get. He decides to ask Delphi to advise him only on whether or not BEM will gain acceptance in the market-place in the sense in which he has defined it; he will back Chee Khoo's judgement about the effects of the introduction of BEM on the sales of LOG. If Delphi advises him that the product will not be accepted he will not proceed further. Delphi have told him that their fee for this work would be £100,000.

You are required to show whether Mr Rover should instruct Delphi Associates to carry out the market research proposals. **(4 marks)**

(d) Preliminary discussions with Delphi suggest that Delphi's forecasts will not be entirely reliable. They believe that, if they indicate that BEM will gain acceptance, there is only a 90% chance that they will be right and, if they indicate failure to gain acceptance, there is only a 70% chance that they will be right. This implies a 75% chance overall that Delphi will indicate acceptance, in line with Mr Rover's estimate.

You are required to show the maximum amount that Mr Rover should be prepared to pay Delphi to undertake the market research, given the new estimates of the reliability of their advice. **(8 marks)**

(e) Outline briefly the strengths and limitations of your methods of analysis in (a) – (d) above. **(5 marks)**

(Total: 25 marks)

Question 3: Homeworker Ltd

Homeworker Ltd is a small company that manufactures a lathe attachment for the DIY market called the 'Homelathe'.

The data for manufacturing the attachment are as follows:

	For each batch of 10 Homelathes					
	Components					*Total*
	A	*B*	*C*	*D*	*E*	
Machine hours	10	14	12			36
Labour hours				2	1	3
	£	£	£	£	£	£
Variable cost	32	54	58	12	4	160
Fixed cost (apportioned)	48	102	116	24	26	316
Total component costs	80	156	174	36	30	476

General-purpose machinery is used to make components A, B and C and is already working to the maximum capability of 4,752 hours and there is no possibility of increasing the machine capacity in the next period. Labour is available for making components D and E and for assembling the product.

The marketing department advises that there will be a 50% increase in demand next period so the company has decided to buy one of the machine-made components from an outside supplier in order to release production capacity and thus help to satisfy demand.

A quotation has been received from General Machines Ltd for the components but, because this company has not made the components before, it has not been able to give single figure prices. Its quotation is as follows:

	Pessimistic		*Most likely*		*Optimistic*	
	Price	*Probability*	*Price*	*Probability*	*Price*	*Probability*
	£		£		£	
Component A	96	0.25	85	0.5	54	0.25
Component B	176	0.25	158	0.5	148	0.25
Component C	149	0.25	127	0.5	97	0.25

It has been agreed between the two companies that audited figures would be used to determine which one of the three prices would be charged for whatever component is bought out.

As management accountant of Homeworker Ltd, it is your responsibility to analyse the financial and production capacity effects of the proposed component purchase.

Required:

(a) Show in percentage form the maximum increased production availability from the three alternatives, i.e. buying A or B or C. **(4 marks)**

(b) Analyse the financial implications of the purchase and, assuming a risk neutral attitude, recommend which component to buy out, noting that the production availability will be limited to a 50% increase. **(6 marks)**

(c) Prepare a profit statement for the period assuming that the component chosen in (b) is bought out and that the extra production is made and sold (show your workings). **(6 marks)**

(d) State three other factors you would consider if you were advised that management had decided to avoid risk as much as possible when buying out a component. (Calculations are not required for this section.) **(4 marks)**

(Total: 20 marks)

Question 4: Z Ltd

Z Ltd is considering various product pricing and material purchasing options with regard to a new product it has developed. Estimates of demand and costs are as follows:

If selling price unit is:	£15 per unit	£20 per unit
	Sales volume (000 units)	*Sales volume* (000 units)
Forecasts probability		
Optimistic 0.3	36	28
Most likely 0.5	28	23
Pessimistic 0.2	18	13
Variable manufacturing costs (excluding materials) per unit	£3	£3
Advertising and selling costs	£25,000	£96,000
General fixed costs	£40,000	£40,000

Each unit requires 3 kg of material and because of storage problems any unused material must be sold at £1 per kg. The sole suppliers of the material offer three purchase options, which must be decided at the outset, as follows:

(i) any quantity at £3 per kg

(ii) a price of £2.75 per kg for a minimum quantity of 50,000 kg

(iii) a price of £2.50 per kg for a minimum quantity of 70,000 kg.

You are required, assuming that the company is risk neutral, to:

(a) prepare calculations to show what pricing and purchasing decisions the company should make, clearly indicating the recommended decisions; **(15 marks)**

(b) calculate the maximum price you would pay for perfect information as to whether the demand would be optimistic or most likely or pessimistic. **(5 marks)**

(Total: 20 marks)

For the answers to these questions, see the 'Answers' section at the end of the book.

Feedback to activities

Activity 1

	Production level		
Possible demands	*100*	*200*	*300*
100	800	600	400
200	800	1,600	1,400
300	800	1,600	2,400

When supply equals demand the contribution = £15 – 7 = £8. So, in the first cell, demand = supply = 100 and total contribution = 100 × £8 = £800.

Similarly if demand exceeds supply, the same contribution applies, e.g. supply = 100, demand = 300, still only 100 sold giving £800.

If supply exceeds demand then the surplus will be sold off at a loss of £(7–5) = £2 per unit, e.g. supply = 300, demand = 100.

Contribution for the 100 supplied	=	£800
Less loss on 200 @ £2	=	£400
		£400

Activity 2

(a) Using maximin a production level of 100 would be chosen as this maximises the smallest possible pay-off. This occurs at a demand level of 100.

(b) Using maximax a production level of 300 would be chosen as this has the highest possible pay-off. This occurs at a demand level of 300.

(c) Using minimax regret, first calculate a regret table showing the maximum regret at each demand level.

Regret table	*Production level*		
Possible demands	*100*	*200*	*300*
100	0	200	400
200	800	0	200
300	1,600	800	0

So, for example at a demand level of 200, the maximum pay-off is 1,600. If a production level of 100 is chosen the pay-off earned will be only 800 and there will be a regret of 800.

The lowest maximum regret is 400 at a production level of 300 hence this will be the choice using the minimax regret criterion.

Activity 3

Possible demands	*Probability*	*100*	*200*	*300*
100	0.3	800	600	400
200	0.6	800	1,600	1,400
300	0.1	800	1,600	2,400
Expected values		800	1,300	1,200

Working: e.g. expected value for last column:

$$400 \times 0.3 + 1{,}400 \times 0.6 + 2{,}400 \times 0.1 = 1{,}200$$

Maximum expected value is 1,300 in the 200 column, hence produce 200 items only.

Note from your answers to Activities 2 and 3 that each different production level has now been chosen depending on the decision model used. From the same pay-off data different action would be taken depending on a manager's attitude to risk.

Activity 4

Demand	*Produce 100 (x)*	x^2	*Produce 200 (x)*	x^2	*Produce 300 (x)*	x^2
100	800	640,000	600	360,000	400	160,000
200	800	640,000	1,600	2,560,000	1,400	1,960,000
300	800	640,000	1,600	2,560,000	2,400	5,760,000
	$\Sigma x = 2,400$	$\Sigma x^2 =$ 1,920,000	$\Sigma x = 3,800$	$\Sigma x^2 =$ 5,480,000	$\Sigma x = 4,200$	$\Sigma x^2 =$ 7,880,000

$$\text{Hence } \sigma \text{ (produce 100)} = \sqrt{\frac{1,920,000}{3} - \left(\frac{2,400}{3}\right)^2}$$

$$= 0$$

(This could in fact be seen from the data as there is no variation in the pay-offs.)

$$\sigma \text{ (produce 200)} = \sqrt{\frac{5,480,000}{3} - \left(\frac{3,800}{3}\right)^2}$$

$$= 471.4$$

$$\sigma \text{ (product 300)} = \sqrt{\frac{7,880,000}{3} - \left(\frac{4,200}{3}\right)^2}$$

$$= 816.5$$

The standard deviation is highest for if 300 units are produced indicating that this choice would carry the highest risk.

Activity 5

	Production level		
Possible demands	*100*	*200*	*300*
100	800	600	400
200	800	1,600	1,400
300	800	1,600	2,400
Average	800	1,266.7	1,400
Standard deviation	0	471.4	816.5
Coefficient of variation	0	37.2%	58.3%

The option to produce 300 units has the greatest coefficient of variation and therefore is, relatively, the most variable.

Activity 6

(a) 14 cm

(b) 8 cm

Activity 7

(a)

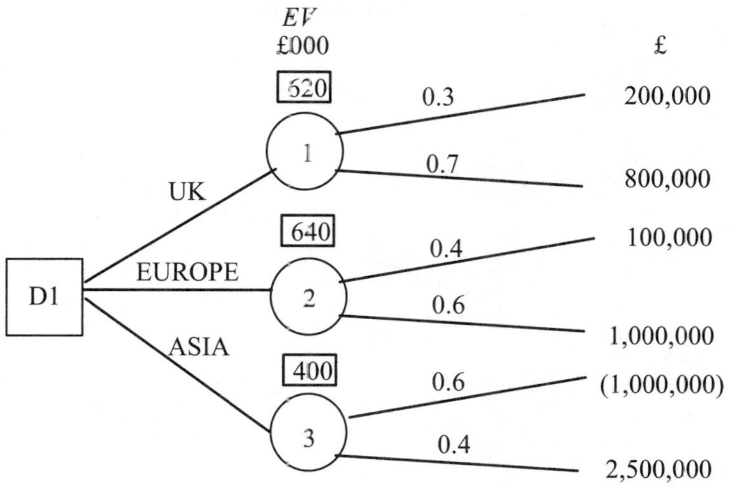

EV (1) = 0.3 × 200,000 + 0.7 × 800,000 = £620,000

EV (2) = 0.4 × 100,000 + 0.6 × 1,000,000 = £640,000 maximum

EV (3) = 0.6 × (1,000,000) + 0.4 × 2,500,000 = £400,000

Maximum expected value is the Europe option at £640,000. Therefore, reject UK and Asia and accept expansion in Europe.

(b) The expected value approach ignores risk. If the Asia option had worked out to give the highest expected value, and the Asia option had been adopted there would be a risk that a loss of £1,000,000 of contribution could occur. In the above context it may also ignore currency fluctuations.

Activity 8

When using sensitivity analysis one variable has to be changed at a time. So firstly consider the initial capital cost of 'build big'.

From the original diagram the value at B = 7.12 and at C = 3.3. To be indifferent:

EMV (build big) = EMV (build small)

So 7.12 – capital cost = 3.3 – 1.3 = 2.0

The capital cost can increase to £5.12m, an increase of (5.12-3.0)/3.0 = 70.7%. This is a high value so the decision is not very sensitive to changes in the capital cost of the 'build big' project.

Considering the sensitivity of the initial capital costs of the 'build small' option. The EMV of 'build big' is 4.12m. As the expected contribution before capital costs of the 'build small' option is only £3.3m there is no value of capital costs which could change the decision.

Activity 9

(a) **Probability tree**

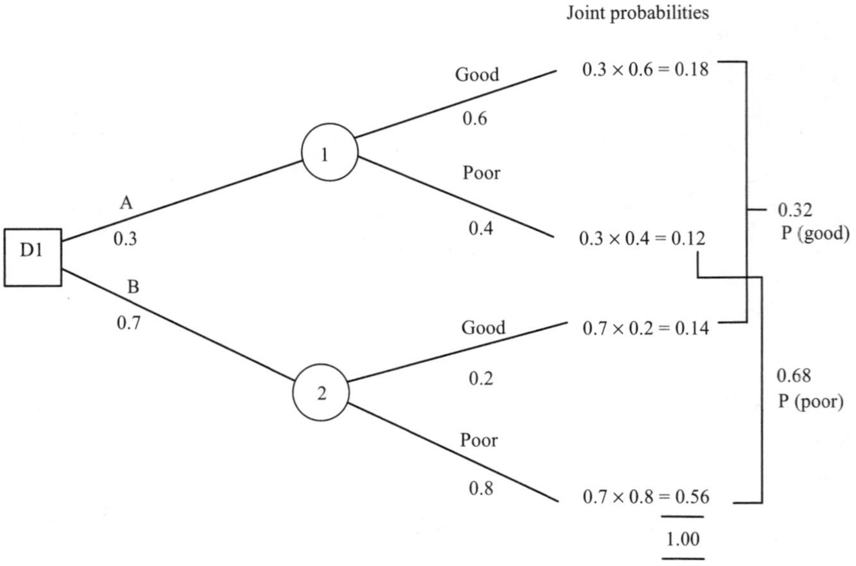

Joint probability table

	Good	*Poor*	*Row totals*	
A	0.18	0.12	0.30	←P(A)
B	0.14	0.56	0.70	←P(B)
Column totals	0.32	0.68	1.00	
	↑ P(good)	↑ P(poor)		

(b) (i) P(A and good) = 0.18 from table or tree

(ii) P(good) = 0.32 from table or tree

(iii) P(A/good) = $\frac{0.18}{0.32}$ = 0.562

Chapter 8

THE MODERN BUSINESS ENVIRONMENT

Syllabus content

This chapter covers the following syllabus content.

- Value analysis and quality function deployment.
- The benefits of just-in-time production, total quality management and theory of constraints and the implications of these methods for decision making in the new manufacturing environment.
- Kaizen costing, continuous improvement and cost of quality reporting.
- Learning curves and their use in predicting product/service costs, including derivation of the learning rate and the learning index.

Contents

1 The modern business environment

1.1 The development of the modern factory

The historical trend in manufacturing progress in the western industrial world was for greater automation and greater economies of scale. The great emphasis in a world of full employment and militant workers was to increase output through more mechanisation. Now, however, faced with intense competition, the emphasis has changed. The successful manufacturer will have to compete by responding rapidly to changing market conditions, **tailoring products** to meet different tastes and quickly introducing **new and innovative products**. All this has to be accomplished at much reduced costs in a very much more competitive market place.

An important factor in achieving this is **flexibility** of manufacturing facilities, that allow a diversity of output at a cost normally associated with mass production. Economies of scale can still be enjoyed, without limiting the scope of products.

The aim is to maximise return from minimum resources. The solution is to invest in new technology and adopt modern manufacturing management practices.

Quality and reliability of output contribute further to the success of '**world class manufacturers**' who lead the way in the manufacture of innovative products at a low cost.

1.2 World Class Manufacturing (WCM)

DEFINITION

World class manufacturing is a position of international manufacturing excellence, achieved by developing a culture based on factors such as continuous improvement, problem prevention, zero defect tolerance, customer-driven JIT-based production and total quality management. (CIMA *Official Terminology*)

World class manufacturing is a position of international manufacturing excellence, achieved by developing a culture based on factors such as continuous improvement, problem prevention, zero defect tolerance, customer-driven JIT-based production and total quality management. (CIMA *Official Terminology*)

World class companies invest in R&D where appropriate, they are **highly capital intensive** and hence highly productive, and have delayered their corporate bureaucracies. Such companies also have a diversity of products, albeit from standard parts and a **flexible manufacturing system**, high quality, and better delivery, and aim to satisfy customers at a global level. They also have an obsession for staying ahead of the competition through **continuous improvement**.

1.3 Advanced manufacturing technologies (AMTs)

This chapter considers the management accounting implications of the various modern practices and techniques that are being increasingly adopted by major companies of the world:

- **Computer integrated manufacturing (CIM)** and related practices in product design and engineering – the idealistic manufacturing environment within which production is fully automated and controlled entirely by computers.
- **Flexible manufacturing system (FMS)** – the stage to which CIM has developed to date, being an integrated, computer-controlled production system that is capable of producing any of a range of parts, and of switching quickly and economically between them, whilst maintaining maximum quality of output.

- **Just-in-time (JIT) production philosophy** – whereby stock levels and waste are reduced to a minimum by a 'pull through' approach – the purchase of materials and production of components taking place as needed.
- **Materials requirements planning (MRP I) and Manufacturing resources planning (MRP II)** – that aim to improve the efficiency with which resources flow through the system, through the use of a master production schedule to determine materials, machine capacity and labour requirements at each stage of the production process.
- **Enterprise resource planning (ERP)** – extends MRP ideas to the complete range of activities within a business enterprise, covering technology aspects as well as system requirements.
- **Optimised production technology (OPT)** – developed from MRP systems, and requiring similar operational and resource information. It seeks to identify and make optimum use of 'bottleneck' resources – that prevent throughput from being higher. Non-bottleneck resources are scheduled around these, utilised at an appropriate capacity level to avoid excessive stock build up.

An essential system run in parallel to AMTs by world-class manufacturers is that of **total quality management (TQM)**, devised to ensure that goods are produced of the highest quality and reliability.

KEY POINT

Modern manufacturing systems are often geared to flexible manufacturing and producing to meet specific customer demand, making use of focus factories or work cells and flow production.

Modern manufacturing systems are often geared to flexible manufacturing and producing to meet specific customer demand, making use of focus factories or work cells and flow production.

1.4 Focus factories

In 'traditional' manufacturing systems, the products made in a factory all go through the same production departments, with each department handling a separate stage in the overall production process. For example, all products go through the machining department, assembly department and finishing department. Production is often in large batches, so that at each stage in production, there are likely to be batches of part-finished items waiting to go into the next stage. There are often bottlenecks, as delays occur in production, and the production process is slow. Part-finished inventory levels can be extremely high – and costly. Since products are manufactured in large batches, some items are made in anticipation of customer orders that do not yet exist. Finished goods go into storage in a warehouse until a customer order comes in, or until the goods are eventually scrapped as unsaleable.

The modern world class approach, by contrast, divides a factory into smaller units, known as focus factories. Each focus factory is a small factory in its own right, which focuses on the manufacture of a single product or product line. For example, each focus factory might have its own machining, assembly and finishing operations. Focus factories replace the large all-purpose production departments found in traditional manufacturing systems. The entire production of an item happens inside its focus factory. Each focus factory has its own management team, responsible for output and performance.

Benefits of a focus factory organisation can be faster production with fewer hold-ups, and much lower stock levels. It can be used to achieve flow production and lean manufacture.

1.5 Flow production

In traditional manufacturing systems, the aim is to make the most efficient use of plant and machinery. In contrast, flow production is concerned with responsiveness to customer orders. Flow manufacturing is a method of organising production so as to respond quickly to customer orders. On receipt of an order, materials are 'pulled' from suppliers and taken through the production system to make the item the customer has asked for. Flow production is sometimes called one-piece flow. This means a flow of work through production, one unit (or order) at a time, at a pace determined by the needs of customers. This avoids the need to build up stocks of part-finished items at each stage in the production process. Flow production methods are consistent with a just-in-time (JIT) approach to purchasing and production.

1.6 Work cell production

Work cell production has similarities with focus factories. A work cell is a group of machines or workstations within the same small area of the factory floor. The equipment is arranged in processing sequence, so that items are manufactured by moving them from one machine or workstation to the next within the work cell. Each work cell makes a single product, or several similar products, so that the entire production process is under its control. There is also flexible work organisation. The workers are trained to be multi-skilled, and each worker can operate any of the machines in the work cell. A work cell should therefore be capable of a smooth flow of production with minimal transportation of part-finished items and minimal production delays.

By organising production in work cells, the benefits of flow manufacturing (one-piece flow) should be achievable. These are faster production, simpler production scheduling, reduced set-up times and lower stocks of work in progress.

Work cell production also allows a company to adapt readily to variations in customer specifications, so that the production system is capable of customising orders. An ability to customise orders is commonly regarded as an essential factor for success in many competitive markets.

1.7 Lean manufacturing

KEY POINT

Lean manufacturing means producing with only the essential resources and without any 'fat'. It aims at eliminating waste.

Lean manufacturing originated in Japan after 1945. 'Lean' means using less human effort, lower capital investment, less floor space, fewer materials and less time in production. In other words, it means operating with only the essential resources, and without any 'fat'. Lean manufacturing also has a customer-oriented focus. Items are manufactured to meet specific customer orders in small jobs or batch runs.

With lean manufacturing, a systematic approach is taken to identifying and eliminating waste in production. Waste is any activity that either:

- does not add value for the customer, or
- costs more than the value it creates.

Lean manufacturing is closely associated with total quality management. Two essential aspects of lean manufacturing are:

- achieving a flow of production in response to customer demand, and
- a continuous search for small improvements in methods, processes and products. This should be ingrained into the culture of everyone in the organisation. Continuous improvement in Japanese is called 'Kaizen'.

Lean production calls for an attack on waste, and eliminating waste wherever it is found. There are several categories of waste.

- Waste from *over-production*, i.e. producing more than customers have ordered. If customer demand fails to materialise, the excess production has to be discarded, or sold off at a heavily-discounted price.
- Waste from *part-finished work-in-process*. Work-in-process builds up when there is a long lead time in production and delays between one stage in processing and the next. Work in process has a cost, but adds no value.
- Waste from *transporting materials* from one location to another. Any form of motion is waste, whether it involves the movement of people, materials, part-finished items or finished goods. Reducing movement is one of the benefits of work cell production.
- Waste in *production process procedures and methods*. Activities within manufacturing operations that do not add value should be eliminated.
- Waste from *time spent idle waiting for machines* to complete a process. The aim should be to maximise the use of the worker, not the machine.
- Waste from the manufacture of *defective items*. If defective items are spotted before they leave the factory, they must be either scrapped or re-worked. If they are not discovered until after they have been delivered to the customer, costs will arise from handling the complaint and having to take back and replace the item. Even more significantly, poor-quality output risks the loss of customer goodwill.

1.8 Continuous improvement/Kaizen costing

Continuous improvement, or 'Kaizen', is an integral part of the just-in-time management philosophy. 'Kaizen' is a Japanese term meaning to improve processes via small, incremental amounts rather than through large innovations. Kaizen costing is a planning method used during the manufacturing cycle that emphasises reducing variable costs of a period below the cost level in the base period. The target reduction rate is the ratio of the target reduction amount to the cost base.

- The organisation should always seek perfection. Perfection is never achieved, so there must always be some scope for improving on current methods and procedures. Improvements should be sought all the time.
- Improvements will be small and numerous rather than occasional and far-reaching.
- Cost reduction targets are set and applied on a more frequent basis than standard costs, Typically these targets are set on a monthly basis whereas standards within a traditional standard costing system are set annually or perhaps semi-annually.
- Variance analysis involves the comparison of target Kaizen costs versus actual cost reduction amounts achieved. This contrasts sharply with standard costing where the variance analysis involves the comparison of actual and "standard" costs.
- Under Kaizen costing investigation occurs when target reductions are not attained in spite of the fact that improvements may have been made during the period. Under standard costing investigation occurs when standards are not met.

- The search for perfection should involve all employees, and be part of the culture of the organisation. Kaizen costing principles acknowledge that workers are closest to the process and thus may have a superior knowledge of operations. This contrasts with a traditional standard costing system in which standards are developed by managers and engineers.

The continuous improvement philosophy contrasts sharply with the concept underlying business process re-engineering (BPR). BPR is concerned with making far-reaching one-off changes to improve operations or processes.

2 Computer aided systems

2.1 Computer integrated manufacturing (CIM)

DEFINITION

CIM is defined as 'the use of computers and other advanced manufacturing techniques to monitor and perform manufacturing tasks'.

CIM is defined as 'the use of computers and other advanced manufacturing techniques to monitor and perform manufacturing tasks'.

CIM enables a firm to link all its functions (both offices and shop floor) to a system of total automation using computers. As a result, firms will be able to manufacture one-of-a-kind products in small batches for specific customers at short notice. This replaces the much criticised mass production of often defective, unsaleable standard items with a job-shop production of high quality unique items. This approach reduces processing time, cuts finished goods inventory, reduces direct labour costs and speeds up response times.

2.2 CAD, CAE and CAM

The automated factory has to be capable of performing various functions with the aid of computers including product design, engineering and manufacturing.

DEFINITION

Computer Aided Design (CAD) is defined as 'computer based technology allowing interactive design and testing of a manufacturing component on a visual display terminal'.

Computer Aided Design (CAD) is defined as computer based technology allowing interactive design and testing of a manufacturing component on a visual display terminal'.

Designers can move pieces of a design around their drawings and manipulate them to see how the shapes change from various angles on their CAD terminals. Although there is an initial high cost, the benefits are quickly realised.

Computer Aided Engineering (CAE) enables designers to test whether their design can be manufactured on the available machines and ascertain the cost. This has eliminated much of the effort hitherto carried out by production engineers.

DEFINITION

A **CAM system** uses 'computer-based technology to permit the programming and control of production equipment in the manufacturing task.'

Once the CAE system has verified the feasibility of a new design, the necessary information for manufacture can be transmitted to a **Computer Aided Manufacturing system (CAM)**. A CAM system uses 'computer-based technology to permit the programming and control of production equipment in the manufacturing task'.

Such a system cuts the time lag between design and manufacturing, and the time taken setting and retooling machines for a new product.

2.3 Flexible manufacturing system (FMS)

DEFINITION

FMS has been defined as 'a bundle of machines that can be reprogrammed to switch from one production run to another'.

FMS has been defined as 'a bundle of machines that can be reprogrammed to switch from one production run to another'.

FMS consists of a cluster of machine tools and a system of conveyor belts that shuttle the work piece from tool to tool in a similar fashion to the traditional transfer line used in mass (large batch) production. Thus the benefits lie in being able to switch quickly from making one product to another.

The major strength of an FMS system is its ability to manufacture not just a family of parts, but also a family of products.

The following benefits of FMS have been identified:

- **More variety of products** as compared to conventional automation without the low rate of capacity utilisation of a typical job shop system.
- **Better product quality** thanks to accuracy and repeatability of the production process.
- **Shorter machine setup times** for new production runs. This results in reduced lead times to meet customer demands. This, in turn, decreases work-in-progress inventories and plant space.
- **Reduced labour costs and the capital costs** of human environmental protection. This offers a stability in production even with machine breakdown, because of computer scheduling, which also allows instant responses to changes in demand.

3 Resource planning systems

3.1 Material requirements planning (MRP I)

DEFINITION

MRP I – a system that converts a production schedule into a listing of the materials and components required to meet that schedule, so that adequate stock levels are maintained and items are available when needed. (CIMA *Official Terminology*)

MRP I essentially replaces excessive inventories with better information systems. MRP I schedules the production of jobs through the factory and eliminates the excessive WIP inventory levels required to compensate for job-scheduling problems that arise in decoupled cost or operation centres. MRP I releases works orders for parts based upon a master production schedule and the current number and location of parts within the plant.

If there is an order for 100 units of a product, it may be that the economic lot size indicates that 500 should be produced. A Bill of Materials is programmed into the computer.

The computer will record the number of inventory components required along with time standards for moving, any waiting, setting up and running. This information allows production to be time phased so that the final assembly can begin with all the required components at the ready. The key factor in MRP I is that it is demand dependent. Finished products are assembled to order from families of standard components. This is in contrast to traditional systems where components are ordered on the EOQ basis remote from the pattern of final product demand.

3.2 Manufacturing resource planning (MRP II)

DEFINITION

Manufacturing resource planning (MRP II) – expansion of material requirements planning (MRP I) to give a broader approach than MRP I to the planning and scheduling of resources, embracing areas such as finance, logistics, engineering and marketing. (CIMA *Official Terminology*)

KEY POINT

If correctly applied, MRP II provides a common database for the different functional units such as manufacturing, purchasing and finance within a firm.

Manufacturing resource planning (MRP II) is an expansion of material requirements planning (MRP I) to give a broader approach than MRP I to the planning and scheduling of resources, embracing areas such as finance, logistics, engineering and marketing. (CIMA *Official Terminology*, 2000)

MRP II adds the MRP I schedule into a capacity planning system and then builds the information into a production schedule. It is also seen as a link between strategic planning and manufacturing control. The sequence of events is as follows:

Product demand forecast prepared

↓

Manufacturing plan prepared

↓

Master production schedule prepared

- Inventory file
- Product structure file
- Production routing file

↓

Materials requirements demand

(The essential area covered by MRP I: master production schedule prepared, inventory file, product structure file, production routing file)

↓

Time schedule prepared

↓

Production capacity checked

↓

Manufacturing plan executed

3.3 Enterprise resource planning (ERP)

DEFINITION

ERP is a software system which is designed to support and automate the business processes of medium and large enterprises.

In the 1960s the focus of manufacturing systems embraced 'traditional' stock control concepts such as the EOQ. In the 1970s the focus changed to MRP I, enabling sub-assemblies and components to be planned for on a timely basis. In the 1980s this concept evolved into MRP II, extending MRP I first to planning and distribution management. In the 1990s MRP II was further extended into areas such as finance, human resources, project management, etc, and the concept of ERP was born since it encompassed all the activities carried on within the enterprise.

ERP is multi-module application software that helps a manufacturer (or other business) to manage the important components of its business, including product planning, procuring parts, maintaining inventories, dealing with suppliers, providing customer service and tracking orders. It can also include modules to manage the finance and human resources responsibilities of a business.

ERP therefore attempts to provide a **total integrated solution** to integrate the suppliers and customers into the manufacturing environment of the organisation. The current market leader in providing ERP software is the company SAP with its product SAP R/3. Other products are offered by companies such as Oracle and IBM.

Traditional application packages within a business (e.g. payroll, or purchasing) operate independently of each other within the boundaries of their function. The power of an ERP system is that it brings all these packages together, using data stored in a single relational database, so that the data can be used by multiple users and for multiple purposes. Initially the high cost of software and hardware meant that only the largest companies could consider adopting an ERP approach. However, the advent of cheap powerful PCs and development of affordable Relational Database Management Systems (RDBMS) have enabled an increasing number of companies to adopt ERP. The different geographical locations can be linked using Electronic Data Interchange (EDI) or the Internet.

While MRP systems were originally designed for manufacturing companies only, ERP can be implemented in **any type of business organisation**. Benefits are not typically enjoyed immediately, but most companies who have chosen the ERP route believe that the integration of all their activities is a necessary step towards the world class excellence that they are seeking.

4 Cost reduction programmes

4.1 Cost reduction versus cost control

It is important to distinguish between cost control and cost reduction.

Cost control is the system whereby limits (budgets, standards) are set for particular costs and actual costs are monitored against these. The reasons for variances are sought and corrective action taken where necessary.

DEFINITION

Cost reduction is the reduction in unit cost of goods or services without impairing suitability for the use intended (CIMA *Official Terminology*).

Cost reduction is the reduction in unit cost of goods or services without impairing suitability for the use intended (CIMA *Official Terminology*, 2000). Cost reduction relates to the level at which the cost limits are set in the first place. It involves a detailed analysis of the components of the good or service to determine whether any components can be dropped or modified to reduce cost, without detracting from their appeal to the customer.

Cost reduction is achieved through the application of **value engineering**, incorporating **value analysis** and **functional analysis.**

4.2 The value analysis approach

Value analysis is a systematic interdisciplinary examination of factors affecting the cost of a product or service, in order to devise means of achieving the specified purpose most economically at the required standard of quality and reliability (CIMA *Official Terminology*, 2000). Value analysis was described in Chapter 6.

4.3 Functional analysis

DEFINITION

Functional analysis is an analysis of the relationships between product functions, their perceived value to the customer and their cost of provision (CIMA *Official Terminology*).

Functional analysis is an analysis of the relationships between product functions, their perceived value to the customer and their cost of provision (CIMA *Official Terminology*, 2000).

Functional analysis uses the functions of a product as the cost object and is used either in initial designs or in the review of existing products. It can be extended to services, overhead expenses, and organisation structure and even to the overall strategy of the company (Innes et al *Contemporary Cost Management*).

DEFINITION

Value engineering is an activity which helps to design products which meet customer needs at a lower cost while assuming the required standard of quality and reliability.

Functional analysis uses the nine basic steps of **value engineering** as its essential technique. These are:

1	Choose the object of analysis – product, service or overhead area	
2	Select the members of the team (this will be inter-departmental with people either seconded or especially brought in)	
3	Gather information	This is the main sphere of functional analysis
4	Define the functions of the object	
5	Draw a functional family tree	
6	Evaluate the function.	
7	Suggest alternatives and compare these with the current or target (expected) cost	
8	Choose the alternative operations	
9	Review the actual results	

At the end of the exercise, a new product design that may be cheaper, but certainly more profitable, will have been developed. This is the final part of the evaluation. Possible savings might be:

- reduced usage of material, use of cheaper substitute, reduction in the need for storage
- wages might be reduced through further mechanisation (this could also cut inspection costs and reduce reject rates and rework)
- possible reduction in overheads especially if storage and inspection are being reduced.

Innes et al suggest that, to measure the real value of such cost savings, the accountant must explore the impact of changes on future cash flows and ideally translate these into a net present value through discounting them at the corporate cost of capital.

4.4 The traditional approach to cost control and reduction

To survive and be continually successful and competitive, all organisations need to rigorously control their costs. This requires an effective cost control system.

Crowningshield and Gorman identify six requirements of such a system.

(a) **Effective delegation of authority and assignment of responsibility** for incurring costs.

(b) An **agreed plan** that sets up objectives and goals to be achieved.

(c) **Motivation** to encourage individuals to reach the goals established and agreed.

(d) **Timely reporting**.

(e) The **recommendations and action** must follow.

(f) More importantly there must be an **effective system of follow-up** to ensure that the corrective measures are being effectively implemented.

In the light of the above, there is now a strong body of opinion that the real emphasis of cost reduction reports is not the eventual product cost, or the cost saving, but the actual control of cost drivers. This requires laying the cost driver at the door of the person responsible.

5 Just-In-Time (JIT)

5.1 Introduction

DEFINITION

Just-in-time – a system whose objective is to produce or to procure products or components as they are required by a customer or for use, rather than for stock. A just-in-time system is a 'pull' system, which responds to demand, in contrast to a 'push' system, in which stocks act as buffers between the different elements of the system, such as purchasing, production and sales. (CIMA *Official Terminology*)

Just-in-time is a system whose objective is to produce or to procure products or components as they are required by a customer or for use, rather than for stock. A just-in-time system is a 'pull' system, which responds to demand, in contrast to a 'push' system, in which stocks act as buffers between the different elements of the system, such as purchasing, production and sales (CIMA *Official Terminology*, 2000).

This system has gained considerable popularity in both the United States and Europe. It has a wide ranging impact upon many of the traditional organisational functions.

The production of components only when they are needed and in the quantity that is needed shortens lead times and virtually eliminates work in progress and finished goods inventories.

- **Conventional production** provides monthly production schedules to every process including the final assembly line. The preceding process supplies the parts to the subsequent process (**push through system).** Each process must adjust their schedule simultaneously, requiring back up inventory between processes.
- **JIT** does not provide simultaneous schedules to every process, only for the final assembly line. Goods are built for the customer, not for stock. The system works on a **pull through basis**, drawing components through the system. It can respond quickly drawing parts as required. As soon as items are completed in one process, they are passed to the next process and this stimulates production. This is known as a Kanban system.

5.2 Impact on purchasing and production

Suppliers

Under JIT, a buyer can reduce the number of suppliers. Long-term contracts and single sourcing are advocated to strengthen buyer-supplier relationships and tends to result in a higher quality product. Inventory problems are shifted back onto suppliers, with deliveries being made as required.

JIT delivery and transportation

The spread of JIT in the production process inevitably impinges upon those in delivery and transportation.

The use of JIT puts new demands on the schedules of the hauliers. Tighter schedules are required, with penalties for non-delivery. The haulier is regarded as almost a partner to the manufacturer.

Impact on cost systems

Costing systems need to be simpler and more flexible. However, before making any changes, a thorough review of the costing systems is required.

Inventory valuation

The inevitable reduction in inventory levels will reduce the time taken to count inventory and the clerical cost.

As a final point on JIT, the system also renders the EOQ model virtually useless. The student will recall that the optimal EOQ equals:

$$\sqrt{\frac{2C_oD}{C_h}}$$

C_o = variable costs of placing a production/purchase order

D = annual demand for inventory item,

C_h = annual holding costs of one inventory item.

JIT causes the ordering cost to decline towards zero and since the model is optimal when holding costs equal ordering costs, the optimum becomes a virtually zero inventory level.

5.3 Eliminating waste

DEFINITION

Waste is defined as any activity performed within a manufacturing company that does not add value to the product.

Waste is defined as any activity performed within a manufacturing company that does not add value to the product.

JIT attempts to eliminate waste at every stage of the manufacturing process notably by the:

- elimination of WIP by reducing batch sizes (often to one)
- elimination of raw materials inventories by the suppliers delivering direct to the shop floor just in time for use
- elimination of scrap and rework by an emphasis on total quality control of design, of the process, and of the materials
- elimination of finished goods inventories by reducing lead times so that all products are made to order
- elimination of material handling costs by re-design of the shop floor so that goods move directly between adjacent work centres.

The combination of these concepts brings about JIT, which provides a smooth flow of work through the manufacturing plant, a flexible production process which is responsive to the customer's requirements and massive reductions in capital tied up in inventories. The end result of JIT is radical improvements in true productivities with more products of higher quality getting to the customers more quickly at a lower cost.

5.4 The characteristics of an 'ideal' factory layout

Far from 'batching up', JIT manufacturers aim for smaller and smaller batch size (and hence shorter and shorter lead times) in order to become even more reactive to customer demands.

Briefly the characteristics of an ideal system would seem to be the following:

- it should have a short manufacturing cycle time, to minimise work-in-progress inventory and maximise customer service
- it should have manufacturing batch sizes identical to customer order quantities (even if this is one), to minimise finished goods inventory and maximise customer responsiveness
- it should be flexible enough to make products in the same order as the customer wants them, again in order to minimise finished goods inventory and maximise responsiveness

- it should be able to rapidly trap and cure deviations from quality standards in order to maximise customer service and minimise scrap and rework
- it should call in raw materials as late as possible in order to minimise raw material inventory.

5.5 JIT purchase contracts

Obtaining the co-operation of suppliers is a vital first step when implementing a JIT system. A company is a long way towards JIT if its suppliers will give it shorter lead times, deliver smaller quantities more often, guarantee a low reject rate and perform quality assurance inspection at source.

If a company's suppliers make more frequent deliveries of small quantities of material, then it can ensure that each delivery is just enough to meet its immediate production schedule. This will keep its inventory as low as possible.

If suppliers will guarantee the quality of the material they deliver and will inspect it at source, then a company can make enormous savings on both time and labour. Materials handling time will be saved because, as there is no need to move the stock into a store, the goods can be delivered directly to a workstation on the shop floor. Inspection time and costs can be eliminated and the labour required for reworking defective material or returning goods to the supplier can be saved.

In return for this improved service from the supplier, the company can guarantee to give more business to fewer suppliers, place long-term purchase orders and give the suppliers a long-range forecast of its requirements.

5.6 Multifunctional workers

A key element of JIT manufacturing is the flexibility of the workforce. Demarcation of functions must be eliminated and replaced by a team approach where each person is trained in multiple functions and can move quickly within the plant to meet the changing requirements of the customers. The same kind of flexible team approach must also be taken by non-direct personnel such as management accountants. Management accountants must be willing to see their role change significantly as the needs of the business change and, in fact, initiate change as part of the continuous improvement concept of JIT manufacturing.

There must be a clear and shared understanding of what the critical success factors of the business are. There must be recognition throughout all levels of the organisation of what the overall business objectives are, and how each unit or department can contribute to satisfying these objectives. The management process itself must be integrated in the sense of sharing a common purpose and approach.

In order for the business objectives to be understood and accepted by personnel at all levels, communications and training become increasingly important. Organisations must be slimmer, with fewer levels of management and a removal of traditional barriers. Only by doing this is there a possibility that the top management philosophy and objectives will filter down through the organisation. Equally important, it is the only way that the degree of adherence to these objectives at lower levels will become visible to senior management.

5.7 Accounting for costs under JIT

Investment in advanced manufacturing technologies (AMT) dramatically changes cost behaviour patterns. The introduction of computer technicians, software engineers, and programmers replaces traditional direct labour. Most variable costs, other than direct material and energy, also disappear. Overheads, both conversion and non-conversion become an even bigger part of the total cost.

From this outline, the student should observe:

- Costs are only allowed to accumulate when the product is finished. This directs effort and attention towards output rather than production.
- JIT emphasises the elimination of waste. Thus allowances for waste, scrap and rework are removed from the standard costs and detailed reports produced on these items. This means a move to the ideal standard, rather than an achievable standard.
- Output is credited at standard. Thus any difference in input and output is a variance, which can be analysed as either a cost or efficiency variance.

5.8 Cost classification under JIT

In a JIT and hence advanced manufacturing environment, cost classifications will change:

	Traditional	*JIT*
Material handling	Indirect	Direct
Repair & maintenance	Largely direct	Direct
Energy	Indirect	Direct
Operating supplies	Indirect	Direct
Supervision	Indirect	Direct
Production support	Indirect	Largely direct
Depreciation	Indirect	Direct

Inevitably many of these costs will be allocated to products on the basis of their cost drivers, hence using activity based costing.

5.9 Revised performance measures

The introduction of JIT related manufacturing will also change the performance measures.

Traditional	*JIT*
Direct labour (efficiency, utilisation, productivity)	Total Head Count productivity (Note the emphasis on 'people' rather than labour)
Machine utilisation	Days of inventory
Stock turnover	Group or cell incentives
Cost variances	Knowledge and capability based promotion
Individual incentives	Ideas generated and implemented
Seniority	Customer complaints

6 Synchronous manufacturing

6.1 Introduction

The profitability of the modern organisation is dependent on a number of factors, not least of which is the rate at which sales are made. Other factors include the reduction of costs and maximisation of efficiency.

Management must identify what is referred to as 'the bottleneck factor'. This is the factor of production that limits the organisation's ability to increase the rate at which sales are achieved. You should recall that this is similar in principle to the limiting factor used in contribution analysis as part of short-term decision-making.

KEY POINT

The combination of management policies and practices to improve efficiency and identify and alleviate the bottleneck factor are collectively referred to as synchronous management and manufacturing practices.

The combination of management policies and practices to improve efficiency and identify and alleviate the bottleneck factor are collectively referred to as synchronous management and manufacturing practices.

6.2 Optimised production technology and synchronous manufacturing

Optimised Production Technology (OPT) has developed out of MRP systems. It is both a technique, and in its diminutive form of OPT, a computer software package. Although the initials are used interchangeably, the emphasis in this section is upon the technique. Like its precursor, MRP, OPT requires detailed information about inventory levels, product structures, routings and the set-up and operation timing for each and every procedure within each product. However, in stark contrast to MRP, the technique actively seeks to identify what prevents output and hence productivity from being higher by distinguishing between bottleneck and non-bottleneck resources. A bottleneck might be a machine whose capacity limits the throughput of the whole production process. It might be a key department with highly specialist skills that holds up the process.

To avoid large build-ups of inventory, the non-bottleneck areas should be balanced to produce what the bottleneck can absorb in the short term. Thus, if the bottleneck can only absorb 60% of the output of the non-bottleneck areas, then the output should be scaled down to that level, since any excess over that level is only going to increase the piles of work-in-progress inventory standing about. It has also been suggested that overhead should be absorbed on the basis of throughput based upon the duration of production from the initial input of raw materials and components to the delivery of the finished products. By adopting this approach, management can see how costs can be reduced by cutting the throughput time.

6.3 Synchronous manufacturing and the theory of constraints

DEFINITION

Theory of constraints (TOC) is an approach to production management that aims to maximise sales revenue less material and variable overhead cost. It focuses on factors such as bottlenecks which act as constraints to this maximisation.

Synchronous manufacturing is a combination of MRP and OPT and JIT and quality. The term was coined in 1984, as an attempt to widen the perceived limited scope of OPT. The pioneer behind both techniques is a mathematician, Eli Goldratt, famed for his book *The Goal*. Goldratt coined the term 'theory of constraints' (TOC) to describe the process of identifying the constraints that restrict output and then taking steps to eliminate them.

Theory of constraints (TOC) is an approach to production management that aims to maximise sales revenue less material and variable overhead cost. It focuses on factors such as bottlenecks which act as constraints to this maximisation.

The steps to follow in TOC are as follows.

Step 1

Identify the bottlenecks in the system. These are the constraints that restrict output from being increased.

Step 2

Concentrate on each bottleneck in turn to ensure that they are being fully and efficiently utilised.

Step 3

Scale down the throughput of non-bottleneck activities to match what can be dealt with by the bottlenecks.

Step 4

Remove bottlenecks if possible, e.g. by hiring in more skilled workers or buying a larger machine.

Step 5

Since TOC is a continuous improvement process, return to Step 1 and re-evaluate the system now that some bottlenecks have been removed.

Goldratt advises on the use of throughput accounting (TA) to apply TOC principles. This is covered later in this chapter.

Synchronous manufacturing is a wider concept than OPT or TOC. Umble and Srikanth (1990) have defined synchronous manufacturing as:

> '... an all-encompassing manufacturing management philosophy that includes a consistent set of principles, procedures and techniques where every action is evaluated in terms of the common goal of the organisation.'

The use of the term 'philosophy' is deliberate. OPT is perceived as narrow and very technique-based. The use of the term 'optimised' implied that a theoretical optimum existed and could be achieved. While such a goal might be possible, it implies that a level can be achieved where one can be satisfied, content or even complacent. Such a theoretical level is conceptually contrary to the notions of continuous improvement. Equally, the terms 'production' and 'technology' were perceived as failing to encompass the total range of constraints and challenges faced by the firm in trying to achieve its objectives. Markets, logistics, managerial ability, cultural and behavioural problems can all place constraints upon production capacity.

In widening the understanding of terms, it is worth adding that resource is not just confined to materials. Resource means materials, components, the direct labour force and machinery and equipment.

Seven principles are associated with synchronous manufacturing.

- Management should not focus on balancing capacities, but focus on synchronising the flow.
- The marginal value of time at a bottleneck resource is equal to the throughput rate of the products processed by the bottleneck. That is the area of potential savings and improvements.
- The marginal value of time at a non-bottleneck resource is negligible. As we have already seen, lack of synchronisation in these areas merely builds up inventory.

- The level of utilisation of a non-bottleneck resource is controlled by other constraints within the system. (If you cannot get it painted, why build it?)
- Resources must be utilised, not simply activated.
- A transfer batch may not, and many times should not, be equal to a process batch.
- A process batch should be variable both along its route and over time. Thus, batches of work along the line must reflect what can be taken by the next area.

Synchronous manufacturing purports to be an improvement on JIT-based techniques by advocating a more focused approach. JIT works upon the principle of continuous improvement. Such an approach is prone to overlook the capacity constraints upon resources in advance. Rather it waits until the problems occur and disrupt the system. Synchronous manufacturing, by balancing throughput so that there is an even flow and no inventory build-up, has to anticipate where the logjams are, accommodate them in the short term, and then plan for their eventual removal.

7 Throughput accounting

DEFINITION

Throughput is the rate of production of a defined process over a stated period of time. Rates may be expressed in terms of units of products, batches produced, turnover, or other meaningful measurements. (CIMA *Official Terminology*)

KEY POINT

The value of throughput can be measured as:

Sales revenue minus Direct materials costs

Throughput accounting is a method of accounting that focuses on throughput, and relates costs of production to throughput.

Throughput is 'the rate of production of a defined process over a stated period of time. Rates may be expressed in terms of units of products, batches produced, turnover, or other meaningful measurements.' (CIMA *Official Terminology*)

A basic concept in throughput accounting is that the production manager has a quantity of resources available, in the form of labour resources, capital equipment, buildings and so on. The cost of these resources is assumed to be time-related, and so fixed for a given period of time. Resources are used to create throughput. Direct materials are turned into finished items and sold, and the value of throughput can be measured as:

Sales revenue minus Direct materials costs

Throughput is only created when the finished output is sold. If items are produced and put into finished goods stock, no throughput is created. The aim is not production at any price. Throughput accounting focuses on the need to achieve sales with items produced, and stocks are only considered desirable to the extent that they can increase throughput. In this respect, the principles of throughput accounting are consistent with the principles of *just in time production (JIT).*

7.1 Influences on throughput

Factors that affect the value of throughput in any period are:

- the selling price of items sold
- the purchase cost of direct materials
- efficiency in the usage of direct materials
- the volume of throughput.

Constraints on throughput could be:

- selling prices that are too high (thereby limiting sales demand) or too low (thereby restricting sales revenue)
- unreliable product quality (resulting in scrapped items or items returned by customers)
- unreliable supplies of key materials (so that production cannot be scheduled in an optimal way)
- a shortage of production resources (leading to bottlenecks).

DEFINITION

A **bottleneck** is an activity within an organisation which has a lower capacity than preceding or subsequent activities, thereby limiting throughput. (CIMA *Official Terminology*)

Management should aim to maximise throughput with available resources. Some resources might be in short supply, and so act as a constraint on production. Shortages of resources are referred to as bottlenecks. A *bottleneck* is 'an activity within an organisation which has a lower capacity than preceding or subsequent activities, thereby limiting throughput'. (CIMA, *Official Terminology*)

The task of management is to eliminate bottlenecks and other constraints. Removing a bottleneck in one part of the production process should result in higher throughput, although the bottleneck will often switch to another part of the production process. Management should then focus on eliminating the new bottleneck, in order to increase throughput still further.

7.2 Throughput accounting reports

Results in a given period can be reported to management in terms of throughput achieved, as follows.

Products	*A*	*B*	*C*	*D*	*E*	*F*
	£	£	£	£	£	£
Sales						
Direct materials						
Throughput						
Labour costs						
Other production overheads						
Administration costs						
Marketing costs						
Profit						

KEY POINT

Similarity between throughput accounting and marginal costing, but with only direct materials costs treated as a marginal cost item.

Any closing inventory is valued at direct materials cost only, and no direct labour or production overhead costs are added to stock values. You might see a similarity here between throughput accounting and marginal costing, but with only direct materials costs treated as a marginal cost item.

There is no profit, and so no value, in manufacturing for stock unless there is a clear link between producing for stock now in order to have the certainty of increasing future sales. This can happen, for example, when sales are seasonal. Stocks might be built up in advance of the high sales period, in order to meet sales demand when it eventually occurs. (If stocks are not built up in advance, the organisation will not have the resources to meet sales demand in the peak season.)

7.3 Throughput accounting performance measurements

In throughput accounting, only direct materials costs are regarded as variable costs. Direct labour costs and production overheads (conversion costs) are fixed costs, which may be grouped together and labelled as 'total factory costs'.

Performance measures used in throughput accounting are:

- return per factory hour
- throughput accounting ratio.

7.4 Return per factory hour

This is a measure of throughput per hour of the bottleneck resource, and is therefore:

$$\frac{\text{Sales minus direct materials cost}}{\text{Usage (in hours)of the bottleneck resource}}$$

This measurement of performance is similar in concept to the contribution per unit of scarce resource. This is a marginal costing concept, which is used for short-term decision making when a key resource is in scarce supply.

Note: We say 'per hour' but this depends on the process and what is being produced: it may be more appropriate to measure 'return per day' or 'return per minute'.

KEY POINT

The throughput accounting ratio is:

$$\frac{\text{Return per factory hour}}{\text{Total cost per factory hour}}$$

Management should try to achieve a high throughput ratio, i.e. greater than 1.

7.5 Throughput accounting ratio

The throughput accounting ratio is the ratio of the throughput earned and the cost per 'factory hour', where factory hour is measured as the usage in hours of the bottleneck resource. The ratio is therefore:

$$\frac{\text{Return per factory hour}}{\text{Total cost per factory hour}}$$

Management should try to achieve a high throughput ratio, i.e. greater than 1.

Example

A company manufactures a single product which it sells for £10 per unit. The direct materials cost of the product is £3 per unit. Other factory costs total £50,000 each month. The bottleneck factor in production is the assembly of the unit, which is a labour-intensive process. There are 20,000 labour hours available in assembly each month, and each unit takes two hours to assemble.

Required:

Calculate the budgeted rate per factory hour and the throughput ratio each month.

Solution

$$\text{Return per factory hour} = \frac{\text{Sales minus direct materials cost}}{\text{Usage of bottleneck resource}}$$

$$= \frac{£10 - £3}{2\,hours}$$

$$= £3.50$$

$$\text{Cost per factory hour} = \frac{\text{Total factory cost}}{\text{Bottleneck resource hours available}}$$

$$= \frac{£50{,}000}{20{,}000 \text{ hours}}$$

$$= £2.50$$

$$\text{Throughput accounting ratio} = \frac{\text{Return per factory hour}}{\text{Cost per factory hour}}$$

$$= \frac{£3.50}{£2.50}$$

$$= 1.4:1$$

Activity 1

X Limited manufactures a product that requires 1.5 hours of machining. Machine time is a bottleneck resource, due to the limited number of machines available. There are 10 machines available, and each machine can be used for up to 40 hours per week.

The product is sold for £85 per unit and the direct material cost per unit is £42.50. Total factory costs are £8,000 each week.

Required:

Calculate:

(a) the return per factory hour

(b) the throughput accounting ratio.

Feedback to this activity is at the end of the chapter.

7.6 Treatment of bottlenecks

Bottlenecks can be identified by profiling capacity usage through the system. Usually they will be areas of most heavy usage. Thus monitoring build-ups of inventory and traditional idle time and waiting time will indicate actual or impending bottlenecks.

Traditional efficiency measures will be important in managing bottlenecks. Changes in efficiency will indicate the presence of bottlenecks and the need for a response. This may take the form of creating short-term build-ups of stock to alleviate the problem. Another possible solution might be to prioritise the work at bottlenecks to ensure that throughput is achieved. Measures that highlight throughput per bottleneck will need to be developed.

In view of the fact that the JIT philosophy sees all non-value adding activities as potential waste, TA looks for anything that will enhance saleable output. Thus, anything that will reduce costly lead times, set-up times and waiting times will enhance the throughput. Again, these need to be identified and reported on and monitored to see if they are being reduced.

7.7 Other factors

All constraints should be considered in the reporting process. If quality is a throughput constraint, then detailed quality cost reports on rework, scrap levels and returns need to be added to the performance measuring process. Equally, if delivery times are crucial, then failure to meet delivery times needs to be reported. The essence of throughput accounting is contingent on what is needed and the circumstances that prevail.

7.8 Assessment

TA may seem to be going against the trend of emulating Japanese-style methods. It is a highly short-term perspective on costs, regarding only material as variable or directly activity-related. It neglects the costs of overhead and people. As a result, there will always be the risk of suboptimal profit performance. TA will really only work effectively where material remains a high proportion of the cost or selling price. Also, there must be a situation where demand is constant enough or high enough to always put pressure on output and production resources.

It is suggested that TA with its emphasis on direct material is an ideal complement to ABC which can draw attention to the overheads. In that way, a comprehensive cover of costs can be achieved.

KEY POINT

It is suggested that TA with its emphasis on direct material is an ideal complement to ABC which can draw attention to the overheads. In that way, a comprehensive cover of costs can be achieved.

8 Total quality management (TQM)

8.1 Introduction

TQM is 'an integrated and comprehensive system of planning and controlling all business functions so that products or services are produced which meet or exceed customer expectations.' (CIMA *Official Terminology*, 2000) TQM is a philosophy of business behaviour, embracing principles such as employee involvement, continuous improvement at all levels and customer focus, as well as being a collection of related techniques aimed at improving quality such as full documentation of activities, clear goal-setting and performance measurement from the customer perspective. Its origin lies primarily in Japanese organisations and it is argued that TQM has been a significant factor in Japanese global business success.

DEFINITION

TQM is an integrated and comprehensive system of planning and controlling all business functions so that products or services are produced which meet or exceed customer expectations. TQM is a philosophy of business behaviour, embracing principles such as employee involvement, continuous improvement at all levels and customer focus, as well as being a collection of related techniques aimed at improving quality such as full documentation of activities, clear goal-setting and performance measurement from the customer perspective.

The basic principle of TQM is that costs of prevention (getting things right first time) are less than the costs of correction.

KEY POINT

The basic principle of TQM is that costs of prevention (getting things right first time) are less than the costs of correction.

This contrasts with the 'traditional' UK approach that less than 100% quality is acceptable as the costs of improvement from say 90% to 100% outweigh the benefits. Thus in an analysis of quality related costs there may be a trade-off between a lowering of failure at the expense of increased prevention and appraisal costs.

Which view is correct is a matter of debate but the advocates of TQM would argue that in addition to the cost analysis above the impact of less than 100% quality in terms of lost potential for future sales also has to be taken into account.

It is apparent from the rather lengthy definition that TQM goes beyond the isolated notions of statistical quality control into the whole operating process. This means designing in quality manufacturing procedures possibly through the use of CAD/CAM, training all personnel involved with the product/service, continually maintaining equipment to ensure that standards remain up to specification and working with suppliers to eliminate defects. The latter may well involve the use of JIT. It is worth adding that TQM is expected to cross all the company's functional activities, even the accounting function.

8.2 Quality chains

The philosophy of TQM is based on the idea of a series of **quality chains** that may be broken at any point by one person or service not meeting the requirements of the customer.

The key to TQM is for everyone in the organisation to have well-defined 'customers', beyond the customers of the company, to anyone to whom an individual provides a service. Thus the 'paint shop' staff would be customers of the 'assembly shop' staff who would themselves be the customers of the 'machine shop' staff.

The idea is that the supplier-customer relationships would form a chain extending from the company's original suppliers through to its ultimate consumers. Areas of responsibility would need to be identified and a manager allocated to each, and then the customer/supplier chain established.

True to the principle outlined above the quality requirements of each 'customer' within the chain would be assessed, and meeting these would then become the responsibility of the 'suppliers' who form the preceding link in the chain.

8.3 Characteristics of TQM companies

Thackray has indicated the following features of companies that follow TQM:

- Absolute commitment by the chief executive and all senior managers to doing what is needed to change the culture.
- People are not afraid to try new things.
- Communication is excellent and multi-way.
- There is a real commitment to continuous improvement in all processes.
- Attention is focused first on the process and second on the results to encourage employees to look for potential improvements.
- Strict control systems are absent.

8.4 Analysis and restructuring of resources

DEFINITIONS

Discretionary activities are activities such as checking, chasing and other tasks related to product failures.

Core activities add direct value to the business. They use the specific skills of the particular employees being examined and are the reason for their employment.

Support activities are those activities that clearly support core activities and are thus necessary to allow core activities to add value.

In many businesses, employees' time is used up in **discretionary activities** such as checking, chasing and other tasks related to product failures. Some or even most of this time may be capable of being redeployed into the two other categories of work:

- core activities
- support activities.

Core activities add direct value to the business. They use the specific skills of the particular employees being examined and are the reason for their employment. Support activities are those activities that clearly support core activities and are thus necessary to allow core activities to add value.

Analysis of employees' time will provide a clearer view of the costs of poor quality and whether efforts in other departments could reduce the amount of time spent by a department further down the product chain on discretionary activities.

For example, suppose there are seven processes from purchasing of raw materials through various stages of production to delivery of the product to the customer. If each process is 90% effective then there will be only a 48% success rate at the end of the seventh stage (90% × 90% × 90% etc.). What happens in practice, however, may be that personnel employed in stage 4 of the process spend a lot of their time on discretionary activities trying to remedy the effect of defects at earlier stages. It is suggested that it would be more sensible for departments in the earlier stages to **get things right the first time**.

8.5 Quality circles

Quality circles consist of about 10 employees possessing relevant levels of skill, ranging from the shop floor through to management. They meet regularly to discuss the major aspect of quality, but other areas such as safety and productivity will also be dealt with.

The main aim is to be able to offer management:

- ideas connected with improvements and recommendations
- possible solutions and suggestions
- organising the implementation of the first two.

The development of quality circles allows the process of decision making to start at shop floor level, with the ordinary worker encouraged to comment and make suggestions, as well as being allowed to put them into practice. Circle members experience the responsibility for ensuring quality, and have the power to exercise verbal complaint. Quality circles may be applied at any level of organisational activity, being used to cover all aspects and could conceivably involve all employees.

Putting this system into practice can prove difficult. The well established system of hierarchical management is difficult to penetrate, and to some organisations it would present extreme changes. Some systems may not be able to accommodate such change, e.g., the armed forces or police force where a powerful hierarchy has developed.

8.6 Quality control

DEFINITION

Quality control is the process of:

- establishing standards of quality for a product or service
- establishing procedures or production methods that ought to ensure that these required standards of quality are met in a suitably high proportion of cases
- monitoring actual quality
- taking control action when actual quality falls below standard.

Quality control is the title given to the more traditional view of quality.

Quality control is the process of:

- establishing standards of quality for a product or service.
- establishing procedures or production methods that ought to ensure that these required standards of quality are met in a suitably high proportion of cases
- monitoring actual quality
- taking control action when actual quality falls below standard.

The contrast with TQM is that less than 100% quality may be regarded as acceptable. Eradicating the costs of failure of a product should be weighed against higher prevention costs for example. Charts such as **statistical control charts** are often used to monitor quality in such instances, especially in terms of the physical dimensions of the component parts of a product or the strength of a product.

8.7 Measurement of quality

Many companies in industrialised countries are adopting quality improvement as a primary corporate objective. As a management accountant this will impinge upon you in two ways. First, the implementation of TQM on all the company's functional activities. Secondly, and perhaps more important, where quality priorities are tied to enhancing the value of products/services that an entity provides to its customers. This covers a wide range of criteria. Measures that might be used to control and improve quality of performance include:

- proportion of deliveries made on time
- number of sub-standard products
- the amount of reworks
- frequency and length of machine breakdowns
- the launch time of new products
- number and gravity of customer complaints.

8.8 Quality related costs

CIMA *Official Terminology* defines and analyses the types of cost related to quality.

DEFINITION

Cost of quality is defined as the difference between the actual cost of producing, selling and supporting products or services and the equivalent costs if there were no failures during production or usage. (CIMA *Official Terminology*)

Cost of quality is defined as the difference between the actual cost of producing, selling and supporting products or services and the equivalent costs if there were no failures during production or usage. (CIMA *Official Terminology*, 2000)

The cost of quality can be analysed into:

- **Cost of conformance** – The cost of achieving specified quality standards.
  - **Cost of prevention** – The costs incurred prior to or during production in order to prevent substandard or defective products or services from being produced.
  - **Cost of appraisal** – Costs incurred in order to ensure that outputs produced meet required quality standards.
- **Cost of non-conformance** – The cost of failure to deliver the required standard of quality.
  - **Cost of internal failure** – The costs arising from inadequate quality that are identified before the transfer of ownership from supplier to purchaser.
  - **Cost of external failure** – The cost arising from inadequate quality discovered after the transfer of ownership from supplier to purchaser.

KEY POINT

Costs of non-conformance are costs required to evaluate, dispose of and either correct or replace a defective or deficient product.

8.9 Classification of quality costs

From the CIMA definitions quoted above, we can analyse and illustrate the different costs of quality.

(a) Costs of non-conformance are costs required to evaluate, dispose of and either correct or replace a defective or deficient product. Costs of non-conformance can be sub-divided under two headings:

- **Internal failure costs** – Failure costs discovered **before** the product is delivered to customers. Examples include:
  - rework or rectification costs
  - net cost of scrap
  - disposal of defective products
  - downtime or idle time due to quality problems.
- **External failure costs** – Failure costs discovered **after** the product is delivered to the customer. Examples include:
  - complaint investigation and processing
  - warranty claims
  - cost of lost sales
  - product recalls.

The inclusion of **cost of lost sales** emphasises another important feature of TQM, that it crosses the traditional functions within an organisation. Marketing and sales have to be concerned about the quality of the product they are presenting.

Product recalls do little for the image of the product/service. While it does show concern for quality and safety, it emphasises that a procedure failed somewhere and was not detected until too late.

KEY POINT

Costs of conformance are costs required to prevent the production of poor quality goods in the first place.

(b) Costs of conformance are costs required to prevent the production of poor quality goods in the first place. Costs of conformance are also subdivided:

- **Appraisal costs** – Costs of monitoring and inspecting products in terms of specified standards before the products are released to customers. This is very much the traditional view of quality control. Examples might be:
  - the capital cost of measurement equipment
  - inspection and testing
  - product quality audits
  - process control monitoring
  - test equipment expense.
- **Prevention costs** – Investments in machinery, technology, education and training programmes designed to reduce the number of defective products during production. Examples are:
  - customer surveys
  - research of customer needs
  - field trials
  - quality education and training programmes
  - supplier reviews
  - investment in improved production equipment
  - quality engineering
  - quality circles.

In western industrialised countries, products have always been considered defective if they do not conform to internally set and agreed specifications and standards. Today, however, a customer has a higher expectation of the product he is buying and his standards may be higher than that of the manufacturer. The customer of the future will expect a longer guarantee for his durable product, possibly even over life. Thus prevention will be about making design standards that conform to the expectations of customers in the form of 'super-prevention costs'.

9 Learning curves and experience curves

9.1 Introduction

Accountants tend to assume that, within the relevant range of activity, costs display linear characteristics so that the variable cost per unit and the total fixed cost remain unchanged and can be forecast given that the level of activity is known.

This assumption is not always valid, particularly in cases where a **learning curve effect** applies. In such a case, analysis of the learning curve provides a forecasting method which can be used in the standard costing process to estimate direct and indirect labour costs.

9.2 The learning curve rule

It has been observed in some industries, particularly where skilled labour predominates such as in aircraft manufacture, that as more of the same units are produced, there is a reduction in the time taken to manufacture them until the learning process is complete.

DEFINITION

A learning curve is the mathematical expression of the phenomenon that when complex and labour intensive procedures are repeated, unit labour times tend to decrease at a constant rate.

KEY POINT

If, for instance, there is a 60% learning curve, the cumulative average time per unit of output will fall to 60% of what it was before, every time output is doubled.

A learning curve is the mathematical expression of the phenomenon that when complex and labour intensive procedures are repeated, unit labour times tend to decrease at a constant rate.

The learning curve phenomenon states that **each time the number of units produced is doubled, the cumulative average time per unit is reduced by a constant percentage**. If this constant reduction is 20%, this is referred to as an 80% learning curve, and a 10% reduction as a 90% learning curve. This is an important phenomenon that has been empirically observed. Note, the cumulative average time is the average time per unit for all **units produced up to the present time**, including right back to the very first unit made.

If, for instance, there is a 60% learning curve, the cumulative average time per unit of output will fall to 60% of what it was before, **every time output is doubled**.

This will be illustrated by assuming that it has taken 400 direct labour hours to manufacture the first unit of a new product. As in the past for this business it is anticipated that a 75% learning curve will occur. A schedule can be drawn up with the following important headings and calculations:

(1) *Cumulative number of units*	*(2)* *Cumulative average time per unit*	*(1) × (2)* *Cumulative total hours*
1	400	400
2	300 (75% of 400)	600
4	225 (75% of 300)	900

The first two columns form the basis for the calculations as the cumulative total hours in the third column are obtained by multiplying together the figures in columns (1) and (2). As the output doubles the cumulative average time per unit is 75% of the previous figure.

Therefore, if 1 unit has been produced already taking 400 hours, the production of another similar unit will only take (600 – 400), i.e. 200 hours in the situation of a 75% learning curve. Once 2 units have been produced, and the learning process continues, the production of 2 more units will take only (900 – 600), i.e. 300 hours. This represents 150 hours per unit.

Activity 2

Determine the cumulative total hours for 8 units and hence determine the total time to make the last four units.

Feedback to this activity is at the end of the chapter.

9.3 Learning curve graph

The learning curve effect can be shown on a graph, or learning curve, either for unit times or for cumulative average times or costs.

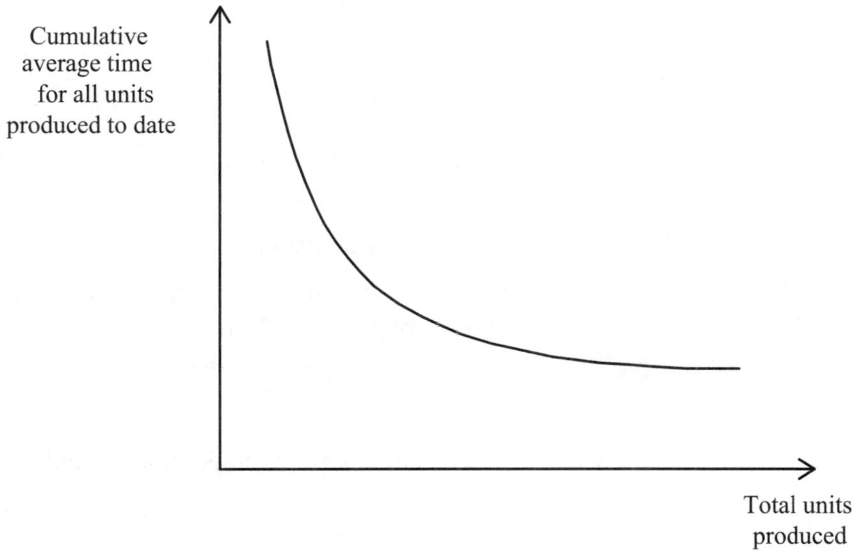

As can be seen on the graph, eventually the curve becomes almost horizontal when many units have been produced, as the learning effect is lost and production time per unit becomes a constant.

9.4 The relevance of the learning effect to standard costing

A standard cost of a product is the planned unit cost of the product during a specific period of time. If the product enjoys a learning effect, but the effect is ignored, then the standard cost will be too high, since the fact that the products will take progressively less labour will have been ignored.

Budgeted costs must therefore take into account any expected learning curve when they are being formulated.

The following example illustrates one possible approach to taking the effect into account.

Example

Rachel plc expects to produce four machines next month. Each machine will require £200 of components to be incorporated into a frame costing £100. The first machine is expected to require 100 hours of labour, although a 90% learning effect will apply throughout the month. Labour is paid £8 per hour, while variable overheads are charged at £12 per hour. Calculate the budgeted average cost per machine produced next month.

Solution

Hours for first machine = 100

∴ Average hours for first four machines $= 100 \times 0.9^2$ = 81 hours

∴ Total hours for first four machines $= 4 \times 81$ = 324 hours

Total cost next month will be:

	£
Materials $4 \times (£200 + £100)$	1,200
Labour $324 \times £8$	2,592
Overheads $324 \times £12$	3,888
	7,680

The budgeted average per machine is $\frac{£7,680}{4} = £1,920$.

9.5 Learning curve equation

The learning curve describing the cumulative average time per unit plotted against cumulative number of units can be represented by an equation of the form (as per the CIMA *Mathematical Tables*):

$Y_X = aX^b$

where Y_X = cumulative average time per unit to produce X units

a = time required to produce the first unit of output

X = cumulative number of units

b = index of learning

The exponent b is defined as:

$$\frac{\text{logarithm of rate of learning}}{\text{logarithm of 2}}$$

Therefore, for a 75% learning curve the coefficient of learning is given by:

$$b = \frac{\log 0.75}{\log 2}$$

$$= \frac{-(0.1249)}{0.3010}$$

$= -0.415$ = coefficient of learning for a 75% learning curve

Note: The log of a number less than one is always negative; therefore b will always be negative.

The following is a calculation check using the figures in the previous illustration, where 1 unit had taken 400 hours and a cumulative of 4 units of production is assumed:

$Y_X = aX^b$

where Y_X	=	cumulative average time per unit
a	=	400
X	=	4
b	=	0.415
Y	=	$400 \times 4^{-0.415} =$ 225.01 hours

Therefore, the cumulative average time per unit when a total of 4 units is produced is 225 hours (as previously determined).

For a cumulative production of 3 units, 1 unit having been produced in 400 hours, the calculations would be as follows:

$$Y = 400 \times (3)^{-0.415}$$

$$= 253.5 \text{ (the cumulative average time per unit)}$$

The cumulative total time for 3 units would be 760.5 hours (3 × 253.5).

Activity 3

If the learning curve rate is 85%, what is the value of b in the learning curve model?

$Y_X = aX^b$

Feedback to this activity is at the end of the chapter.

The following worked example illustrates that the benefit of the learning curve relates to labour and labour-related costs, but not to the cost of materials.

Example

A company wishes to determine the minimum price it should charge a customer for a special order. The customer has requested a quotation for 10 machines, but might subsequently place an order for a further 10. Material costs are £30 per machine. It is estimated that the first batch of 10 machines will take 100 hours to manufacture and an 80% learning curve is expected to apply. Labour plus variable overhead costs amount to £3 per hour. Setting-up costs are £1,000 regardless of the number of machines made.

(a) What is the minimum price the company should quote for the initial order if there is no guarantee of further orders?

(b) What is the minimum price for the follow-on order?

(c) What would be the minimum price if both orders were placed together?

(d) Having completed the initial orders for a total of 20 machines (price at the minimum levels recommended in (a) and (b)), the company thinks that there would be a ready market for this type of machine if it brought the unit selling price down to £45. At this price, what would be the profit on the first 140 'mass-production' models (i.e. after the first 20 machines) assuming that marketing costs totalled £250?

Solution

(a) **Initial order**

If there is no guarantee of a follow-up order, the setting-up costs must be recovered on the initial order. Costs are, therefore, as follows.

	£
Material (10 × £30)	300
Labour and variable overhead (100 × £3)	300
Setting-up cost	1,000
Total	£1,600
Minimum price each (£1,600 ÷ 10)	£160

(b) **Follow-on order**

The setting-up costs have been recovered on the initial order. Output is doubled; therefore, average time for each group of 10 machines is reduced to

$$100 \times 0.8 = 80 \text{ hours}$$

i.e. cumulative time for 20 machines = 160 hours

∴ Time for second group of 10 = time for first 20 – time for first 10
= 160 – 100
= 60 hours

Costs are therefore:

	£
Material (10 × £30)	300
Labour and variable overhead (60 × £3)	180
Total	£480
Minimum price each	£48

(c) **Both orders together**

Total costs are:

	£
Material	600
Labour (160 hours)	480
Setting-up cost	1,000
Total	£2,080
Minimum price each	£104

This is, of course, the mean of the two previous prices: cumulative costs are the same but they are recorded evenly over 20 units instead of most of the cost being 'loaded' onto the first 10 units.

(d) **Mass production**

The time spent on the first 140 mass production models is calculated as follows:

If a 'unit' is a batch of 10 machines, $Y_X = aX^b$ where

$$A = 100$$

$$b = \frac{\log(0.8)}{\log 2}$$

$$= -0.3219$$

Average time/unit for first 2 units (i.e. first 20 machines)

$$= 100 \times 2^{-0.3219}$$

$$= 80 \text{ hours}$$

Total time for first 2 units $= 80 \times 2$

$$= 160 \text{ hours (as before)}$$

Average time per unit for first 16 units (i.e. first 160 machines)

$$= 100 \times 16^{-0.3219}$$

$$= 40.96 \text{ hours}$$

Total time for first 16 units $= 40.96 \times 16$

$$= 655.36 \text{ hours}$$

Hence total time for units 3 to 16 i.e. the 140 mass-produced units)

$$= (655.36 - 160) \text{ hours}$$

$$= 495.36 \text{ hours}$$

Cost of first 140 mass-production models

	£
Material (140 × £30)	4,200
Labour and variable overhead (495.36 × £3)	1,486
Marketing	250
Total cost	5,936
Revenue	6,300
Profit	364

9.6 Limitations of the learning curve effect

The learning curve, whilst being an important factor to be taken into account if it exists, is based on specific assumptions which may or may not apply in a modern manufacturing environment. The model applies if the process is:

- **Labour intensive.** Modern manufacturing environments may be very capital intensive and the labour effect cannot apply if machines limit the speed of labour.
- **New product.** This may be the case in the modern environment as products have short lives and therefore new products will be introduced on a regular basis.

- **Complex.** The more complex the product the more likely that the learning curve will be significant and the longer it will take for the learning curve to reach a plateau (beyond which no more learning can take place).
- **Repetitive.** The learning effect requires that production is repetitive with no major breaks in which the learning effect may be lost. JIT production has moved towards multi-skilled and multi-tasked workers. It is possible that some of the benefits of the learning effect in a single tasking environment may be lost. The production of small batches of possible different products in response to customer demand may also lead to the loss of some of the learning effect.
- **Difficulty in identifying the learning effect in practice.** Even if there are conditions which suggest that a learning effect is present it may be very difficult to forecast the index of learning accurately. Despite this it may be better to incorporate an estimate of the learning effect into budgets and forecasts rather than ignore it completely as the effect can be so great.

In any given scenario you should think carefully about whether the learning effect may be present and be prepared to discuss the limitations of your analysis.

9.7 Experience curves

An experience curve is a function that shows how the full costs of a product (per unit) decline as units of output increase. An experience curve will reflect changes in unit costs in respect of manufacturing, marketing, distribution etc.

The differences between the learning curve and the experience curve are:

- the learning curve relates to a single repetitive operation by an operative while the experience curve relates to the business itself
- the learning curve formula is normally expressed in terms of time taken to perform the repetitive task while the experience curve is normally expressed in terms of costs per unit of output. Time and costs are obviously related. The longer an operative takes to finish a task, the greater will be the labour cost of production of the finished unit. Material costs, however, will not be affected by the learning curve effect. The experience curve applies to the total cost of output.

9.8 Causes of the experience curve

The experience curve is not a natural phenomenon; it needs to be made to work. A number of factors lead to increased experience and these are summarised below.

- **Labour efficiency** – This is really the learning effect, but it extends beyond the operatives to management and administration. (Any students who have sat a number of CIMA examinations will appreciate that each time they have gained additional 'examination experience'.)
- **Workforce organisation** – This results from either increased specialisation or from a structuring of the labour force to meet specific manufacturing situations. (Specialisation does, of course, lead to narrowing of work perspective which in turn results in increased specialist experience.)

- **Production processes** – Innovations and developments in the production process will take place on an ongoing basis and can lead to substantial cost savings.
- **Resource mix** – As comparative costs change, so the resource mix can be varied, e.g. by more sophisticated mechanisation. This is made possible by the extent of scale.
- **Product standardisation** – There is a dichotomy between the production need for standardisation, and the marketing need for variety. Larger volumes can reconcile this problem, which is an aspect of experience.
- **Technical conservatism** – Equipment is usually rated conservatively at first and used with caution. As experience grows it can be worked nearer its limits.
- **Product redesign** – With experience, products can be redesigned to improve production efficiency or to appeal to more customers.
- **Economies of scale and the learning curve** – This is really a separate effect, but overlaps with the experience effect. Not only are there 'static' economies of scale, but the company may advance more quickly down the learning curve if there are large production volumes.

Summary

- World-class manufacturing is a position of internal manufacturing excellence, achieved by developing a culture based on factors such as continuous improvement, problem prevention, zero defect tolerance, customer-driven JIT-based production and total quality management.
- Continuous improvement ('Kaizen') is a process of small, incremental improvements, rather than large innovations.
- Computer integrated manufacturing is the use of computers and other advanced manufacturing techniques to monitor and perform manufacturing tasks.
- Materials requirements planning converts a production schedule into a listing of materials and components required to meet that schedule. Manufacturing resource planning is an expansion of this to embrace areas such as finance, logistics, engineering and marketing.
- It is worth learning the distinctions between cost control and cost reduction, and between utility value and esteem value.
- Just in time is a system designed to produce or procure components as they are required by a customer, or for use, rather than for stock. JIT attempts to eliminate all waste at every stage of the manufacturing process.
- Theory of constraints aims to maximise sales revenue less materials. It is based on the identification and elimination of bottlenecks.
- The throughput accounting ratio measures the return per factory hour as a proportion of the total cost per factory hour and the aim is for this to exceed 1.
- Total quality management is an integrated and comprehensive system of planning and controlling all business functions so that products or services are produced which meet or exceed customer expectations.

- Learning curves describe how unit labour times tend to decrease at a constant rate when labour-intensive procedures are repeated.
- The formula to the learning curve is $Y_X = aX^b$. The letter b in this formula represents a coefficient of learning, which is calculated as the logarithm of the learning rate divided by the logarithm of 2.
- Experience curves describe how full product costs per unit tend to decrease as the units of output increase.

Having completed your study of this chapter you should have achieved the following learning outcomes.

- Compare and contrast value analysis and functional analysis.
- Evaluate the impacts of just-in-time production, the theory of constraints and total quality management on efficiency, inventory and cost.
- Explain the concepts of continuous improvement and kaizen costing that are central to total quality management and prepare the cost of quality reports.
- Explain and apply learning and experience curves to estimate time and cost for new products and services.

Self-test questions

1 What is lean manufacturing? (1.7)

2 Give examples of waste in production. (1.7)

3 Explain the role of computers in an automated factory. (2.2)

4 What is a flexible manufacturing system? (2.3)

5 Explain materials requirements planning. (MRP I). (3.1)

6 Explain the techniques that may be used to effect cost reduction. (4.1)

7 Explain how just-in-time parameters affect supplier relationships. (5.2)

8 Explain the theory of constraints (TOC). (6.3)

9 Define the throughput accounting ratio. (7.5)

10 Give two examples of each of the following quality costs: internal failure, external failure, appraisal, prevention. (8.9)

11 What is the learning curve effect? (9.1)

12 Explain the meaning of each of the items in $Y_X = aX^b$ learning curve equation. (9.5)

13 What is the experience curve? (9.7)

Objective test questions

Question 1

Which of the following describes a system that converts a production schedule into a listing of the materials and components required to meet that schedule on a timely basis?

A Material requirements planning (MRP I)

B Manufacturing resource planning (MRP II)

C Money resource planning (called MRP III by some authorities)

D Enterprise resource planning (ERP)

Question 2

Which of the following might be modules in an ERP system?

I Treasury

II Investment

III Production planning

IV Human resources management

A I, II and III only

B II, III and IV only

C III and IV only

D I, II, III and IV

Question 3

If the first unit takes 40 minutes to produce in a process enjoying a 90% learning effect, then the third unit will take:

A 29.2 minutes

B 29.5 minutes

C 36 minutes

D 101.5 minutes

Question 4

Which of the following is not a characteristic of world-class manufacturing?

A Continuous improvement

B Zero defect tolerance

C Total quality management

D Production-driven scheduling

The following information is relevant to questions 5 and 6.

A company produces a single product which uses three processes as follows;

Machine	Time taken	Machine hours available
1	3 minutes	450
2	5 minutes	575
3	4.8 minutes	500

The company is operating at full capacity.

The revenue and cost data relating to the product are as follows;

	£ per unit
Sales price	3.80
Direct material	1.40
Direct labour	0.90
Variable overhead	0.45

Fixed cost for the period is £8,500

Question 5

Determine the bottleneck for the process and calculate the maximum output possible.

Question 6

Calculate the throughput accounting ratio and comment on your result.

For the answers to these questions, see the 'Answers' section at the end of the book.

Exam-type questions

Question 1: Limitation of traditional management accounting

The new manufacturing environment is characterised by more flexibility, a readiness to meet customers' requirements, smaller batches, continuous improvements and an emphasis on quality. In such circumstances, traditional management accounting performance measures are, at best, irrelevant and, at worst, misleading.

You are required:

(a) to discuss the above statement, citing specific examples to support or refute the views expressed **(10 marks)**

(b) to explain in what ways management accountants can adapt the services they provide to the new environment. **(7 marks)**

(Total: 17 marks)

Question 2: Learning curve for PQ plc

PQ plc manufactures domestic toasters. It is investigating whether or not to accept a one-year contract to make a new de-luxe model for sale through a supermarket chain. New machinery costing £7,000 would have to be bought at the start of the contract. The contract uses skilled labour that cannot be increased above that currently available and PQ plc will receive a fixed price of £45 per toaster for all the toasters it can produce in the year. The following estimates have been made:

Materials	£30 per toaster
Labour	£6 per hour
Cost of capital	15%

The factory manager knows from experience of similar machines that there will be a learning effect for labour. He estimates that the learning rate will be 90%.

He estimates that the first 500 toasters will take 800 hours to produce and that the fixed amount of labour available will enable 4,000 toasters to be produced in the first year. Fixed overheads of £25,000 will be payable each year.

Based upon net cash flows should the contract be accepted? **(10 marks)**

Question 3: Devon Ltd

Devon Ltd manufactures specialised electronic instruments for the medical profession. The company's major problem is finding sufficient suitably trained staff. Thanks to an extensive training programme Devon has managed to maintain a steady workforce of 40 assembly staff but sees no chance of increasing that number.

A contract is being considered by the board to supply a new type of dartmeter for the next four years. The meter will sell for £2,000, will require components costing £300 and will take two days to assemble and test. The company is only prepared to put 25% of its staff on production of the dartmeter. Even this will mean that they will have to be taken from other work which will result in a loss of contribution of £120 per man day (calculated after charging the £80 per day labour cost).

Devon Ltd feels that it will be able to sell all the output that this team can produce in the 250 working days a year.

The figures of £300 for components and two days for production are initial basic estimates. If output exceeds 2,600 units in any one year, the components supplier will reduce the cost by 10%. Two days is the time that it is anticipated that the first component will take a member of staff to produce. Learning effects will cause this to fall in the conventional manner according to the equation:

$Y_X = aX^b$

where:	Y_X	=	overall average time per unit
	a	=	time taken for first unit (2 days)
	X	=	cumulative production
	b	=	$\frac{\text{log of the learning rate}}{\text{log 2}}$

The learning rate for Devon staff is 90%, but learning stops once a member of staff has produced 50 units.

The project will require an initial investment of £3½ million and additional fixed costs of £850,000 will be incurred over each of the four years. Devon's cost of capital is 10% per annum and you may assume that all cash flows occur annually in arrears.

You are required to calculate the NPV of the dartmeter contract. **(17 marks)**

For the answers to these questions, see the 'Answers' section at the end of the book.

Feedback to activities

Activity 1

(a) Return per factory hour = (£85 – £42.50)/ 1.5 hours = £28.33

(b) Cost per factory hour = £8,000/(10 × 40 hours) = £20

Throughput accounting ratio = £28.33: £20 = 1.4165:1

Activity 2

Cumulative number of units	*Cumulative average time per unit*	*Cumulative total hours*
8	168.75 (75% of 225)	1,350

Therefore, time for last 4 items = 1,350 – 900 = 450 hours.

Activity 3

$$b = \frac{\log(0.85)}{\log 2}$$

$$b = \frac{-0.0706}{0.3010} = -0.234$$

Chapter 9

ACHIEVING COMPETITIVE ADVANTAGE

Syllabus content

This chapter covers the following syllabus content.

- Target costing.
- Life cycle costing and implications for marketing strategies.
- The value chain and supply chain management, including the trend to outsource manufacturing operations to Eastern Europe and the Far East.
- Gain sharing arrangements in situations where because of the size of the project, a limited number of contractors or security issues (e.g. in defence work), normal competitive pressures do not apply.

Contents

1 Target costing

1.1 Target pricing

Target pricing is a term which implies that the firm has a sufficient knowledge of the conditions of the market for its product and for the production factors that it uses to be able to set a price which it calculates will achieve a desired target.

Possible targets might include the following.

- **Short- or long-run profit maximisation** – In practice these are not normally considered to be specific targets and are not usually regarded as being within the scope of target pricing.
- **Sales maximisation** – This may be regarded in a similar light to that of profit maximisation. Strictly it does not represent a specific target.
- **A desired rate of return on capital invested in a product** – This is, perhaps, the most common target, chiefly because investment decisions are based on comparisons of future returns and on estimates of attainable returns. Managers will, therefore, seek to achieve the projections made when the decision was being reached.
- **Market share** – This is rarely an end in itself; more often it is the necessary pre-condition for the firm to achieve the price and cost combination it desires.
- **Achieve a given rate of growth** – Growth may be an important objective of the firm but, because of the costs and risks of obtaining capital, a steady growth rate is desired because this can be obtained from available capital funds. An objective of growth at a particular rate is also likely to require the achievement of a profit rate considered acceptable to the finance markets. The firm cannot go to the capital market for additional finance unless it can prove to that market that it has achieved a satisfactory rate of profit on its existing capital. What is 'satisfactory' depends on a range of influences and conditions at any particular time.
- **Keep out competitors** – This involves the use of price as a barrier to the entry of market competitors. This may mean that some degree of monopoly profit may be sacrificed in the desire to keep price below the level at which it would become profitable for a new firm to enter the market

KEY POINT

In target costing, we determine an acceptable market price and a desired profit level. The difference is the target cost that must be achieved.

1.2 Target costing

Target costing should be viewed as an integral part of a strategic profit management system. The initial consideration in target costing is an estimate of the selling price for a new product which will enable a firm to capture its required share of the market. Then it is necessary to reduce this figure to reflect the firm's desired level of profit, having regard to the rate of return required on new capital investment and working capital requirements. The deduction of required profit from the proposed selling price will produce a target cost that must be met in order to ensure that the desired rate of return is obtained.

Target costing will necessitate comparison of current estimated cost levels against the target level which must be achieved if the desired levels of profitability, and hence return on investment, are to be achieved. Thus where a gap exists between the current estimated cost levels and the target cost, it is essential that this gap be closed. This may not be possible in the short term but continuous improvement, economies of scale by achieving a large market share, or learning curve effects may make it possible in the long term. Organisations should recognise that it is far easier to 'design out' cost during the pre-production phase than to 'control out' cost during the production phase. Thus cost reduction at this stage of a product's life cycle is of critical significance to business success.

A number of techniques may be employed in order to help in the achievement and maintenance of the desired level of target cost. Attention should be focussed upon the identification of value added and non-value added activities with the aim of eliminating the latter. The product should be developed in an atmosphere of "continuous improvement". In this regard, total quality techniques such as the use of quality circles may be used in attempting to find ways of achieving reductions in product cost.

Value engineering techniques can be used to evaluate necessary product features such as the quality of materials used. It is essential that a collaborative approach is used by the management of organisations and that all interested parties such as suppliers and customers are closely involved in order to engineer product enhancements at reduced cost.

1.3 Target costs and standard costs

There are some similarities between target costs and standard costs but the significance of a target cost lies in the process of how it is developed. They both provide unit cost targets but here the similarity ends and significant differences include:

- the focus upon what a product **should** cost in the long term. In constructing the target cost of a new item consideration should first be given to the price at which the product should be sold in order to attract the desired market share. Once this selling price has been determined the required profit margin needs to be deducted in order to arrive at the target cost. A standard cost would tend to be based on attainable standards of efficiency whereas a target cost may incorporate a cost gap which can only be achieved over a longer term.

- A market orientated approach. The use of standard costs which have been derived from target costs ensures that external factors that are related to the marketplace are taken into account. A standard cost is usually based on production cost information only.

- Focus on continual improvement. The target cost may incorporate a series of cost targets which are continuously reduced until the target is achieved. A standard is normally set at the outset of production and may not be reviewed on a regular basis.

- Team approach. Target costing requires that all departments working on the product should be involved in the target costing exercise and should contribute to the target cost being achieved. This includes research and development, marketing and sales as well as production. This contrasts with standard costs which are normally production costs only.

- A target cost will be set before major development costs are incurred. This allows cost reductions to be designed into the product or a decision to be made to abandon the product if the required cost target cannot be achieved. In contrast, standards are set when production commences, by which time 70 – 80% of costs may already be committed.

2 Product life cycle costing

2.1 Introduction

DEFINITION

Life cycle costing refers to the forecasting and management of all costs and revenues over the product life

Life cycle costing is similar to target costing in that it may also be viewed as a strategic profit management system. It refers to the forecasting and management of all costs and revenues over the product life from the development stage, through the growth and maturity phases to the decline stage. Life cycle costing has been influenced by a dramatic reduction in product life in the modern environment. It has been estimated that there is a need to bring the break-even point of a product down from an average of five years to two. With the reduction in life span comes an increase in the disproportionate cost outflows during the early stages of the product life cycle. A primary objective must be to match the high costs with the revenues and maximise profit over the product life cycle.

2.2 Changing pattern of costs

As production techniques have advanced, the cost of production has declined relative to the other costs. Improved reliability has reduced the amount of warranty work needed, so post-production costs have declined. Potential problem areas have been designed out of the products, while costs have been further reduced by using components from standard families.

Since it is estimated that between 50% and 80% of the total life cycle cost may be committed before production ever takes place, to have accurate estimates of the cost at the outset is extremely valuable in a competitive market. Ways of reducing costs can be found and even as production progresses, further cost reduction can be encouraged.

Points which need careful consideration in life cycle costing include:

- Every effort should be made to reduce **development costs**. As a guide, the spend on development should not exceed the savings made in subsequent production and post-production activities.
- **Development costs** are frequently treated as period costs in financial accounts. SSAP13 does allow development for a specific product that is expected to be profitable to be carried forward. However, prudence often dictates that these costs have already been written off. Writers advocate that these costs should be recorded as a product cost so that a more accurate profit can be calculated over the whole product life.
- **Over-engineering should be avoided**. The customer perception of value needs to be clearly understood. This could mean ensuring that the product is made to be durable, fairly long lived, but cheap to maintain.
- The use of **cost tables**. These are seen as a vital method of improving control during the product life cycle. Cost tables are computerised cost relational data bases that function as decision support systems. In many respects they are similar to the traditional planned estimates used by the electronics industry, or the 'Red Book' of costs of the western automobile industry. They are particularly useful for pre-production cost estimation and hence control in an area of high and increasing costs. Japanese firms use cost tables both to estimate the cost of new products, and to control and reduce the costs of existing products. All component activities are included to enable decisions to be taken about alternative methods of manufacture especially where volumes and specifications may differ. Cost tables can also be used for indirect activities as well as providing choices of design that require different mixes of direct and indirect costs.

DEFINITION

A **cost table** is a database containing all the costs associated with the production of a product, broken down to include the costs of functions and/or components and sub-assemblies. They also incorporate the cost changes that would result from a number of possible changes in the input mix.

- As production costs have declined, non-production costs have increased in significance. It is important that there is a strategic marketing plan and that pricing and marketing decisions will result in maximising profit over the life cycle. Careful consideration should be given to whether a penetration or skimming approach is more profitable. Advertising, product support and eventual withdrawal costs should all be allocated to the product.

2.3 The life cycle cost budget

The application of life cycle costing requires the establishment of a life cycle cost budget for a given product which in turn necessitates identification of costs with particular products. Actual costs incurred in respect of the product are then monitored against life cycle budget costs.

A company is in a weak position if all its products are at the same phase of the life cycle. If they are all in the growth phase there are problems ahead; if they are all in one of the other phases there are immediate difficulties.

Companies try to overcome this problem by introducing new products that are growing as the old products are declining and by having products with life cycles of different lengths.

In applying life cycle costing a supplier will recognise that the life of the product commences prior to its introduction to the marketplace. Indeed up to 90% of costs result from decisions made prior to its 'launch' concerning issues such as functions, materials, components and manufacturing methods to be adopted.

Life cycle costs may be classified as follows:

- development costs
- design costs
- manufacturing costs
- marketing costs, and
- distribution costs.

A pattern of costs will emerge over the life cycle of the product. Invariably the absolute level of costs will rise and this trend should "track" the pattern of sales of the product. The supplier will always be monitoring relevant costs and revenues in an attempt to ensure that the rise in resultant sales revenues is greater than the rise in the attributable costs of the product. Moreover, the supplier will expect reductions to occur in the unit cost of a product as a consequence of economies of scale and learning and experience curves. In order to maximise the profits earned by a product over its life cycle management need give consideration to minimising the time required to get the product to the marketplace. This may enable an organisation to "steal a march" on its competitors who will invariably attempt to launch a rival product at the earliest available opportunity. Hence "time to market" assumes critical significance since it affords an organisation who is first to the marketplace with an opportunity to make profits prior to arrival of competitor products.

Once the product has reached the marketplace management attention should be focused upon maximising the length of the product's life cycle. In this regard "time to market" is also critical since by definition the earlier a product reaches the marketplace the longer will be its resultant life cycle. Management should always be searching for other potential uses of the product and/or finding alternative markets for the product. Whilst it may be difficult to envisage other potential uses for product at the planning stage it may be possible for an organisation to draw up a plan which involves the staggered entry of the product into geographically separate markets with the resultant effect of increasing the overall life cycle of the product. A major benefit of this staggered approach which is often adopted by global players lies in the fact that the income streams from one market may be used to fund the launch of the product into another market.

The application of life cycle costing requires management to consider whether the anticipated cost savings that were expected to be achieved via the application of cost reduction techniques, both prior to and following the product's introduction, have actually been achieved. Its use may also assist management in allocating resources to non-production activities. For example, a product which is in the mature stage may require less marketing support than a product which is in the growth stage.

3 The value chain

The meaning of the word profitability can be extended to include anything that is beneficial or advantageous to an organisation. This wider perspective stems from the concept of "value chain analysis" developed by Professor Michael Porter of Harvard Business School. A value chain may be regarded as a linear map of the way in which value is added through a process from raw materials to finished, delivered product (including continuing service after delivery).

Porter's approach may be summarised as follows:

- Within an industry many business units produce products or services that are very similar if not actually identical to those of their competitors.
- There are two generic strategies that may be employed by a business unit in order to create a competitive advantage over its rivals, namely "cost leadership" and "differentiation". "Cost leadership" means that a business unit has a significant cost advantage over its competitors and is the lowest cost producer within the industry in which it operates. "Differentiation" implies that the product or service offers some unique attribute or characteristic which is valued by existing and potential purchasers.
- The activities of the business unit can be categorised into five primary and four support activities each of which may contribute to the overall competitive advantage of the business unit. These activities comprise the value chain as shown in the figure below.
- Each activity within the value chain provides inputs which after processing constitute added value to the output, which the customer ultimately receives in the form of a product or service or as the aggregate of values at the end of the value chain.
- Each primary support activity has the potential to contribute to the competitive advantage of the business unit by enabling it to produce, market and deliver products or services which meet or surpass the value expectations of purchasers in comparison with those resulting from other value chains.

Porter's Value Chain

The value chain

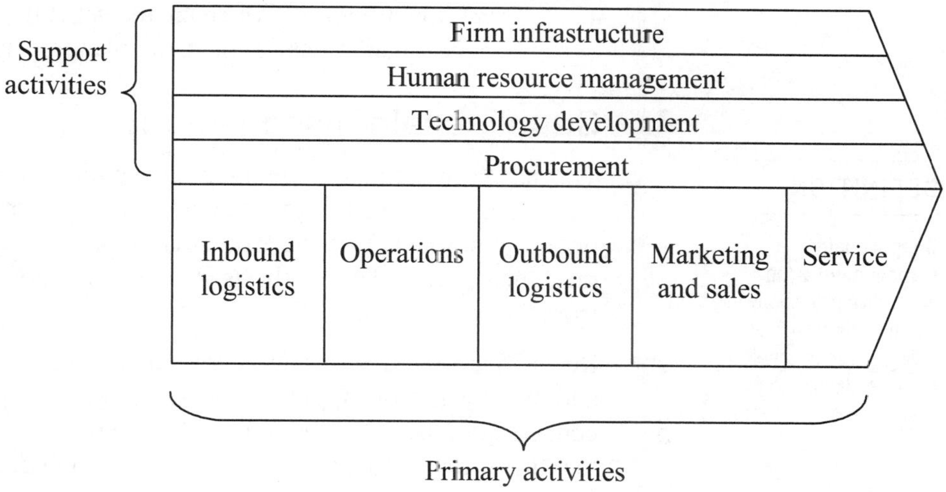

The activities which comprise the value chain are as follows.

Primary activities

These are the activities which involve the physical movement of raw materials and finished products, production of goods and services, marketing sales and subsequent services to outputs of a business unit.

1. Inbound logistics – which entails receiving, storing, materials handling, warehousing, inventory control, vehicle scheduling, returns to suppliers.
2. Operations – which entails transferring inputs into final product form (e.g. machining, packaging, assembly, equipment maintenance, testing, printing and facility operations.
3. Outbound logistics – which entails distributing the finished product (e.g. finished goods warehousing, material handling, operation of delivery vehicles, order processing and scheduling).
4. Marketing and sales – which entails inducing and facilitating buyers to purchase the product, e.g. advertising, activities of sales personnel, preparation of quotations, channel selection, channel relations, pricing of goods and services.
5. Service – which entails maintaining or enhancing the value of the product after the sale has taken place, installation, commissioning, repair, training, parts supply and product adjustment.

Support activities

Support activities are those activities that provide support to the primary activities and also to each other.

1. Procurement – which entails purchasing of raw materials, consumable items and capital items.
2. Technology development – which entails the use of know how, procedures to be applied and the technological inputs required in every activity which forms part of the value chain.

3. Human resource management – which entails the selection, retention and promotion of staff, the appraisal of staff and performance-rewards linkage, management development and employee relations.

4. Firm infrastructure – which entails general management, accounting and finance, quality management and planning activities.

4 Supply chain management

DEFINITION

Supply chain management is 'an integrative philosophy to manage the total flow of a distribution channel from the supplier to the ultimate user'.

This has been defined as 'an integrative philosophy to manage the total flow of a distribution channel from the supplier to the ultimate user'. Today's organisations have become aware that improved supply chain management will raise their profits. The emphasis is upon the removal of inefficient processes from the supply-chain.

Recent decades have seen an increasing rate of globalisation of the economy and thereby also of supply chains. The days when products were produced and consumed in the same geographical area are long past. In fact it is often the case that the different components of a product come from all over the globe. Such a trend causes longer and more complex supply chains and thus changes the requirements within supply chain management. This, in turn, affects the effectiveness of the IT systems employed within the supply chain. A longer supply chain often results in a lengthening of order-to-delivery lead times.

Supply chain decisions fall into two broad categories depending whether they are strategic or operational in nature. As one might expect, strategic decisions concern a longer time horizon and this is where a decision to source goods and services nationally or internationally must be made if value added benefits are to be derived. Such decisions are inextricably linked to corporate strategy. The focus of attention in the making of such decisions is the effective and efficient management of the product flow in the strategically planned supply chain.

Supply chain management requires consideration of four major decision areas, each of which has strategic and operational aspects.

1. Location
2. Production
3. Inventory
4. Distribution

An organisation with international trading interests must be aware of the decisions made by firms in the international arena regarding each of these areas. This knowledge will enable them to operate in an "understood environment" and manage their particular supply requirements in a more effective manner.

The following is a summary of the main considerations.

Location

The first step in creating a supply chain lies in the situation of production facilities, together with stocking and sourcing points. The decision regarding the location of manufacturing facilities is primarily strategic in nature because not only is such a decision invariably irreversible, at least in the short to mid-term, but also it requires a major commitment of resources to a longer-term plan. The determination of the size, number and location of production facilities will determine the possible paths by which products can flow to the ultimate customer. Such decisions are of fundamental importance to an organisation since in essence they underpin the basic strategy for accessing customer markets and have a major impact on resultant revenues, costs and levels of service provision. Such decisions need to consider many factors including production costs and limitations, tax duties and tariffs, local considerations and distribution costs, if a sub-optimal decision is to be avoided.

Production

The strategic considerations that need to be addressed by management include which products to produce and where they should be produced. Further considerations include the allocation of suppliers to production plants and to customer markets. Again these decisions will have a major impact on revenues, costs and customer service levels of the organisation. Such decisions are made on the assumption that production facilities are already in existence and proceed to determine the exact route(s) through which a product flows to and from these facilities. The availability of manufacturing capacity assumes critical significance and this may be largely dependent upon the extent of vertical integration that has been achieved within the organisation. Detailed production scheduling comprises the primary focus of operational decisions. These necessitate consideration of matters such as master production schedules, scheduling production on machines and planned maintenance routines. Other considerations include the operation of effective quality control procedures and the determination of balanced workloads within each facility.

Inventory

Inventories are a feature of every stage of the supply chain, either as raw materials, part finished goods or finished goods. They can also be in process between locations, their primary purpose being to act as an insurance buffer against any uncertainties that might exist in the supply chain. The holding costs associated with inventories are significant and can comprise up to 40% of their value. Efficient management of inventories therefore assumes critical significance in supply chain operations. Insofar as the top tier of management set goals relating to inventory management then one might contend that the inventory management is strategic in nature. However, most writers approach inventory management from an operational standpoint which includes consideration of the adoption of 'push' or 'pull' strategies, control policies, the determination of economic order quantities, reorder points and safety stock levels in respect of each facility. Students should appreciate that these levels are critical since they are the principal determinants of resultant customer service levels.

Distribution

The choice of transport mode(s) is of strategic significance to the organisation. Such decisions are closely linked to inventory decisions since the choice of mode will involve a detailed cost analysis of the indirect costs of inventory that are attributable to that mode. Air shipments are fast, reliable but comparatively expensive in spite of the reduced need for the maintenance of safety stocks. Shipping by sea or rail is much cheaper than air shipments, but slower and less reliable. For this reason organisations tend to hold much larger amounts of inventory. Geographic location and customer service levels are important in such decisions. Transportation costs comprise more than 30% of total logistics costs, hence it is crucial that management choose correct options in this sphere of operations. The firm's transport strategy will include consideration of shipment sizes, routing and scheduling for each facility.

5 Outsourcing

5.1 The nature of outsourcing

To survive in today's marketplace, firms need to be flexible and pro-active, creating maximum added value for the customers. This accounts for the growth of outsourcing during recent years.

KEY POINT

Outsourcing involves the buying in of components, sub-assemblies, finished products and services from outside suppliers rather than supplying them internally.

Outsourcing involves the buying in of components, sub-assemblies, finished products and services from outside suppliers rather than supplying them internally. It may be regarded as a management strategy by which an organisation delegates major non-core functions to specialised, efficient service providers.

Traditionally the insourcing/ outsourcing decision was focused on a make or buy decision for manufacturing functions. However companies are now beginning to apply the decision analysis to nearly all functions and activities.

Examples of functions now coming under the outsourcing spotlight:

- sales
- design and development
- IT
- distribution.

Advantages and disadvantages of insourcing

Advantages	Disadvantages
• Higher degree of control over inputs	• Requires high volumes
• Increases visibility over the process	• High investment
• Economies of Scale/scope uses integration	• Dedicated equipment has limited flexibility
	• Not a core competence

Advantages and disadvantages of outsourcing

Advantages	Disadvantages
• Greater flexibility	• Possibility of choosing wrong supplier
• Lower investment risk	• Loss of visibility & control over process
• Improved cash flow	• 'Hollowing out' of company
• Concentrate on core competence	• Possibility of increased lead times
• Enables more advanced technologies to be used without making investment	

The keys to successful outsourcing fall into five main areas.

- strategic analysis
- market analysis
- selecting a supplier

- managing the relationship
- internal change management.

International purchasing

Many organisations are finding they are conducting and managing international commercial relationships. Although the underlying management philosophy is (and should be) the same as with domestic suppliers there are aspects of the relationship that are specific to the global environment that require careful thought.

Globalisation is a trend away from distinct national units and toward one huge global market. There are a variety of elements of globalisation but primarily they fall into two key areas, namely the globalisation of markets and production.

Globalisation of markets

Traditionally national markets are becoming global as consumer tastes and wants are influenced by a global perspective

Globalisation of production

Companies are sourcing products (and services) worldwide taking advantage of national differences in cost of production and labour force.

Examples of organisations who have chosen this sourcing option are US automotive companies moving production to Mexico, Dyson moving production to Eastern Europe, and the transfer of call centres to India.

Drivers for globalisation include:

- breaking down of trade and investment barriers
- technological changes
- telecommunication
- internet
- transportation.

5.2 Outsourcing manufacturing operations to Eastern Europe and the Far East

During recent years foreign investment has begun to pour into Eastern European countries as West European and U.S. companies look for lower-cost manufacturing bases close to the European Union. Today, as these and other countries have joined the EU, the East and Central Europeans themselves are looking in an easterly direction for low-cost manufacturing. As rising wages force them to find ways to become more competitive, some are setting up plants or outsourcing their production to subcontractors in places such as Bosnia, Romania, Russia and Ukraine. The investment farther east is increasing, and economists and trade experts expect it to increase substantially in the next few years as both living standards and manufacturing costs continue to rise. Taxation is also a major consideration (Russia has attractive tax rates, as low as 13%) but cheaper labour is the major factor.

UK and other European based organisations are aware that assembly costs in Eastern European countries are far lower than at home. This fact is leading to the transfer of production to such territories.

Some companies are already looking to China and other parts of Asia, where labour costs are even lower. An organisation which makes sports and leisure gear, now sources 70 – 80% of its production in China, India, Taiwan, Turkey and Vietnam and only uses national manufacturers for sophisticated products and small orders that would be uneconomical to produce in Asia. It is crucial that organisations maintain their ability to compete and thus as production costs in the new EU member states start to approach those in Western Europe, more and more firms could be eastward bound.

Contract manufacturing has always been about cutting costs, and today that means rapid expansion of, for example, the electronic manufacturing services (EMS) industry into China, Eastern Europe and other low-wage areas. At the same time, hand-in-hand with that expansion is contraction, as organisations cut back operations in high-wage areas such as the United States. With original equipment manufacturers (OEMs) increasingly outsourcing printed circuit boards and finished systems, a significant amount of that manufacturing is especially likely to find its way to China. Indeed, it is highly probable that a major trend over the next few years will be the migration to low-cost manufacturing centres, particularly China.

Competitive pressure forces OEMs and contract manufacturers to do all they can to take costs out of their businesses, and consequently many organisations are heading in the direction of Eastern Europe and China in an attempt to do so. As far as China is concerned, not only are costs low but also, in addition to making products there to be sold around the world, firms can also entertain the possibility of sales into the Chinese market.

6 Gain-sharing arrangements

KEY POINT

Under a gain-sharing arrangement, vendors typically guarantee customers will achieve a certain amount of cost savings or top-line improvement.

While risk-sharing/gain-sharing arrangements can take different forms, vendors typically guarantee customers will achieve a certain amount of cost savings or top-line improvement. If targets are not met, the vendor commits to making up the difference in cash. If targets are exceeded, the vendor may also receive a pre-specified percentage of the gains.

These agreements are attractive to vendors because they can provide insulation from the cutthroat price competition that characterises today's technology marketplace. Vendors that guarantee cost savings and top-line improvement can command a price premium in the marketplace. Such risk-sharing agreements are attractive to customers because they reduce the business risk and cost associated with implementing new technologies, systems, and services.

While companies across a number of industries (including hospital supplies, automotive parts manufacturing, and transportation and logistics) have benefited greatly by deploying risk-sharing/gain-sharing agreements, many vendors have been slow to adopt such practices. There are several reasons for this. First, the management team may not have any hands-on experience in structuring such agreements. This may be because these agreements were not judged to be critical to the sales and marketing efforts. Moreover the agreements themselves can be difficult to put into practice. Parties to a potential gain sharing arrangement must agree on project scope, what criteria will be measured, and how performance will be tracked.

However, whilst structuring risk-sharing/gain-sharing agreements is difficult, it is not impossible. Modern day organisations operate in very competitive industries, and yet are able to create and maintain impressive records of growth and earnings performance. Their success, in large part, is due to the fact that they have made risk-sharing/gain-sharing agreements a key element of their sales and marketing strategy.

Enterprises must be willing to cooperate in the research processes related to their sphere of operations and those that do will expect to benefit from both vendors' and customers' insights and recommendations regarding potential process improvements and cost-saving opportunities.

Putting a successful risk-sharing/gain-sharing strategy in place requires dedicated commitment of senior management teams but experience suggests that the rewards for both vendors and customers more than justify the time and expense invested.

Gain sharing is an approach to the review and adjustment of an existing contract, or series of contracts, where the adjustment provides benefits to both parties. It is a mutual activity requiring the agreement of both parties to the contract adjustment. Consideration of a gain sharing proposal will be limited to just that area affected by the proposal.

The sharing of benefits provides an incentive on both parties to a contract to explore gain sharing possibilities. In the UK, the Ministry of Defence is committed to, and industry supports, gain sharing as one of a number of approaches to improve the efficient use of the defence procurement budget.

Gain sharing arrangements are popular where there exists the potential to achieve mutual benefit among the parties concerned. The gain, benefit or advantage to be shared might not be financial in nature, though financial benefits are likely to feature strongly. The period of application of the sharing arrangement will need to be agreed. The sharing arrangement may apply only to the current contract; or the effects of the agreement, and the sharing arrangements, may be carried forward into future contracts.

A successful gain sharing proposal may be achieved through an amendment to the existing contract(s) and thus can be introduced only by the agreement of both parties. Thus the decision on whether to proceed with any gain sharing proposal will need to be taken by both parties to a contract.

Gain sharing opportunities may be found in various areas within a contract and its supply chain. Areas which may be susceptible to change include:

Specification and statement of requirements

It may be possible to obtain better value by reducing or increasing the technical specifications or levels of performance required. This could arise from advances in technology, or matching performance requirements to changing customer needs. Opportunities for gain sharing can affect whole-life costs and hence have a significant impact on the attractiveness of a contract.

Delivery

A revised programme or timing of a service may lead to improved performance.

Development programmes

Changes in a development programme could help to reduce the level of costs or facilitate the achievement of improved performance.

Asset utilisation

Opportunities for the generation of an additional income stream from the use of assets could emerge or be developed.

Supply chain

Opportunities may be found within the supply chain for gain sharing between contractors. Indeed most contracts contain the scope for the application of gain sharing arrangements – there are very few limitations. For example, gain sharing can be applicable across the range of defence procurement contracts, irrespective of the procurement agency. Increasingly, new contracts will include incentives where appropriate.

As far as the handling and content of gain sharing proposals relating to Ministry of Defence contracts is concerned, then such proposals are administered in accordance with the relevant principles set out in the *Code of Practice on the Handling of Innovative Proposals* published as Guidelines for Industry No 12 (GFI 12).

Mutual trust and cooperation between contracting parties is essential since assessment of the financial benefit of a Gain sharing proposal will require both parties to provide each other with access to relevant cost data to provide the basis for the valuation of the benefit and to facilitate the calculation and sharing of that benefit.

Gain sharing represents a reward for innovative thinking by the contractor; it is important that the nature of any change proposal is agreed at the outset in the light of this principle. Once a gain sharing proposal is agreed, the concept of sharing the benefits will be fundamental to further discussion and agreement; neither party will seek to secure all the benefits.

Summary

- In target costing, we determine an acceptable market price and a desired profit level. The difference between these is the target cost that must be achieved.
- Life cycle costing is the forecasting and management of all costs and revenues over the product life from the development stage, through the growth and maturity phases to the decline stage. Professor Michael Porter identified a 'value chain' comprising five primary activities and four support activities.
- Supply chain management is concerned with the total flow of a distribution channel from the supplier to the ultimate user.
- Outsourcing involves the buying in of components, sub-assemblies, finished products, and services from outside suppliers rather than supplying them internally.
- Under a gain-sharing arrangement, vendors typically guarantee that customers will achieve a certain amount of cost savings or top-line improvements.

Having completed your study of this chapter you should have achieved the following learning outcomes.

- Explain how target costs can be derived from target prices and describe the relationship between target costs and standard costs.
- Explain the concept of life cycle costing and how life cycle costs interact with marketing strategies at each stage of the life cycle.
- Explain the concept of the value chain and discuss the management of contribution/profit generated throughout the chain.
- Discuss gain sharing arrangements whereby contractors and customers benefit if contract targets for cost, delivery, etc are beaten.

Self-test questions

1 Explain the principles of target costing (1.2)

2 Explain the principles of life cycle costing. (2.1)

3 Identify and describe the activities which comprise the value chain. (3)

4 What are the four major decision areas that require consideration in the management of an organisation's supply chain? (4)

5 Identify the advantages and disadvantages of insourcing and outsourcing. (5.1)

6 Why has Eastern Europe become a popular manufacturing location for Western European manufacturing organisations? (5.2)

Objective test questions

Question 1

Which of the following may be classified as life-cycle costs?

A Development costs and manufacturing costs only

B Marketing and manufacturing costs only

C Marketing, manufacturing and distribution costs only

D Development, marketing, manufacturing and distribution costs

Question 2

Which of the following statements regarding the value chain is true?

1 The activities of an organisation may be categorised into five primary and four support activities.

2 Support activities only provide support to primary activities.

3 Each activity within the value chain provides inputs which after processing constitute added value to the output.

4 Each primary activity has the potential to contribute to the competitive advantage of an organisation.

A 1 and 2 only

B 1, 2 and 3 only

C 1, 3 and 4

D All four statements

Exam-type question

NN Ltd

NN Ltd specialises in the manufacture of micro-digital equipment. It is planning to introduce a micro DVD player/camera called the 'MDVDC' into its home market. The new product development team are shortly to commence work on the MDVDC and the management of NN Ltd is currently preparing a budget in respect of the product life cycle of the MDVDC. The marketing director has stated that the product is expected to have a life cycle of three years. The following information relating to sales and costs has been collated by the management accountant of NN Ltd:

	Year 1	*Year 2*	*Year 3*
Sales units (000)	365	1,460	1,095
Unit selling price (£)	200	175	175
Products per batch	500	625	625
Research & Development costs (£000)	6,000	1,500	–
Production costs			
Variable costs per 'MDVDC' unit (£)	95	80	80
Variable costs per batch (£)	6,250	5,500	5,500
Fixed costs (£000)	25,000	25,000	25,000
Marketing costs			
Variable costs per 'MDVDC' unit (£)	20	18	18
Fixed costs (£000)	10,000	8,000	8,000
Distribution costs			
'MDVDC's per batch	250	200	150
Variable costs per 'MDVDC' unit (£)	4	4	4
Variable costs per batch (£)	480	480	480
Fixed costs (£000)	6,000	6,000	6,000
Customer service costs per 'MDVDC' (£)	8	6	6

Required:

(a) Prepare a summary which clearly shows the profit/loss attributable to each year of the product's life cycle and also shows the whole-life profit/loss that will results as a result of the decision to manufacture the 'MDVDC'. **(10 marks)**

(b) Tarot Ltd, which is a market research organisation, has undertaken a study on behalf of NN Ltd which indicates that if the projected selling price per unit was reduced by £10 in each of the three years the sales volumes of 'MDVDC' would increase by 20% in each of the first two years, and by 5% during the third year of the product's life.

In order to accommodate the increased sales volumes, NN Ltd plans to increase its production batch size by 20% in each of the three years of the product's life cycle as a consequence of this increase. A major reorganisation of distribution activities would result in the doubling of the batch size in each year of the project. However, in order to achieve such a sizeable increase in the distribution batch size, it is estimated that fixed distribution costs would increase by £1,000,000 per year.

Advise management of NN Ltd whether the proposed selling prices of the MDVDC should be reduced. **(10 marks)**

(c) Discuss the potential benefits to be gained by organisations who undertake product life cycle costing exercises. **(5 marks)**

(Total: 25 marks)

For the answers to these questions, see the 'Answers' section at the end of the book.

Chapter 10

ACTIVITY-BASED TECHNIQUES

Syllabus content

This chapter covers the following syllabus content.

- Activity-based management in the analysis of overhead and its use in improving efficiency of repetitive overhead activities.
- The use of direct and activity-based cost methods in tracing costs to 'cost objects' such as customers or distribution channels, and the comparison of such costs with appropriate revenues to establish 'tiered' contribution levels, as in the activity-based costing hierarchy.
- Pareto analysis.

As direct costs (e.g. direct labour) become smaller and indirect costs (e.g. quality control overheads) become larger, so it becomes increasingly important to allocate overheads to cost units accurately. Activity-based costing (ABC) is a development with just this aim in mind. Supporters of ABC claim that traditional overhead absorption is inappropriate in the modern business environment and that ABC should be used instead.

Contents

1 Activity-based approaches to cost analysis

1.1 Introduction

Activity-based costing (ABC) is an approach to the costing and monitoring of activities which involves tracing resource consumption to cost units. Resources are assigned to activities and activities to cost objects based on consumption estimates. The latter utilise cost drivers to attach activity costs to outputs. (CIMA *Official Terminology*)

DEFINITION

A **cost driver** is any factor that causes a change in the cost of an activity. (CIMA *Official Terminology*)

A **cost driver** is any factor that causes a change in the cost of an activity. (CIMA *Official Terminology*)

1.2 The origins of activity-based costing (ABC)

Activity-based costing (ABC) has its origins in the 1950s, when some US firms made efforts to allocate their selling and distribution overheads between products in a more 'accurate' and meaningful way. Over time, as manufacturing methods changed, growing attention was given to overhead costs, and the problem of how overhead costs should be allocated between products or services, in order to obtain a more reliable assessment of the profitability of different products or services. It was recognised that traditional absorption costing did not necessarily provide a reliable analysis of product costs and profitability.

KEY POINT

In a modern manufacturing environment, production overhead costs are high relative to direct labour costs, and the consumption of resources in overhead activities is not driven by direct production activity.

At one time, the main elements of cost in manufacturing were direct materials and direct labour. Production overhead costs were relatively low, and the use of resources by overhead activities was largely driven by activities in the direct production departments. It was therefore reasonable to allocate production overheads to product costs on the basis of a rate per direct labour hour or as a percentage of direct labour cost. Modern manufacturing systems are very different, and the cost of 'support functions' or 'service functions' can be very high, as a proportion of total costs. Whereas direct labour costs might be fairly low in a highly automated environment, support activities might use a large amount of resources. Support activities include order processing, the costs of setting up new production batches for processing, customer services, materials handling, inspection costs, the cost of logistics (transportation and storage), and so on.

In a system of traditional absorption costing, the largest allocation of overheads is typically charged to the high-volume or high-value products. This is because these products use up a relatively large proportion of direct labour time or machine time in the production department. However, use of the resources of support activities is often unrelated to the volume of production or the value of sales. For example, a small rush order for a low value item could use up large amounts of resource in order processing, customer services, batch set up time and inspection costs. The nature of support activities varies between different firms and industries, but here are some examples of how resource consumption is not related to the volume or value of production and sales.

- Set-up costs. Production runs might be in a mix of small and large batch runs, or a mixture of small and large jobs. Set-up costs could well be the same regardless of whether the next job is a short or a long one. It would therefore seem likely that the costs of setting up, if these are substantial, are more likely to relate to the number of jobs or batches rather than to the overall volume of production.

- Order handling costs. A large amount of resources might be required to deal with customer orders. An order has to be taken and recorded. The time and resources needed to handle small orders might be the same as for larger orders. Taking an order, processing the order, handling customer queries, chasing the order, and despatching the order might all be much the same, regardless of order size.

Activity-based costing developed out of an awareness that traditional absorption costing, which typically recovers overheads in product costs on the basis of a direct labour hour rate, does not allocate overheads in a fair way between products. As a result, information about product costs and profitability is unreliable.

Cost information should indicate which products or activities are really profitable, and which might be making losses because they use up large amounts of overhead resources that are not recovered sufficiently in the product's selling price. Some products that might seem profitable when costed by traditional methods might seem much less profitable when a closer analysis is made of the overhead resources they consume.

ABC attempts to charge overhead costs more accurately to the products or services that, directly or indirectly, consume resources and give rise to the expenditures. It does this by charging overhead costs in a way that reflects the activities that influence those costs.

1.3 The mechanics of ABC

ABC is a form of absorption costing system, but with much greater analysis of overhead costs. It tries to identify those activities that give rise to resource consumption and overhead expenditures.

The collection of overhead costs is done in the same way as with traditional overhead costing.

The next step is to allocate overhead costs to cost pools or activity pools. There is a cost pool for each activity that consumes significant amounts of resources. Costs in each cost pool might arise in a number of different departments. (Costs are not allocated or apportioned to production and service departments, so in this respect ABC differs significantly from traditional absorption costing.)

Examples of resource-consuming activities might be materials handling, procurement, quality inspection and set-up of batches or jobs. The selection of cost pools will vary according to the nature of the business operations, the markets and management's judgement.

For each activity pool, there should be a *cost driver*. A cost driver is an item or an activity that results in the consumption of resources, and so results in costs being incurred. For the costs in the cost pool, overheads are then allocated to product costs on the basis of a recovery rate per unit of cost driver.

Examples of cost drivers

There are no rules about what the cost driver should be for any particular activity or cost pool. An organisation should identify the cost driver that seems best suited for the particular activity.

The following are examples of possible cost drivers.

Activity	*Cost driver*
Materials procurement	Number of purchase orders
Materials handling	Number of materials movements
Quality control	Number of inspections
Engineering services	Number of change orders
Maintenance	Number of breakdowns
Line set-up	Number of set-ups/batch runs
Order processing	Number of customer orders

For the service sector, cost drivers can also vary widely. Here are illustrative examples taken from the field of health care. The following cost drivers might be used to establish a basis for charging patients for particular services.

Activity	*Cost driver*
Patient movement	Number of in-patients
Booking appointments	Number of patients
Patient reception	Number of patients
X-ray:	
Equipment preparation	Time taken
Patient preparation	Time taken
Patient aftercare	Time taken
Film processing	Number of images
Film reporting	Number of images

(From Kirton: '*ABC at Luton & Dunstable Hospital'* CIMA 1992).

Having established the total costs for an activity pool, and having chosen the cost driver for that pool, a *cost per unit of cost driver* is then calculated. This is an overhead recovery rate that will be used to allocate overhead costs to products or services. As with traditional absorption costing, the overhead rate per unit of cost driver can be pre-determined in the budget, and calculated as:

$$\frac{\text{Budgeted costs for the cost pool}}{\text{Budgeted activity level (units of cost driver)}}$$

For each activity pool, costs are allocated to products and services, on the basis of:

Units of cost driver used up x Cost per unit of cost driver.

ABC is a form of absorption costing, and so has similarities with traditional absorption costing. However, the cost driver represents the factor that has the greatest influence on the behaviour of costs in the activity pool, and the consumption of resources. For example, if 50% of orders received and processed are for one particular product and there is a cost pool for order handling costs, the product should attract 50% of the total costs of order handling.

Example

Oceanides has four departments who make use of the procurement function. The total cost of the function is £12,000,000 per annum. The four departments use the function in the following way:

Department	*No. of orders*	*Cost allocation*
		£
A	200,000	8,000,000
B	50,000	2,000,000
C	40,000	1,600,000
D	10,000	400,000
	300,000	12,000,000

Simply dividing the total cost by the cost driver we get:

$$\frac{£12,000,000}{300,000} = £40\text{per order}$$

Activity 1

Pelleas has the following indirect costs:

	£	
Quality control	90,000	450 inspections
Process set-up	135,000	450 set-ups
Purchasing	105,000	1,000 purchase orders
Customer order processing	120,000	2,000 customer orders
Occupancy costs	150,000	75,000 machine hours
	600,000	

Calculate the charge out rates for each of the activities.

Feedback to this activity is at the end of the chapter.

Example

Pelleas (the company in Activity 1) makes a standard product called the Melisande.

The cost details are as follows:

Unit material cost	£0.50
Unit labour cost	£0.40
Total production for the coming year	1,000,000 units
No. of production runs	50
No. of purchase orders required	50
No. of customer orders	10
Unit machine time	3 minutes

The product is inspected once at the end of each production run.

You are required to calculate the standard cost of a Melisande.

Solution

Using the cost driver rates calculated in Activity 1, draw up a grid for the overheads.

Function	*Rate × annual usage*		£
Quality control	£200 × 50	=	10,000
Process set-up	£300 × 50	=	15,000
Purchasing	£105 × 50	=	5,250
Customer orders	£60 × 10	=	600
Occupancy	£2 × 50,000	=	100,000
			130,850

Dividing the total overhead cost by the number of units produced we get:

$$\frac{130{,}850}{1{,}000{,}000} \quad = \quad £0.1385 \text{ (say £0.14)}$$

Thus the standard unit cost for a Melisande is:

	£
Material	0.50
Labour	0.40
Overhead	0.14
	1.04

A typical examination question might ask candidates to calculate overhead rates in the traditional manner and using the ABC method and compare the results over two or more products, one like the Melisande (standard and with long runs), and others which are likely to be non-standard with short runs.

1.4 Value added and ABC

In ABC, product costs are assembled by allocating a cost for each of the activities required to make a product or provide a service, based on the consumption or use of those activities. ABC can therefore be used, with care, to identify activities and costs that are not contributing to the value of the products the organisation makes or the services it provides. The following questions can be asked:

- What is the purpose of this activity?
- Who benefits from the activity, and how?
- Why are so many people needed?
- What might reduce the number of staff needed?
- Why is overtime needed?

ABC can also be used as the basis for one-off exercises to identify activities that do not add value to products or services, or to identify ways in which activities might be re-organised. One-off investigations using ABC analysis are referred to as 'activity-based management'.

1.5 ABC and long-run variable costs

Many of the overhead costs in activity pools might be variable costs, in the sense that the total costs of the activity will rise as the amount of the activity increases. However, many costs are more likely to be variable in the longer term rather than in the immediate short term. For example, if the ABC cost of setting up a batch production run is estimated at £400, the actual cost of setting up 10 batches is unlikely to be £4,000. This is because many overhead costs are fixed in the short term.

However, in the longer term, all costs are variable. By identifying activities that use up resources that give rise to costs, ABC can provide useful information about product profitability, for controlling overhead costs over the longer term. Traditional absorption costing does not do this because there is no relationship between the overhead costs allocated to products and the consumption of overhead resources.

Since costs are allocated to products on the basis of resource-consuming activities, ABC provides useful information about the economic cost of products, and which products are more profitable than others.

1.6 Problems with ABC

There are several problems with ABC. A major problem is the cost of setting up and operating a system. An ABC system costs more to set up and maintain than a traditional absorption costing system. This is because the activities in each cost pool have to be monitored and measured. The system should also be reviewed periodically, to check that the selection of activity pools and cost drivers is still appropriate.

There can be a danger of taking the analysis of activities and cost pools to excessive detail. For example, purchasing might be a major activity, in which case an ABC cost per purchase order might be calculated for the purchasing cost pool. However, purchasing might be broken down into a number of different cost pools, such as new supplier selection, purchase requisitioning, placing purchase orders and so on. A different cost driver could then be selected for each of these separate activities within purchasing. This would add to the complexity of the system, and the cost of operating it. To prevent an ABC system from becoming too complex and expensive, the number of cost pools and cost drivers should be kept to a small and manageable number.

Another problem with ABC is the risk that ABC costs will be seen as 100% accurate economic costs of products or services. This is not the case. ABC is a form of absorption costing, and although it attempts to trace overhead costs to products more accurately, there will inevitably be some element of shared cost apportionment. It is impossible to trace *all* costs objectively to specific products or services.

2 Activity-based management (ABM)

2.1 Cost visibility

DEFINITION

Activity-based management is a system of management which uses ABC information for a variety of purposes including cost reduction, cost modelling and customer profitability analysis. (CIMA *Official Terminology*)

Activity based management is a 'system of management which uses activity based cost information for a variety of purposes including cost reduction, cost modelling and customer profitability analysis'. (CIMA *Official Terminology*, 2000) The activity-based approach brings costs out into the open and helps management see what they get for the commitment of resources.

For example, the buying department ties up people, equipment (office space, desks, filing cabinets) and uses stationery, telephones etc. and produces purchase orders.

The effectiveness of the department can be monitored in terms of delays, reductions in lead times and errors. This would enable the purchasing function to be monitored effectively and improved upon. In addition, a purchasing department is not just concerned with buying. It will have input from the design area, perhaps being told to find standard parts for specialist products, it will obviously buy and track prices, it may be responsible for receiving and it will pass invoices to accounting. How quickly and effectively it performs these tasks can all be used to monitor performance and control costs.

2.2 Activity cost profile

ABC is perhaps most useful in monitoring how effectively the traditional overhead departments operate. Since a factory needs material, it follows that it needs buyers. It is tempting to say that they are indispensable and not track the cost. What ABC does do is enable management to really ask whether or not any department is as cost effective as it could be. One way of doing this is to create cost profiles to measure resource consumption.

This is not a new idea. Students should already be familiar with traditional overhead reporting statements which show last year's figures as a comparison. The profile is merely a different approach.

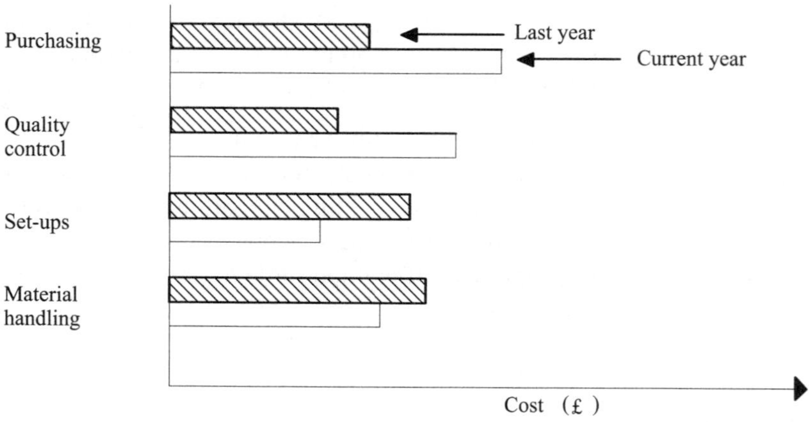

From the profile, it can be asked 'Why has purchasing cost gone up?'. This could be because of increased volume, diversity of products, change in mix of production runs, etc.

The dramatic increase observed in the cost of quality control may be offset by fewer external failures, fewer warranty claims and fewer recalls. It may be due to the changing expectation of the customer, demanding a higher quality product. Similar analyses can be performed on set-up and material handling costs.

DEFINITION

Value added = 'sales value less the cost of purchased materials and services. This represents the worth of an alteration in form, location or availability of a product or service.'

2.3 Identifying value added

Value added is 'sales value less the cost of purchased materials and services. This represents the worth of an alteration in form, location or availability of a product or service.' However, not all costs incurred add value to the basic bought in good or service.

The table below illustrates some of the cost categories that could be scrutinised under this form of analysis.

Activity	*Value added*	*Non-value added*
Purchasing		
Vetting suppliers	X	
Producing orders	X	
Returning goods		X
Correcting orders		X
Customer order processing		
Assessing credit rating		X
Liaising with customer	X	
Expediting delivery		X
Dealing with returns inwards		X
Quality control		
Supplies received		X
In process		X
On completion		X

Activity	*Value added*	*Non-value added*
Material scheduling		
Identifying line needs	X	
Storage		X
Movement from store to line		X

In theory, all costs that do not add value to the product should be targets for elimination. However, some, such as quality control, are essential to the running of the business in the short term. Quality control ensures that the product is up to customer expectation. It does not add value, but its removal could further add costs. Some judgement may be seen to be needed in the classification. Expediting delivery could mean ensuring that orders do not fall behind (non-value adding) or saying we can deliver to your schedule but at a premium cost.

A further development in this form of analysis breaks activities into three components – core, support and discretionary. In the case of sales costs, time spent with customers and potential customers would be core work. That is the essential business of winning orders for the firm. Travelling time would be a support activity while dealing with sales order processing errors would be purely discretionary. Thus effective cost management is about reducing the amount of resources that are being expended on non-core activities. This may mean changing territories to reduce travel time or travel costs, or changing the order process system to minimise errors.

2.4 Cost behaviour patterns

The student should be familiar with the traditional narrow view of cost behaviour patterns. In essence a linear assumption is made that is based upon one variable, e.g. production or possibly sales volume. Common sense indicates that not all costs vary in a direct linear relationship with activity. One obvious example is the telephone. It may actually be used far more if activity is slack in order to drum up more business.

Fixed costs have increased in proportion to the total but have also not remained unchanged. More resources are being committed to elements of the fixed cost structure. What is required is an analysis of what is driving these increases. One approach to investigating and exploring ways of reducing these costs is to establish a hierarchy that classifies types of activity and identifies how costs are driven.

Level 1	Unit basis	Costs depend on the volume of production, e.g. machine power.
Level 2	Batch basis	Costs depend upon the number of batches, e.g. set-up and monitoring.
Level 3	Process level	Costs depend upon the existence of the process, e.g. quality control and supervision.
Level 4	Product level	Costs depend upon the existence of a group or line, e.g. product management and parts administration.
Level 5	Facility level	Costs depend on the existence of a facility of plant, e.g. rent, rates, general management.

This approach highlights the pattern of costs as one moves further away from the product. It also highlights the position in the hierarchy of decision-making. The fixed set-up cost can be reduced by longer runs, but at the expense of increased storage if there is no immediate demand. Further up the hierarchy, consideration can be given to reducing the number of processes, merging lines and changing facility capacity. Such an approach requires a different view of costs which traditional analysis does not give. Traditional analysis with its subjective apportionments assumes that the product drives all the costs. By definition, fixed costs cannot be product-driven and what is required is to find out how they are driven and if they add value to the product. It also provides an attention-directing signal that highlights the cost of resources consumed by a product in order to gain a particular market price. Such a signal enables consideration of future strategies towards volumes and product development.

2.5 Customer-driven costs

This is an area that has been traditionally neglected. All the emphasis has been upon manufacturing costs with over-emphasis on direct labour. It may come as a shock that the labour cost content of a \$18,000 (£12,000) car is about \$840 (£560) while the selling and distribution cost is about 30% of the showroom price, i.e. \$5,400 (£3,600) (*Fortune 4 April 1994*). Major potential cost savings can be achieved in this hitherto almost sacred area. The following customer-driven costs have been identified.

- **Supply and delivery patterns** – A JIT system will need more but smaller deliveries compared with a customer who maintains high buffer inventories.
- **Customer location** – Distribution, communication and contact costs are all influenced by distance.
- **Quality provided** – Different customers may require different standards, both of supply and product.
- **Provision of after sales service** – This will have been negotiated with the individual customer. Obviously, the customer who wants 24 hours support for his PCs is going to pay a premium over the customer who is happy to buy the cheapest "box" from a specialist supermarket.
- **Required documentation** – This may be determined by the needs of the customer.
- **Sales and promotion effort** – This again may be geared to different types of customers, who may be attracted to different attributes of the product on offer.
- **Discounts given** – Repeat business, special relationships, offers or promptness of paying can all differ among customers.

Illustrative example

Diomed manufactures a single product with a production cost of £40 per unit which is sold to three customers at a price of £75 per unit. The details are:

Sales pattern:	Customer	X	10,000 units per annum
		Y	10,000 units per annum
		Z	10,000 units per annum

Non-production overhead is:

	£
Delivery	220,000
Quality inspection	200,000
Salespeople	80,000
After sales service	100,000
	600,000

This is currently apportioned on the basis of a rate on the production cost. The MD is unhappy about this and asks for an analysis based upon ABC methods.

The following period activity volumes have been identified.

Customer	*X*	*Y*	*Z*
No. of deliveries	2,500	50	12
No. of inspections	10,000	500	0
No. of salesmen visits	200	24	6
After sales visits	200	100	50

Required:

Calculate the profit or loss arising from each customer.

Solution

Cost driver rates:

Delivery	$\frac{£220,000}{2,562}$	=	£85.87 per delivery
Inspection	$\frac{£200,000}{10,500}$	=	£19.05 per inspection
Salespeople	$\frac{£80,000}{230}$	=	£347.83 per visit
After sales	$\frac{£100,000}{350}$	=	£285.71 per after sales visit

Analysing these costs:

Customer			*X*	*Y*	*Z*
			£	£	£
No. of deliveries	2,500 @	85.87	214,675		
	50 @	85.87		4,294	
	12 @	85.87			1,030
Inspection	10,000 @	19.05	190,500		
	500 @	19.05		9,525	
Sales visits	200 @	347.83	69,566		
	24 @	347.83		8,348	
	6 @	347.83			2,087
After sales visits	200 @	285.71	57,142		
	100 @	285.71		28,571	
	50 @	285.71			14,286
			531,883	50,738	17,403

Final unit cost analysis (10,000 units are sold to each customer):

	Production cost	*Non-production cost*	*Total cost*	*Selling price*	*Profit (loss)*
	£	£	£	£	
Customer X	40	53.19	93.19	75.00	(18.19)
Customer Y	40	5.07	45.07	75.00	29.93
Customer Z	40	1.74	41.74	75.00	33.26

Thus the MD's misgivings were justified. The high cost of serving customer X effectively wipes out the profit being made on producing and selling the product and some consideration has to be given to the quality of service offered for the price charged.

2.6 Impact upon the budget process: activity-based budgeting (ABB)

DEFINITION

Activity-based budgeting is a method of budgeting based on an activity framework and utilising cost-driven data in the budget setting and variance feedback process.

Activity-based budgeting is a method of budgeting based on an activity framework and utilising cost-driven data in the budget setting and variance feedback process.

The introduction of ABC to the budgeting process is not dissimilar to the impact of the zero-based budgeting (ZBB) approach in so far as each method draws upon the use of cost-driven data in the budget setting process. You will recall from your previous studies that 'Zero based budgeting (ZBB) is a method of budgeting that requires each cost element to be specifically justified, as though the activities to which the budget relates were being undertaken for the first time. Without approval, the budget allowance is zero'. (CIMA *Official Terminology*, 2000) For effective activity-based management within the confines of the budget process the following guidelines are advocated:

- Identification of the activities to which resources will be committed. This may require consideration of the hierarchy of levels discussed earlier.
- Examination of the value of activities to the organisational objectives, leading to a prioritisation ranking for scarce resource provision in the budgeting process. This again will require reference back to what adds value to the product. Any activity that does not add value will need careful review. (Again compare with ZBB.)
- Assessment of the possible levels of service required from these activities, including the zero option.
- A meaningful match between areas of responsibility or 'ownership' and costs. This approach is akin to responsibility accounting.
- Estimation of the cost implications of alterations to activities either by reorganisation or changed workloads that will enable objective analysis to be made. Again, this is close to ZBB. Like ZBB it poses the second, often neglected question 'Can we do things differently?'. The obvious example from ZBB texts is security. Policing a shopping mall requires manpower that is expensive and limited. The use of cameras with connections into a rapid response police station may be cheaper and more effective.

KEY POINT

The use of cost drivers in the budget-reporting process enables effective measures of costs against capacity and would highlight over-provision rather than pure overspend.

The use of cost drivers in the budget-reporting process enables effective measures of costs against capacity and would highlight over-provision rather than pure overspend.

3 Business process re-engineering (BPR)

Business process re-engineering (BPR) is a technique that many organisations have employed in order to improve organisational performance. BPR involves a detailed appraisal and overhaul of existing business practices. The scope of its application is far-reaching and encompasses not only manufacturing activities but also an extensive range of administrative and operational activities. BPR takes a holistic customer-focused systems view and necessitates changing the way in which an organisation conducts its activities. BPR contrasts with the "continuous improvement" philosophies that underpin kaizen costing and total quality management. Such initiatives place a focus upon methods which enable improvements to be achieved in business processes so as to obtain gradual, incremental improvements. However, during recent years several factors have accelerated the need to improve business processes. The most obvious is technology. New technologies (like the Internet) bring new capabilities to businesses, thereby raising the level of competition and reinforcing the need to improve business processes dramatically.

Another apparent trend is the opening of world markets and increased free trade. Such changes bring more companies into the marketplace, and competing becomes harder and harder. In today's marketplace, major changes are required just to stay even. It has become a matter of survival for most companies.

As a result, companies have sought out methods for faster business process improvement. Moreover, companies want breakthrough performance changes, not just incremental changes, and they require such changes sooner rather than later. Because the rate of change has increased for everyone, few businesses can afford a slow change process. Thus in order to enhance their competitive position a large number of organisations have adopted BPR methodologies in pursuit of rapid change and dramatic improvement.

The primary focus will be upon the needs of the customer. In a large number of cases BPR will entail a shift of emphasis from transactions processing to decision making and controlling the activities of an organisation. Information systems may require changing in order to furnish those responsible for managing a programme involving process re-engineering with the information that will enable them to understand their environment and manage the new processes that result from the programme. In this sense the format and content of information becomes critical since managers need to rapidly assimilate and understand such information.

Proponents of BPR argue that it is good for business since it provides an appropriate focus for the sphere of operations that should be conducted and leads to cost advantages that enhance the competitive posture of an organisation. Moreover, it encourages management to take a more strategic view of the business and in particular to question those operational processes that are currently employed which may well result in the provision of increased 'added value' to its customers. BPR may result in the simplification and streamlining of processes throughout the entire organisation which can help counteract the myopia which all too often stems from undue concentration upon functional boundaries which act as impediments to improved organisational performance.

Management of organisations who wish to employ BPR need to be aware that it might be met with cynicism by staff who view its application as little more than a cost reduction exercise. In essence BPR programmes are not primarily concerned with reductions in the level of operating costs although such reductions can result. BPR requires top management support (as does any change management programme) and management should seek to ensure that such a programme is regarded as a matter of ongoing interest within an organisation.

4 Customer profitability analysis (CPA)

4.1 Problems of measurement

The example Diomed above illustrated how different customers' behaviours can lead to different levels of profitability from the same level of sales. No accountant is under any illusion that the same level of profit is derived from all customers. There are obvious distinguishing features among groups of customers or channels of distribution and there can also be differences in effective selling prices and variations in the mix of products purchased. Generally customers are another example of the Pareto distribution in action: often it can be found that 80% of profits are earned from just 20% of the population of customers. (We discuss Pareto analysis later in this chapter.)

The differences in selling prices may be much less important than the varying levels of customer service that are supplied to each category of customer or market segment. It could be that the lower selling prices charged to one segment of the market are more than justified by cost savings which are generated by the way in which these customers are serviced. Hence these customers may, in reality, be more profitable than those in areas where the higher selling prices achieved are more than offset by the increased costs incurred in achieving the sales.

If the business is to be able to allocate its limited resources most effectively in the future so as to achieve its corporate profit objectives, it must have reliable information on which of its current and potential future customer groupings are its most profitable, and whether there are any existing areas in which the business actually makes a loss, or looks like making one. The senior managers need tailored financial information which helps them to assess the effectiveness of their existing activities in the different market segments and this information would enable sound decisions to be taken with regard to the future allocation of both sales and marketing resources and new product development priorities.

Clearly this financial analysis needs to go beyond a simplistic comparison of the relative gross margins achieved in each market segment but, equally, neatly splitting the existing net profit of the total business exactly across these different areas would provide a very bad basis for future strategic decisions.

4.2 Customer profitability analysis

DEFINITION

Customer profitability analysis (CPA) is the analysis of the revenue streams and service costs associated with specific customers or customer groups.

It is the widespread introduction of ABC techniques that has, for the first time, enabled customer profitability analysis to be accurately carried out. Customer profitability analysis (CPA) is the analysis of the revenue streams and service costs associated with specific customers or customer groups.

In the past customer-related expenses have been split between the various customers on a more or less arbitrary basis. ABC allows the resources used by particular customers to be charged to them, so that those customers who place numerous small orders or demand non-standard components can either be educated to change their behaviour or else charged appropriately on a transparent objective basis.

Many companies refer explicitly to their customers as 'the most important assets which the organisation has', even if they do not feature in the balance sheet. Phrases like customer orientation and customer focus now proliferate not only in business strategy books but in company mission statements and the related business plans.

In recent years there has been a shift towards customer segmentation, with different customer demands in such things as pricing, distribution, sales support and specialised packaging. Without the implementation of sophisticated financial analysis techniques, the company may not be able to decide on the relative costs associated with doing business in these segments. This has led to the development of customer-orientated segment profitability analysis, or customer profitability analysis (CPA).

As Bob Scarlett (*CIMA Insider*, May 2003) says: 'In recent years many firms have claimed to have moved from being "product-centric" to being "customer centric". Customer relationship management (CRM) initiatives are usually at the forefront of their efforts. Their belief is that understanding customer behaviour and profitability is the key to gaining a competitive advantage.'

The essence of CPA is that it provides a guide for actions to be taken through a CRM initiative. It focuses on profits generated by customers and does not automatically equate increases in sales revenues with increases in profitability.

4.3 Customer profitability in practice

If an analysis of customer profitability is possible then marketing decisions are more easily made on such matters as:

- discounts
- special credit terms
- special after sales servicing
- whether any efforts are required on a sector given its lack of profitability.

The layout of a customer profitability statement can be similar to a product profitability statement:

	Customer Segment A	*Customer Segment B*	*Total*
	£	£	£
Sales	X	X	X
Variable manufacturing cost	X	X	X
	–	–	–
Manufacturing contribution	X	X	X
Variable marketing costs			
Sales commissions	X	X	X
Selling expenses	X	X	X
	–	–	–
Gross contribution	X	X	X
Fixed but direct marketing costs			
Advertising	X	X	X
Sales salaries	X		X
Telemarketing		X	
	–	–	–
Customer net contribution	X	X	X
	–	–	
Indirect marketing costs			
Corporate advertising			X
			–
Marketing contribution			X
Other fixed costs:			
Administration			X
			–
Net profit			X
			–

4.4 Benefits of CPA

The major benefits which can be and are obtained from CPA are in the area of strategic planning and decision-making. This is because knowledge of the relative profitability of different customer groups can enable a company to focus its resources either on those areas which can generate the most profitable growth for the business or on rationalising areas which are making an unsatisfactory return. It should enable companies to identify unexpected differences in profitability among customer groups and to investigate the reasons for these differences.

Also, in the face of aggressive negotiating by specific customers, the company should be able to quantify the financial impact of any proposed changes and hence argue from a position of relative strength, at least in terms of knowing how much any such changes will cost it.

For example, consider the situation where one segment or category of customer is considering doing away with the services of field sales support of its suppliers and is trying to negotiate an appropriate discount to reflect the savings to be made to the supplier. From the suppliers' point of view, the potential discount should reflect the avoidable cost of the salesforce which will obviously be saved if the change is made. However, this cost will not be the same as the historic actual cost which may have been apportioned to this category or segment of customer, as this will include some shared costs, such as sales managers, which will not change if this is the only customer that stops using the support service. The CPA analysis will reflect the increasing levels of attributable costs as the customer segments are made more general – so that if a change is made to the whole distribution channel, the savings would be much greater. The analysis would also highlight that the potential cost saving may not be equal to the potential incremental cost which would be incurred if a single customer or group of customers wanted to begin using the field salesforce service.

4.5 Information for CPA

The above example should have outlined the sort of problems which are likely to be encountered in collecting the information required for a comprehensive system of CPA. Costs must be allocated at varying levels of customer groupings depending on how the cost changes but, more importantly, it may not be relevant to include the actual historic level of cost at all.

The costs required may be hypothetical as in the above illustration of the customers negotiating to stop using the field salesforce. However, the key here is to design a good CPA system which will enable a comparison of relative costs and profitability. Consequently if some customers do not use the field salesforce while other similar ones do, it should be possible to extract the differences in their relative cost levels in respect of the salesforce and hence estimate an approximate avoidable cost involved in ceasing to use it. For this comparison of relative cost levels to generate accurate answers, it is important that each customer analysis is computed on a consistent basis and that there is no attempt to spread the total costs incurred in any area across the customers because, if apportionment is done, the differences will cease to represent the appropriate form of attributable cost which is required.

Some businesses may wish to include some elements of such apportioned costs, particularly if they are likely to have a material impact on the relative levels of customer profit contributions. However it is clear that an even apportionment of such costs will not have any such material impact on relative levels of CPA. Consequently, these shared costs need only be incorporated in the CPA analysis if significantly different levels of cost can genuinely be apportioned to different categories of customers.

4.6 Distribution channel profitability

Strategic cost management recognises that costs are driven not only by products produced, but also by the customers served and the channels through which the products are sold (e.g. distributors, catalogues, mega-stores, direct mail, e-commerce, etc.). This method separates costs into three different types: product-related costs, customer-related costs, and channel-related costs.

It is clear that activity-based costing is a method that measures cost of a product/service, based on the activities performed to produce the product/service. The underlying assumption is that activities drive the cost, which are driven by the product or customer. This radically differs from the conventional costing systems, which is built on the assumption that product drives the cost directly. ABC system drives indirect and support expenses, first to the activities and processes and then to products, services and customers, giving managers a clearer picture of profitability of their operations and services.

The ABC methodology can be extended in order to enable customer profitability analysis to be undertaken. It can also be applied to monitor distribution channel profitability. The importance of distribution channels cannot be overstated. Indeed, according to Michael Porter access to distribution channels can be a source of competitive advantage.

Management can develop accurate channel costs in much the same way as customer costs. In this respect they are aided by the separation of the organisation's cost structure into activity-related and non activity-related costs. Management can thus identify the cost behaviour of all costs, activity-related and otherwise, and trace these costs to the individual products, customers and distribution channels. From these actions management will gain an invaluable insight into the organisation by translating the product, customer and distribution channel cost elements into a total cost view of the business.

The activities which drive distribution costs vary from organisation to organisation, being dependent upon the organisational structure adopted by an organisation and the importance of individual activities to its operations. Management need recognise that the customer or final consumer must be the primary consideration when designing their channels of distribution. Therefore when making decisions concerning the distribution of its products, an organisation should give consideration to size, geographic distribution, usage patterns, purchasing habits and outlet preferences. In this respect management should be mindful that consumer product channels can be much longer than industrial product channels because not only is the number of customers far greater but also they tend to purchase products in much lower quantities and are spread over far larger geographical areas. Given the fact that distribution costs constitute a significant cost of virtually all organisations, it is easy to envisage that the application of activity-based costs to distribution channel profitability analysis will prove as beneficial to organisations as product and customer profitability analysis can do so.

5 Direct product profitability (DPP)

5.1 Introduction

In a similar way that CPA tries to assess the profitability of particular customer segments using ABC techniques where possible, direct product profitability (DPP) is a method of analysing the profitability of particular product segments by comparing the unit price charged for each product with a fair total of the costs that can be directly allocated to each unit.

DEFINITION

Direct product profitability is used primarily within the retail sector and it involves the attribution of costs other than purchase price (e.g. distribution, warehousing, retailing) to each product line. Thus a net profit, as opposed to gross profit, can be identified for each product. The cost attribution process utilises a variety of measures (e.g. warehousing space, transport time) to reflect the resource consumption of individual products. (CIMA *Official Terminology*)

DPP is used primarily within the retail sector and it involves the attribution of costs other than purchase price (e.g. distribution, warehousing, retailing) to each product line. Thus a net profit, as opposed to gross profit, can be identified for each product. The cost attribution process utilises a variety of measures (e.g. warehousing space, transport time) to reflect the resource consumption of individual products. (CIMA *Official Terminology*)

The method will be illustrated using an example.

Example

Captains plc produces high quality model figures from a central manufacturing plant. Output is stored in the warehouse before being delivered to shops around central England. Overheads last year were as follows.

	Total
	£000
Warehouse costs	1,728
Head office costs	336
	2,064

The following information is available for three models.

	Kirk	*Pickard*	*Janeway*
Boxed units per cubic metre	200	240	100
Average time in warehouse (weeks)	4	2	1
Production costs per model	£2	£3	£5
Selling price per model	£5	£7	£10

The total volume of goods produced per week by the company as a whole is $600m^3$.

There are 48 working weeks in a year. The company currently examines the contribution to sales ratio from each model to assess the relative profitability of different products.

Required:

(a) Compare the profitability of the three products under the company's current method with the profit per item using the DPP method.

(b) Suggest ways in which the company's profitability could be improved.

Solution

(a) Current method shows:

	Kirk	*Pickard*	*Janeway*
	£	£	£
Sales price per unit	5	7	10
Production costs	(2)	(3)	(5)
Contribution	3	4	5
C/S ratio	60%	57%	50%

In relative terms, the Kirk is the most profitable, followed by the Pickard, with the Janeway the least profitable.

Using a DPP method, the warehouse costs can be allocated among the units produced, while the head office costs remain unallocated.

Note: DPP only allocates costs for which some causal link exists between the cost and the product. Compare this with conventional total absorption costing which would allocate both the warehouse costs and the head office costs on some necessarily arbitrary basis.

Weekly warehouse cost: £1,728,000 ÷ 48 ÷ 600 = £60/m^3

The DPP analysis is therefore as follows:

	Kirk	*Pickard*	*Janeway*
	£	£	£
Contribution	3	4	5
Allocated warehouse cost			
£60 ÷ 200 × 4 weeks	(1.2)		
£60 ÷ 240 × 2 weeks		(0.5)	
£60 ÷ 100 × 1 week			(0.6)
Direct product profit	1.8	3.5	4.4
Profit / sales ratio	36%	50%	44%

In terms of the direct product profit to the sales ratio, the Pickard is now the most profitable, with the Janeway second, and the Kirk the least profitable. The change in rankings is largely due to the Kirk spending four weeks in the warehouse and thus being charged with more use of warehouse space than the other products.

(b) The company's profitability could be improved by:

- increasing the sales prices achieved per unit
- reducing the direct production costs incurred per unit
- reducing the warehouse costs, perhaps by shipping the products out to shops more quickly, thus reducing the volume of product in storage; a smaller warehouse could then be used or the unused space in the existing warehouse could be hired out
- reducing the head office costs, by bearing down on non-value added activities.

5.2 Conclusion

Direct product profitability analysis is similar to activity-based costing in that costs are related to products on the basis of the causal activities that give rise to such costs. Total absorption costing fails to achieve this accuracy since costs in absorption costing are related to cost centres rather than the activities that give rise to the costs.

Management decisions concerning product pricing and promotion, etc. should therefore be more accurate if DPP is adopted rather than traditional absorption costing.

6 Pareto analysis

A Pareto distribution is a frequency distribution describing what percentage of value or resources is accounted for by a given percentage of items. In general, the Pareto concept (sometimes called the 80: 20 rule) says that 20% of causal factors (or resources) account for 80% of the result. For example, a Pareto 80/20 distribution would indicate that 20% of items sold accounted for 80% of total sales by value. This can be shown on a typical Pareto graph as follows:

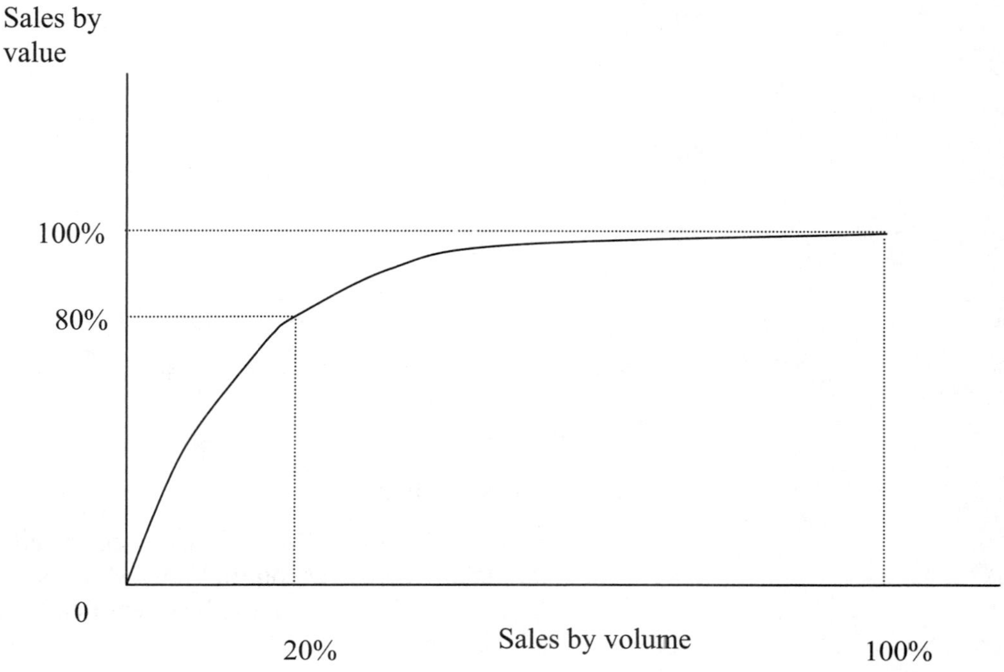

In this example, 20% of the firm's sales accounts for 80% of the firm's total revenue.

There are two important points to note:

(a) The percentages are not necessarily 20%: 80%. However, where this analysis is relevant, the percentages will typically be skewed in this way (maybe 30%: 70% or something similar, but not 50: 50).

(b) There is no logic or calculation that leads to this result. It is just observed in many situations and leads to management action to use the situation to the company's advantage.

One frequent application is to enable a company to identify its most important items of stock, i.e. the items to which the company should pay particular attention as regards stock reorder levels, optimum order sizes, security etc.

The method used to identify these items is usually referred to as the 'ABC plan', but do not be confused by terminology as this has nothing to do with activity based costs. The 'ABC plan' is simply another name for Pareto analysis. The ABC plan of stores control classifies all the stock items into one of three groups 'A', 'B', 'C') and establishes separate systems of control for each group. Group 'A' comprises the more expensive materials, whereas group 'C' includes the small value items. The dividing lines between groups are chosen arbitrarily, but a useful guide is that 'A' covers roughly the top 50% of total stockholding turnover value and 'C' comprises the top 50% of the turnover in units.

Illustration – Stock Control

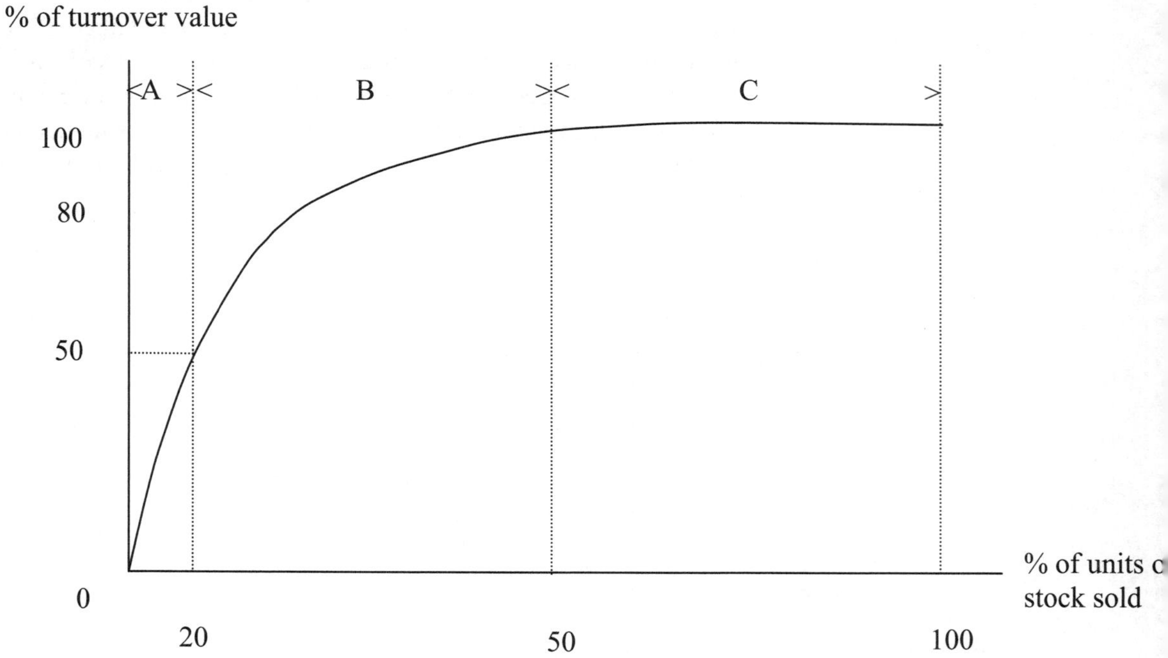

Using the ABC plan

(a) *Group 'A' stocks* – The items in group 'A' are very closely controlled through carefully set control limits which are regularly reviewed. The EOQ for each item will also be scientifically determined after considering all the relevant factors.

(b) *Group 'B' stocks* – Control of 'B' items is exercised through the establishment of EOQ, together with a safe reorder level for each stock item.

(c) *Group 'C' stocks* – The simplest physical controls are introduced for group 'C' items. It must be noted, however, that although these items represent a small investment and are less important from the 'stewardship' point of view they may represent a high percentage of physical usage and the goods must be available when required.

Summary

- A cost driver is any factor that causes a change in the cost of an activity.
- Activity-based costing uses cost drivers to attach activity costs to outputs.
- Activity-based management uses ABC information for a variety of purposes including cost reduction, cost modelling and customer profitability analysis.
- Business process re-engineering involves a detailed appraisal and overhaul of existing business practices.
- Customer profitability analysis is the analysis of the revenue streams and service costs associated with specific customers or customer groups.
- Direct product profitability is a method of analysing the profitability of particular product segments by comparing the unit price charged for each product with a fair total of the costs that can be directly allocated to each unit.
- Pareto analysis helps managers to focus on the particular members of a population that most deserve managerial attention.

Having completed your study of this chapter you should have achieved the following learning outcomes.

- Apply the techniques of activity-based management in identifying cost drivers/activities and explain how process re-engineering can be used to eliminate non-value adding activities and reduce activity costs.
- Apply activity-based costing ideas to analyse direct customer profitability and extend this analysis to distribution channel profitability.
- Apply Pareto analysis as a convenient technique for identifying key elements of data and in presenting the results of other analyses, such as activity-based profitability calculations.

Self-test questions

1 What is activity-based costing? (1.1)

2 What is a cost driver? (1.1)

3 State the problems with activity-based costing. (1.6)

4 Explain activity-based management. (2.1)

5 What is an activity cost profile? (2.2)

6 Explain the effects of activity-based costing on the budgeting process. (2.6)

7 Define customer profitability analysis (CPA). (4.2)

8 Are all overheads allocated to products under DPP? (5.1)

Objective test questions

Question 1

A company produces two products, A and B. The following information is available:

		Product A	*Product B*
Budgeted production (units)		500	2,250
Machine hours per unit		6	8
Number of production runs required		10	4
Number of components		12	5
Number of inspections		6	6
Production set-up costs (total)	£118,000		
Stock handling costs (total)	£28,000		
Inspection costs	£80,000		

Overheads are currently absorbed on the basis of machine hours.

If the company changed to an activity based costing system, the overhead charged to product A would:

A remain unchanged

B fall by £10.76 per unit

C increase by £20.56 per unit

D increase by £223.54 per unit.

Question 2

Which of the following features are typical of business process re-engineering?

1 Continuous improvement

2 Elimination of bottlenecks

3 A holistic customer focused systems view of improvements

A 1 and 3

B 2 and 3

C 3 only

D All of these

Question 3

The ABB approach is similar to:

A fixed budgeting

B zero-based budgeting

C incremental budgeting

D participative budgeting.

For the answers to these questions, see the 'Answers' section at the end of the book.

Exam-type question

ABC terms

(a) In the context of activity-based costing (ABC), it was stated in *Management Accounting – Evolution not Revolution* by Bromwich and Bhimani, that

'Cost drivers attempt to link costs to the scope of output rather than the scale of output thereby generating less arbitrary product costs for decision-making.'

You are required to explain the terms 'activity-based costing' and 'cost drivers'. **(8 marks)**

(b) XYZ plc manufactures four products – namely A, B, C and D – using the same plant and processes.

The following information relates to a production period:

Product	*Volume*	*Material cost per unit*	*Direct labour per unit*	*Machine time per unit*	*Labour cost per unit*
A	500	£5	½ hour	¼ hour	£3
B	5,000	£5	½ hour	¼ hour	£3
C	600	£16	2 hours	1 hour	£12
D	7,000	£17	1½ hours	1½ hours	£9

Total production overhead recorded by the cost accounting system is analysed under the following headings:

Factory overhead applicable to machine-oriented activity is £37,424.

Set-up costs are £4,355.

The cost of ordering materials is £1,920.

Handling materials is £7,580.

Administration for spare parts is £8,600.

These overhead costs are absorbed by products on a machine hour rate of £4.80 per hour, giving an overhead cost per product of:

A = £1.20 B = £1.20 C = £4.80 D = £7.20

However, investigation into the production overhead activities for the period reveals the following totals:

Product	*Number of set-ups*	*Number of material orders*	*Number of times material was handled*	*Number of spare parts*
A	1	1	2	2
B	6	4	10	5
C	2	1	3	1
D	8	4	12	4

Required:

(i) Compute an overhead cost per product using activity-based costing, tracing overheads to production units by means of cost drivers. **(6 marks)**

(ii) Comment briefly on the differences disclosed between overheads traced by the present system and those traced by activity-based costing. **(3 marks)**

(Total: 17 marks)

For the answer to this question, see the 'Answers' section at the end of the book.

Feedback to activity

Activity 1

Quality control	90,000	÷	450	=	£200 per inspection
Process set-up	135,000	÷	450	=	£300 per set-up
Purchasing	105,000	÷	1,000	=	£105 per order
Customer order processing	120,000	÷	2,000	=	£60 per customer order
Occupancy costs	150,000	÷	75,000	=	£2 per machine hour

Note that occupancy cost has been allocated on traditional machine hours. The cost driver there is product volume and therefore the same cost driver is chosen as would have been chosen using absorption costing.

Chapter 11

INVESTMENT APPRAISAL TECHNIQUES

Syllabus content

This chapter covers the following syllabus content.

- The techniques of investment appraisal: payback, discounted payback, accounting rate of return, net present value and internal rate of return.

- Application of the techniques of investment appraisal to project cash flows and evaluation of the strengths and weaknesses of the techniques.

Contents

1 Time value of money

1.1 Introduction

Investment appraisal techniques are used to make long-term decisions. The costs and benefits of projects are calculated and evaluated and decisions must be made with respect to:

- whether a project is worthwhile
- which is the best alternative given a range of mutually exclusive alternatives or limited capital.

1.2 The time value of money

A simple method of comparing two investment projects would be to compare the amount of cash generated from each – presumably, the project that generates the greater net cash inflow (taking into account all revenues and expenses) is to be preferred. However, such a simple method would fail to take into account the time value of money, the effect of which may be stated as the general rule below:

> 'There is a time preference for receiving the same sum of money sooner rather than later. Conversely, there is a time preference for paying the same sum of money later rather than sooner.'

The reasons for time preference are threefold.

(a) **Consumption preference** – money received now can be spent on consumption.

(b) **Risk preference** – risk disappears once money is received.

(c) **Investment preference** – money received can be invested in the business or invested externally.

If consideration is given to these factors it can be seen that inflation affects time preference but is not its only determinant. Higher inflation for instance, will produce greater consumption preference and thus greater time preference, all else being equal. It is best to ignore inflation initially when considering DCF techniques.

Discounted cash flow (DCF) techniques of investment appraisal seek to adjust for the time value of money.

The discounting analysis is based on (c), and in particular the ability to invest or borrow and receive or pay interest. The reason for this approach is that, even where funds are not actually used and borrowed in this way, interest rates do provide the market measure of time preference.

The analysis, therefore, proceeds in terms of the way interest payments and receipts behave.

DEFINITION

Simple interest arises when interest accruing on an investment is paid to the investor as it becomes due, and is not added to the capital balance on which subsequent interest will be calculated.

Compound interest arises when the accrued interest is added to the capital outstanding and it is this revised balance on which interest is subsequently earned.

1.3 Compound interest

Simple interest arises when interest accruing on an investment is paid to the investor as it becomes due, and is not added to the capital balance on which subsequent interest will be calculated.

Compound interest arises when the accrued interest is added to the capital outstanding and it is this revised balance on which interest is subsequently earned.

The discounting process that is fundamental to DCF calculations is analogous to compound interest in reverse. A short compound interest calculation is included here as revision.

Example

Barlow places £2,000 on deposit in a bank earning 5% compound interest per annum.

Required:

(a) Find the amount that would have accumulated:

- (i) after one year
- (ii) after two years
- (iii) after three years.

(b) Find the amount that would have to be deposited if an amount of £2,500 has to be accumulated:

- (i) after one year
- (ii) after two years
- (iii) after three years.

Solution

(a) **Terminal values**

Although compound interest calculations can be produced using common sense, some may prefer to use a formula:

$$V = X(1 + r)^n$$

where V = final amount accumulated (terminal value)

X = principal (initial amount deposited)

r = interest rate per annum (as a decimal – i.e. 10% is expressed as 0.1)

n = number of years principal is left on deposit

(i)	After one year, V	=	£2,000 × (1.05) =	£2,100
(ii)	After two years, V	=	£2,000 × 1.05 × 1.05	
		=	£2,000 × 1.05^2 =	£2,205
(iii)	After three years, V	=	£2,000 × 1.05^3 =	£2,315.25

(b) **Present values**

In this case the final amount, V, is known and the principal, X, is to be found. Again the formula could be used, rearranging it to become:

$$\text{Principal, } X = \frac{V}{(1+r)^n}$$

(i) If £2,500 is required in one year's time, a principal, X, has to be invested such that:

$$X \times 1.05 = £2,500$$

$$X = £2,500 \times \frac{1}{1.05} = £2,380.95$$

(If £2,380.95 is invested for a year at 5% interest, 5% of £2,380.95 or £119.05 is earned making the total amount £2,500 as required.)

(ii) If £2,500 is required in 2 years' time:

$$X \times 1.05^2 = £2,500$$

$$X = £2,500 \times \frac{1}{1.05^2} = £2,267.57$$

(It can be checked that £2,267.57 will accumulate to £2,500 after two years.)

(iii) If £2,500 is required in three years' time:

$$X = £2,500 \times \frac{1}{1.05^3} = £2,159.59$$

KEY POINT

DCF calculations are based on present values of future cash flows.

This second group of calculations is the mechanics behind DCF calculations, the calculation of a present value. For example in (b) (i) one would be equally happy with receiving £2,500 in one year's time or £2,380.95 now. Although the immediate receipt is less than £2,500, if invested for a year at 5% it would amount to £2,500 hence the indifference between the two sums. £2,380.95 is called the present value (at 5%) of a sum of £2,500 payable or receivable in one year's time.

1.4 PV formula

The present value (PV) of a single sum, S receivable in n years' time, given an interest rate (a discount rate) r, is given by:

$$PV = S \times \frac{1}{(1+r)^n}$$

Compare this with the two formulae shown in section 3.4.

Illustration

Find the present values of:

(a) £1,000 receivable in one year's time given a discount rate of 10%

(b) £4,000 receivable in two years' time given a discount rate of 5%

(c) £10,000 receivable in five years' time given a discount rate of 8%.

In each case the process of reducing the cash flows to find that sum with which one would be equally happy now follows a procedure similar to compound interest backwards.

(a) PV = $£1,000 \times \frac{1}{1.10}$ = £909.09

(One would be equally happy with £909.09 now as £1,000 in one year's time. With £909.09 available now to invest for one year at 10%, £90.91 interest is earned and the whole sum accumulates to £1,000 in one year's time.)

(b) PV = $£4,000 \times \frac{1}{(1.05)^2}$ = £3,628.12

(Check for yourself that £3,628.12 will accumulate to £4,000 in two years if interest is earned at 5% pa.)

(c) PV = $£10,000 \times \frac{1}{(1.08)^5}$ = £6,806

(It is conventional to state present values to the nearest £ and inappropriate to assume too great a level of accuracy.)

1.5 Annuities

It may be the case that certain types of cash flow are expected to occur in equal amounts at regular periods over the life of a project. Calculating the present value of annuities can be made simpler by use of a second formula.

Illustration

Find the PV of £500 payable for each of three years given a discount rate of 10% if each sum is due to be paid annually in arrears.

The PV can be found from three separate calculations of the present value of a single sum.

$$PV = \left[£500 \times \frac{1}{(1.10)}\right] + \left[£500 \times \frac{1}{(1.10)^2}\right] + \left[£500 \times \frac{1}{(1.10)^3}\right]$$

Although this can be evaluated:

$$= £455 + £413 + £376 = £1,244$$

it might be worth looking again at the expression for the PV and restating it as:

$$PV = £500 \times \left[\frac{1}{(1.10)} + \frac{1}{(1.10)^2} + \frac{1}{(1.10)^3}\right]$$

This can be evaluated:

$$= £500 \times 2.48685 = £1,243$$

(The difference is attributable to rounding.)

The last expression for the PV might be recognised as a geometric progression and a formula can be produced (which could be proved although there is no need to do so) for the PV of an annuity:

$$PV = a \times \frac{1}{r}\left(1 - \frac{1}{(1+r)^n}\right) \text{ or } a \times \left(\frac{1}{r} - \frac{1}{r(1+r)^n}\right)$$

As given in the *CIMA Mathematical Tables and Formulae*, with t instead of n

where now a is the annual cash flow receivable in arrears.

In this case:

$$PV = £500 \times \frac{1}{0.10}\left(1 - \frac{1}{(1.10)^3}\right)$$

$$= £500 \times \frac{1}{0.10}(1 - 0.7513148)$$

$$= £500 \times 2.48685 = £1,243$$

1.6 Present value and annuity factor tables

To make investment appraisal calculations simpler, tables are produced of discount factors and annuity factors. The formulae to calculate PVs and annuity factors are included in the heading of each table. A copy of the tables issued in the exam appears at the front of this text. These provide values of:

Individual discount factors = $\frac{1}{(1+r)^n}$ (or $(1 + r)^{-n}$)

Cumulative discount factors for annuities = $\frac{1}{r}\left(1 - \frac{1}{(1+r)^n}\right)$

Tutorial note: These should always be used in an exam question, except in the relatively unusual situation that the required discount factor lies outside of the range of the table, as there is a considerable time saving.

To illustrate the use of tables recalculate the examples in paragraphs 1.5 and 1.6 using tables to find appropriate discount factors.

1.7 Perpetuities

Sometimes it is necessary to calculate the PVs of annuities that are expected to continue for an indefinitely long period of time – 'perpetuities'. The PV of £a, receivable for n years given a discount rate, r, is:

$$a \times \frac{1}{r}\left(1 - \frac{1}{(1+r)^n}\right)$$

What happens to this formula as n becomes large? As n tends to infinity, $(1 + r)^n$ also tends to infinity and $\frac{1}{(1+r)^n}$ tends to zero. The cumulative discount factor tends to $\frac{1}{r}(1 - 0)$ or $\frac{1}{r}$.

This makes life very simple. For example, the PV of £5,000 receivable annually in arrears at a discount rate of 8% is:

$$= \frac{£5,000}{0.08} = £62,500.$$

To summarise, the PV of an annuity, a, receivable in arrears in perpetuity given a discount rate, r, is given by:

$$\text{PV perpetuity} = \frac{a}{r}\left(= \frac{\text{annual cash flow}}{\text{discount rate (as a decimal)}}\right)$$

1.8 Discounted cash flow techniques

The principle of discounting is used in three different investment appraisal techniques which are explained later in the chapter:

- net present value
- internal rate of return
- discounted payback.

Each of these techniques uses relevant cash flows to assess whether a project is worthwhile.

2 Net Present Value (NPV)

The net present value is 'the difference between the sum of the projected discounted cash inflows and outflows attributable to a capital investment or other long term project'. (CIMA *Official Terminology*)

The NPV method therefore calculates the present value of all of the costs and benefits of a project and deducts the PV of costs from the PV of benefits. If the net present value is:

- Positive – the investment is worthwhile at the company's cost of capital and should be accepted
- Negative – the investment is not worthwhile at the company's cost of capital and should be rejected
- Zero – the investment is just worthwhile at the company's cost of capital and should be carried out.

If there is limited capital or mutually exclusive projects the project with the highest NPV should be chosen.

Example

Ex plc has a cost of capital of 10% and is considering investing in a project which has the following cash flows.

Year	*Capital*	*Revenue*
0	(5,000)	
1		2,500
2		4,000
3		3,000
4		2,000

Calculate the NPV of the project and recommend whether Ex plc should invest in the project.

Solution

NPV calculation:

Year	*Net cash flows*	*DCF 10%*	*NPV £*
0	(5,000)	1.000	(5,000)
1	2,500	0.909	2,273
2	4,000	0.826	3,304
3	3,000	0.751	2,253
4	2,000	0.683	1,366
			4,196

Recommendation; as the NPV is positive the project should be undertaken.

Note: The convention in capital investment appraisal is that cash flows occur at the end of the year. Thus the year 1 cash flow of £2,500 is assumed to occur at the end of year 1. This is to enable discount factors to be applied to the cash flows. The end of year 1 is considered to be the same as the beginning of year 2. So if you were given information relating to a cash flow at the beginning of year 2 you should include this as a year 1 cash flow in your analysis. Year 0 means now ie the beginning of year 1. Initial capital expenditure is often shown as a cash outflow now, in year 0.

Activity 1

Lindsay Ltd wishes to make a capital investment of £1.5m but is unsure whether to invest in one of two machines each costing that amount. The net cash inflows from the two projects are shown below.

Time	*1*	*2*	*3*
Denis plc Machine (£'000)	900	600	500
Thomson plc Machine (£'000)	700	700	700

Evaluate which machine should be chosen using the net present value technique. Assume that the company has a cost of capital of 10%.

Feedback to this activity is at the end of the chapter.

3 Internal rate of return (IRR)

3.1 Definition

DEFINITION

The **internal rate of return (IRR)** is the annual percentage return achieved by a project, at which the sum of the discounted cash inflows over the life of the project is equal to the sum of the discounted cash outflows, i.e. the IRR is the discount rate at which the NPV = 0. (CIMA *Official Terminology*)

The internal rate of return (IRR) is the annual percentage return achieved by a project, at which the sum of the discounted cash inflows over the life of the project is equal to the sum of the discounted cash outflows, i.e. the IRR is the discount rate at which the NPV = 0. (CIMA *Official Terminology*)

It is sometimes known as the yield, or DCF yield, or internal yield, but these terms are confusing and their use is not recommended.

In an exam, it is necessary to compute the IRR by trial and error, that is to compute NPVs at various discount rates until the discount rate is found which gives an NPV of zero (since the IRR is the discount rate at which the NPV = 0). (In real life you can use a spreadsheet, for instance the IRR function in Excel.)

The IRR can be thought of as the return generated by the project. If the return is greater than the company's cost of capital then the project should be accepted.

KEY POINT

The IRR can be thought of as the maximum rate of interest that can be paid on the finance for a project without making a loss.

3.2 Finding the IRR – the graphical method

Example

Find the IRR of the Denis machine that Lindsay (Activity 1) decided not to acquire.

Solution

The net present value at 10% was £190,000.

The aim is to find the discount rate that gives an NPV of zero. Since the project has a positive NPV at 10%, the cash flows have not been discounted enough, and a higher discount rate must be chosen – try 15%.

$$\text{NPV at 15\% (£000)} = -1{,}500 + \frac{900}{1.15} + \frac{600}{(1.15)^2} + \frac{500}{(1.15)^3} = 65$$

This is clearly closer to the IRR than 10%, but not that close. However, rather than continue to try ever-increasing discount rates, an approximate shortcut can be taken. If the two discount rates and NPVs are plotted on a graph, the following is seen.

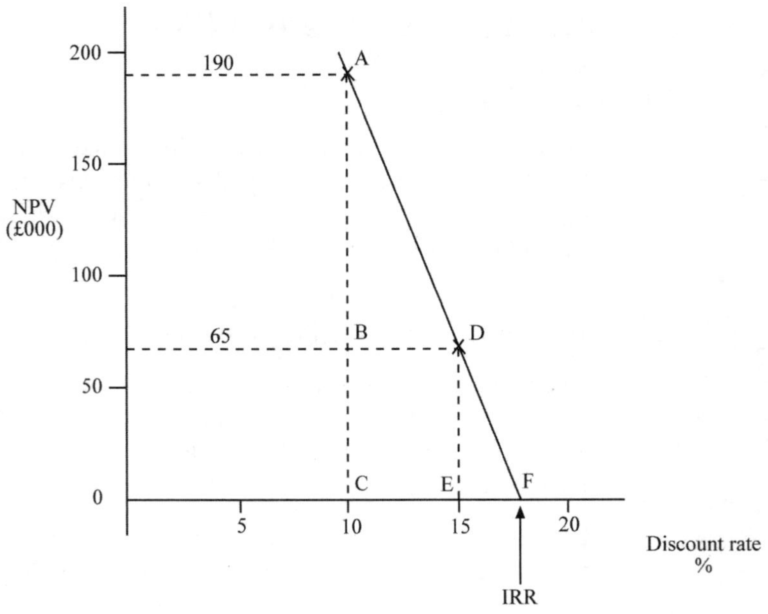

From the graph the IRR appears to be about 17½%.

In reality the graph is unlikely to be linear so this method can only give a very rough approximation.

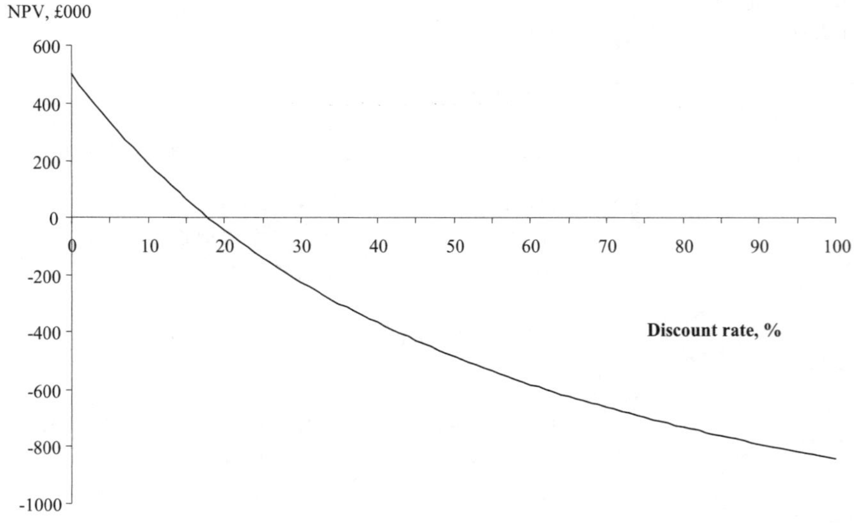

Graph of NPV v discount rate (showing non-linearity)

3.3 Finding the IRR – the formula method

Continuing the example of Lindsay, an estimate of the IRR could be found logically:

- NPV has fallen from 190 to 65 (by 125) as the discount rate has increased by 5% (from 10% to 15%) – this is a fall of 25 per percentage point increase
- to find the IRR the NPV needs to fall another 65
- to achieve this, the discount rate must be increased by (65/125) × 5% = 2.6%.

The IRR is approximately 15% + 2.6% = 17.6%.

Using this logic a formula to find the IRR can be derived as follows:

$$IRR \approx A + (B - A)\frac{N_A}{N_A - N_B}$$

where	A	=	lower discount rate	(10%)
	B	=	higher discount rate	(15%)
	N_A	=	NPV at rate A	(190)
	N_B	=	NPV at rate B	(65)

KEY POINT

The IRR formula is not given in the CIMA *Mathematical Tables* so a useful mnemonic is:

A BANANA-NB

Notes:

- If you like mnemonics it is very useful to remember that the IRR formula spells (roughly):

  A BANANA–NB

  … but you still have to remember what to add, subtract, divide and multiply, and what A, B, N_A and N_B stand for!
- The formula applies whether the discount rates chosen both give positive NPVs, both give negative NPVs, or give one of each.
- If negative NPVs appear, be careful with signs.
- The formula is only approximate since it assumes that the relationship between NPV and discount rate is linear; as the graph below shows, this assumption is false. It is not worth quoting an IRR found in this way to more than one decimal place (and even that might be too much).
- The closer the two rates (A and B) are to the true IRR, the more accurate will be the result.
- It is sometimes suggested that the IRR can only be found if one NPV is positive and one negative; this is not so and may lead to inaccuracy or wasting time in exams as attempts are made to produce these types of result. Don't dither over this in exams: just take the rate given in the question and a rate 10% higher.

Activity 2

The Thomson machine required an outlay of £1.5m to produce three inflows of £0.7m. At 10% the NPV of this project was £241,000. Find the IRR using the method above and taking 20% as the next discount rate.

Feedback to this activity is at the end of the chapter.

3.4 Even annual cash flows

A simpler approach can be used to find the IRR of simple projects in which the annual cash inflows are equal. The IRR can be found via a cumulative discount factor as the following exercise with the Thomson machine project shows.

NPV calculation

		Cash flow	*(c)% Discount factor*	*Present value*
		£000		£000
Time				
0	Investment	(1,500)	1	(1,500)
1 – 3	Inflow	700	(b)	(a)
Net present value (£000)				NIL

The aim is to find the discount rate that produces an NPV of nil; therefore the PV of inflows (a) must equal the PV of outflows, £1,500,000.

Step 1

Find the cumulative discount factor $\dfrac{\text{initial investment}}{\text{annual inflow}}$.

If the PV of inflows (a) is to be £1,500,000 and the size of each inflow is £700,000, the discount factor required must be 1,500,000 ÷ 700,000 = 2.140.

Step 2

Find the life of the project, n.

In this example it is three years.

Step 3

Look along the n year row of the cumulative discount factors until the closest value to cumulative discount factor is found.

Looking along the three-year row of the cumulative discount factors a value of 2.140 is included under the 19% column.

Step 4

The column in which this figure appears is the IRR.

19% in this case.

Activity 3

A company is considering investing in a project that has outflows in years one and two of £35,000 followed by annual inflows in years three to eight of £17,000. The company's cost of capital is 10%.

Keeping your workings as short and simple as possible decide whether the company should invest in this project.

Feedback to this activity is at the end of the chapter.

3.5 Perpetuities

Just as it is possible to calculate the PV of a perpetuity, so it is a simple matter to find the IRR of a project with equal annual inflows that are expected to be received for an indefinitely long period.

Formula

$$\text{The IRR of a perpetuity} = \frac{\text{annual inflow}}{\text{initial investment}} \times 100$$

This can be seen by looking at the formula for the PV of a perpetuity and considering the definition of IRR.

Illustration

Find the IRR of an investment that costs £20,000 and generates £1,600 for an indefinitely long period.

$$\text{IRR} = \frac{\text{annual inflow}}{\text{initial investment}} \times 100 = \frac{£1{,}600}{£20{,}000} \times 100 = 8\%$$

4 NPV v IRR

4.1 Different types of investment decision

Two different basic DCF methods have been seen – NPV and IRR. When used to analyse a project, the decision is easily made:

- if a project has a positive NPV it should be accepted
- if a project has an IRR greater than the required rate of return, accept it.

Since the two basic DCF methods are based on the same underlying principle – the time value of money – one would expect them to give identical investment decisions. This is not always so. Below we look at cases where NPV and IRR appear to be inconsistent.

4.2 Mutually exclusive investments

Organisations may often face decisions in which only one of two or more investments can be undertaken; these are called mutually exclusive investment decisions. In these circumstances NPV and IRR may give conflicting recommendations.

Example

Barlow Ltd is considering two short-term investment opportunities which it has called project A and project B and which have the following cash flows.

Time	*0*	*1*
Project A (£000)	(200)	240
Project B (£000)	(100)	125

Barlow has a cost of capital of 10%. Find the NPVs and IRRs of the two projects.

Solution

		NPV	*IRR*
		£000	%
Project A:	240 ÷ 1.10 – 200	18.18	20
Project B:	125 ÷ 1.10 – 100	13.64	25

The IRRs could be found either by trial and error or by using a formula. It would be easier to notice that project A, over one year, earns £40,000 on an investment of £200,000 (a 20% return) whilst project B earns £25,000 on £100,000 (25%).

It is worth noticing that A has the higher NPV whilst B has the higher IRR – a conflict.

Graphical explanation

If the NPVs of the two projects were calculated for a range of discount rates and two graphs of NPV against rate plotted on the same axes, it would look as shown below.

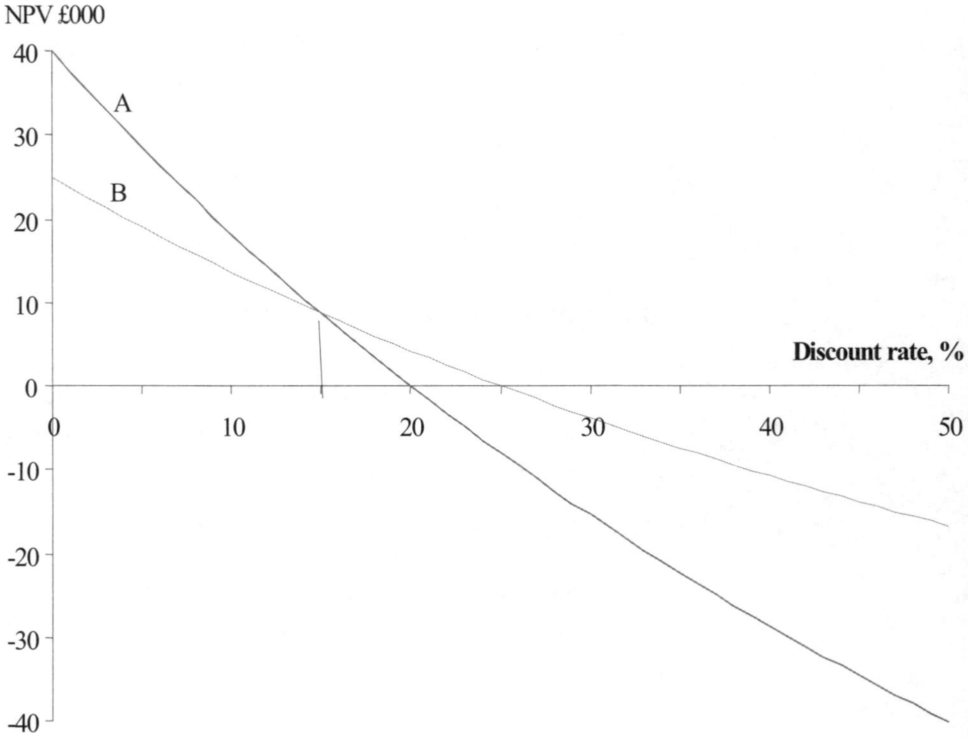

The lines cut the horizontal axis at their IRRs of 20% and 25% and intersect at (what seems to be) 15%. Project B has the higher IRR whereas, at the cost of capital of 10% (in fact at any rate below 15%) project A has the higher NPV.

4.3 Mutually exclusive projects – rationale and resolution

Although NPV and IRR are based on the same principle of the time value of money, they are calculated in different ways. The reasons for different rankings are:

KEY POINT

When NPV + IRR give a different ranking for mutually exclusive projects, the project with the highest NPV should be accepted.

- **absolute and relative measures** – the NPV is an absolute measure but the IRR is a relative measure of a project's viability. In our example, Project A is twice the size of Project B. Even though A's *percentage return* is less than B's, in absolute terms it is more valuable than B.
- **reinvestment assumption** – the two methods are sometimes said to be based on different assumptions about the rate at which funds generated by the projects are reinvested. NPV assumes reinvestment at a firm's cost of capital; IRR assumes reinvestment at the IRR.

When deciding between the two projects it must be realised that it is only their nature that causes us to choose between them, not shortage of funds (see capital rationing later). These might represent two alternative uses of the same building that can't be carried out together. Going for B or, more particularly A, does not restrict our ability to accept other profitable projects that become available. In view of this the decision should be to accept the project with the larger NPV.

The reasons for this are:

- **better reinvestment assumption** – if the relevance of reinvestment is accepted, the NPVs assumption is more realistic than that of the IRR
- **achieving corporate objectives** – use of the NPV method is consistent with achieving a firm's corporate objective of maximising share price (maximising shareholder wealth).

In addition to these two reasons in favour of using the NPV, the futility of the IRR could be seen if the firm, Barlow Ltd, surrendered their chance to accept either of these two projects in exchange for the possibility of a third project, project C.

	Time	*Cash flow*
		£
Project C:	0	(10)
	1	14

This project has a much higher IRR (40%) than either of the first two, but its NPV at 10% ([£14 ÷ 1.10] – £10) of £2.73 will not have much effect on any company's market value.

4.4 Annualised cash flows

You may be faced with a situation where you have to decide between projects of different durations.

Example

A company has three mutually exclusive investment possibilities and the management accountant has produced the following analysis.

Project	*X*	*Y*	*Z*
	£	£	£
Initial investment	130,000	242,000	310,000
Cash inflow for X, years 1 to 3	64,000		
Cash inflow for Y, years 1 to 6		64,000	
Cash inflow for Z, years 1 to 9			64,000
NPV at 10%	29,168	36,720	58,576
Ranking	3	2	1
IRR	22.35%	15.03%	14.58%
Ranking	1	2	3

The NPVs suggest that project Z should be undertaken, but the IRRs suggest that project X is the one to choose. However, no account has been taken of the duration of the projects.

One approach might be simply to divide the NPVs by the number of years the project lasts, 3, 6, and 9 respectively. However, as Carol Cashmore, a previous CIMA examiner, said in her article in *CIMA Insider* (September 2002): 'this would not be quite correct because the cash flows have been discounted. Instead, the NPVs should be divided by the sum of the annual discount rates, which can be obtained from present value tables.'

Project	*X*	*Y*	*Z*
NPV at 10%	29,168	36,720	58,576
Cumulative discount rate	2.487	4.355	5.759
Annualised cash flow	11,728	8,432	10,171
Ranking	1	3	2

4.5 Projects with multiple yields

A weakness of the IRR method is that projects may either have no IRR or several IRRs.

Example

Consider the following projects with cash flows over a three-year period.

Time	*Project A*	*Project B*	*Project C*
	£	£	£
0	(5,000)	(10,000)	(100,000)
1	2,000	23,000	360,000
2	2,000	(13,200)	(431,000)
3	2,000	(1,000)	171,600

You are required to calculate the NPV of these projects over the range 0 – 40% at 5% intervals and plot the results on three separate graphs. (***Note: Tables can be used for discount factors up to 20%. Formulae must be used for discount factors above 20%.***)

Solution

The NPV at 0% is found by adding up the (undiscounted) cash flows.

Rate	*0*	*5*	*10*	*15*	*20*	*25*	*30*	*35*	*40*
NPV_A	1,000	447	(26)	(434)	(787)	(1,096)	(1,368)	(1,608)	(1,822)
NPV_B	(1,200)	(932)	(751)	(639)	(579)	(560)	(574)	(612)	(671)
NPV_C	600	162	0	(25)	0	19	0	(76)	(219)

The three graphs are shown below.

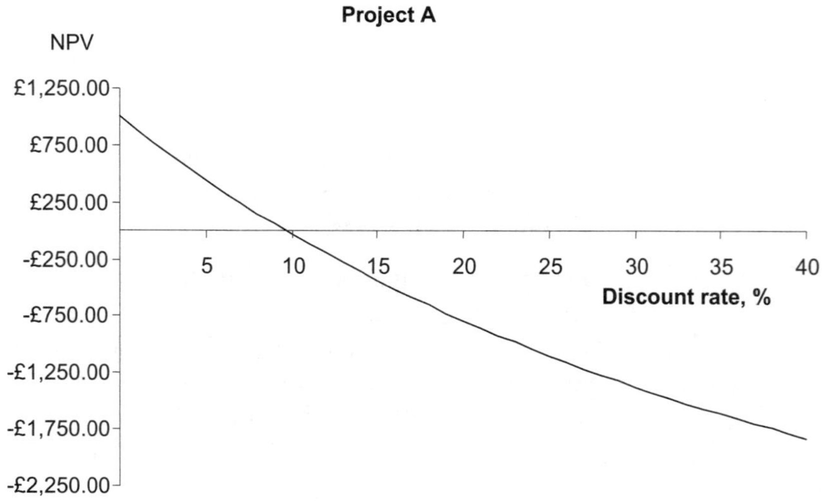

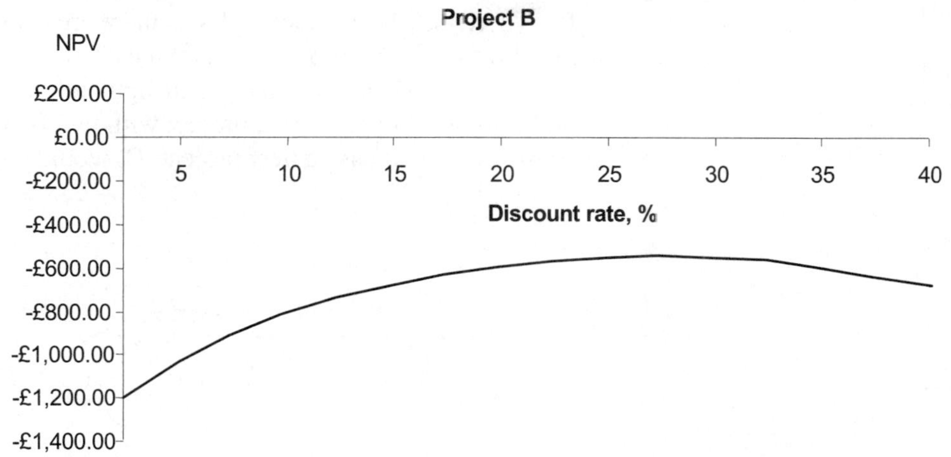

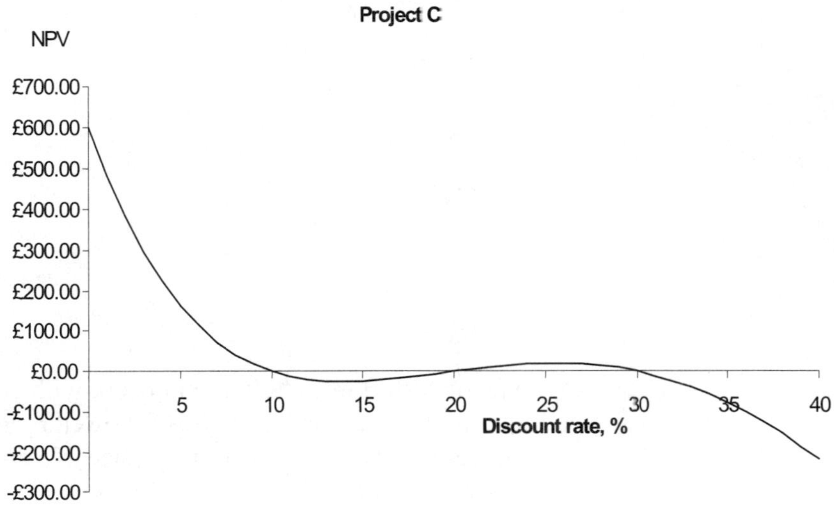

Notes

- Project A is a 'conventional' project, with one outflow followed by several net inflows, and shows the expected pattern of NPV decreasing as discount rate increases.

  Project A has one IRR at 10%.

- Project B's cash flows could be described as unconventional with outflows of a significant size appearing at the beginning and end of the 'project' (which is always unprofitable but is least unprofitable at 25%).

  Project B has no IRR.

- Project C's cash flows alternate between being outflows and inflows and the graph of NPV v discount rate alternately falls and rises.

  Project C has three IRRs at 10%, 20% and 30%.

Since the graph of NPV against discount rate bears no relation to a straight line, the formula shown previously should not be used to calculate the IRR of projects that look as if they will have multiple yields. Either use trial and error or a graphical approach.

4.6 The problem of non-conventional cash flows

The feature of projects that causes the graph of NPV v discount rate to change from the standard shape as shown by project A is more than one 'change in sign'. Project A had an outflow followed by inflows (one change in sign), whereas project B had outflows then inflows (a first change in sign), but then further outflows (two changes in sign).

Rule: There may be as many IRRs as there are changes in sign in the patterns of cash flows. Clearly project C has three changes in sign and has three IRRs; although project B has two changes in sign but no IRRs. Project B's cash flows could be adjusted to produce a project with two IRRs simply by ignoring the last outflow. In that case a new project, D, would show the following graph.

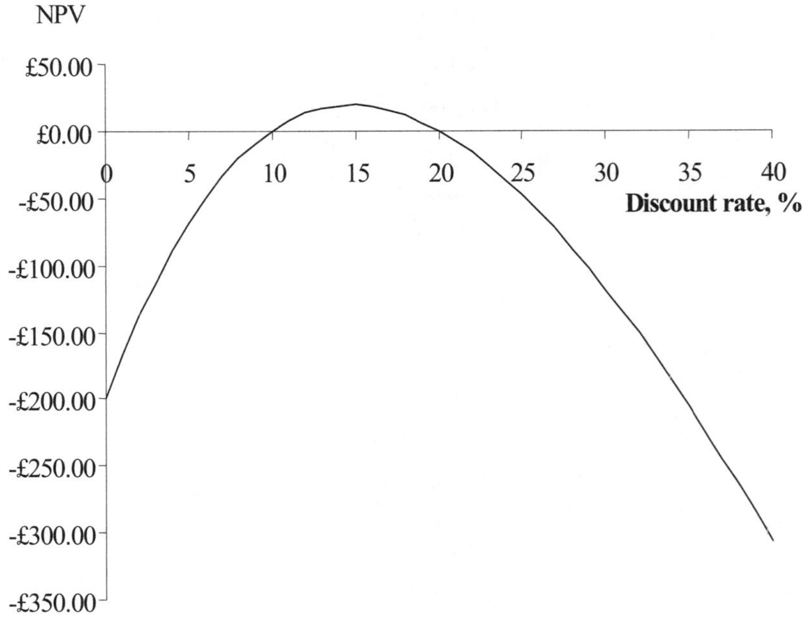

This type of cash flow pattern might occur with projects such as mining or oil exploration. An initial investment is followed by receipts from sales for a few years but, at the end of the project, the sizeable cost of reparations has a major effect on the project.

Clearly it is difficult to use the IRR method in these circumstances. Attempts can be made to modify the cash flows in such a way as to be able to find a single IRR without invalidating the analysis. However, multiple yields merely provide further evidence that the NPV method is superior to IRR. Despite having several IRRs projects will have only one NPV at the required rate of return which will be either positive or negative (or zero).

KEY POINT

Clearly it is difficult to use the IRR method in these circumstances. Attempts can be made to modify the cash flows in such a way as to be able to find a single IRR without invalidating the analysis. However, multiple yields merely provide further evidence that the NPV method is superior to IRR. Despite having several IRRs projects will have only one NPV at the required rate of return which will be either positive or negative (or zero).

5 Payback and discounted payback

5.1 Payback period

DEFINITION

Payback refers to the time required for the cash inflows from a capital investment project to equal the cash outflows. (CIMA *Official Terminology*)

Simple payback refers to the time required for the cash inflows from a capital investment project to equal the cash outflows. (CIMA *Official Terminology*)

The payback method is a useful screening process that assesses liquidity. However, it has weaknesses and should not be used as the main decision criterion (and certainly not for choosing between alternative investment opportunities).

In the simplified case of a project with equal annual cash inflows, it is easy to find the payback period:

$$\text{Payback period} = \frac{\text{Initial payment}}{\text{Annual cash inflow}}$$

For example if £2m is invested to earn £500,000 per annum for seven years (these being net cash earnings) the payback period (P) is given by:

$$P = \frac{£2,000,000}{£500,000} = 4 \text{ years}$$

However, if cash inflows are uneven (a more likely state of affairs), the payback has to be calculated by working out the cumulative cash flow over the life of a project.

5.2 Payback period with uneven cash flows

Illustration

A project has the following cash flows.

You are required to calculate the project payback period.

Year	*Cash flow* £000	*Cumulative cash flow* £000
0	(2,000)	(2,000)
1	500	(1,500)
2	500	(1,000)
3	400	(600)
4	600	Nil
5	300	300
6	200	500

The payback period is exactly four years.

For such a project it is possible that the payback period does not give a realistic measure of its 'worthwhileness' – the point being that no account is taken of the time value of money. As far as payback is concerned, the shorter the payback period the better the project. However, the limitations of the technique can be seen when it is used to appraise several projects together and hence compare them.

Further illustration

Year		*Cash flow*					
	Project	*A*	*B*	*C*	*D*	*E*	*F*
0		(100)	(100)	(100)	(100)	(80)	(80)
1		10	10	40	40	40	40
2		20	20	30	30	(20)	40
3		30	30	20	20	30	30
4		40	40	10	10	10	20
5		–	10	10	40	20	20
6		–	40	40	10	40	(40)
Payback period (years)		4	4	4	4	4 or 5	2?

The payback period for all of projects A, B, C and D is four years – and thus in terms of this measure the four projects are equivalent. However, since there is a time value to money the projects are not equivalent. In particular:

- B is preferred to A because of the extra receipts in years 5 and 6
- C is preferred to B because the cash inflows in years 1, 2, 3 and 4 are received more rapidly
- D is preferred to C because the post-payback period receipts are greater in the earlier years.

Additional problems arise when determining the payback period for projects E and F. For project E, the payback may be deemed to be four years (the length of time taken for the cash receipts to cover the initial outlay) or five years (the length of time before cumulative cash flows are zero). For project F the initial outlay is recovered by the end of the second year, but it seems very imprudent to totally ignore the cash flow arising at the end of year 6. (Of course, in line with the nature of conservative accountants, positive cash flows arising after the payback period have been ignored in projects B to E also.)

5.3 Merits of simple payback period as an investment appraisal technique

(a) **Simplicity**

As a concept, it is easily understood and is easily calculated.

(b) **Rapidly changing technology**

If new plant is likely to be scrapped in a short period because of obsolescence, a quick payback is essential.

(c) **Improving investment conditions**

When investment conditions are expected to improve in the near future, attention is directed to those projects that will release funds soonest, to take advantage of the improving climate.

(d) **Payback favours projects with a quick return**

It is often argued that these are to be preferred for three reasons.

- Rapid project payback leads to rapid company growth – but in fact such a policy will lead to many profitable investment opportunities being overlooked because their payback period does not happen to be particularly swift.

- Rapid payback minimises risk (the logic being that the shorter the payback period, the less there is that can go wrong). Not all risks are related to time, but payback is able to provide a useful means of assessing time risk (and only time risk). It is likely that earlier cash flows can be estimated with greater certainty.
- Rapid payback maximises liquidity – but liquidity problems are best dealt with separately, through cash forecasting.

(e) **Cash flows**

Unlike ARR it uses cash flows, rather than profits, and so is less likely to produce an unduly optimistic figure distorted by assorted accounting conventions which might permit certain costs to be carried forward and not affect profit initially.

5.4 Weaknesses of payback period

- **Project returns may be ignored** – In particular, cash flows arising after the payback period are totally ignored.
- **Timing ignored** – Cash flows are effectively categorised as pre-payback or post-payback, but no more accurate measure is made. In particular, the time value of money is ignored.
- **Lack of objectivity** – There is no objective measure as to what length of time should be set as the minimum payback period. Investment decisions are therefore subjective.
- **Project profitability is ignored** – Payback takes no account of the effects on business profits and periodic performance of the project, as evidenced in the financial statements. This is critical if the business is to be reasonably viewed by users of the accounts.

Activity 4

A project requires an initial investment of £550,000 and will bring the following cash receipts.

Year	1	2	3	4	5	6
Receipts (£000)	100	200	200	100	75	25

You are required to calculate the project's payback period.

Feedback to this activity is at the end of the chapter.

5.5 Discounted payback

One of the major criticisms of using the payback period is that it does not take into account the time value of money. The discounted payback technique attempts to overcome this criticism by measuring the time required for the present values of the cash inflows from a project to equal the present values of the cash outflows.

Example

W Ltd is considering investing in a project which has the following cash flows:

Year	*Cash flow (£)*
0	(2,250)
1	750
2	1,000
3	1,250
4	850

The company's cost of capital is 10%.

Required:

Calculate the NPV, payback period and the discounted payback period of the project.

Solution

Year	*Cash flow*	*Cumulative cash flow*	*Discount factor*	*Present value*	*Cumulative present value*
	£000	£000		£000	£000
0	(2,250)	(2,250)	1	(2,250)	(2,250)
1	750	(1,500)	0.909	681.75	(1,568.25)
2	1,000	(500)	0.826	826	(742.25)
3	1,250	750	0.751	938.75	196.5
4	850	1,600	0.683	580.55	777.05
			NPV	777.05	

The NPV is £777,050. The payback period is two years and (500/1250 × 12) five months approximately, assuming cash flows accrue evenly throughout the year. The discounted payback period is two years and (742.25/938.75 × 12) 9.5 months approximately.

5.6 Conclusions on payback

Payback is best seen as an initial screening tool. For example, a company might decide that no project with a payback of more than ten years is to be considered.

It is an appropriate measure for relatively straightforward projects, e.g. those which involve an initial outlay followed by constant long-term receipts.

However, in spite of its weaknesses and limitations the payback period is one of the most common initial methods of investment appraisal in use in the UK. It is not, however, often used exclusively but rather in conjunction with other methods.

6 Accounting rate of return (ARR)

6.1 Definition

The accounting rate of return (ARR) expresses the profits from a project as a percentage of capital cost. However, the figure for profit and for capital cost used may vary. The most common approach produces the following definition:

$$\text{ARR} = \frac{\text{average annual (post depreciation) profits}}{\text{initial capital costs}} \times 100$$

In the absence of any instructions to the contrary, this is the method that should be used (profits before interest and tax, but after depreciation). Other possible methods include the following:

- using the first year's profits
- using the total profits over the whole of the project's life
- using the average book value of the assets over their life (instead of the initial capital costs).

Example

A project involves the immediate purchase of an item of plant costing £110,000. It would generate annual cash flows of £24,400 for five years, starting in year 1. The plant purchased would have a scrap value of £10,000 in five years, when the project terminates. Depreciation is on a straight-line basis.

You are required to calculate the ARR.

Solution

Annual cash flows are taken to be profit before depreciation.

Average annual depreciation	=	(£110,000 – £10,000) ÷ 5
	=	£20,000
Average annual profit	=	£24,400 – £20,000
	=	£4,400
ARR	=	$\frac{\text{average annual profit}}{\text{initial capital cost}} \times 100$
	=	$\frac{£4,400}{£110,000} \times 100 = 4\%$

6.2 Using average book values of investments

This variation on the calculation of an ARR produces a figure which is, under certain circumstances, closer to the conventional financial accounting view of return on capital employed (and is the way the ARR is defined in the CIMA *Official Terminology*).

Example

Using the figures in the previous example, produce revised calculations based on the average book value of the investment.

Solution

The calculations are as follows:

Average annual profits (as before) = £4,400

$$\text{Average book value of assets} = \frac{\text{initial capital cost} + \text{*final scrap value}}{2}$$

$$= \frac{£110{,}000 + £10{,}000}{2} = £60{,}000$$

$$\text{ARR} = \frac{£4{,}400}{£60{,}000} \times 100 = 7\tfrac{1}{3}\%$$

* Note that the scrap value increases the average book value.

6.3 Merits of accounting rate of return for investment appraisal

- **Simplicity** – As with the payback period, it is easily understood and easily calculated.
- **Link with other accounting measures** – Return on capital employed, calculated annually to assess a business or sector of a business (and therefore the investment decisions made by that business), is widely used and its use for investment appraisal is consistent with that. The ARR is expressed in percentage terms with which managers and accountants are familiar. However, neither this nor the preceding point necessarily justify the use of ARR.

6.4 Criticisms of ARR

There are a number of specific criticisms of the ARR.

- It fails to take account of either the project life or the timing of cash flows (and time value of money) within that life.
- It will vary with specific accounting policies, and the extent to which project costs are capitalised. Profit measurement is thus 'subjective', and ARR figures for identical projects would vary from business to business.
- It might ignore working capital requirements.
- Like all rate of return measures, it is not a measurement of absolute gain in wealth for the business owners.
- There is no definite investment signal. The decision to invest or not remains subjective in view of the lack of an objectively set target ARR.

KEY POINT

It is concluded that the ARR does not provide a reliable basis for project evaluation.

It is concluded that the ARR does not provide a reliable basis for project evaluation.

Activity 5

A project requires an initial investment of £800,000 and then earns net cash inflows of:

Year	1	2	3	4	5	6	7
Cash inflows (£000)	100	200	400	400	300	200	150

In addition, at the end of the seven-year project the assets initially purchased will be sold for £100,000.

Required:

(a) Calculate the project's payback period.

(b) Determine its ARR.

Feedback to this activity is at the end of the chapter

Summary

- Discounted cash flow techniques may be used to compute a net present value and/or an internal rate of return. Usually the calculations are simplified by the use of present value tables.
- In case of conflict, the NPV criterion should be followed in preference to the IRR criterion.
- Payback period is the time required for the cash inflows from a capital investment project to equal the cash outflows. It may be used as an initial screening criterion, but it does not take account of the time value of money.
- The accounting rate of return expresses the profits from a project as a percentage of capital cost. Its main disadvantage is that it is based on profits rather than cash.

Having completed your study of this chapter you should have achieved the following learning outcomes.

- Explain the financial consequences of dealing with long-run projects. In particular, the importance of accounting for the 'time value of money'.
- Evaluate project proposals using the techniques of investment appraisal.
- Compare, contrast and evaluate the alternative techniques of investment appraisal.

Self-test questions

1 Explain what is meant by the time value of money. (1.2)

2 What formula gives the present value of a perpetuity? (1.7)

3 What is an internal rate of return? (3.1)

4 How can an IRR be calculated? (3.2, 3.3)

5 Why might NPV and IRR give conflicting conclusions and how should this be resolved? (4.3)

6 Under what circumstances may a project have more than one IRR? (4.5)

7 Despite its limitations, why is the payback period a popular means of investment appraisal? (5.3)

8 What are the limitations of the use of the accounting rate of return? (6.4)

Objective test questions

Question 1

Borg plc is considering a new project costing £167,500 with the following expected cash flows:

Year	*Cash flow*
	£000
1	40
2	50
3	60
4	70

The payback period is:

A 3 years

B 3¼ years

C $3\frac{5}{7}$ years

D 4 years

Question 2

Given a discount rate of 10%, the discounted payback period in the above example is:

A 3 years

B 3.71 years

C 3.94 years

D infinite

Question 3

The NPV of the above project is:

A £0

B £3,030

C £52,500

D £170,530

Question 4

The IRR of the above project is closest to:

A 10%

B 11%

C 12%

D 13%

For the answer to these questions, see the 'Answers' section at the end of the book.

Exam-type questions

Question 1: Paradis plc

Stadler is an ambitious young executive who has recently been appointed to the position of financial director of Paradis plc, a small listed company. Stadler regards this appointment as a temporary one, enabling her to gain experience before moving to a larger organisation. Her intention is to leave Paradis plc in three years' time, with its share price standing high. As a consequence, she is particularly concerned that the reported profits of Paradis plc should be as high as possible in this third and final year with the company.

Paradis plc has recently raised £350,000 from a rights issue, and the directors are considering three ways of using these funds. Three projects (A, B and C) are being considered, each involving the immediate purchase of equipment costing £350,000. One project only can be undertaken and the equipment for each project will have a useful life equal to that of the project, with no scrap value. Stadler favours project C because it is expected to show the highest accounting profit in the third year. However, she does not wish to reveal her real reasons for favouring project C and so, in her report to the chairman, she recommends project C because it shows the highest internal rate of return. The following summary is taken from her report.

Years				*Net cash flows* (£000)					*Internal rate of return*
Project	*0*	*1*	*2*	*3*	*4*	*5*	*6*	*7*	*8*	%
A	(350)	100	110	104	112	138	160	180	-	27.5
B	(350)	40	100	210	260	160	-	-	-	26.4
C	(350)	200	150	240	40	-	-	-	-	33.0

The chairman of the company is accustomed to projects being appraised in terms of payback and accounting rate of return, and he is consequently suspicious of the use of the internal rate of return as a method of project selection. Accordingly, the chairman has asked for an independent report on the choice of project. The company's cost of capital is 20% and a policy of straight-line depreciation is used to write off the cost of equipment in the financial statements.

Required:

(a) Calculate the payback period for each project. **(3 marks)**

(b) Calculate the accounting rate of return for each project. **(5 marks)**

(c) Prepare a report for the chairman with supporting calculations indicating which project should be preferred by the ordinary shareholders of Paradis plc.

(12 marks)

Note: Ignore taxation. **(Total: 20 marks)**

Question 2: Khan Ltd

Khan Ltd is an importer of novelty products. The directors are considering whether to introduce a new product, expected to have a very short economic life. Two alternative methods of promoting the new product are available, details of which are as follows.

- **Alternative 1** would involve heavy advertising and the employment of a large number of agents. The directors expect that an immediate cash outflow of £100,000 would be required (the cost of advertising) which would produce a net cash inflow after one year of £255,000. Agents' commission amounting to £157,500 would have to be paid at the end of two years.

- **Alternative 2** would involve a lower outlay on advertising (£50,000, payable immediately) and no use of agents. It would produce a net cash inflow of zero after one year and £42,000 at the end of each of the subsequent two years.

Mr Court, a director of Khan Ltd, comments 'I generally favour the payback method for choosing between investment alternatives such as these. However, I am worried that the advertising expenditure under the second alternative will reduce our reported profit next year by an amount not compensated by any net revenues from sale of the product in that year. For that reason I do not think we should even consider the second alternative.'

The cost of capital of Khan Ltd is 20% per annum. The directors do not expect capital or any other resource to be in short supply during the next three years.

Required:

(a) Calculate the net present values and estimate the internal rates of return of the two methods of promoting the new product. **(10 marks)**

(b) Advise the directors of Khan Ltd which, if either, method of promotion they should adopt, explaining the reasons for your advice and noting any additional information you think would be helpful in making the decision. **(8 marks)**

(c) Comment on the views expressed by Mr Court. **(7 marks)**

(Total: 25 marks)

For the answer to these questions, see the 'Answers' section at the end of the book.

Feedback to activities

Activity 1

The calculation without using tables would be carried out as follows:

Cash inflows from Denis machine:

$$\text{PV} = \frac{£900{,}000}{1.10} + \frac{£600{,}000}{1.10^2} + \frac{£500{,}000}{1.10^3}$$

$$= £818{,}182 + £495{,}868 + £375{,}657 = £1{,}689{,}707$$

Cash inflows from Thomson machine:

$$\text{PV} = \frac{£700{,}000}{1.10} + \frac{£700{,}000}{1.10^2} + \frac{£700{,}000}{1.10^3}$$

$$= £700{,}000 \times \frac{1}{0.10} \times \left(1 - \frac{1}{(1.10)^3}\right)$$

$$= £700{,}000 \times 2.48685 = £1{,}740{,}796$$

Simple projects such as these two can be analysed by calculations taking a single line; but in general it is better to use a tabular layout as follows.

Denis machine

		Cash flow £000	*10% discount factor*	*Present value* £000
Time				
0	Capital cost	(1,500)	1	(1,500)
1	Inflow	900	$\frac{1}{1.10}$	818
2	Inflow	600	$\frac{1}{1.10^2}$	496
3	Inflow	500	$\frac{1}{1.10^3}$	376
Net present value (£000)				190

Thomson machine

		Cash flow £000	*10% discount factor*	*Present value* £000
Time				
0	Capital cost	(1,500)	1	(1,500)
1 – 3	Inflow	700	2.48685	1,741
Net present value (£000)				241

The two NPV calculations for Lindsay, using the CIMA tables might look as follows.

Denis machine (using the one year present value table)

NPV (£000) $= -1{,}500 + [900 \times 0.909] + [600 \times 0.826] + [500 \times 0.751]$

$= 189$

Thomson machine (using the cumulative present value table)

NPV (£000) $= -1{,}500 + [700 \times 2.487]$

$= 241$

It can be seen that there is a time saving by using the tables.

Despite the earlier receipts from the Denis machine, the extra £100,000 in total receipts gives the Thomson machine the advantage.

Since the PV of the inflows exceeds the (PV of) initial cost, the Thomson machine project is worthwhile. (It has an NPV of £1,740,796 – £1,500,000 = £240,796.)

Notes:

- PVs have been rounded to the nearest £000; it is not worth stating them to the nearest penny and, when using tables, round to the nearest three significant figures (perhaps to the nearest £000 or £m if that is not too different from three significant figures) although only the first two significant figures are really accurate.
- Again brackets are used for outflows.

Activity 2

$$\text{NPV at 20\% (£000)} = -1{,}500 + \frac{700}{1.20} + \frac{700}{(1.20)^2} + \frac{700}{(1.20)^3} = -25.$$

In using 20%, a discount rate has been found that is slightly higher than the IRR. The IRR can be estimated using:

$$\text{IRR} \approx 1 + (B - A)\left(\frac{N_A}{N_A - N_B}\right)$$

$$\approx 10 + (20 - 10)\left(\frac{241}{241-(-25)}\right)$$

$$\approx 10 + 10 \times \left(\frac{241}{241+25}\right) = 19\%$$

(Note that a cumulative discount factor, 2.10648 or 2.11 to two decimal places, could have been used to find the NPV at 20% but would have given the same IRR.)

Activity 3

Because the cash flows are the same each year you can save time and space by calculating appropriate cumulative discount rates from the tables. This approach is recommended by the examiner (*CIMA Insider,* September 2002), so learn it, don't be nervous of it.

For years one and two, which both have an outflow of £35,000, use the cumulative discount factor for year 2 (1.736). For years three to eight you have inflows of £17,000 each year and that means you can calculate a single cumulative discount factor by finding the year eight factor and subtracting the year 2 factor: 5.335 – 1.736 = 3.599.

Years	*Cash flows*	*Discount rate*	*PV*
1 – 2	(£35,000)	1.736	(£60,760)
3 – 8	£17,000	3.599	£61,183
		NPV	£423

The company should invest in this project because it has a positive NPV.

Activity 4

The payback period could be found by inspection or by tabulating cumulative cash flows.

Year	0	1	2	3	4	5	6
Cumulative cash flows (£000)	(550)	(450)	(250)	(50)	50	125	150

After three years £50,000 is still 'outstanding'; the inflow over the fourth year is £100,000. If cash inflows accrue evenly over the year, the payback period is 3½ years.

Activity 5

(a) **Payback period**

Cumulative cash flows are tabulated below.

Year	0	1	2	3	4	5	6	7
Cumulative (£000)	(800)	(700)	(500)	(100)	300	600	800	950

The payback period appears during the fourth year in which £400,000 arises. Since £100,000 still has to be paid off at the start of the fourth year, the payback period is 3¼ years.

(b) **Accounting rate of return**

This uses profits rather than cash flows.

Average annual inflows = £1,750,000 ÷ 7 = £250,000

Average annual depreciation = (£800,000 – £100,000) ÷ 7 = £100,000

(A net £700,000 is being written off as depreciation over seven years.)

Average annual profit = £250,000 – £100,000 = £150,000

$$\text{ARR} = \frac{\text{average annual profit}}{\text{initial investment}} \times 100 = \frac{£150{,}000}{£800{,}000} \times 100 = 18.75\%$$

Note: If ARR had been based on the average book value of assets, £150,000 would have been divided by the average of initial capital cost, £800,000, and final scrap value, £100,000, i.e. £450,000, to give an accounting rate of return of $33\frac{1}{3}\%$.

Chapter 12

EVALUATION OF INVESTMENT PROJECTS

Syllabus content

This chapter covers the following syllabus content.

- The process of investment decision making, including origination of proposals, creation of capital budgets, go/no go decisions on individual projects (where judgements on qualitative issues interact with financial analysis), and post audit of completed projects.
- Generation of relevant project cash flows taking account of inflation, tax and 'final' project value where appropriate.
- Activity-based costing to derive approximate 'long-run' costs appropriate for use in strategic decision making.

Contents

1 The process of investment decision making

1.1 The capital budgeting process

A common feature of industrial activity is the need to commit funds by purchasing land, buildings, machinery, etc. in anticipation of being able to earn, in the future, an income greater than the funds committed. This indicates the need for an assessment of the size of the outflows and inflows of funds, the life of the investment, the degree of risk attached (greater risk being justified perhaps by greater returns) and the cost of obtaining funds.

The basic stages in the capital budgeting process are identified below.

Step 1

Needs for expenditure are forecast.

Step 2

Projects to meet those needs are distinguished.

Step 3

Alternatives are appraised.

Step 4

Best alternatives are selected and approved.

Step 5

Expenditure is made and monitored.

Step 6

Deviations from estimates are examined.

Step 3 occupies a major place in the theory and practice of management decision-making, and it will be examined later in considerable depth. The rest of this section will concentrate on summarising the main stages in capital budgeting.

1.2 Types of capital project

Reasons for capital expenditure vary widely. Projects may be classified into the following categories:

- **maintenance** – replacement of worn-out or obsolete assets, safety and security, etc.
- **profitability** – cost savings, quality improvement, productivity, relocation, etc.
- **expansion** – new products, new outlets, research and development, etc.
- **indirect** – office buildings, welfare facilities, etc.

A particular investment project, of course, could combine any number or all of the above classifications.

Note that not all expenditure will be termed capital according to accepted accountancy definitions. For example, it may be decided to write off expenditure in the year in which it is incurred, rather than capitalising it and writing it off over a period of years. In this context, most organisations have a *de minimis* rule, under which any asset costing less than a given sum, say £1,000, is not capitalised but is written off in the year of purchase, despite the fact that it may be used for several years to come (for example, pocket calculators in an accountant's office are unlikely to be capitalised). However, the important consideration is that cash is being spent now in the expectation of future cash profits. For example, whether the decision is to spend on a new machine or to relocate an existing machine, identical considerations will apply – size of cash outflows and inflows, timing of cash flows, life of project, etc.

Even those projects that are not likely to earn profits must be subjected to investment appraisal, in order to choose the best way of achieving the project. For example, investment appraisal can be used to find the cheapest method for constructing a staff canteen, although such a project is unlikely to earn profits.

1.3 Working capital

In most industrial projects, investment is required, both in fixed assets and in working capital, although the risk attached to working capital is less than that for fixed assets. Values of land and buildings may appreciate and so present less risk, but money invested in machinery is a sunk cost, which is unlikely to be recovered, save for perhaps minimal scrap values.

In project appraisal, accurate estimates of working capital requirements are desirable, not only for assessment of project profitability, but also to facilitate forecasting of capital requirements.

1.4 Capital expenditure forecast

In preparing budgets, it is necessary to consider how much money can or must be allocated to capital expenditure. Capital development schemes may be started because a surplus of cash resources is revealed by the long-term plan, but usually management decide on a capital development scheme and then seek the means to finance it.

Initially, the budget will be an expression of management's intention to allocate funds for certain broad purposes. In the budget period, money will be required:

- for previously authorised existing projects
- for new projects, full details of which may not yet be available.

The forecasts will indicate whether sufficient funds are available, and perhaps when additional funds will need to be obtained. It is advisable, therefore, for managers to submit long-term capital expenditure forecasts, say for two to five years ahead; consequently, the possibility of obsolescence (and the direction of the future development of the firm) must be borne in mind.

KEY POINT

The importance of this aspect of planning cannot be over-emphasised, because present capital investment will determine the structure and profitability of the company in the near future. Errors made in forecasting and planning will, therefore, have serious results, and may prove difficult to rectify.

The capital budget is the outcome of a dual process:

- higher management allocating funds to various areas in relation to the corporate plan, i.e. according to the long-term objectives of the company
- individual managers seeking to utilise the funds for specific projects.

The importance of this aspect of planning cannot be over-emphasised, because present capital investment will determine the structure and profitability of the company in the near future. Errors made in forecasting and planning will, therefore, have serious results, and may prove difficult to rectify.

1.5 Methods of appraising capital investment projects

The most important step in the capital budgeting process is determining whether the benefits from investing large capital sums outweigh the large initial costs of those investments. A range of methods is used in reaching these investment decisions. Broadly speaking they fall into two categories: traditional (non-discounting) methods and discounted cash flow (DCF) methods.

Traditional (non-discounting) methods are:

- payback period
- accounting rate of return (ARR).

DCF methods involve finding:

- a net present value (NPV), or
- an internal rate of return (IRR).

These techniques were the subject of the previous chapter.

2 Project control, evaluation and post audit

2.1 Capital expenditure committee

In order to control investment decisions, a capital expenditure committee may be formed, either as a sub-committee of the budget committee or as a separate meeting of the entire budget committee.

The functions of such a committee are to:

- co-ordinate capital expenditure policy
- appraise and authorise capital expenditure on specific projects
- review actual expenditure on capital projects against the budget.

In many organisations, multidisciplinary teams, or working parties, are set up to investigate individual proposals and report back to top management on their findings. Such a team might comprise:

- project engineer
- production engineer
- management accountant
- relevant specialist, e.g.
  - personnel officer, for a project involving sports facilities or canteens
  - safety officers, etc
- economist.

2.2 Capital expenditure decision

The seriousness of all decisions relating to capital expenditure must be stressed. Today's decisions will affect the direction and pace of the company's future growth or, indeed, its very survival. If a wrong decision is made it will be difficult to correct, particularly where special purpose plant is involved.

It has frequently been reported that, in both the private and public sectors, investment decisions are made rather casually and that this laxity is one of the major causes of lack of growth within an economy. Of all the decisions taken by management, those concerned with investment are the most crucial: once made, they may fix the future of the company in terms of its technological role, cost structure and market effort required, i.e. once the product has been selected and the plant built, the company is committed to the specific cost structure that accompanies that particular type of plant and the product made.

2.3 Authorisation of capital projects

The capital budget will not necessarily be based on a detailed analysis of required projects. It is likely that managers will be asked to forecast their capital expenditure requirements for inclusion in the budget but, even if such figures are included, it is still necessary for detailed proposals to be submitted to the committee before the projects may be started.

Many projects will incur fairly small expenditure and, in order not to involve the committee in unnecessary detail, broad guidelines ought to be laid down regarding the amounts of expenditure that may be committed by each level of management. Top management must see that the types of expenditure to be treated as capital are clearly defined and that every subordinate or committee knows precisely the limits to which they can approve capital expenditure.

Capital expenditure requiring approval by the committee must be formulated by the managers. The amount of detail should be stipulated by the committee and would generally cover the following:

- outline of the project, including the budget classification and how it is linked, if at all, with other projects
- reason for the expenditure – if a new project – and the departments affected; an assessment of intangible benefits or disadvantages
- the amount of capital expenditure required (fixed and working capital), including a breakdown by budget periods and an estimate of any internal work required
- a complete statement of incremental costs and revenue arising from the project, and the budget periods affected; an assessment of the effect of taxation ought to be made
- estimated life of the project
- assessment of risks to which the project is sensitive – political, economic, competitors, natural hazards, etc.
- projects that are feasible alternatives, and comparative data
- effect of postponement or rejection of project.

Major projects would probably be subjected to a comprehensive financial evaluation, as part of the committee's consideration; less important projects could be submitted, accompanied by an economic justification.

KEY POINT

Major projects would probably be subjected to a comprehensive financial evaluation, as part of the committee's consideration; less important projects could be submitted, accompanied by an economic justification.

2.4 Capital expenditure control

Strict control of large projects must be maintained and the accountant must submit periodic reports to top management on progress and cost. A typical report would include such data as:

- budgeted cost of the project, date started and scheduled completion date
- cost and over or under-expenditure to date
- estimated cost to completion, and estimated final over or under-expenditure
- estimated completion date and details of penalties, if any.

The capital expenditure committee will seek explanations for any overspending that may have arisen. Where projects are incomplete and actual expenditure exceeds the authorisation, additional authority must be sought to complete the project. In so doing, the committee must consider the value of the project as it then stands and the additional value that will be gained by completing it, compared with the additional expenditure to completion.

A vital consideration is the adequacy of funds available. Where existing projects are overspending their allocation, other perhaps more desirable projects may be delayed. When reviewing progress, therefore, the committee must consider the funds available, in the light of which it may become necessary to revise the order of priority in which funds are awarded to projects.

2.5 Network planning in project control

Traditional budget approaches have a number of disadvantages when applied to the monitoring and control of capital projects:

- they are tied to budget periods that are unrelated to the stages in processes
- the functional classifications are unlikely to coincide with activities within a total project
- the accumulation of costs under budget heads fails to provide advance warning of cost overruns
- budgets only concentrate on costs, and fail to identify the critical factor of completion dates for each activity.

Network planning (critical path analysis) provides a much better system. This latter approach has also been developed to control the inherent uncertainty in projects.

2.6 Post-completion appraisal

On completion of a project, an investigation should be undertaken to examine its profitability and compare it with the plan.

DEFINITION

A **post-completion audit** is an objective and independent appraisal of the measure of success of a capital expenditure project in progressing the business as planned.

'A post-completion audit is an objective and independent appraisal of the measure of success of a capital expenditure project in progressing the business as planned.

The appraisal should cover the implementation of the project from authorisation to commissioning and its technical and commercial performance after commissioning. The information provided is also used by management as feedback that aids the implementation and control of future projects.' (CIMA *Official Terminology*)

There are three reasons for undertaking these post-mortems:

- to discourage managers from spending money on doubtful projects, because they may be called to account at a later date
- it may be possible over a period of years to discern a trend of reliability in the estimates of various managers
- a similar project may be undertaken in the future, and then the recently completed project will provide a useful basis for estimation.

3 Relevant cash flows

3.1 Costs to ignore

Before looking at those cash flows that should be included in any DCF analysis, it is worth emphasising those items that should be excluded.

- **Depreciation** – this is not a cash flow and any depreciation charges should be excluded from DCF calculations. If profit figures after depreciation have been provided, the profit needs to be increased by adding back the depreciation.
- **Apportioned fixed costs** – the cost of producing an item may include an apportionment of factory-wide fixed costs using some standard basis for absorption. These should be excluded; fixed costs may appear in a DCF calculation, but only if it is known that they will increase as a result of accepting a project.
- **Book values of assets** – these fall into the same category as depreciation, they are not cash flows and must be ignored.
- **Interest payments** – in most cases it can be assumed that the cost of interest has been taken into account by the discounting process. Interest payments should be ignored since to do otherwise would be 'double counting'.
- **Sunk costs** – any sums that have already been spent or committed and cannot be influenced by the investment decision should be ignored.

3.2 Cash flows to include

The cash flows that should be included are those which are specifically incurred as a result of the acceptance or non-acceptance of the project. In some cases, these may be opportunity costs.

When deciding what figure should be included in any DCF calculation it sometimes helps to tabulate for a particular element of cost.

Cash flow if project accepted	–	Cash flow if project rejected	=	Relevant cash flow

3.3 Absolute and incremental cash flows

When deciding between two projects, only one of which can be accepted (i.e. mutually exclusive projects), two approaches are possible:

- discount the cash flows of each project separately and compare NPVs
- find the differential (or incremental) cash flow year by year, i.e. the difference between the cash flows of the two projects. Then use the discounted value of those differential cash flows to establish a preference.

Either approach will lead to the same conclusion.

Example

Two projects, A and B, are under consideration. Either A or B, but not both, may be accepted. The relevant discount rate is 10%.

You are required to recommend A or B by:

(a) discounting each cash flow separately

(b) discounting relative (incremental or differential) cash flows.

The cash flows are as follows.

Time	*Project A*	*Project B*
	£	£
0	(1,500)	(2,500)
1	500	500
2	600	800
3	700	1,100
4	500	1,000
5	Nil	500

Solution

(a) **Discounting each cash flow separately**

Time	*PV factor at 10%*	*Project A Cash flow*	*Project A PV*	*Project B Cash flow*	*Project B PV*
		£	£	£	£
0	1.000	(1,500)	(1,500)	(2,500)	(2,500)
1	0.909	500	455	500	455
2	0.826	600	496	800	661
3	0.751	700	526	1,100	826
4	0.683	500	342	1,000	683
5	0.621	Nil	Nil	500	311
NPV			£319		£436

Project B is preferred because its NPV exceeds that of A by £(436 – 319) = £117

(b) **Discounting relative cash flows**

Time	*Project A*	*Project B*	*Incremental cash flow*	*PV factor at 10% B – A*	*PV of incremental cash flow*
0	(1,500)	(2,500)	(1,000)	1.000	(1,000)
1	500	500	Nil	0.909	Nil
2	600	800	200	0.826	165
3	700	1,100	400	0.751	300
4	500	1,000	500	0.683	342
5	Nil	500	500	0.621	310
NPV of incremental cash flow					£117

In other words, the present value of the cash flows of project B is £117 greater than those of project A. B is preferred. Note the result is exactly the same in (a) and (b). This gives a useful shortcut to computation when comparing two projects as long as it is known in advance that one of the projects must be undertaken. However, where this is not the case, care should be taken with the 'differential' approach or the technique may result in acceptance of a project with a negative NPV (the other project having a larger negative NPV). There must be a tacit third option from A and B, namely to do neither.

The following example is typical of the type of problem relating to incremental cash flows.

Example

Smith Ltd has decided to increase its productive capacity to meet an anticipated increase in demand for its products. The extent of this increase in capacity has still to be determined, and a management meeting has been called to decide which of the following two mutually exclusive proposals – A or B – should be undertaken.

The following information is available.

	Proposal A	*Proposal B*
	£	£
Capital expenditure:		
Buildings	50,000	100,000
Plant	200,000	300,000
Installation	10,000	15,000
Net income:		
Annual pre-depreciation profits (note (1))	70,000	95,000
Other relevant income/expenditure:		
Sales promotion (note (2))	–	15,000
Plant scrap value	10,000	15,000
Buildings disposable value (note (3))	30,000	60,000
Working capital required over the project life	50,000	65,000

Notes:

1 The investment life is ten years.

2 An exceptional amount of expenditure on sales promotion of £15,000 will have to be spent in year 2 of proposal B. This has not been taken into account in calculating pre-depreciation profits.

3 It is the intention to dispose of the buildings in ten years' time.

Using an 8% discount rate, you are required to evaluate the two alternatives.

Solution

Since the decision has been made to increase capacity (i.e. 'to do nothing' is not an alternative), the easiest approach is to discount the incremental cash flows.

The tabular approach of the previous chapter is still appropriate particularly as the project lasts for ten years (other forms of presentation will appear later).

Time		*A*	*B*	*B – A*	*8%*	*PV*
		£000	£000	£000	*Factor*	£000
0	Capital expenditure	(260)	(415)	(155)	1	(155)
0	Working capital	(50)	(65)	(15)	1	(15)
2	Promotion	–	(15)	(15)	0.857	(13)
1–10	Net income	70	95	25	6.710	168
10	Scrap proceeds	40	75	35	0.463	16
10	Working capital	50	65	15	0.463	7
	Net present value (£000)					8

The present value of proposal B exceeds that of proposal A by £8,000 at 8% and therefore proposal B is preferred.

Assumptions

- The disposal value of buildings is realistic and all other figures have been realistically appraised.
- Expenditure on working capital is incurred at the beginning of the project life and recovered at the end.
- Adequate funds are available for either proposal.
- All cash flows occur annually in arrears on the anniversary of the initial investment.

3.4 More on opportunity costs in project appraisal

If there are scarcities of resources to be used on projects (e.g. labour, materials, machines), then consideration must be given to revenues that could have been earned from alternative uses of the resources.

DEFINITION

Opportunity cost is the value of the benefit sacrificed when one course of action is chosen in preference to an alternative. The opportunity cost is represented by the forgone potential benefit from the best rejected course of action.

Opportunity cost is the value of the benefit sacrificed when one course of action is chosen in preference to an alternative. The opportunity cost is represented by the forgone potential benefit from the best rejected course of action.

For example, the skilled labour that is needed on the new project might have to be withdrawn from normal production causing a loss in contribution. This is obviously relevant to the project appraisal. The cash flows of a single department or division cannot be looked at in isolation. It is always the effects on cash flows of the whole organisation that must be considered.

Example

A new contract requires the use of 50 tons of metal ZX81. This metal is used regularly on all the firm's projects. There are 100 tons of ZX81 in stock at the moment that were bought for £200 per ton. The current purchase price is £210 per ton, and the metal could be disposed of for net scrap proceeds of £150 per ton. With what cost should the new contract be charged for the ZX81?

Solution

The use of the material in stock for the new contract means that more ZX81 must be bought for normal workings. The cost to the organisation is therefore the money spent on purchase, no matter whether existing stock or new stock is used on the contract. Assuming that the additional purchases are made in the near future, the relevant cost to the organisation is current purchase price, i.e.:

50 tons × £210 = £10,500

Example

Suppose the organisation has no use for the ZX81 in stock. What is the relevant cost of using it on the new contract?

Solution

Now the only alternative use for the material is to sell it for scrap. To use 50 tons on the contract is to give up the opportunity of selling it for:

50 × £150 = £7,500

The contract should therefore be charged with this amount.

Example

Suppose that there is no alternative use for the ZX81 other than a scrap sale, but that there is only 25 tons in stock.

Solution

The relevant cost of the 25 tons in stock is £150 per ton. The organisation must then purchase a further 25 tons, and assuming this is in the near future, it will cost £210 per ton.

The contract must be charged with:

	£
25 tons @ £150	3,750
25 tons @ £210	5,250
	9,000

Activity 1

A mining operation uses skilled labour costing £4 per hour, which generates a contribution, after deducting these labour costs, of £3 per hour.

A new project is now being considered that requires 5,000 hours of skilled labour. There is a shortage of the required labour. Any used on the new project must be transferred from normal working. What is the relevant cost of using the skilled labour on the project? What contribution cash flow is lost if the labour is transferred from normal working?

Feedback to this activity is at the end of the chapter.

Activity 2

Suppose the facts about labour are as in the previous activity, but there is a surplus of skilled labour already employed (and paid) by the business which is sufficient to cope with the new project. The presently idle men are being paid full wages.

What contribution cash flow is lost if the labour is transferred to the project from doing nothing?

Feedback to this activity is at the end of the chapter.

3.5 Layout

When deciding between Smith Ltd's proposal A and proposal B (see Section 3.3) to increase capacity, most of the cash flows were constant over the life of the project that went on for ten years. These two features, constant cash flows and lengthy projects, make the sort of presentation used in our solution the most appropriate. However, once opportunity cost and other considerations (such as inflation, or product life cycles) are introduced then a new layout may be preferable. If projects are relatively short, up to five or six years, and cash flows change frequently from year to year, an alternative form of presentation is preferable – one that resembles a cash budget.

A pro-forma might show:

Time	*0*	*1*	*2*	*3*	*4*
	£000	£000	£000	£000	£000
Capital cost	(X)	(X)	–	–	X
Materials	(X)	–	(X)	(X)	–
Labour	–	(X)	(X)	(X)	(X)
Overheads	–	(X)	(X)	(X)	(X)
Revenue		X	X	X	X
Net cash flows	(X)	X	X	X	X
X% discount factor	1.00	X	X	X	X
Present value	(X)	X	X	X	X
Net present value (£'000)	=	X			

4 Project abandonment

4.1 Relevant costs and the decision to abandon

During our initial consideration of project appraisals, it was noted that past costs were irrelevant to any decision regarding the future of a project. This remains true for those occasions when the company has already started a project and wishes to establish whether it should continue with it, or whether it should abandon the project part way through its life.

The only relevant costs are future costs: these will be compared with future revenues to decide the viability of abandonment. Management is often reluctant to take a decision to abandon a project half-way through, as it is often considered to reflect a poor past decision; however true this may be, it would be even worse to compound the error by making another poor decision. Projects must, therefore, be kept constantly under review.

4.2 Cash flow patterns and the decision to abandon

We shall now consider two basic patterns of cash flow:

(a) negative cash flows followed by positive cash flows

(b) a mixture of positive and negative cash flows throughout a project's life.

Pattern (a) is the 'conventional' pattern, where, for example, a factory is built and then used to manufacture goods that will recoup the outlay.

Time	*0*	*1*	*2*	*3*	*4*	*5*	*6*
Cash flow (£000)	–500	–1,000	–200	+750	+600	+500	+400

In this example, it would be unlikely that the project would be abandoned before time 3 unless it transpired, at any point of reappraisal, that estimates of inflows were wildly inaccurate and it became apparent that future incremental cash flow expenditure would not be appropriately covered by future cash inflows. Similarly, once time 3 is reached, there would seem to be little point in abandoning the project, as it is expected to generate further inflows.

It is, however, important to keep estimates under review to ensure their accuracy. It would probably be disastrous for the project, for instance, if at time 3 a net outflow of 100 was achieved instead of an inflow of 750, as this would indicate that the estimated revenues were inaccurate.

Pattern (b) might take the following form.

Time	*0*	*1*	*2*	*3*	*4*	*5*	*6*
Cash flow (£000)	–100	+150	–70	+60	+80	–100	+150

Such a flow might occur, for example, if substantial replacements were necessary at times 2 and 5, or if opportunity costs arose at those times.

This project would not be abandoned immediately after a negative cash flow, if positive flows were expected in later periods. Thus, we would not abandon at time 2 or 5. We would have to consider at time 1, whether we should proceed to time 3 or 4; and at time 4, whether we should proceed to time 6.

4.3 Factors in the decision to abandon

The following considerations must be taken into account in deciding whether to continue or abandon a project:

- the costs, and cost cash flows, of proceeding with the project
- the revenues, and revenue cash flows, associated with the project
- revenues that would arise if the project were abandoned
- other projects, which may be:
  - alternatives to the project under consideration
  - more profitable uses of funds tied up in the project under review.

Each of these factors must be consciously assessed at each stage of the project's life and, if it is seen that abandoning the project would be more beneficial than proceeding with it, then an abandonment decision must be made.

Activity 3

A company with a cost of capital of 10% is undertaking a capital project with the cash flows estimated from the start of the project being as follows:

Time	*0*	*1*	*2*	*3*	*4*	*5*	*6*
Cash flow (£000)	–500	–1,000	–200	+750	+600	+500	+400

We are now approaching the end of the first year, during which £390,000 was spent rather than the £500,000 forecast. The next £1m is just about to be spent and managers are happy about the accuracy of the inflows originally forecast for times 3 to 6 of the project. However they now believe that the outflow at time 2 is more likely to amount to £450,000 rather than the original estimate of £200,000. Should the project now be abandoned before the next £1m is spent?

Feedback to this activity is at the end of the chapter.

4.4 Initial analysis

Any capital investment project will have to be constantly monitored to ensure that it continues to be profitable. It is important that all costs of discontinuing are taken into account (such as redundancy costs) and that a realistic view of cost savings is taken (premises may be difficult to sell and their costs may not be avoided). However, at the start of a project, expected to last, say, ten years, it is worth determining whether the project should be terminated earlier to avoid increasing maintenance cost for equipment for instance. This requires the sorts of calculations carried out for replacement decisions, discussed in the next chapter.

5 Inflation

DEFINITION

For the purpose of this subject, **inflation** may be defined as a general increase in prices, or a general decline in the real value of money.

5.1 The effect of inflation

For the purpose of this subject, **inflation** may be defined as a general increase in prices, or a general decline in the real value of money.

Inflation generally alters the cash flows in projects. In general, the effects are that:

- revenues increase
- costs increase
- interest and debt liabilities may well increase.

In a period of increasing inflation lenders will require an increasing return. Interest rates typically comprise two components, a real underlying interest rate, and an allowance for inflation.

Example

An investor lends £100 now, for repayment in one year of the principal, plus £15.50 interest. During the intervening year a rate of inflation of 5% is expected.

Analyse the interest charge between real interest and the allowance for inflation.

Solution

The investor has £100 now. In order to maintain the purchasing power of the money £100 + 5% will be needed in one year, i.e. £105.

To the investor:

- £105 purchases the same quantity of goods in one year's time as £100 now.
- £115.5 therefore purchases the equivalent of $\frac{£115.5}{£105} \times £100$, or £110 now.

The investor has therefore experienced a 10% return in real terms (i.e. in terms of the quantity of product that can be purchased).

Put another way, the real interest is:

£115.5 – £105 = £10.5

Expressed as a percentage, this is:

$$\frac{£10.5}{£105} \times 100 = 10\%$$

Thus:

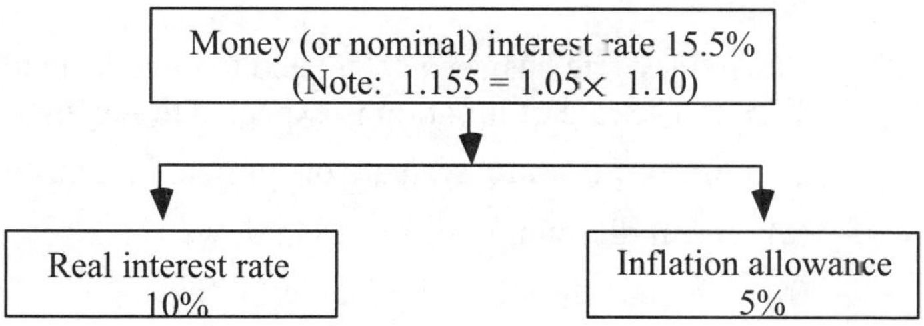

From this example you should note two key concepts.

KEY POINT

Analysis can take place in either money or real terms, as long as the two are not muddled.

(a) Money interest rates and cash flows include the effect of inflation.

Real interest rates and cash flows exclude the effect of inflation.

(b) Analysis can take place in either money or real terms, as long as the two are not muddled.

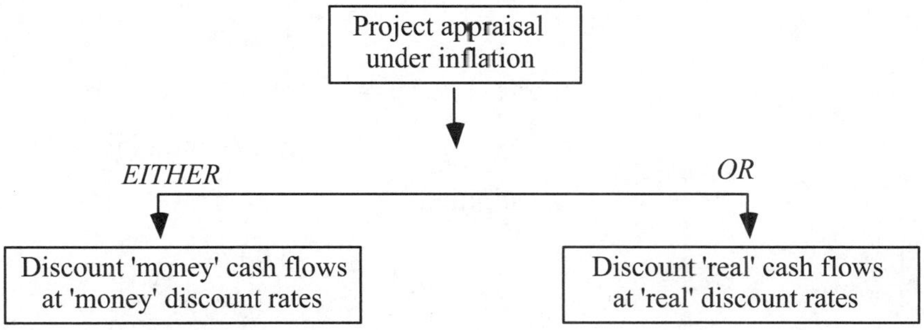

It is further worthy of note that you may obtain real rates of return using:

$$(1 + r) = \frac{(1+m)}{(1+i)}$$

where r, m, and i are the real, money, and inflation rates, respectively. In the last example:

$$(1 + r) = \frac{(1+0.155)}{(1+0.05)} = 1.1,$$ giving the real rate of return as 10%.

Activity 4

Consider the level of interest rates current at the time that you are reading this. How much of the money interest rate is the real interest rate and how much the effects of inflation?

Feedback to this activity is at the end of the chapter.

Example

A project has the following cash flows before allowing for inflation.

Year	*Cash flow*
	£
0	(750)
1	330
2	242
3	532

These are not, therefore, the flows expected if all figures grow in line with inflation.

The money rate has been calculated to include an allowance for inflation at 15.5%. The rate of inflation is expected to remain constant at 5%.

You are required to evaluate the project in terms of:

(a) real discount rates and cash flows

(b) money discount rates and cash flows.

Solution

(a) **Real discount rates and cash flows**

The money rate as per the question of 15.5% includes an investor's/lender's inflation expectation of 5%.

Hence 'real' discount rate, r, is given by:

$$1+r = \frac{1+m}{1+i}$$

where m = money interest rate

i = rate of inflation

Substituting:

$$1+r = \frac{1+0.155}{1+0.05} = 1.10$$

and r is once again 0.10 or 10%.

Discounting the cash flows as per the question:

Year	*Cash flow* £	*PV factor @ 10%*	*Present value* £
0	(750)	1.000	(750)
1	330	0.909	300
2	242	0.826	200
3	532	0.751	400
Net present value			150

(b) **Money discount rates and cash flows**

The discount rate as per the question of 15.5% is the money discount rate. Cash flows, however, need to be increased by 5% compound each year from year 0, to allow for inflation.

Year	*Real cash flow*	*Inflation factor*	*Money* cash flow*	*Discount factor @ 15.5%*	*Present value*
(i)	*(ii)*	*(iii)*	*(iv) = (ii) × (iii)*		
	£		£		
0	(750)	1	(750)	1.000	(750)
1	330	1 + 0.05	346	0.866	300
2	242	$(1 + 0.05)^2$	267	0.750	200
3	532	$(1 + 0.05)^3$	616	0.649	400
Net present value					150

KEY POINT

When appraising a project, either discount actual (money) cash flows using actual (money) discount rates, or real cash flows using real discount rates.

Provided a constant rate of inflation applies to all factors, either approach yields identical conclusions (allowing for rounding). When appraising a project, either discount actual (money) cash flows using actual (money) discount rates, or real cash flows using real discount rates.

5.2 Varying impact of inflation on costs and revenues

In practice, inflation does not affect all costs to the same extent. Some may increase at above and some below the 'average' rate of inflation. Clearly, in relation to a given project, such variations are important and must be taken into account. This is much more easily dealt with by using money cash flows and discount rates.

Example

A company is considering a cost-saving project. This involves purchasing a machine costing £7,000, which will result in annual savings on wage costs of £1,000 and on material costs of £400.

The following forecasts are made of the rates of inflation each year for the next five years.

Wage costs	10%
Material costs	5%
General prices	6%

The cost of capital of the company, in money terms, is 15%.

Evaluate the project, assuming that the machine has a life of five years and no scrap value.

Solution

The first stage is to calculate money cash savings each year.

Year	*Labour cash savings*				*Material cash savings*				*Total savings*
	£			£	£			£	£
1	1,000 ×	1.1	=	1,100	400 ×	1.05	=	420	1,520
2	1,000 ×	$(1.1)^2$	=	1,210	400 ×	$(1.05)^2$	=	441	1,651
3	1,000 ×	$(1.1)^3$	=	1,331	400 ×	$(1.05)^3$	=	463	1,794
4	1,000 ×	$(1.1)^4$	=	1,464	400 ×	$(1.05)^4$	=	486	1,950
5	1,000 ×	$(1.1)^5$	=	1,610	400 ×	$(1.05)^5$	=	510	2,120

Net present value evaluation

Year	*Cash flow*	*PV factor @ 15%*	*PV of cash flow*
	£		£
0	(7,000)	1.000	(7,000)
1	1,520	0.870	1,322
2	1,651	0.756	1,248
3	1,794	0.658	1,180
4	1,950	0.572	1,115
5	2,120	0.497	1,054
Net present value			(1,081)

Therefore the project is not worthwhile.

Note: The general rate of inflation has not been used in, and is irrelevant to, this calculation.

5.3 Deflation

Many western economies have very low rates of inflation at present and some are even experiencing deflation. Deflation may also apply to certain hi-tech materials which get considerably cheaper when they go into mass production.

Suppose an economy is experiencing 5% deflation and the money rate is 1%.

$$1 + r = \frac{1+m}{1+i}$$

where m = money interest rate

i = rate of inflation

Substituting, and remembering that the inflation rate is negative:

$$1 + r = \frac{1+0.01}{1-0.05} = 1.063$$

In other words the real rate is about 6.3%.

As Bob Scarlett said in a recent article in *CIMA Insider*: 'The impact of general price deflation on performance appraisal is the mirror image of the impact of inflation'. In other words revenues will decrease, costs will decrease and so on.

As Scarlett says, deflation may affect business decision making in several ways.

- Investing in projects that have long payback periods may require some courage.
- Borrowing to finance the purchase of assets that are going to fall in value may also require some courage: money rates will be low, but real rates are higher.
- It may be difficult to reduce some costs – especially wages – in line with deflation.
- Consumers may defer purchasing decisions if they anticipate that prices will fall.

6 Taxation

6.1 The effect of taxation

Taxation has two major effects.

- Project cash flows will give rise to taxation that itself has an impact on project appraisal. There will be natural differences between the cash flows earned and the level of profits on which the payment of taxation is based, particularly as regards capital expenditure, but in general cash receipts will give rise to tax payable and *vice versa*.
- The relief on interest payments will reduce the effective rate of interest that a firm pays on its borrowings, and hence the opportunity cost of capital.

6.2 Net-of-tax cash flows from projects

The effects of taxation are complex, and are influenced by a number of factors including:

- the taxable profits and tax rate
- the company's accounting period, and tax payment dates
- the allowable rate of tax depreciation
- losses available for set-off.

Information relating to the tax rates and tax payments dates should be given in the exam question and, unless information is given to the contrary, you should also assume that:

- Where a tax loss arises from the project, there are sufficient taxable profits elsewhere in the organisation to allow the loss to reduce any relevant (subsequent) tax payment (and thus may be treated as a cash inflow).
- The first tax depreciation claim is made in the year of purchase. Normally half of the tax payable is paid in the year that the profit is earned and half paid in the following year but you should read the question carefully for specific instructions.
- The company's financial year commences at the start of the project and that it will have sufficient taxable profits to obtain full benefit from capital allowances.
- There are balancing adjustments on the disposal of all assets.

Whenever tax is relevant to an appraisal, careful reading of the question and stating of any assumptions is essential.

6.3 Calculation of corporation tax and writing down allowances (WDAS)

Common exam questions will give cash flows arising from a project and information concerning the calculation of corporation tax and WDAs. You will be required to calculate and include in the project cash flows for discounting:

- corporation tax due on project profits
- tax depreciation available that results in tax relief.

Example

KL Ltd is considering manufacturing a new product. This requires machinery costing £20,000, with a life of four years and a terminal value of £5,000. Profits before depreciation from the project will be £8,000 pa. However, there will be cash flows that will differ from profits by the build-up of working capital during the first year of operations and its run-down during the fourth year, amounting to £2,000.

The machine qualifies for tax depreciation at the rate of 25% pa on a reducing balance basis. At the end of the project's life a balancing charge or allowance will arise equal to the difference between the scrap proceeds and the tax written-down value.

50% of tax is payable in the year on which it is based and the balance one year later. The corporation tax rate is 35% and the start of the project is also the start of the accounting year.

The after-tax cost of capital is 15%.

Should the project be accepted?

Solution

The first step will be to calculate the corporation tax due on project profits. Note that the profit figure should be before depreciation charges as these are disallowable for tax purposes (and are replaced by tax depreciation).

(W1) Tax due/paid on profits earned:

Year	*Profit*	*Tax due (35%)*	*Year tax paid*				
			1	*2*	*3*	*4*	*5*
1	8,000	2,800	1,400	1,400			
2	8,000	2,800		1,400	1,400		
3	8,000	2,800			1,400	1,400	
4	8,000	2,800				1,400	1,400
			1,400	2,800	2,800	2,800	1,400

The next step is to calculate the tax relief available: (W2)

Year	*Bal b/f*	*Tax depr 25%*	*Tax relief 35%*	*Year relief received*				
				1	*2*	*3*	*4*	*5*
1	20,000	5,000	1,750	875	875			
2	15,000	3,750	1,312		656	656		
3	11,250	2,812	984			492	492	
4	8,438	3,438*	1,203				602	601
Disposal	5,000							
Balancing allowance	3,438							
		15,000		875	1,531	1,148	1,094	601

Balancing allowance of £8,438 less disposal value of £5,000.

These figures can then be incorporated into a schedule which records all of the cash flows relating to the project. A tabular approach is usually the best method of presentation.

All figures £	*Year 0*	*Year 1*	*Year 2*	*Year 3*	*Year 4*	*Year 5*
Profit		8,000	8,000	8,000	8,000	
Working capital		(2,000)			2,000	
Capital	(20,000)				5,000	
Tax paid (W1)		(1,400)	(2,800)	(2,800)	(2,800)	(1,400)
Tax relief (W2)		875	1,531	1,148	1,094	601
Net cash flow	(20,000)	5,475	6,731	6,348	13,294	(799)
DF at 15%	1	0.870	0.756	0.658	0.572	0.497
Present values	(20,000)	4,763	5,089	4,177	7,604	(397)
Net present value						1,236

It is therefore concluded that the project is worthwhile.

Activity 5

W Ltd is considering investing in a new machine which has a capital cost of £25,000. It has an estimated life of four years and a residual value of £5,000 at the end of four years. The machine qualifies for tax depreciation at the rate of 25% per year on a reducing balance basis.

An existing machine would be sold immediately for £8,000 if the new machine were to be bought. The existing machine has a tax written down value of £3,000.

The existing machine generates annual net contribution of £30,000. This is expected to increase by 20% if the new machine is purchased.

W Ltd pays corporation tax on its profits at the rate of 30%, with half of the tax being payable in the year that the profit is earned and half in the following year.

The company's after tax cost of capital is 15% per year.

Evaluate whether the investment is worthwhile.

Feedback to this activity is at the end of the chapter.

7 Activity-based costing in longer-term decisions

Activity-based costing (ABC) has been discussed in an earlier chapter. In this section we briefly discuss the role of ABC in longer-term decision making.

ABC systems are primarily designed to furnish management with cost information relating to an organisation's products. However, the production of this information is not an end in itself. Indeed it is the use to which such activity-based information is put that represents its real purpose and its value should be assessed against this end-result.

An ABC system furnishes the management of an organisation with historic information relating to its products or service provision which is of much assistance to management in analysing and explaining an organisation's profitability. However, many commentators including Robert Kaplan and Robin Cooper have viewed ABC as supporting major areas of strategic decision making with organisations, these being:

- decisions concerning product pricing strategy
- changes to the range and mix of products via the promotion and discontinuance of current lines, and
- new product development.

When ABC information is used in the above ways then it will underpin policy decisions of senior management and will therefore have a significant influence upon the longer-term prosperity of an organisation. Advocates of the use of ABC for strategic decision making maintain that its value lies in greater accuracy attaching to product costing which in turn increases the degree of reliability of cost information used for the above purposes. They further maintain that the use of ABC may give an indication of the long-term variable cost of products which arguably is the most relevant cost information for use in decisions of the above type. Given the inherent uncertainty involved in strategic decision making, management may use ABC information in decision-modelling and sensitivity analysis to assist in the making of such decisions.

The end product of an ABC system is an estimate of the historic cost of each of an organisation's products. However, strategic decision making involves future time periods and thus it is future outlay costs that need to be taken into consideration as opposed to historic costs. Therefore, it is arguable that the results obtained from an ABC system should only be used as a starting point in the determination of cost information that is aimed at assisting in the making of longer-term decisions. This is especially the case if ABC based product costs are viewed as estimates of longer term product costs as 'nothing is forever' and historic costs are susceptible to substantial change since all factors of production become variable in the longer term.

Any cost information which has been produced based on past activities must be used with caution with regard to longer-term decisions. Even so, ABC information may provide a sound starting point for the preparation of cost information to be used in strategic decision making. It has been argued that a significant advantage of ABC over conventional costing systems lies in its suitability for strategic decision making. Kaplan has argued that for decisions of a strategic nature a long-term perspective is usual and maintains that an ABC system gives product cost information which matches this requirement particularly well. This is evidenced by his assertion that 'conventional notions of fixed and variable costs are ignored because, for the purposes of product cost analysis, the time period is long enough to warrant treatment of virtually all costs as variable'.

Summary

- The process of investment decision making can be analysed in six steps.
- Because of the financial amounts involved, investment projects should be subject to control procedures, such as approval by a capital expenditure committee and formal evaluation once the project is ended.
- In arriving at an investment decision, only relevant costs and benefits should be included. Costs such as depreciation, apportioned fixed costs and sunk costs should be ignored.
- Review of estimated costs and benefits should continue once the project has been launched. In some cases this may lead to abandonment of the project.
- Where inflation affects project cash flows, either discount real cash flows at real discount rates, or discount money cash flows at money discount rates.
- Taxation has two major effects on project cash flows: corporation tax payments or rebates may arise; and WDAs may give tax relief.
- In longer-term decisions, activity based costing may provide useful information for decision making.

Having completed your study of this chapter you should have achieved the following learning outcomes.

- Explain the processes involved in making long-term decisions.
- Apply the principles of relevant cash flow analysis to long-run projects that continue for several years.
- Calculate project cash flows, accounting for tax and inflation, and apply perpetuities to derive 'end of project' value where appropriate.
- Apply activity-based costing techniques to derive approximate long-run product or service costs appropriate for use in strategic decision making.

Self-test questions

1 What are the functions of a capital expenditure committee? (2.1)

2 What information about capital expenditure should be submitted to the committee? (2.3)

3 What are the three reasons for undertaking post-project audits? (2.6)

4 What costs should be ignored in any DCF calculation? (3.1)

5 If using an incremental approach to decide between two alternative investment opportunities, what tacit third option must not exist? (3.3)

6 What is the general impact of inflation on evaluation of a capital project? (5.1)

7 Distinguish between real cash flows and money cash flows. (5.1)

8 What are the two major effects of taxation on a capital project? (6.1)

Objective test questions

Question 1

Which of the following should be included in a DCF analysis as a relevant cash flow?

A A sunk cost

B Depreciation charge

C Apportioned fixed costs

D Irrecoverable VAT on the purchase of a fixed asset

Question 2

The decision to abandon a partly completed project should be taken by comparing:

A past costs with past revenues

B past costs with future revenues

C future costs with past revenues

D future costs with future revenues

Question 3

If the nominal interest rate offered by a bank account is 6%, while inflation stands at 1.5%, then the real interest rate offered is most accurately stated as:

A 1.5%

B 4.4%

C 4.5%

D 6%

For the answers to these questions, see the 'Answers' section at the end of the book.

Exam-type questions

Question 1: AB plc

AB plc is considering a new product with a three-year life. The product can be made with existing machinery, which has spare capacity, or by a labour-saving specialised new machine that would have zero disposal value at the end of three years.

The following estimates have been made at current prices.

Sales volume	1 million units per annum
Selling price	£15 per unit
Labour cost (without m/c)	£6 per unit
Material cost	£2 per unit
Variable overheads	£2 per unit

Additional fixed overheads for the new product are estimated to be £3 million per year.

The new machine would cost £5 million now and would halve the labour cost per unit.

Because of competition, selling price increases will be limited to 2% per annum, although labour cost is expected to rise at 12% per annum and all other costs at 8% per annum.

The company's money cost of capital is 15% and, apart from the cost of the new machine, all other cash flows can be assumed to arise at year ends.

Required:

Evaluate whether the new machine should be purchased.

(10 marks)

Question 2: J plc

J Plc is considering whether to buy or lease a new machine. The machine would cost £500,000 and a lease could be arranged costing £150,000 per annum for four years, payable in advance.

Corporation tax is payable at the rate of 30% of profits and is paid in two equal instalments: the first in the year that profits arise and the second in the following year. Tax depreciation is available at 25% each year on a reducing balance basis. The machine is expected to have a useful life of four years with no residual value.

The company has sufficient profits to take advantage of all available tax relief and the cost of capital is 8%.

Required:

Evaluate whether the company should buy or lease the machine. **(10 marks)**

For the answers to these questions, see the 'Answers' section at the end of the book.

Feedback to activities

Activity 1

	£
Contribution per hour lost from normal working	3
Add back: labour cost per hour that is not saved	4
Cash lost per labour hour as a result of the labour transfer	£7
The contract should be charged with 5,000 × £7	£35,000

Activity 2

Nothing.

The relevant cost is zero.

Activity 3

The new cash profile is as follows.

Time	*0*	*1*	*2*	*3*	*4*	*5*
Cash flow (£000)	–1,000	–450	+750	+600	+500	+400
10% discount factor	1.000	0.909	0.826	0.751	0.683	0.621
Present value (£000)	–1,000	–409	+620	+451	+342	+248

NPV = £252,000.

So the project still has a positive expected NPV and therefore should not be abandoned.

Activity 4

For example, suppose the gross yield on long gilts was 8.18% while inflation was 1.90% pa.

m = money rate of interest = 8.18%

i = inflation rate = 1.90%

∴ real rate of interest, r, is given by:

$$1+r=\frac{1+m}{1+i}=\frac{1.0818}{1.0190}=1.0616$$

The real rate of interest is 6.16% pa.

Activity 5

(W1) The incremental increase in contribution earned as a result of using the new machine is £30,000 × 40% = £12,000 per year.

(W2) Tax due/paid on incremental contribution earned:

Year	*Inc contr*	*Tax due (30%)*	*Year tax paid* *1*	*2*	*3*	*4*	*5*
1	12,000	3,600	1,800	1,800			
2	12,000	3,600		1,800	1,800	1,800	
3	12,000	3,600			1,800	1,800	
4	12,000	3,600				1,800	1,800
			1,800	3,600	3,600	3,600	1,800

(W3) Tax depreciation/ tax relief

Existing machine

The sale of the existing machine leads to a balancing charge of £8,000 – £3,000 = £5,000. Tax payable on this is £5,000 × 30% = £1,500. Assume this is paid half in year 0 and half in year 1.

New machine

Year	*Bal b/f*	*Tax depr 25%*	*Tax relief 30%*	*Year relief received* *1*	*2*	*3*	*4*	*5*
1	25,000	6,250	1,875	937	938			
2	18,750	4,688	1,406		703	703		
3	14,063	3,515	1,055			528	527	
4	10,547	5,547	1,664				832	832
Disposal	5,000							
Balancing allowance	5,547							
		20,000		937	1,641	1,231	1,359	832

All figures £	*Year 0*	*Year 1*	*Year 2*	*Year 3*	*Year 4*	*Year 5*
Incremental contribution (W1)		12,000	12,000	12,000	12,000	
Capital	(25,000)				5,000	
Tax paid (W2)		(1,800)	(3,600)	(3,600)	(3,600)	(1,800)
Tax paid on existing machine (W3)	(750)	(750)				
Tax relief on new machine (W3)		937	1,641	1,231	1,359	832
Net cash flow	(25,750)	10,387	10,041	9,631	14,759	(968)
DCF at 15%	1	0.870	0.756	0.658	0.572	0.497
Present values	(25,750)	9,037	7,591	6,337	8,442	(481)
Net present value						5,176

The net present value is positive and therefore it is worthwhile purchasing the machine.

Chapter 13

FURTHER ASPECTS OF INVESTMENT APPRAISAL

Syllabus content

This chapter covers the following syllabus content.

- Sensitivity analysis to identify the input variables that most effect the chosen measure of project worth (payback, ARR, NPV or IRR).
- Methods of dealing with particular problems: the use of annuities in comparing projects with unequal lives and the profitability index in capital rationing situations.

If the previous chapters provided mainly a revision of previous studies, in this chapter more of the practical aspects of investment appraisal are introduced that you may not have seen earlier. The object is to concentrate less on the mechanics of discounting and more on the way in which those mechanics are applied to the investment decisions that are faced by companies.

Contents

1 Sensitivity analysis

1.1 Introduction

A major problem with capital investment decisions is that the figure reached in any calculation (a positive or negative NPV) is only as reliable as the estimates used to produce that figure. One only has to look at the revisions made to estimates of large capital sums in major investment programmes such as the Millennium Dome or road or rail investment to see how unreliable some of these estimates can be. Estimating the long-term benefits presents even greater problems.

One way of providing useful supplementary information for an investment decision is to consider a range of figures for various estimates and establish whether these give positive or negative NPVs. With the increased use of spreadsheet packages, this exercise is easy to perform, sometimes being referred to as posing 'What if?' questions; however, it is important to be able to determine what variations in estimates are reasonable and what are unlikely. This analysis is usually applied to one estimate at a time, although it can be applied to each estimate simultaneously.

A more concise form of analysis takes each estimate in turn and assesses the percentage error that would be required to alter our decision on the investment. It is customary to apply this approach to single estimates although, if any relationship between variables is known, it can be applied to groups of figures. It is this form of sensitivity analysis that is considered here.

1.2 Illustration of sensitivity analysis

Example

Bacher Ltd is considering investing £500,000 in equipment to produce a new type of ball. Sales of the product are expected to continue for three years, at the end of which the equipment will have a scrap value of £80,000. Sales revenue of £600,000 per annum will be generated at a variable cost of £350,000. Annual fixed costs will increase by £40,000.

Required:

(a) Determine whether, on the basis of the estimates given, the project should be undertaken assuming that all cash flows occur at annual intervals and that Bacher Ltd has a cost of capital of 15%.

(b) Find the percentage changes required in the following estimates for the investment decision to change:

- (i) initial investment
- (ii) scrap value
- (iii) selling price
- (iv) sales volume
- (v) cost of capital.

Solution

Although part (a) could be completed most efficiently by finding net annual inflows (£600,000 – £350,000 – £40,000) of £210,000, separate present values are needed for part (b).

(a) **NPV calculation**

Time		*Cash flow* £000	*15% discount factor*	*Present value* £000
0	Equipment	(500)	1	(500)
1–3	Revenue	600	2.283	1,370
1–3	Variable costs	(350)		(799)
1–3	Fixed costs	(40)		(91)
3	Scrap value	80	0.658	53
Net present value (£'000)				33

The project should, on the basis of these estimates, be accepted.

(b) **Sensitivity analysis**

KEY POINT

To find the percentage change required in an estimate to change an investment decision, find:

$$\frac{\text{NPV of project}}{\text{PV of those figures that vary with estimate concerned}}$$

To find the percentage change required in an estimate to change an investment decision, find:

$$\frac{\text{NPV of project}}{\text{PV of those figures that vary with estimate concerned}}$$

(i) ***Initial investment***

For the decision to change, the NPV must fall by £33,000. For this to occur the cost of the equipment must rise by £33,000. This is a rise of:

$$\frac{33}{500} \times 100 \quad = \quad 6.6\%$$

(ii) ***Scrap value***

If the NPV is to fall by £33,000, the present value of scrap proceeds must fall by £33,000. The PV of scrap proceeds is currently £53,000; it must fall by:

$$\frac{33}{53} \times 100 \quad = \quad 62.26\%, \text{ say } 62\%$$

(This would bring the scrap proceeds down by 62.26% to £30,000; the PV of the scrap proceeds would be £20,000, i.e. £33,000 less than in (a). There are some slight differences from rounding due to the use of 3 decimal place tables.)

(iii) ***Sales price***

If sales price varies, sales revenue will vary (assuming no effect on demand). If the NPV of the project is to fall by £33,000, the selling price must fall by:

$$\frac{33}{1,370} \times 100 \quad = \quad 2\%$$

(iv) ***Sales volume***

If sales volume falls, revenue and variable costs fall (contribution falls); if the NPV is to fall by £33,000, volume must fall by:

$$\frac{33}{(1{,}370-799)} \times 100 \quad = \quad 6\%$$

(v) ***Cost of capital***

If NPV is to fall, cost of capital must rise; the figure to which the cost of capital has to rise – that gives an NPV of zero – is the project's IRR. To find the IRR, which is probably not much above 15%, the NPV at 20% can be found using the summarised cash flows.

$$\text{NPV (£'000)} \quad = \quad -500 + [210 \times 2.106] + [80 \times 0.579]$$

$$= \quad -11$$

We can then use the formula:

$$\text{IRR} \quad \approx \quad A + (B - A)\left(\frac{N_A}{N_A - N_B}\right)$$

$$\approx \quad 15 + (20 - 15) \times \left(\frac{33}{33+11}\right)$$

$$\approx \quad 18.75\%$$

The cost of capital would have to increase from 15% to 18.75% before the investment decision changes.

(***Note*** do not calculate percentages of percentages!)

Activity 1

(a) Using the data in the previous example about Bacher's new equipment, estimate:

(i) the percentage changes in unit variable cost, and

(ii) annual fixed cost needed to change the investment decision.

(b) Comment on the significance of the sensitivity analysis carried out.

Feedback to this activity is at the end of the chapter.

2 Replacement theory

2.1 The nature of replacement problems

The replacement problem is concerned with the decision to replace existing operating assets. The two questions to be evaluated are:

- when should the existing equipment be replaced?
- what should be the replacement policy thereafter (i.e. the future replacement cycle)?

This may be represented diagrammatically.

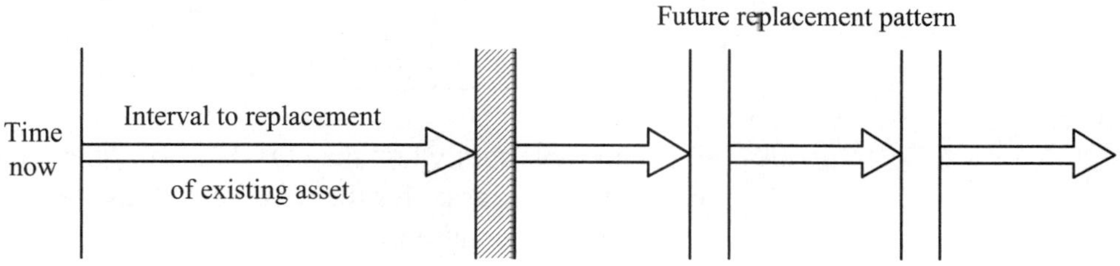

KEY POINT

It is difficult to determine the replacement policy of an existing asset in isolation, because that decision will be dependent on the cost of the future replacement pattern.

It is difficult to determine the replacement policy of the existing asset in isolation, because that decision will be dependent on the cost of the future replacement pattern, a fact that will be demonstrated in the sections that follow.

2.2 Relevance of replacement decisions

Within the UK, it is estimated that 50% to 60% of total investment incorporates replacement. Yet the evidence also suggests that replacement appraisal is somewhat haphazard. In particular:

- there is a failure to take account of the timescale problems
- techniques such as payback and accounting rate of return are used, which are unsuitable for replacement decisions
- taxation and investment incentives are ignored
- inflation is ignored.

This section is concerned with developing a systematic approach to replacement analysis.

2.3 Factors in replacement decisions

The factors to be considered include the following.

(a) **Capital cost of new equipment** – the higher cost of equipment will have to be balanced against known or possible technical improvements.

(b) **Operating costs** – operating costs will be expected to increase as the machinery deteriorates over time. This is referred to as operating inferiority, and is the result of:

  (i) increased repair and maintenance costs

  (ii) loss of production due to 'down-time' resulting from increased repair and maintenance time

  (iii) lower quality and quantity of output.

(c) **Resale value** – the extent to which old equipment can be traded in for new.

(d) **Taxation and investment incentives**.

(e) **Inflation** – both the general price level change, and relative movements in the prices of inputs and outputs.

2.4 The timescale problems

A special feature of replacement problems is that they involve comparisons of alternatives with different timescales. If the choice is between replacing an item of machinery every two or three years, it would be meaningless simply to compare the NPV of the two costs.

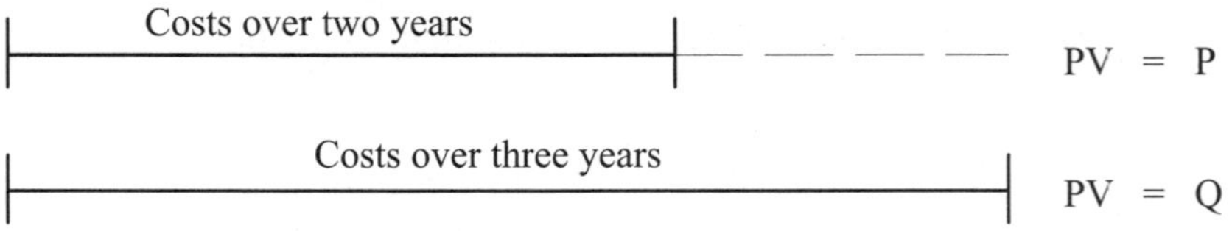

P is almost certainly less than Q. However, this does not take account of the cost of providing an asset for the third year. A method of calculating an equivalent annual cost is required.

Three methods are available to take account of this.

Lowest common multiple (LCM)

The LCM of the various replacement cycles is computed (in this case the LCM of two and three is six) and the PV of costs over this period is computed, i.e. the cost of 3 × 2-year cycles is compared with those of 2 × 3-year cycles.

The method rapidly becomes unwieldy – for a machine that can be replaced every five or seven years the LCM is 35 years.

Finite time horizon

To avoid the problem of very long periods to be considered under the LCM method it is possible to consider costs only over a finite period – say, ten years. Thus the PV of costs incurred over this finite period are compared and the costs arising after this time are ignored on the basis that they will be discounted heavily anyway and thus their PV will be negligible.

The problem with this method is that strictly, like is not being compared with like. For example, in the case of a machine that could be replaced every five or seven years, then at the end of a ten-year period the five-year cycle would end up with a five-year old machine, and the seven-year cycle would end with a three-year old machine.

Equivalent annual cost (EAC)

The neatest solution is to compute the PV of costs over one cycle and then turn it into an EAC by the use of an annuity factor. Thus, the costs associated with any particular cycle can be considered as equivalent to having to pay this EAC every year throughout the cycle and throughout subsequent cycles. This will be made clearer by use of the following example.

Example

A decision has to be made on replacement policy for vans. A van costs £12,000 and the following additional information applies.

Interval between replacement (years)	*Trade in allowance*	*Maintenance cost paid at year end*
	£	£
1	9,000	Nil
2	7,500	2,000
3	7,000	3,000

Calculate the optimal replacement policy at a cost of capital of 15%. There are no maintenance costs in the year of replacement. Ignore taxation and inflation.

Solution

The solution will be calculated using the three techniques discussed in the last section.

It is assumed that a brand new van is owned at the beginning of the cycle, and therefore must be owned at the end of the cycle.

(a) **Lowest common multiple**

Since replacement is possible every one, two or three years the LCM is six and hence a six-year period will be considered.

(i) Replace every year

Time	*0*	*1*	*2*	*3*	*4*	*5*	*6*
	£	£	£	£	£	£	£
Capital cost	(12,000)	(12,000)	(12,000)	(12,000)	(12,000)	(12,000)	(12,000)
Trade in all'ce	–	9,000	9,000	9,000	9,000	9,000	9,000
Maintenance	–	–	–	–	–	–	–
	(12,000)	(3,000)	(3,000)	(3,000)	(3,000)	(3,000)	(3,000)
15% factor	1	0.870	0.756	0.658	0.572	0.497	0.432
PV	(12,000)	(2,610)	(2,268)	(1,974)	(1,716)	(1,491)	(1,296)

NPV = £(23,355)

(ii) Replace every other year

Time	*0*	*1*	*2*	*3*	*4*	*5*	*6*
	£	£	£	£	£	£	£
Purchase	(12,000)	–	(12,000)	–	(12,000)	–	(12,000)
Trade in	–	–	7,500	–	7,500	–	7,500
Maintenance	–	(2,000)	–	(2,000)	–	(2,000)	–
Net	(12,000)	(2,000)	(4,500)	(2,000)	(4,500)	(2,000)	(4,500)
15% factor	1	0.870	0.756	0.658	0.572	0.497	0.432
PV	(12,000)	(1,740)	(3,402)	(1,316)	(2,574)	(994)	(1,944)

NPV = £(23,970)

(iii) Replace every third year

Time	*0*	*1*	*2*	*3*	*4*	*5*	*6*
	£	£	£	£	£	£	£
Purchase	(12,000)	–	–	(12,000)	–	–	(12,000)
Trade in	–	–	–	7,000	–	–	7,000
Maintenance	–	(2,000)	(3,000)	–	(2,000)	(3,000)	–
Net	(12,000)	(2,000)	(3,000)	(5,000)	(2,000)	(3,000)	(5,000)
15% factor	1	0.870	0.756	0.658	0.572	0.497	0.432
PV	(12,000)	(1,740)	(2,268)	(3,290)	(1,144)	(1,491)	(2,160)

NPV = £(24,093)

It is concluded under the LCM approach that annual replacement has the lowest PV of costs.

It could be argued that the first or last £12,000 should be ignored so that six complete cycles only are included, but note that, had we excluded the £12,000 initial cost at year 0 under each option, the decision would have been exactly the same.

(b) **Finite time horizon**

In an examination question the finite time horizon method would probably be inappropriate because the LCM method gives a period of only six years to be considered. It is included in this example for completeness. A time period of five years will be considered ignoring the common initial cost of £12,000.

		One-year cycle		*Two-year cycle*		*Three-year cycle*	
Time	*15% discount factor*	*Cash flow*	*PV*	*Cash flow*	*PV*	*Cash flow*	*PV*
		£	£	£	£	£	£
1	0.870	3,000	2,610	2,000	1,740	2,000	1,740
2	0.756	3,000	2,268	4,500	3,402	3,000	2,268
3	0.658	3,000	1,974	2,000	1,316	5,000	3,290
4	0.572	3,000	1,716	4,500	2,574	2,000	1,144
5	0.497	3,000	1,491	* 3,000	1,491	* 4,500	2,237
Net present value			£10,059		£10,523		£10,679

Again, it is concluded that annual replacement gives the lowest level of costs.

* It is assumed that the one or two year old van will be traded in at the end of the five-year period under review.

(c) **Equivalent annual cost**

The costs incurred over a single cycle are computed and the EAC is found as follows.

(i) Replace every year

NPV of a single cycle $= -£12{,}000 + \dfrac{£9{,}000}{1.15} = £(4{,}174)$

1 year 'annuity' factor $= 0.87$

Equivalent annual cost $= \dfrac{\text{NPV}}{\text{annunity factor}} = \dfrac{£(4{,}174)}{0.870} = £(4{,}798)$

(ii) Replace every two years

NPV of a single cycle $= -£12{,}000 - \dfrac{£2{,}000}{1.15} + \dfrac{£7{,}500}{1.15^2} =$

£(8,068)

2 year 'annuity' factor $= 1.626$

Equivalent annual cost $= \dfrac{£(8{,}068)}{1.626} = £(4{,}962)$

(iii) Replace every three years

NPV of a single cycle $= -£12{,}000 - \dfrac{£2{,}000}{1.15} - \dfrac{£3{,}000}{1.15^2} + \dfrac{£7{,}000}{1.15^3} = £(11{,}405)$

3 year 'annuity' factor = 2.283

Equivalent annual cost $= \dfrac{£(11{,}405)}{2.283} = £(4{,}996)$

The optimal replacement period is every year (as in the previous two instances).

Note: The EAC is that sum that could be paid annually in arrears to finance the three replacement cycles. It is equivalent to the budget accounts that various public services encourage customers to open to spread the cost of those services more evenly. The present value of annual sums equal to the EACs is the same as the PV of the various receipts and payments needed to buy and maintain a van.

In this case there was no conflict between the three methods adopted. However, in other questions, the finite time horizon method may give a result that is different to the other two. In an examination this will not matter. It is always more important to show your workings and that the solution was approached in a valid logical manner, rather than to achieve any particular result.

Activity 2

A company with a cost of capital of 12% wishes to determine the optimum replacement policy for its computers. Each computer costs £5,000 and can either be traded in at the end of the first year for £3,000 (no maintenance cost paid) or traded in at the end of the second year for £2,000 (£500 maintenance paid after one year). Calculate the equivalent annual cost of each policy and recommend which should be implemented.

Feedback to this activity is at the end of the chapter.

2.5 Incorporation of deterioration and obsolescence

In many situations, as the machine ages, a predictable gap, or operating inferiority, between it and new machines emerges (i.e. in addition to its scrap value falling and maintenance cost rising, its ability to produce falls). As the machine ages, the annual cost of operating inferiority becomes greater. On the other hand, the capital cost declines as an annual cost with machine age. The optimal replacement policy will be the minimum cost combination.

Example

The capital cost of an item of new equipment is £5,000. It has no value once installed except from continued use, and it has a maximum life of seven years. However, every year of use there is a cost of operating inferiority (made up of maintenance costs and production losses) that increases at £500 pa. This cost may be treated as a cash outflow occurring annually starting two years after installation.

Calculate the optimal replacement interval. The cost of capital is 10%. Ignore taxation, incentives and inflation.

Solution

The data above must be tabulated to calculate the two cost elements for each alternative replacement cycle up to seven years:

Year	*1*	*2*	*3*	*4*	*5*	*6*	*7*
	Cost of operating inferiority for year	*PV of operating inferiority @ 10%*	*Cumulative PV of operating inferiority*	*Annuity factor for year @ 10%*	*Equivalent annual cost for life*		
					Operating inferiority [(3)÷(4)]	*Capital cost [£5,000÷(4)]*	*Total [(5)+(6)]*
	£	£	£		£	£	£
1	–	–	–	0.909	–	5,501	5,501
2	500	413	413	1.736	238	2,880	3,118
3	1,000	751	1,164	2.487	468	2,010	2,478
4	1,500	1,025	2,189	3.170	691	1,577	2,268
5	2,000	1,242	3,431	3.791	905	1,319	2,224
6	2,500	1,413	4,844	4.355	1,112	1,148	2,260
7	3,000	1,539	6,383	4.868	1,311	1,027	2,338

This analysis can be presented graphically.

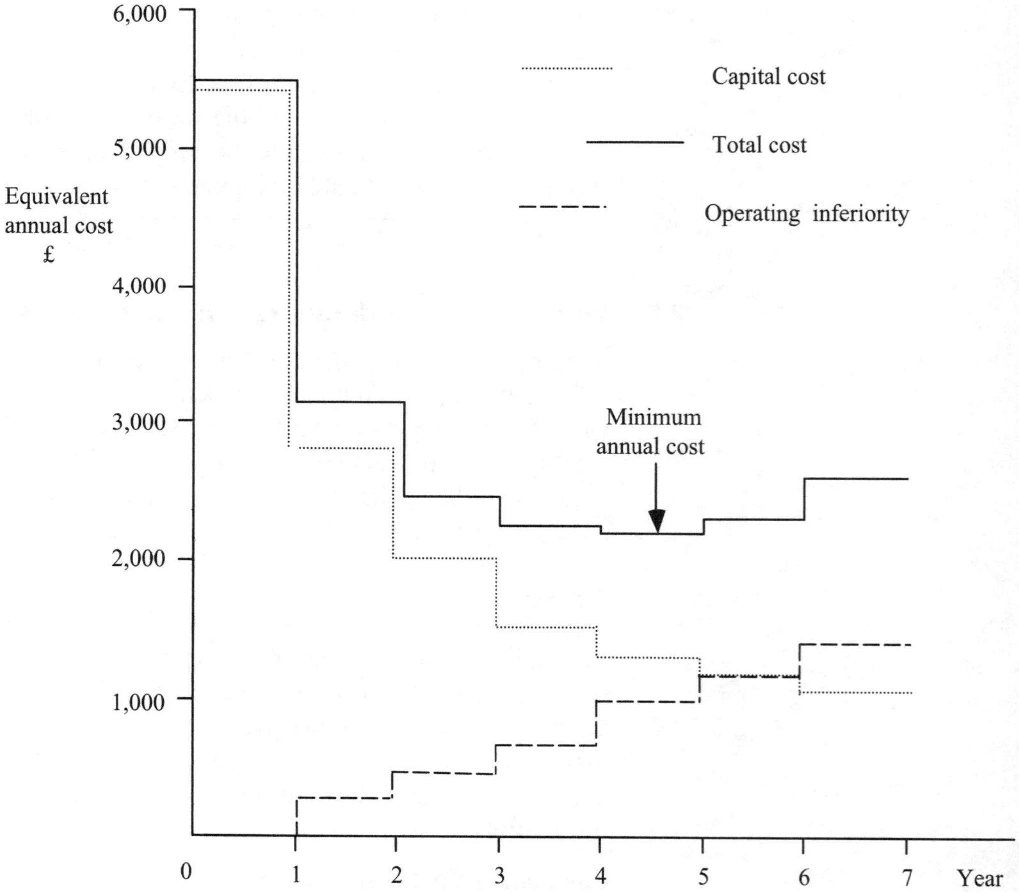

The cost is minimised with a five-year (year 0 to year 5) replacement policy.

2.6 One-off replacement decisions

In addition to the long-term replacement problem, there is also the one-off replacement decision.

Example

Using the data in the previous example, the company has currently installed and been running a two-year old machine. It has received a one-off offer of £2,500 for the machine, if it sells now.

Should it accept the offer or wait until the normal replacement date?

Solution

This is an exercise in differential costing. It is known from the calculations above that the equivalent annual cost from the time of the next replacement is £2,224.

The costs arising after the third year may be ignored as 'common costs'. Thus, assuming, for convenience, that the machine was to have been kept for a further three years, the incremental costs and revenues as a result of deciding to sell the machine now are tabulated below.

An equivalent annual cost $= \dfrac{\text{NPV of one replacement cycle}}{\text{cumulative discount factor}}$

Time	*0*	*1*	*2*	*3*
	£	£	£	£
Sale proceeds received	2,500			
Operating inferiority avoided	–	1,000	1,500	2,000
Cost of replacement machine (annualised)	–	(2,224)	(2,224)	(2,224)
Net cash flow	2,500	(1,224)	(724)	(224)
10% discount factors	1.000	0.909	0.826	0.751
Present value	2,500	(1,113)	(598)	(168)

NPV = £621.

This positive NPV indicates that the incremental project is worthwhile so it is worth replacing the machine now, receiving £2,500 although it means higher costs for the next three years.

DEFINITION

Capital rationing arises when an organisation is restricted in the amount of funds available to initial all worthwhile projects (i.e. projects that have a positive net present value).

3 Capital rationing

Capital rationing arises when an organisation is restricted in the amount of funds available to initiate all worthwhile projects (i.e. projects that have a positive net present value).

The fact that capital needs to be rationed is a situation that has to be appreciated when looking at capital budgeting.

There are two causes of capital rationing, as follows:

- **hard (external) capital rationing** – Although, theoretically, finance is always available at a price, in practice most lending institutions decide that there is a point beyond which they will not lend, at any price. This may provide an absolute limit to the funds available.
- **soft (internal) capital rationing** – Particularly following a period of economic depression, many firms may be more concerned with survival than growth. In order to minimise risk, they adopt conservative growth and financing policies. Also, they want to maintain stable dividends rather than use cash for expansion.

Whether the restriction is caused by internal or external causes does not affect the analysis.

Capital rationing might therefore exist for reasons other than inability to obtain additional capital.

- A company might be aware that when proposals are made for new capital investments, the managers who put forward the proposals are often over-optimistic in their expectations and with their forecasts. Imposing capital spending limits can be a way of weeding out weak or marginal projects, by making them compete for funds with stronger and more profitable projects. This can be a crude but effective way of reducing the risk of making poor investments.
- A company might be able to raise new finance externally, but might prefer a strategy of organic growth. An advantage of organic growth is that the benefits of growth should all be enjoyed by the existing shareholders. However, a strategy of organic growth inevitably places restrictions on the amount of investment capital available.
- A company might be able to raise additional capital by borrowing externally. However, higher borrowing has implications for financial risk, through higher financial gearing. A company might therefore impose limits on its external borrowing by setting a limit to its gearing level.

3.1 Types of capital rationing

Two types of capital rationing may be distinguished:

- **Single period** – shortage of funds now, but funds are expected to be freely available in all later periods.
- **Multi-period** – where the period of funds shortage is expected to extend over a number of years, or even indefinitely.

3.2 Project divisibility

Projects may be divided into two categories.

- **Divisible projects** – either the whole project, or any fraction of the project, may be undertaken. If a fraction only is undertaken, then both initial investment and cash inflows are reduced pro rata. Quoted shares represent a divisible investment – varying numbers of shares may be purchased, with resultant prorating of investment returns.
- **Indivisible projects** – either the project must be undertaken in its entirety, or not at all. Decisions about introducing new product ranges are indivisible – either new products are introduced or they are not.

In reality, almost all projects are indivisible. However, the assumption of divisibility enables the easier use of mathematical tools. Its implications are reconsidered later.

The approaches to the combinations of rationing and project types that you will be expected to deal with are summarised as follows:

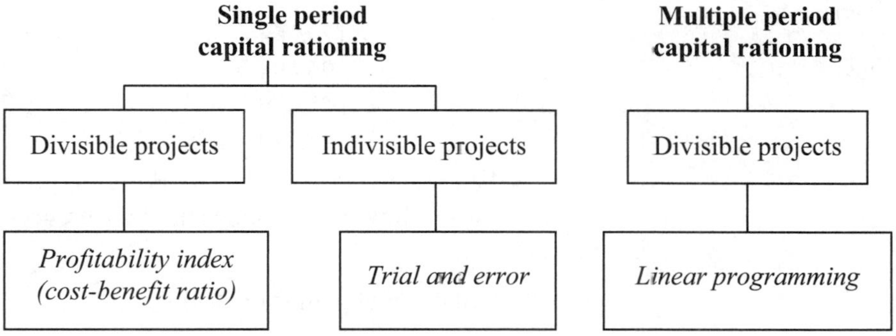

KEY POINT

The **objective** of all capital rationing exercises is the maximisation of the total NPV of the chosen projects' cash flows at the cost of capital.

The **objective** of all capital rationing exercises is the maximisation of the total NPV of the chosen projects' cash flows at the cost of capital.

3.3 Single period capital rationing, divisible projects

Maximising NPV is achieved in these circumstances by ranking projects according to their **profitability index (cost-benefit ratio)**, then allocating funds accordingly until they are exhausted.

DEFINITION

The **profitability index (PI)** of a project is the NPV per £ invested.

The **profitability index (PI)** of a project is the NPV per £ invested.

By comparing NPV with initial cash outflows, a measure of returns relative to size is obtained. This is comparable with the IRR approach. It suffers from the same criticisms as the latter in that it measures relative, not absolute, returns. In the capital rationing situation, however, this is what is required, since a selection of projects with the highest profitability indices will result in the maximum net present value for limited funds available.

Example

C Ltd, with a cost of capital of 10%, has £40,000 available for investment in Year 0. Four divisible projects are available.

Project	*Outlay*		*Receipts (cash flows)*		
	Year 0	*Year 1*	*Year 2*	*Year 3*	*Year 4*
	£	£	£	£	£
1	100,000	40,000	100,000	80,000	60,000
2	30,000	40,000	40,000	40,000	40,000
3	20,000	40,000	30,000	40,000	50,000
4	40,000	20,000	30,000	30,000	30,000

You are required to calculate the optimal investment policy.

KEY POINT

For a single period capital rationing between divisible projects, use the PI to rank projects.

Solution

Project	*Net present value at 10%*	*Profitability indices – net present value per £1 of outlay at 10%*	*Ranking*
	£	£	
1	120,255	1.203	III
2	96,894	3.230	II
3	105,479	5.274	I
4	46,079	1.152	IV

Note: When reviewing your own workings to pre-worked NPV figures in this or any other text, allow for possible small differences due to rounding of present value factors.

Summary of optimal plan for C Ltd:

Project	*Fraction of project accepted*	*Outlay at time 0*	*Net present value*
		£	£
3	1.00	20,000	105,479
2	2/3	20,000	64,596*
Capital used and available		40,000	
Net present value obtained			170,075

* Two-thirds of £96,894.

The opportunity cost of the capital rationing is £198,632 (368,707 – 170,075).

You might think that the IRR approach, as a measure of relative profitability, could be used to rank projects in a capital rationing situation. In fact this approach does not always give the correct ranking, but it may be used in the examination if profitability indices cannot be calculated from the information given.

3.4 Single period capital rationing, indivisible projects

In these circumstances, the objective can only be achieved by selecting from amongst the available projects on a trial and error basis. Because of the problem of indivisibility this may leave some funds unutilised.

Example

PQ Ltd has £50,000 available to invest. Its cost of capital is 10%. The following indivisible projects are available:

Project	*Initial outlay*	*Return pa to perpetuity*
	£	£
1	20,000	1,500
2	10,000	1,500
3	15,000	3,000
4	30,000	5,400
5	25,000	4,800

Solution

The first stage is to calculate the NPV of the projects.

Project	*Initial outlay*	*PV of cash flows* **	*NPV*
	£	£	£
1	20,000	15,000	(5,000)
2	10,000	15,000	5,000
3	15,000	30,000	15,000
4	30,000	54,000	24,000
5	25,000	48,000	23,000

$$** \text{ PV of perpetuity} = \frac{\text{Annual receipt}}{\text{Discount rate as a proportion}}$$

The approach is then one of considering all possible combinations of projects under the investment limit of £50,000.

KEY POINT

For single period capital rationing between indivisible projects, use trial and error.

The optimum selection of projects is as follows.

Projects	*Initial outlay*	*NPV*
	£	£
2	10,000	5,000
3	15,000	15,000
5	25,000	23,000
	50,000	43,000
Unused funds	Nil	
Funds available	50,000	

This may be compared to the ranking, if these were divisible projects:

Project	*Cost/benefit ratio*			*Ranking*	*Fraction of project accepted*	*NPV*
				£		
1	−5/20	=	−0.25	V	-	
2	5/10	=	0.50	IV	-	
3	15/15	=	1.00	I	1.00	15,000
4	24/30	=	0.80	III	1/3	8,000
5	23/25	=	0.92	II	1.00	23,000
						46,000

The projects selected do not coincide with this ranking because of the fact that they are not divisible. Given there is this constraint, and that for finance, no solution will give a higher NPV than £43,000.

3.5 Investment of surplus funds

In addition to specific investment opportunities, there may be a general opportunity to invest surplus funds on the market. Assuming equal risk levels, the rate of interest earned cannot, in the long run, be higher than the cost of the capital of the company, otherwise the cost of capital would be found to increase.

The rate of interest payable on surplus funds is therefore likely to be below the cost of capital. In a single period capital rationing situation, there is rarely any advantage in investing surplus funds at below the cost of capital (i.e. in projects with negative NPVs). However, if a project with a negative NPV has a cash inflow at year 0, rather than an outflow, investment could be worthwhile as it might free up funding for investment in other profitable projects which would otherwise be rejected under the capital rationing constraints.

As well as the specific investment opportunities available, consideration should also be given to investing surplus funds arising in one period, even at rates lower than the cost of capital, in order to increase funds available in later periods.

KEY POINT

For **multi-period** capital rationing, divisible projects, a **linear programming** approach may be suitable.

3.6 Multi-period capital rationing, divisible projects

This has already been defined as the situation where the cash shortage extends into a number of future periods. The problem is too complex to be suitable for a trial-and-error approach.

However, it may be defined so as to be suitable for a **linear programming** approach. For linear programming to be suitable, the following conditions must apply:

- The proportions undertaken of each of the projects available are the variables.
- Projects are assumed to be divisible.
- There are only two projects being considered. If there are more than two projects, then the simplex technique is required. A solution would be provided in the form of a final simplex tableau which would require interpretation.
- NPVs are linearly related to the proportion of each project accepted.
- Cash limits year by year form the constraints.
- The objective is to maximise the NPV of cash flows at the cost of capital.

You should also note that the linear programming problems examined assume that projects cannot be deferred, and have cash outflows extending over several periods.

To demonstrate the technique, an artificially simple example with only two projects will be examined.

Example

A company is proposing to invest in two projects. The projects are divisible, i.e. they can be accepted in whole or in part. If accepted in part, both cash outflows and subsequent cash receipts are reduced pro rata.

The two projects and associated cash flows are as follows:

Year	*Project A Cash flow* £	*Project B Cash flow* £
0	(10,000)	(20,000)
1	(20,000)	(10,000)
2	(30,000)	-
3	100,000	60,000

The company's cost of capital is 10%. All cash flows occur at exactly 12 month intervals, starting in year 0.

The funds available are restricted as follows:

Year 0	£20,000
Year 1	£25,000
Year 2	£20,000

Funds not utilised in one year will not be available in subsequent years. Projects cannot be deferred.

You are required to find the company's optimum investment policy.

Solution

It is first necessary to calculate the NPV of each project at 10%.

Year	*10% discount factor*	*Project A Cash flow*	*Project A Present value*	*Project B Cash flow*	*Project B Present value*
		£	£	£	£
0	1.000	(10,000)	(10,000)	(20,000)	(20,000)
1	0.909	(20,000)	(18,180)	(10,000)	(9,090)
2	0.826	(30,000)	(24,780)	-	-
3	0.751	100,000	75,100	60,000	45,060
NPV			22,140		15,970

Let a be the proportion of project A accepted.

Let b be the proportion of project B accepted.

The constraints are formulated as follows.

Year 0	10,000a	+	20,000b	≤	20,000	or	a	+	2b	≤ 2
Year 1	20,000a	+	10,000b	≤	25,000	or	4a	+	2b	≤ 5
Year 2	30,000a			≤	20,000	or	3a			≤ 2

General non-negativity constraints: $0 \leq a \leq 1$
$0 \leq b \leq 1$

The objective is to maximise NPVs from investment, i.e.22,140a + 15,970b

The problem may be viewed graphically:

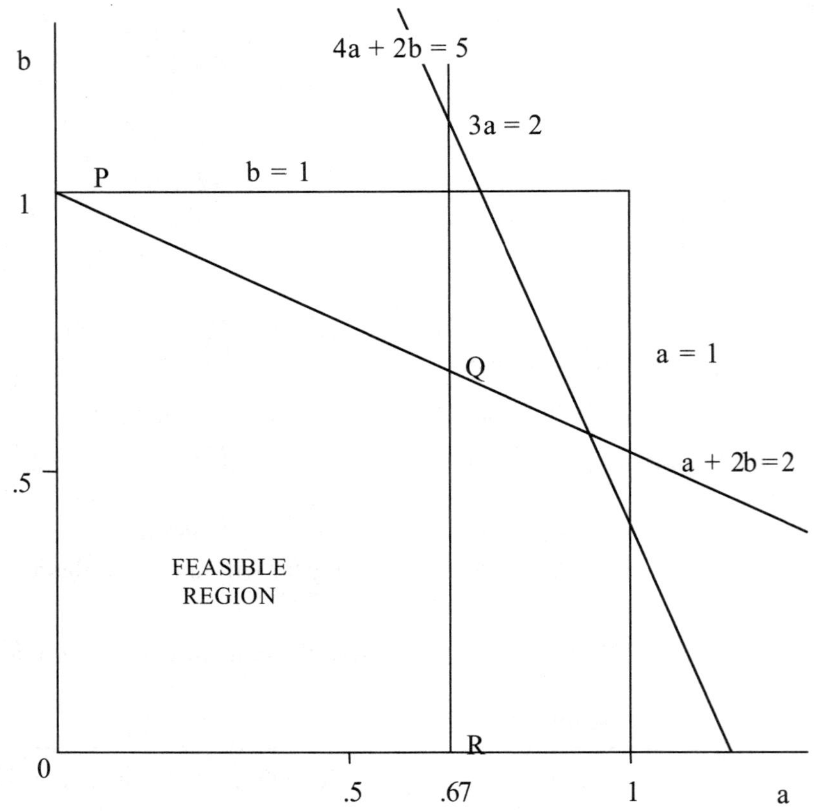

The feasible region (0PQR) has three corners as well as zero: P, Q and R. Proportions accepted, and resulting NPVs, are as follows:

Corner	*Value of*		*Interpretation*	*NPV*
	b	*a*		£
P	1	Nil	Accept B entirely and A not at all	15,970
Q	2/3	2/3	Accept 2/3 of each project	25,406
R	Nil	2/3	Accept 2/3 project A only	14,760

Clearly the optimum solution is to invest in 2/3 of each project – i.e. the solution suggested at point Q.

Workings

At Q two equations are satisfied.

a + 2b	=	2----------- (1)
3a	=	2----------- (2)
(2) becomes a	=	2/3
Substitute (2) in (1) 2b	=	1 1/3------ (3)
b	=	2/3

Note that this solution leaves funds unused in year 1. This poses the question of whether it would be worthwhile to hold funds available from year 1 to year 2, even if they have to be invested below 10% – even say at Nil%.

Activity 3

Availability of investment opportunities below the cost of capital

In the above example, suppose £1,000 of the funds spare in year 1 can be held at a zero rate of interest until year 2.

Does this alter the optimal investment policy?

Feedback to this activity is at the end of the chapter.

3.7 More than two projects

The example above has enabled the problems to be handled computationally. However, the technique is only relevant in reality where there are a number of projects, i.e. where there are more than two.

You are not likely to be asked to solve such problems numerically, but it will be helpful if you can formulate the objective and constraint equations (i.e. the linear programming model).

Example

A company has four divisible projects available. The cash outlays and NPVs are as follows:

Project	*Outlay*		*Net present*
	Year 0	*Year 1*	*value at 10%*
	£000	£000	£000
1	20	–	10
2	40	20	30
3	50	80	60
4	30	30	15

Capital rationing is expected to extend over the next two years, with £100,000 available now and £80,000 next year before accepting any of the projects.

Solution

Let x_1 be the proportion of project (1) accepted

x_2 be the proportion of project (2) accepted

x_3 be the proportion of project (3) accepted

x_4 be the proportion of project (4) accepted

Hence x_i can take any value between 0 and 1, i.e.

$0 \geq x_i \geq 1$ where $i = 1 - 4$

Objective: to maximise net present value = $10x_1 + 30x_2 + 60x_3 + 15x_4$

Constraints:

Year	*Funds available*	*Funds utilised*
0	$100 \geq$	$20x_1 + 40x_2 + 50x_3 + 30x_4$
1	$80 \geq$	$20x_2 + 80x_3 + 30x_4$

Logic (non-negativity) constraints:

$0 \geq x_1 \geq 1 \quad 0 \geq x_2 \geq 1$ etc.

The optimum solution can now be found by one of the standard techniques for manipulating linear programming problems, e.g. the Simplex method.

3.8 The importance of qualitative factors

The emphasis in this chapter has been on investment appraisal as a computational exercise: known numbers are inserted into formulae and a numerical result is produced. But it would be wrong to end without mentioning the sorts of qualitative factors that must also be borne in mind in the investment appraisal exercise.

Consider the typical example of the proposed purchase of a new machine in a manufacturing plant. The machine offers both quantitative and qualitative costs and benefits, as below.

Quantitative costs include:

- the purchase price of the machine
- installation and training costs.

Quantitative benefits include:

- lower direct labour costs
- lower scrap costs and items requiring rework
- lower stock costs.

Qualitative costs include:

- increased noise level
- lower morale if existing staff have to be made redundant.

Qualitative benefits include:

- reduction in product development time
- improved product quality and service
- increase in manufacturing flexibility.

Because the qualitative factors are difficult to state in numerical terms, they are conventionally ignored in the investment appraisal exercise. However such an approach is flawed. If a question asks you to carry out a DCF analysis and then comment on what you have done, be certain to point out the qualitative factors that could additionally be brought into the decision.

Summary

- Sensitivity analysis is an analysis of how far our estimates must be in error before our decision is affected. If a minor error in our estimate of a variable (e.g. our estimate of expected sales volumes) makes a large difference to our conclusion we say that the variable is sensitive. Managers should focus their attention on obtaining good estimates of variables that are sensitive.

- There are three main methods of tackling replacement decisions: lowest common multiple method, finite time horizon method, and equivalent annual cost method.

- Capital rationing arises when an organisation is restricted in the amount of funds available to initiate all worthwhile projects.

- Capital rationing may apply to just a single period or to multiple periods.

Having completed your study of this chapter you should have achieved the following learning outcomes.

- Evaluate and rank projects that might be mutually exclusive, involve unequal lives and/or be subject to capital rationing.
- Apply sensitivity analysis to cash flow parameters to identify those to which net present value is particularly sensitive.
- Produce decision support information for management, integrating financial and non-financial considerations.

Self-test questions

1 What calculation must be performed to determine a project's sensitivity to the choice of discount rate? (1.2)

2 What three approaches could be used to tackle a replacement problem when deciding whether to replace every year, every two years or every three years? (2.4)

3 How is the problem of single period rationing with indivisible projects tackled? (3.4)

4 Give at least four conditions for the linear programming technique to apply. (3.6)

Objective test questions

Question 1

N Ltd is considering an investment in a project which requires an immediate outlay in respect of plant and equipment which will be used to manufacture a wide variety of garden decorative products, e.g. garden gnomes. Which of the following estimated factors may affect the outcome of a capital investment decision?

A Initial outlay and residual value only

B Sales volume and selling price only

C Cost of capital

D All of the above

Question 2

Which of the following reasons may explain why investment decisions may be undertaken in a sub-optimal manner.

A Use of inappropriate techniques such as payback and accounting rate of return

B Failing to take into account the impact of inflation and taxation

C Failing to take into account the problems associated with different timescales

D All of the above

Question 3

Which of the following statements is true in respect of multi-period capital rationing?

1 In practice most lending organisations decide that there is a point at which they will not lend at any price

2 Capital rationing might exist for reasons other than the inability to raise additional capital

3 Multi-period capital rationing concerns situations where there is likely to be a funds shortage for a number of years or even indefinitely

4 Multi-period capital rationing concerns a situation where there is an immediate shortage but funds are expected to become freely available in all later periods

A 1 and 2 only

B 1, 2 and 3 only

C 1, 2 and 4

D All four statements.

Exam-type questions

Question 1: NAW Transport Services

The management of NAW Transport Services has decided to purchase a new Luxury Overnight Coach which it is estimated will travel 90,000 kilometres per year. They are currently evaluating two mutually exclusive models, details of which are as follows:

- The 'Oregon' which will have a life of five years and a capital cost of £40,000; the running cost would be 25 pence per kilometre during the first year of operation and is forecast to rise by 6 pence per kilometre for each year that the coach is in operation. The coach will require a major overhaul at a cost of £9,000 at the end of the third year of its operation.
- The 'Sante-Fe' which has a life of seven years and costs £60,000. Running costs are expected to be 20 pence per kilometre during the first year of its operation and will rise by 3 pence per kilometre for each year that the coach is in operation.

The company has a cost of capital of 9%

Required:

Advise the management of NAW Transport Services which Coach should be purchased. **(15 marks)**

Question 2: ATZ plc

ATZ plc supports the concept of terotechnology or life cycle costing for new investment decisions covering its engineering activities. The financial side of this philosophy is now well established and its principles extended to all other areas of decision-making.

The company is to replace a number of its machines and the Production Manager is torn between the Exe machine, a more expensive machine with a life of 12 years, and the Wye machine with an estimated life of 6 years. If the Wye machine is chosen it is likely that it would be replaced at the end of 6 years by another Wye machine. The pattern of maintenance and running costs differs between the two types of machine and relevant data are shown below.

		Exe		*Wye*
		£		£
Purchase price		19,000		13,000
Trade-in value		3,000		3,000
Annual repair costs		2,000		2,600
Overhaul costs	(at year 8)	4,000	(at year 4)	2,000
Estimated financing costs averaged over machine life		10% pa		10% pa

Required:

(a) Recommend, with supporting figures, which machine to purchase, stating any assumptions made. **(10 marks)**

(b) Describe an appropriate method of comparing replacement proposals with unequal lives. **(4 marks)**

(Total: 14 marks)

For the answers to these questions, see the 'Answers' section at the end of the book.

Feedback to activities

Activity 1

(a) (i) **Change in unit variable cost**

The project's NPV must fall by £33,000, therefore the PV of the variable costs must rise by £33,000. Since the PV of variable costs is £799,000, a rise of £33,000 is an increase of:

$$\frac{33}{799} \times 100 = 4\%$$

(ii) **Change in annual fixed costs**

The percentage increase in annual fixed costs required:

$$= \frac{\text{NPV of project}}{\text{PV of annual fixed costs}} \times 100$$

$$= \frac{33}{91} \times 100 = 36\%$$

(b) The analysis shows that project is particularly sensitive to changes in the sales price, unit variable cost and the sales volume. Very small percentage changes in these variables will lead to the project becoming unviable. Management may decide that the risk is too great and seek to invest in an alternative project. Alternatively, management may monitor these particular variables very closely and be prepared to take corrective action if actual performance diverges from the forecast.

Activity 2

(i) **Replace every year**

$$\text{NPV of one cycle} = -£5,000 + \frac{£3,000}{1.12} = £(2,321)$$

$$\text{EAC} = \frac{£(2,321)}{0.893} = £(2,599)$$

(ii) **Replace every other year**

NPV of one cycle $= -£5,000 - \dfrac{£500}{1.12} + \dfrac{£2,000}{1.12^2} = £(3,852)$

EAC $= \dfrac{£(3,852)}{1.690} = £(2,279)$

Replacing every two years is the cheaper option.

Activity 3

Increasing the funds available in year 2 would change the constraint for that year to $30,000a \leq 21,000$ or $3a \leq 2.1$.

Relaxing this constraint would alter the shape of the feasible region at the cost of tying up £1,000 of capital between years 1 and 2. The cost of this would be equivalent to the net present value of an outflow of that amount at the end of year 1 (£1,000 × 0.909) less the value of an inflow at the end of year 2 (£1,000 × 0.826) = £909 – 826 = £83.

This change will have no effect on corner P. The remainder of the table, ignoring the additional cost of tying up capital, can be restated as follows:

Corner	*Value of* *b*	*a*	*Interpretation*	*NPV* £
P	1	Nil	Accept B entirely and A not at all	15,970
Q	0.65	0.7	Accept 65% of B and 70% of A	25,879
R	Nil	0.7	Accept 70% of project A only	15,498

Relaxing this binding constraint offers the opportunity to increase the NPV of the investments from £25,406 to £25,879, an increase of £473. This exceeds the additional cost of capital arising from tying up £1,000 at 0% interest for a year.

Chapter 14

ANSWERS TO END-OF-CHAPTER QUESTIONS

Chapter 1

Objective test questions

Question 1

The correct answer is D.

The difference between the stock valuations of these systems is the treatment of the fixed overhead costs. It is this which causes the profit difference. The question cannot be answered without an analysis of the fixed and variable costs.

Question 2

B Fixed overheads = $\frac{1}{4} \times 16$ = £4 per unit

Difference between marginal costing and absorption costing profit is:

(closing stock – opening stock) × fixed OAR

= (2,500 – 0) × £4 = £10,000

As stock has increased, absorption costing profit will be bigger.

Question 3

The profit reported under an absorption costing system is £47,000.

Workings

		Absorption costing		
	Units	£	£	£
Sales	9,000	20		180,000
Production	11,000	12	132,000	
Closing stock	2,000	12	–24,000	
				108,000
				72,000
Over-absorbed	1,000	4		4,000
				76,000
Variable selling	9,000	1	9,000	
Fixed selling cost	10,000	2	20,000	
				29,000
				47,000

The profit reported under a marginal costing system is £39,000.

Workings

		Marginal costing		
	Units	£	£	£
Sales	9,000	20		180,000
Production	11,000	8	88,000	
Closing stock	2,000	8	–16,000	
				72,000
				108,000
Fixed production overhead	1,000		40,000	
Variable selling	9,000	1	9,000	
Fixed selling cost	10,000	2	20,000	
				69,000
				39,000

Exam-type questions

Question 1: Rayners plc

(a) **Operating statement**

	Year 1		*Year 2*		*Year 3*	
	£000	£000	£000	£000	£000	£000
Marginal costing						
Sales		1,080		1,320		1,140
Opening stock @ £5	Nil		50		50	
Add: Production cost @ £5	500		550		450	
	500		600		500	
Less: Closing stock @ £5	50		50		25	
Cost of sales		(450)		(550)		(475)
Contribution		630		770		665
Less: Fixed costs:						
Production overhead	270		270		270	
Administration overhead	20		20		20	
		(290)		(290)		(290)
Profit		340		480		375
Absorption costing						
Sales		1,080		1,320		1,140
Opening stock @ £8	Nil		80		80	
Add: Production cost @ £8	800		880		720	
	800		960		800	
Less: Closing stock @ £8	80		80		40	

Cost of sales	(720)	(880)	(760)
	360	440	380
Over absorption (see working)	30	60	Nil
Administration overhead	(20)	(20)	(20)
Profit	370	480	360

Working

	Year 1 £000	*Year 2* £000	*Year 3* £000
Fixed production overhead absorbed:			
100,000 units × £3	300		
110,000 units × £3		330	
90,000 units × £3			270
Fixed production overhead incurred:			
90,000 units × £3	270	270	270
Over absorption	30	60	-

(b) The difference in profit arises because of the difference in the amount of fixed production overhead included in stock under the absorption costing system.

When the opening and closing stock includes the same amount of fixed overheads (i.e. here when the volume of opening and closing stock is the same, in year 2) profit is the same under both techniques. Where volume of stock has gone up (year 1) and the amount of fixed production overhead in stock has increased then profit is higher under absorption costing and *vice versa*.

Question 2: Miozip Co

Tutorial notes:

1 An average standard question but having no 'units' with which to work does present problems.

2 Part (a) is the standard question about absorption costing with changing stock levels resulting in different profits.

3 Part (b) is not difficult, but with no variable costs per unit with which to work, it is necessary to use total amounts after deducting the fixed factory overhead.

4 Part (c) is reasonably straightforward. Remember the problem of using predetermined absorption rates in periods of changing activity levels.

5 Concentrate on the usefulness of marginal costs in decision-making but full cost systems ensure that no costs are ignored.

(a) **REPORT**

To: The board of directors, Miozip Co

From: The company accountant

Date: XX–XX–20XX

Subject: Profitability

From the summarised profit and loss accounts (estimated 20X2, budgeted 20X3), it is apparent that two periods with equal sales revenue are reporting profits/losses which differ by £210,000. The difference can be entirely attributed to the valuation of opening/closing stock.

The factory cost of goods sold for 20X2 is £60,000 lower than that expected for the level of sales achieved because of the lower overhead absorption rate used in 20X1. Some of the goods produced in this period, being attributed with a lower cost, were sold in 20X2. All units budgeted to be sold in 20X3 carry the full £3.60 overhead.

In addition, the level of activity budgeted in 20X3 (100,000 direct labour hours) is only two-thirds of that achieved in 20X2. This will result in an increased under-absorption of overhead charge of £150,000. This, together with the £60,000 above, accounts for the £210,000 differential.

(b) **Marginal costing statement**

Workings

	£	%
20X1		
Factory cost of production	1,000,000	100.00
Fixed factory overhead absorbed (£600,000 – £300,000)	300,000	30.00
∴ Other variable factory costs	700,000	70.00
20X2 (similar percentage for 20X3)		
Factory cost of production	975,000	100.00
Fixed factory overhead absorbed (£600,000 – £150,000)	450,000	46.15
∴ Other variable factory costs	525,000	53.85

Based on marginal costs:

	Actual 20X1		*Estimated 20X2*		*Budgeted 20X3*	
	£	£	£	£	£	£
Sales		1,350,000		1,316,250		1,316,250
Opening stock	70,000		140,000		192,500	
Variable factory cost of production	700,000		525,000		350,000	
	770,000		665,000		542,500	
Closing stock	(140,000)		(192,500)		(70,000)	
Variable cost of goods sold		630,000		472,500		472,500
Contribution		720,000		843,750		843,750
Fixed costs:						
Factory overheads		(600,000)		(600,000)		(600,000)
Administrative and financial costs		(220,000)		(220,000)		(220,000)
Net profit/(loss)		(100,000)		23,750		23,750

(c) **Potential problems**

The decision to increase the selling price by using the cost-plus formula without considering the effect upon demand from customers could result in an increase in the under-absorbed overhead. The higher price might result in a fall in demand and a fall in the number of direct labour hours worked. Thus, the absorption of overheads would fall with the reduction in direct labour hours and a larger proportion of the overheads incurred would not be absorbed.

(d) **Use of absorption and marginal costing**

Management accounting theorists favour marginal costing because it will tend to give the most relevant costs to assist a decision-maker. Marginal costs are usually differential, incremental costs and are important in most decisions, including pricing special orders, production scheduling with limiting factors, and make or buy decisions. By contrast, full costing systems, by including fixed costs in product costs, can often lead to suboptimal decisions being taken if the effect of 'fixed costs per unit' is not fully understood.

However, full costing systems appear to be used extensively in practice. This could be because:

- a full costing system automatically ensures compliance with SSAP 9
- a full costing system provides more realistic matching of total costs with revenues
- a large part of the costs of most companies are now fixed – using marginal costing may result in these substantial costs being overlooked, e.g. under-pricing using a marginal cost-plus formula resulting in losses
- analysis of under/over-absorbed overhead is useful to identify inefficient utilisation of production resources.

Chapter 2

Objective test questions

Question 1

	Sales revenue	*Joint costs*
	£	£
UB-1 (208,000 × 0.30)	62,400	35,862
UB-2 (192,000 × 0.40)	76,800	44,138
	£139,200	£80,000

Closing stock valuation = $35,862 \times \frac{8}{208} + (44,138 + 38,400) \times \frac{12}{192} = £6,537$

Therefore C is the correct answer.

Question 2

B

Total output 25,000 kg

Joint cost per kg $= \dfrac{£100{,}000}{25{,}000\text{ kg}}$

$= £4$

Profit per unit of X $= £10 - £4$

$= £6$

Question 3

C

	Output	*Selling price*	*Sales value* £
X	5,000	£10	50,000
Y	10,000	£4	40,000
Z	10,000	£3	30,000
			120,000

Cost per £ of sales $= \dfrac{£100{,}000}{£120{,}000} = 0.83$

Profit of Y

	£
Sales	40,000
Cost	33,333
Profit	6,667

Question 4

D

A is incorrect. The percentage profit margin is the same if the joint costs are apportioned on sales value.

B is incorrect. Total profits will be the same whatever method of apportionment is used.

Exam-type questions

Question 1: Mineral Separators Ltd

(a)

	Tonnes produced	*Selling prices per tonne*	*Sales value*
		£	£
W	700	40	28,000
X	600	90	54,000
Y	400	120	48,000
Z	100	200	20,000
	1,800		150,000

Total cost of production

	£
Material	75,000
Labour	24,000
Overhead (25% of labour)	6,000
	105,000

Joint costs as a percentage of sales value are £105,000/150,000 = 70%

Profit per unit

	W	*X*	*Y*	*Z*	*Total*
Sales units	670	580	320	95	
Sales (£)	26,800	52,200	38,400	19,000	136,400
Cost of sales (£)	18,760	36,540	26,880	13,300	95,480
Profit (£)	8,040	15,660	11,520	5,700	40,920

(b) The profit figures calculated in (a) show all products earning the same profit margin of 30%. This is due to the method of apportioning joint costs and is meaningless for decision-making purposes. The nature of joint products is such that a choice to produce a different combination of products is not possible. Either all of the products must be produced or none. The ratio of products also cannot be easily changed, if at all. In this case the process shows a healthy total profit of £40,920 and, unless there is a better alternative use of scarce resources, the process should be continued.

Question 2: XY Ltd

(a) **Joint costs apportioned on weight of products**

	Product *A*	*B*	*C*	*D*	*Total*
	000 kg	000 kg	000 kg	000 kg	000 kg
Sales	140	95	55	180	470
	£	£	£	£	£
Sales	98,000	57,000	33,000	243,000	431,000
Less: Cost of sales	64,400	34,200	30,800	127,800	257,200
Gross profit	33,600	22,800	2,200	115,200	173,800

Less: Administration costs		45,000
Less: Selling costs:	Fixed	35,000
	Variable	4,700
		84,700
Net profit		89,100

Workings

$$\text{Joint cost per kg} = \frac{\text{Costs}}{\text{Weight produced}}$$

$$= \frac{£180,000}{500,000}$$

$$= 0.36$$

As closing stocks are ready for sales, cost of sales is valued at joint plus additional costs, i.e.

Product	*Joint* £	*Cost per kg additional* £	*Total*	*Sales '000 kg*	*Cost of sales* £
A	0.36	0.10	0.46	140	64,400
B	0.36	–	0.36	95	34,200
C	0.36	0.20	0.56	55	30,800
D	0.36	0.35	0.71	180	127,800

(b) **Joint costs apportioned on net sales value of production**

	Product				*Total*
	A £	*B* £	*C* £	*D* £	£
Sales	98,000	57,000	33,000	243,000	431,000
Less: Cost of sales	56,000	28,500	22,000	153,000	259,500
Gross profit	42,000	28,500	11,000	90,000	171,500
Less: Administration and selling costs:					84,700
Net profit					86,800

Workings

	Product				*Total*
	A 000 kg	*B* 000 kg	*C* 000 kg	*D* 000 kg	000 kg
Production	150	110	60	180	500
	£	£	£	£	£
Selling prices	0.70	0.60	0.60	1.35	
Sales value of production	105,000	66,000	36,000	243,000	450,000
Less: Additional costs	15,000	–	12,000	63,000	90,000
Net sales value of production	90,000	66,000	24,000	180,000	360,000

Apportioned joint cost (50%)	45,000	33,000	12,000	90,000	180,000
Additional costs	15,000	–	12,000	63,000	90,000
Production costs	60,000	33,000	24,000	153,000	270,000
Closing stock	$(\frac{10}{150})$4,000	$(\frac{15}{110})$4,500	$(\frac{5}{60})$2,000	–	10,500
Cost of sales	56,000	28,500	22,000	153,000	259,500

(c) **Price comparison**

	Product A	C	D
	£	£	£
Existing price per kg	0.70	0.60	1.35
Less: Additional costs per kg	0.10	0.20	0.35
Net revenue per kg	0.60	0.40	1.00
Overseas offer	0.65	0.52	0.90
Gain/(loss) per kg	0.05	0.12	(0.10)
Reduction in variable selling costs per kg	0.004	0.004	0.004
Net gain/(loss) per kg	0.054	0.124	(0.096)

Recommendation: Sell Products A and C to the overseas customer.

(d) **Increase in annual net profit**

	£
Additional revenue:	
Product A 50,000 kg @ £0.05	2,500
Product C 50,000 kg @ £0.12	6,000
	8,500
Add: Reduction in variable selling costs 100,000 kg @ £0.004	400
Net profit increase	8,900

Note: All other costs and revenue will be unaffected.

Chapter 3

Objective test questions

Question 1

Contribution is in the ratio 60,000:50,000:20,000.

26,000 ÷ [(6 + 5 + 2) ÷ 6] × ½ = 6,000

Therefore A.

Question 2

$$\text{Breakeven number of units} = \frac{\text{Fixed costs}}{\text{Contribution per unit}}$$

If selling price per unit and variable cost per unit rise by 10%, then contribution per unit rises by 10%.

∴ Breakeven number of units will decrease

(assuming a positive contribution in the first place!)

Therefore C.

Question 3

$$\text{Contribution margin} = \frac{SP - VC}{SP} = \frac{SP - 60}{SP} = 0.52$$

$$SP - 0.52SP = 60$$

$$SP = 60/0.48$$

$$SP = £125$$

Profit this year = (125 – 60) × 1,000 – 25 × 1,000 = £40,000

Increases	Selling price	=	125 × 1.08	=	£135
	Variable costs	=	60 × 1.05	=	£63
	Fixed costs	=	25 × 1,000 × 1.05	=	£26,250

$$\text{Breakeven point in units} = \frac{26{,}250 + 40{,}000}{(135 - 63)} = 921$$

Therefore D.

Question 4

The total contribution required is £350,000 + £75,000 = £425,000.

The total C/S ratio is 25% × 35% + 35% × 20% + 40% × 30% = 27.75%.

BEP(£) = £425,000/0.2775 = £1,531,532

Therefore the answer is A.

Question 5

The weighted average C/S ratio is 30% × 50% = 70% × 28% = 34.6%.

BEP = £350,000/0.346 = £1,011,561

Therefore the answer is D.

Question 6

Let c = the missing C/S ratio for product C.

1/3 × 40% + 1/3 × 35% + 1/3 × c = 42%

13.33% + 11.66% + 1/3 × c = 42%

1/3 c = 42% – 13.33% – 11.66% = 17%

c = 17% × 3 = 51%

Question 7

The new total C/S ratio can be calculated as follows;

A	50% × 40%	20%
B	35% × 35%	12.25%
C	15% × 51%	7.65%
Total		39.90%

Exam-type question

JK Ltd

(a)

	Product				
	J	*K*	*L*	*M*	*Total*
	£000	£000	£000	£000	£000
Sales	200	400	200	200	1,000
Variable costs	140	80	210	140	570
Contribution	60	320	(10)	60	430

Calculate the contribution/sales ratios and plot each product starting with the product having the greatest C/S ratio.

J	*K*	*L*	*M*
30%	80%	(5%)	30%

Contribution – Sales Graph

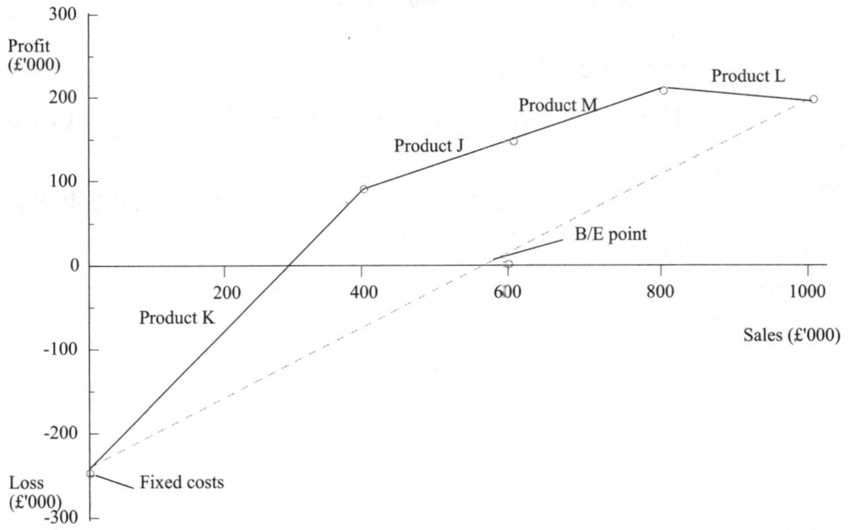

(b) The products are plotted in the order of their C/S ratios. The steeper the line for an individual product the greater the C/S ratio for that product. Thus it can be seen that product K provides the greatest contribution with respect to sales value.

It can be seen from the graph that product L should be dropped as it provides negative contribution.

The breakeven point can be calculated using the C/S ratio of the mix. This can also be approximately seen from the graph.

$$\text{B/E} = \frac{\text{Fixed costs}}{\text{c/s ratio of the mix}}$$

$$= \frac{240{,}000}{430/1{,}000}$$

$$= £558{,}140$$

The overall ratio could be improved by:

(i) increasing the selling prices

(ii) decreasing the sales of products J, L or M

(iii) automating the process. This would increase fixed costs but would reduce variable costs thus increasing contribution.

Chapter 4

Objective test questions

Question 1

B The original cost is irrelevant. The material could be sold now for scrap for £12,500. If reworked, it could be sold for a net £10,000. The incremental effect of reworking is therefore a loss of £2,500.

Question 2

Since material R is in regular use and is readily available in the market, its relevant cost is the replacement price of £6/kg.

So 1,000 kg × £6/kg = £6,000

Question 3

The relevant cost is the lower of the relevant costs of each option.

		£
Recruitment:	4 employees @ £40,000 =	160,000
Manager (no change)		Nil
		160,000
Retrain and replace:	Training	15,000
	Replacement	100,000
		115,000

Therefore the relevant cost is £115,000.

Exam-type questions

Question 1: Mike Limited

Relevant cost statement

	Note	£
Material V	1	900
Material I	2	6,500
Material C	3	2,050
Department 1	4	–
Department 2	5	26,000
Overheads	6	–
Minimum contract price		35,450

Notes

1 The historical cost of £10 is not relevant, as it is a sunk cost. The relevant cost is the opportunity cost relating to lost scrap proceeds:

= 300 × £3 = £900.

2 Again, the historical cost is irrelevant, as it is a sunk cost. Since the material is in continuous use in the business, the relevant cost is the current replacement cost of the material:

= 1,000 × £6.50 = £6,500.

3 Since there is only 300 kg in stock, 250 kg would need to be purchased at the current replacement cost = 250 × £4 = £1,000. If the current stock of 300 kg is not used for the contract, it would be used to replace material Y in an alternative production process.

Therefore the relevant cost for the stock of 300 kg is = 300 × £7/2 = £1,050, bearing in mind the 2-for-1 substitution.

Total relevant cost for material C = £1,000 + £1,050 = £2,050.

4 Since there is spare capacity in this department, there is no relevant cost.

5 For this department, the two alternatives need to be considered:

Cost of working overtime = 2,000 × £10 ×1.5 = £30,000

Cost of diverting labour = 2,000 × (£10 + £3) = £26,000

It would be cheaper to divert the labour from the other production processes, so the relevant cost for department 2 is £26,000.

6 There will be an increase in overhead expenditure for the relevant costs.

7 The minimum price is the price that just covers the relevant costs of the contract.

Question 2: Fiona Ltd

First of all we must restate the figures so that they present the situation in its true light. This will enable each department to be readily evaluated on its locally controllable performance.

Appendix

Department	*1*	*2*	*3*	*Total*
Sales volume (units)	5,000	6,000	2,000	13,000
Sales value (£)	150,000	240,000	24,000	414,000
Cost of sales				
Direct material	75,000	150,000	10,000	235,000
Direct labour	4,846	5,815	1,939	12,600
Overhead	3,000	3,000	1,500	7,500
Expenses	9,000	9,000	6,000	24,000
Contribution (£)	58,154	72,185	4,561	134,900
Other costs				
Labour				(50,400)
Overhead				(7,500)
Expenses				(16,000)
Net profit				61,000

To: **Management**

From: **Management Accountant**

Date: **18/04/X6**

Subject: **Report to management on the advisability of closing department 3**

Introduction

In response to the request to appraise the advisability of closing department 3, we have first considered the way the original financial information was presented. This was found to be misleading, since the figures included apportioned fixed costs over which the operations managers had no control. Indeed, the method of apportionment was such as to actually penalise an effective manager especially when her sales volumes were considerably higher than those of her colleagues irrespective of the contribution those sales might make to the overall business. Consequently we have restated the figures, eliminating from the contribution calculations all figures which cannot be objectively allocated to the departments and over which the local managers have no control. This identifies the overall contribution made by each department to the corporate entity. It makes no difference to the final bottom line.

Findings

From the restated figures it can be seen that department 3 is making a contribution of £4,561 to the overall profit of the business. The apparent loss arises purely from inappropriate apportionment of overheads and expenses. If the department were closed, there would be a loss of £4,561 contribution to the business and, on the assumption there would be no further saving on fixed costs, the profit would be reduced to £56,439.

Other considerations

The figures make no allowance for the closure of department 3 and the redundancy costs and losses on any equipment disposal. Nor do they consider the possible loss of business due to products from department 3 being unavailable to customers who buy from the other departments at the same time.

Conclusions and recommendations

Department 3 should be kept open since it makes a small but useful contribution to the business. It may be necessary to review whether it is making a meaningful use of the assets committed to it.

Consideration must be given to the effectiveness of the reporting methodology and cost apportionment procedures, since they are likely to mislead management in their present form. To that end, control reporting should be done on a marginal costing basis, with operations management assessed for effectiveness on sales and the costs for which they are responsible and can control.

Other costs should be looked at very carefully to see what value the company is deriving from them. At present, over 20% of the costs structure cannot be assigned directly to products and could be construed as being costs which do not add value. These need careful attention.

Chapter 5

Objective test questions

Question 1

Scarce resource – 7,000 labour hours

	A	*B*	*C*
Labour hours per unit	2.5	6	7.5
Contribution per unit	£6.50	£6.80	£15
Contribution per labour hour	£2.60	£1.13	£2
Ranking	1	3	2

Production plan

		Hours
Maximum demand for		
A	1,000 units × 2.5	2,500
C	200 units × 7.5 hours	1,500
B	500 units × 6 hours	3,000 (balance)

Therefore C.

Question 2

	Kilts	*Skirts*	*Dresses*
Contribution per labour hour	4	5.50	7

Therefore C.

Question 3

Product	*X*	*Y*	*Z*
Contribution/unit	£41	£54	£50
Materials (kg/unit)	2	1	3
Contribution/kg	£20.50	£54	£16.66
Ranking	2	1	3

The correct answer is B.

Question 4

The correct answer is A.

Question 5

The company should produce 250 As and 167 Bs. The maximum contribution that can be achieved is £10,010.

Question 6

A shadow price is the extra contribution that could be earned by having one more unit of a scarce resource. In this example the constraints represented by the slack variables S1 and S3 are scarce resources. If one extra unit of S1 became available contribution would increase by £12. This would be achieved by producing an extra 0.4 of product B. If an extra unit of S3 became available contribution would increase by £20. This would be achieved by producing an extra 0.8 of product B and o.2 less of product A.

Exam-type questions

Question 1: Flintstones

(a) From the tabulated information given, per week:

No. of hours unskilled labour per Chip $= \frac{12}{3} =$ 4 hours

No. of hours unskilled labour per Dale $= \frac{15}{3} =$ 5 hours

No. of hours skilled labour per Chip $= \frac{50}{5} =$ 10 hours

No. of hours skilled labour per Dale $= \frac{20}{5} =$ 4 hours

No. of Dinos per Chip $= \frac{20}{10} =$ 2

No. of Dinos per Dale $= \frac{20}{10} =$ 2

Contribution per Chip = £(127 – 97) = £30

Contribution per Dale = £(100 – 75) = £25

As each Dale requires 2 units of B, and only 300 units of B are available, this limits the number of Dales to 150.

There is no constraint on the amount of material A.

Fixed costs will be the same, whatever mix of Chip and Dale is produced, hence they can be ignored for the purpose of obtaining the optimum product mix, but must be included in the calculation of profit.

Let	C	=	number of Chips produced per week.
Let	D	=	number of Dales produced per week.
Let	Z	=	total contributions per week.

The objective function then is to maximise contribution to fixed overheads, i.e.

Maximise: $Z = 30C + 25D$

						Constraint Number	
Subject to:	4C	+	5D	≤	800	(1)	Unskilled labour
	10C	+	4D	≤	1,000	(2)	Skilled labour
	2C	+	2D	≤	400	(3)	Dinos
			D	≤	3C	(4)	Production policy
			2D	≤	300	(5)	Material B
			C, D	≥	0		

Note: There is a constraint that appears confusing at first, that of company policy with regard to the production of Chips and Dales. However, it can be dealt with simply by taking the expression of the policy, as expressed in words, and turning it into symbols, thus:

The production of Dales is to be not more than (i.e. less than or equal to) three times the production of Chips.

$$D \leq 3c$$

or $-3c + D \leq 0$

For graph see below. The feasibility region is CBA0 (outlined in bold).

The solution is at the intersection of constraints (1) and (2), the two labour constraints. The solution can be found by solving (1) and (2) simultaneously.

4C + 5D	=	800	(1)	
10C + 4D	=	1,000	(2)	
5 × (2) – 4 × (1) gives 34C	=	1,800		
C	=	52.94	≈	53
D	=	117.65	≈	118

Contribution = 30C + 25D = £30 × 52.94 + £25 × 117.65

= £4,529.50

Thus, profit = £4,530 – £3,000 = £1,530 per week

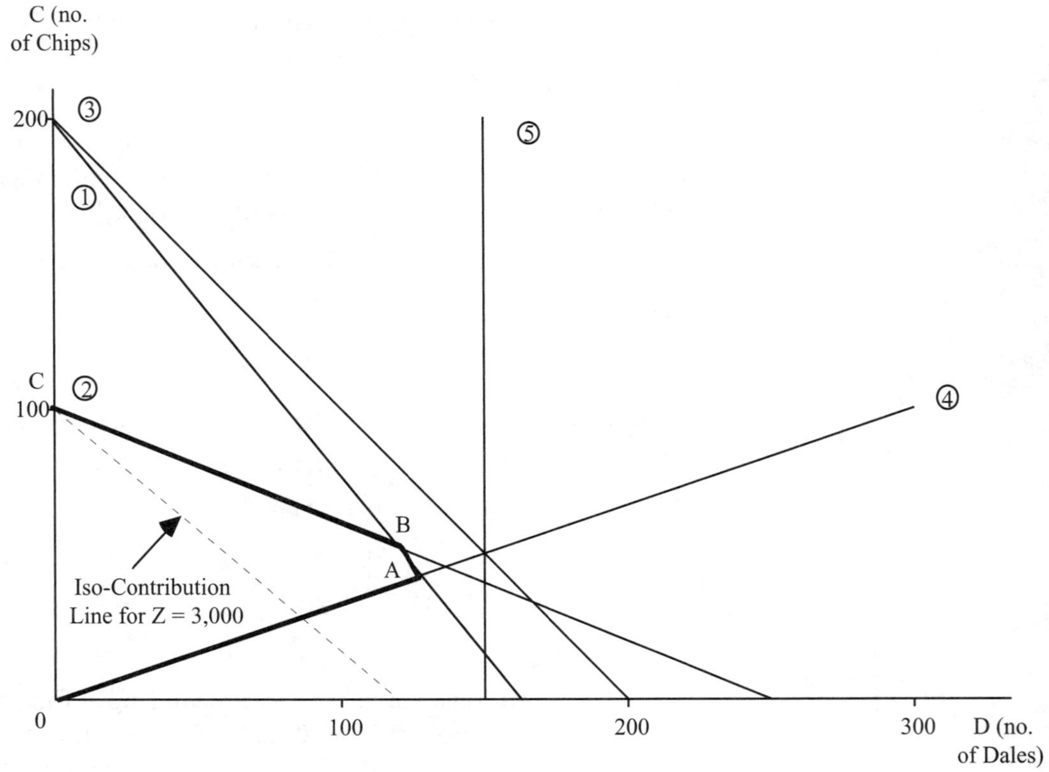

(b) The shadow price of a resource is the extra contribution which can be earned from one extra unit of a scarce resource. For Flintstones the scarce resources are unskilled and skilled labour.

To calculate the shadow price of an hour of unskilled labour a new solution must be calculated relaxing the unskilled labour constraint by one hour. This can be found by solving the simultaneous equations;

4C + 5D	=	801	(1)
10C + 4D	=	1,000	(2)
5 × (2) – 4 × (1) gives 34C	=	1,796	

So C = 52.82 and D = 117.94

The new contribution is £30 × 52.82 + £25 × 117.94 = £4,533.1

Contribution has increased by £3.60 and this is the shadow price of an unskilled labour hour. This means that management would be prepared to pay a premium of up to £3.60 per hour, perhaps in overtime payments, to secure more indirect labour.

This shadow price will hold until another resource becomes a binding constraint. It can be seen from the graph that this will occur when the unskilled labour constraint moves out beyond the intersection of the skilled labour constraint and the production policy constraint. At this point the production plan would be found by solving the simultaneous equations:

D		=	3C	(1)
10C + 4D		=	1,000	(2)
Rearranging (1) gives	3C – D	=	0	(3)
(2) + 4 x (3) gives 22C		=	1,000	

So C = 45.45 and D = 136.36

For this production plan the unskilled labour hours required would be:

4 x 45.45 + 5 x 136.36 = 863.6.

The shadow price of £3.60 will therefore hold for labour hours from 800 to 863.6. Beyond this, unskilled labour hours are no longer a limiting factor and therefore there is no longer a shadow price.

A similar analysis can be carried out for skilled labour hours to find the shadow price and the limit to which the shadow price is valid.

It should be noted that at the optimum solution only unskilled labour and skilled labour will have a shadow price as there is slack available in all of the other resources.

Question 2: Electronic component mix

Let number of X components = x

Let number of Y components = y

Let contribution = £C

Objective function: this is the total contribution, given by

$C = 10x + 15y$

which is to be maximised.

Constraints:

(i) Assembly time:

$x + 2y \leq 600$

(ii) Inspection:

$$\frac{7.5}{60}x + \frac{30}{60}y \leq 100$$

$0.125x + 0.5y \leq 100$

Multiply through by 8 to clear fractions:

$x + 4y \leq 800$

(iii) Package time:

$$\frac{3}{60}x + \frac{20}{60}y \leq 60$$

Multiply through by 60 to clear fractions:

$3x + 20y \leq 3{,}600$

(iv) Engineering limitation on X

$x \leq 500$

(v) Non-negativity

$x \geq 0$

$y \geq 0$

Calculations for graph

(i)	x + 2y =	600			
	When x =	0,	y	=	300
	When y =	0,	x	=	600
(ii)	x + 4y =	800			
	When x =	0,	y	=	200
	When y =	0,	x	=	800
(iii)	3x + 20y	=	3,600		
	When x =	0,	y	=	180
	When y =	0,	x	=	1,200

The x scale must go to 1,200 and the y scale to 300

Iso-contribution line:

Let C	=	1,500, giving 10x + 15y	=	1,500
When x	=	0, y	=	100
When y	=	0, x	=	150

Linear programme for production of components X & Y

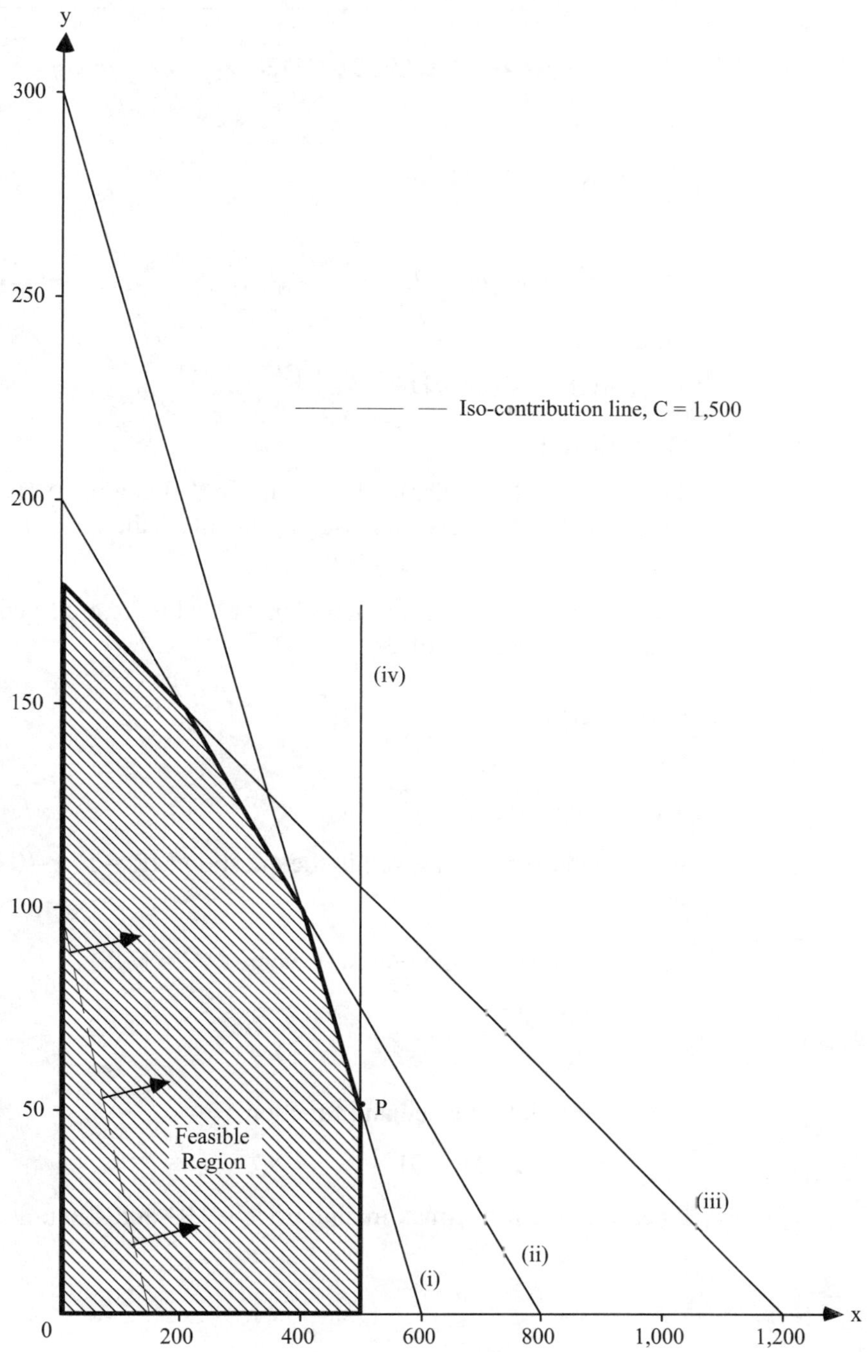

Moving the iso-contribution line away from the origin, keeping the same slope, the last point of the feasibility region to be reached is P, where x = 500, y = 50.

Hence for maximum contribution, produce 500 X and 50y per week.

Contribution	=	$10 \times 500 + 15 \times 50$	(£)
	=	£5,750 per week	

Chapter 6

Objective test questions

Question 1

The correct answer is D.

Question 2

The correct answer is B.

Question 3

The correct answer is D.

Question 4

The variables in the demand curve mean that at a price of £175 demand would be zero and that for every increase in price of £1 the quantity demanded will fall by 0.2.

The variables in the cost function mean that there are fixed costs of £12,500 and variable cost per unit of £7

Question 5

If $P = 175 - 0.2\ Q$

$TR = 175Q - 0.2Q^2$

From the information given in the question $MR = 175 - 0.4Q$

$MC = 7$

The profit-maximising output is where MC = MR

So $175 - 0.4Q = 7$

$Q = 420$

Substituting into the demand function

$P = 175 - 0.2 \times 420 = 91$

Therefore the profit-maximising price is £91 and 420 units will be sold.

Exam-type question

Scenic Snaps Ltd

(a) **Pricing decisions**

(i) **Full cost-plus pricing on current basis**

	£000
Direct costs:	
Materials	24
Labour	16
	40
Production overheads @ 100% direct costs	40
Factory cost	80
Administration and marketing overhead @ 25%	20
Full cost	100
Profit @ 20%	20
Revenue from 10,000 units	120

$$\text{Price per unit} = \frac{120{,}000}{10{,}000} = £12$$

(ii) **Revising budget allowing for shortfall in sales (prior to special order)**

	£000	£000
Sales revenue 75% × £600		450
Costs:		
Materials 75% × £120	90	
Labour 75% × £80	60	
	150	
Production overheads:		
Per original budget = £200,000		
Half of these are fixed ∴ no saving	100	
The other half are reduced by 25%	75	
	325	
Administration and marketing overheads:		
No variation over wide ranges of activity		
∴ as per original budget	100	425
Profit		25

	£000	£000
Original budgeted profit		100
Revised budgeted profit		25
Shortfall to be recovered on special order		75
Marginal cost of production:		
Materials	24	
Labour	16	
	40	
Overheads: 50% × direct costs	20	60
		135

$$\text{Price per unit} = \frac{135{,}000}{10{,}000} = £13.50$$

(iii) **Absorption rate for overheads**

	£000
Per original budget: total overheads	
Production	200
Administration and marketing	100
Total	300

$$\text{Absorption rate per unit} = \frac{£300{,}000}{40{,}000} = £7.50$$

Basing price on this recovery rate:

	£000
Direct costs:	
Materials	24
Labour	16
Overheads: 10,000 × £7.5	75
	115
Profit @ 20%	23
Total revenue	138

$$\text{Price per unit} = \frac{138{,}000}{10{,}000} = £13.80$$

(b) **Advice to management**

For a full analysis of the pricing situation much more information would be necessary, particularly regarding demand patterns. Presumably, there will be some form of resistance to very high levels of prices, otherwise there is no need to settle for any price calculated by the previous methods. Without knowing the levels of prices which the market will bear, it is difficult to give full advice.

Any method of pricing based on cost-plus is arbitrary and the above three methods show three different ways of using the same general principle. Of these, methods (ii) and (iii) probably give indirectly the most useful figures, as they isolate the marginal cost of production, and this is the level below which prices must not be allowed to fall. If there is some reason why the existing budget should be realised, e.g. shareholders' image of the company, etc. then perhaps method (ii) would provide the most useful figures. Methods (i) and (ii) rely on recovery of overheads on rates determined from the original budget, method (i) on an expenditure basis and method (iii), the special order, has a cost structure entirely different from the current production and the units would not appear, therefore, to be comparable.

One of the main considerations in setting the price of this special order will be the expectations of the customer. The price must be set sufficiently low to attract customers, but not so low that they will expect similarly low prices for future orders, which may result in a loss. Gauging the expectations of the customer in this respect may prove difficult, although a skilful salesperson may be able to get an impression of expected price from discussions with customers, or, alternatively, some judicious sounding out of the market may be possible.

Chapter 7

Objective test questions

Question 1

The correct answer is A.

$$\text{Coefficient of variation (\%)} = \frac{\text{Standard deviation}}{\text{Mean}} \times 100$$

Process

W	$^{10}/_{100}$	×	100	=	10
X	$^{5}/_{40}$	×	100	=	12.5
Y	$^{8}/_{80}$	×	100	=	10
Z	$^{12}/_{150}$	×	100	=	8

Question 2

The correct answer is C.

The co-efficient of variation measures the relative dispersion of the given data.

Question 3

The correct answer is A.

In a histogram you are not comparing the height of the bar, but the area represented by each bar. If the class intervals are different then the frequencies must be adjusted, otherwise the histogram will show a distorted picture.

In this example, the histogram class interval is one and a half times as large as the others, so the frequency must be divided by 1½. Assuming a frequency of one:

$$\frac{1}{1\frac{1}{2}} = 0.67$$

So the frequency must be multiplied by 0.67.

Question 4

The correct answer is A.

Question 5

(i) The correct answer is B.

EV for launch of A = (0.6 × 3,000) + (0.4 × 1,000) = £2,200
EV for launch of B = (0.7 × 3,000) + (0.3 × 1,800) = £2,640

Therefore product B should be launched.

(ii) The correct answer is C.

Question 6

The correct answer is B.

EV without the information	=	£120
EV with the information	=	£200
∴ EVI	=	£80

Exam-type questions

Question 1: Tripe

(a) **Decision tree**

The chance forks shown could be arranged in different orders. The tree could be shown with net present values, or incremental cashflows (i.e. reduce each cashflow by £30,000 and do not show the middle branch of the tree).

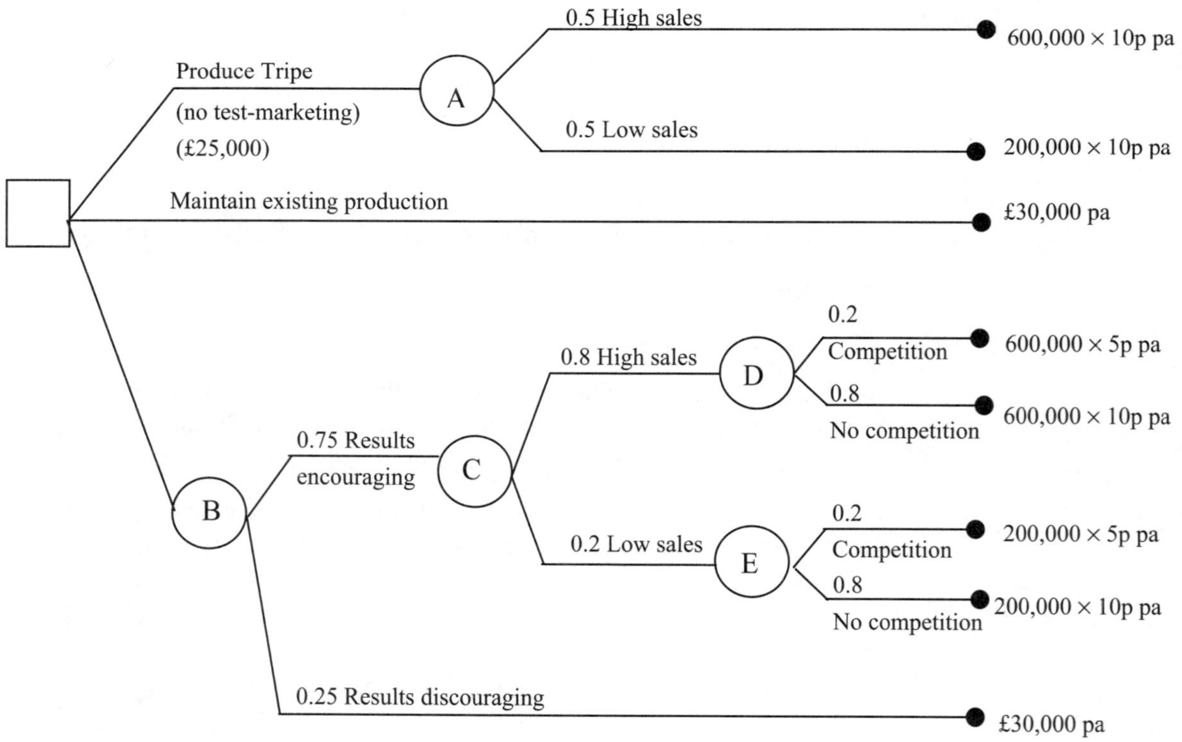

(b) **Expected net present values**

(1) *Produce Tripe, no test-marketing*

Expected NPV = £[(0.5 × 60,000) + (0.5 × 20,000)] × 4 – £25,000

= £135,000

(2) *Maintain existing production*

Expected NPV = 4 × £30,000 = £120,000

(3) *Test market*

Expected NPV at D = £[(0.2 × 30,000) + (0.8 × 60,000)] × 4 = £216,000

Expected NPV at E = £[(0.2 × 10,000) + (0.8 × 20,000)] × 4 = £72,000

Expected NPV at C = (0.8 × £216,000) + (0.2 × £72,000) = £187,200

Expected NPV = 0.75 × (£187,200 – £25,000) + (0.25 × 4 × £30,000) –£7,000 = £144,650

(c) **Maximum price for test-marketing**

The maximum price that the company will pay for test-marketing is the increase in the expected net present value that results from carrying out the test-marketing. The difference in NPVs is £144,650 – £135,000, ie £9,650. (This includes the £7,000 current price of the test-marketing.)

Maximum price = £7,000 + £9,650 = £16,650.

(d) **Limitations on the calculations of expected net present values**

The use of probability forecasts of the outcome of a project enable the expected net present value to be calculated. The word 'expected' is, however, something of a misnomer. The calculated figure is in fact an average of the possible outcomes weighted by their relative probabilities. As such, it is a hypothetical figure – in fact one or other of the outcomes must occur, not some average. If the project were carried out many times, the average results **would** equal the expected value. However, the technique is often applied to projects which will only be done once.

There are other problems associated with expected values. One important factor is that they ignore the decision maker's attitude towards risk. Risk averse decision makers will often accept considerable reductions in expected value for only small decreases in risk.

Calculations of the expected net present values do not of themselves give any idea of the nature of the dispersion of possible outcomes around the expected value. Where uncertainty is present, the investor needs to know more than just what the expected return would be from the investment. The expected net present value does not tell us the maximum possible loss which could be incurred, or how rapidly the proceeds would fall with a decrease in business activity. Furthermore, it may be necessary to consider the relationship between the return on the current investments and the return on other investments already made – for example, would something which causes a low return from the other investments also cause a low return on the investment under consideration?

Also consider the validity of the probability distributions themselves. If an organisation has been through many similar situations in the past, it can tabulate the results of each previous similar situation to obtain an objective measure of the probability of each range of possible outcomes. If, however, the situation were changing – say, the operation were becoming more efficient with each recurrence – then earlier outcomes would be of little use in predicting the likely outcome in other conditions. In practice, business decisions are likely to be made in a changing environment and hence a probability estimated from a long run of similar activities is rarely applicable.

Finally, the use of expected net present values as a basis for investment decisions is almost certain to rest on the use of 'subjective' probabilities, as opposed to 'objective' probabilities derived from empirical research. This in itself is a major limitation of the technique.

(e) In this situation, the advantages largely depend on the quality of the market research undertaken. No survey can ever precisely determine the level of demand for a product but any result that reduces uncertainty can be useful. The major advantages may be summarised as follows:

(i) The reduction in uncertainty will ease a company's planning problems. Cash budgets, production schedules, manpower plans and capital requirements may all be projected with more accuracy and hence a firm can operate more efficiently.

(ii) Although the risk reduction effects may not be of great consequence to shareholders in the context of a well-diversified portfolio, they can be of particular value to other interested parties. Management, employees, suppliers and customers would all welcome a reduction in the total risk of a firm, assuming the costs of the research were not too high.

(iii) A well-researched proposal can often make it easier for a firm to raise new finance. Banks and other suppliers of finance are likely to be more impressed with a well thought-out plan backed by an independent research company rather than simply relying on a firm's own estimates. This is particularly true in a highly competitive market such as, for example, micro-computers.

(iv) It is likely that any reputable market research survey will yield more information than just the size of the market. Information on why the market is of a certain size is also likely to result. This could allow a company to adjust its pricing, quality, promotion and distribution policies to increase the profitability of the project.

Question 2: Butterfield Ltd

(a) Expected contribution = (0.75 × 1,000,000) – (0.25 × 400,000) = £650,000

Mr Rover should give the project further consideration.

(b) Contribution from BEM — Loss of contribution from LOG

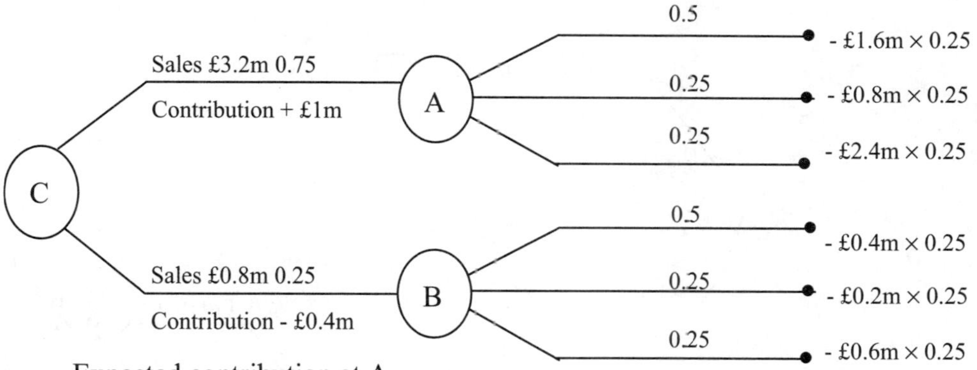

Expected contribution at A

= (-0.5 × 1.6 × 0.25) – (0.25 × 0.8 × 0.25) – (0.25 × 2.4 × 0.25) in £m

= –£0.4m

Expected contribution at B

= (–0.5 × 0.4 × 0.25) – (0.25 × 0.2 × 0.25) – (0.25 × 0.6 × 0.25) in £m

= –£0.1m

Expected contribution at C

= [(1 – 0.4) × 0.75] + [(–0.4 – 0.1) × 0.25] in £m

= £325,000

Mr Rover should give the project further consideration.

(c) With perfect information available and using the figures calculated in part (b) the following tree applies:

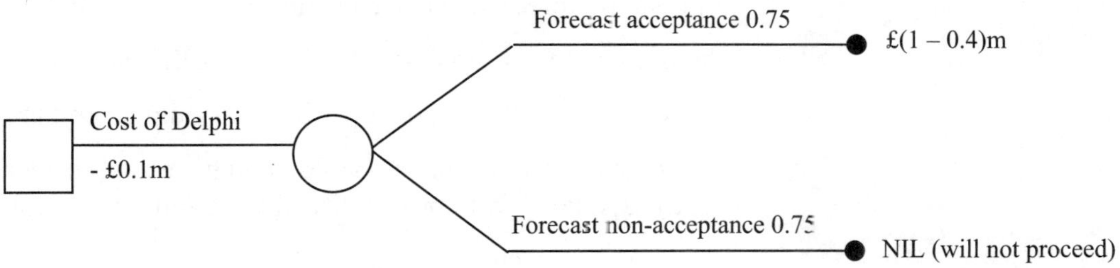

Expected contribution = [0.75 × (1 – 0.4)] – 0.1 = £450,000 – £100,000

= £350,000

Since this is £25,000 greater than the expected contribution without the information, Mr Rover should instruct Delphi to carry out the market research.

(d) It is not clear from the question whether the decision not to proceed further if Delphi predicts a non-acceptance of BEM in the market still applies when the information is not perfect.

Therefore, the following tree determines what decision Mr Rover should make on the basis of Delphi's advice in addition to calculating the value of the information.

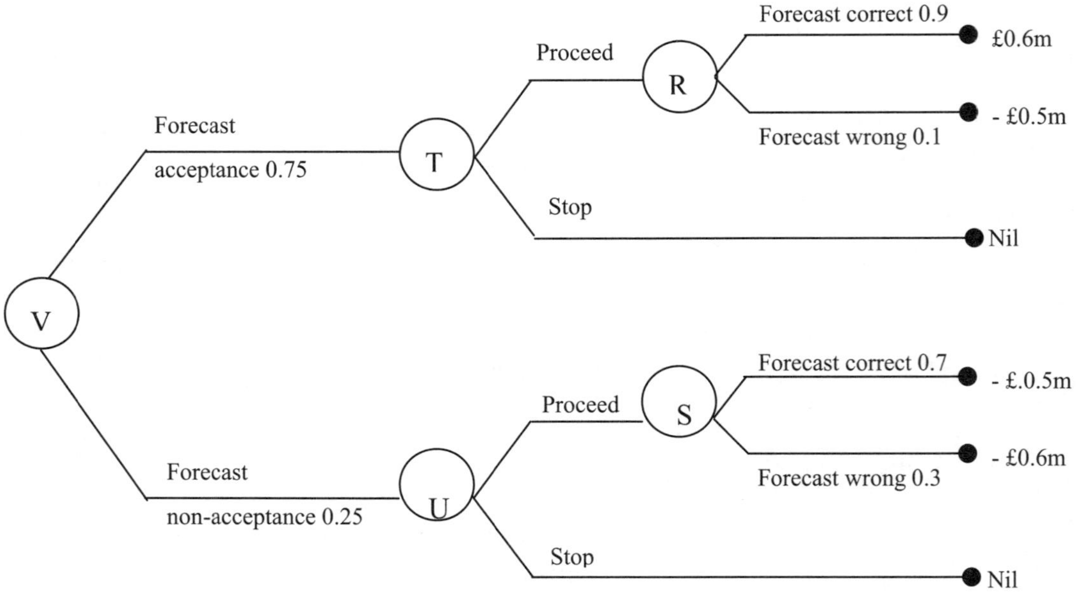

Expected contribution at R

$= (0.9 \times 0.6) - (0.1 \times 0.5) = £490{,}000$

This is preferable to nil and therefore the decision at T will be to proceed.

Expected contribution at S

$= (-0.7 \times 0.5) + (0.3 \times 0.6) = -£170{,}000$

This is worse than nil and therefore the decision at U will be not to proceed.

Expected contribution at V

$= (0.75 \times 0.49) + (0.25 \times 0) = £367{,}500$

Without the forecast, expected contribution = £325,000

Therefore value of forecast = £367,500 – £325,000 = £42,500

This is the maximum amount Mr Rover should be prepared to pay to Delphi.

(e) The advantages of expected values, which are simple averages (arithmetic mean) calculated from probability distributions, are as follows:

(i) easy to calculate and understand

(ii) produce a single representative figure instead of several

(iii) will show what happens in the long run for repeated projects.

The disadvantages of expected values are:

(i) they may be inapplicable to one-off decisions since they only reflect what will happen in the long run if the investment is repeated many times

(ii) they give no indication of risk as this is measured by the spread of possible values in the probability distribution

(iii) usually they give an 'impossible' figure for the investment which cannot occur from a single project.

In addition the methods used, like all project appraisal methods, rely on estimates which may be inaccurate.

Question 3: Homeworker Ltd

(a) **Increased production availability**

Present production 4,752 hours ÷ 36 machine hours = 132 batches

Buying out A

Production capacity 4,752 hours ÷ 26 machine hours = 182.77 batches

INCREASE = 38.46%

Buying out B

Production capacity 4,752 hours ÷ 22 machine hours = 216 batches

INCREASE = 63.64%

Buying out C

Production capacity 4,752 hours ÷ 24 machine hours = 198 batches

INCREASE = 50%

(b) **Financial implications**

Assuming a risk neutral attitude, the appropriate cost price for the bought out components is the 'expected' purchase price.

Expected purchase price:

Component A	96 (0.25) + 85 (0.5) + 54 (0.25)	= £80
Component B	176 (0.25) + 158 (0.5) + 148 (0.25)	= £160
Component C	149 (0.25) + 127 (0.5) + 97 (0.25)	= £125

Contribution possibilities:

	Present position	*Buy out Component A*	*Buy out Component B*	*Buy out Component C*
Number of batches	132	182.8	198*	198
	£	£	£	£
Per batch:				
Variable cost A	32	80	32	32
Variable cost B	54	54	160	54
Variable cost C	58	58	58	125
Variable cost D + E	16	16	16	16
Assembly costs	40	40	40	40
	200	248	306	267
Selling price	600	600	600	600
Contribution	400	352	294	333
Total contribution	52,800	64,346	58,212	65,934

* Only a 50% increase in demand next period.

Decision: Buy out C to maximise contribution.

Note: An incremental approach would have been equally satisfactory.

(c) **Revised profit statement**

	Per batch	Total (198 batches)
	£	£
Sales	600	118,800
Variable cost (as per part (b))	267	52,866
Contribution	333	65,934
Fixed costs (316 × 132 batches)		41,712
Profit		24,222

(d) **Other factors to consider to avoid risk**

(i) **Component prices**. The expected price for component C is £125. It could be as high as £149. There appears to be no incentive for General Machines Ltd to keep down costs.

(ii) **Dealing with risk**. The use of expected values is only one way of dealing with risk. A calculation of the worst possible outcome may have suggested a different choice.

(iii) **Uncertainty of sales estimate**. The sales estimate was assumed to be certain. A range of probabilities should have been used.

(iv) Would fixed costs remain constant with a 50% increase in output?

(v) There will be an **added risk** in obtaining an essential component from only one outside supplier.

Note: Only three factors are required. You should choose the three considered most pertinent to the question.

Question 4: Z Ltd

(a) **At price £15 per unit**

Demand	*Material*	*Material cost (£000) for purchase option:*			*Probability*
	(kg)	*(i)*	*(ii)*	*(iii)*	
36,000	108,000	324	297	270	0.3
28,000	84,000	252	231	210	0.5
18,000	54,000	162	148.5	159	0.2
Expected cost:		255.6	234.3	217.8	

The best purchasing option is (iii) with an expected material cost of £217,800.

Notes:

1 Material costs are calculated as in the following example:

Demand: 18,000 units; Purchase option (iii)

Material requirement = 18,000 × 3 kg = 54,000 kg

70,000 kg purchased, surplus = 70,000 – 54,000 = 16,000 kg

	£000
Cost of 70,000 kg @ £2.50	175
Less: revenue from sale of surplus @ £1	16
Net cost	159

2 As actual demand is not known, the decision as to which purchasing option to use is based on the option that gives the lowest expected cost, where

Expected cost = S (material cost × demand probability)

Calculation of profit

Expected demand = S (demand × probability)

= (36,000 × 0.3) + (28,000 × 0.5) + (18,000 × 0.2)

= 28,400 units

	£000	£000
Sales (28,400 @ £15)		426
Less: Material costs	217.8	
Manufacturing costs (28,400 @ £3)	85.2	
Advertising + selling costs	25	
Fixed costs	40	
Total cost		368
Net profit		58

At price £20 per unit

Demand	*Material*	*Material cost (£'000) for purchase option:*			*Probability*
	(kg)	*(i)*	*(ii)*	*(iii)*	
28,000	84,000	252	231	210	0.3
23,000	69,000	207	189.75	174	0.5
13,000	39,000	117	126.5	144	0.2
Expected cost:		202.5	189.475	178.8	

The optimum purchasing option is (iii), expected cost £178,800.

Profit calculation

Expected demand = (28,000 × 0.3) + (23,000 × 0.5) + (13,000 × 0.2)

= 22,500

	£000	£000
Sales (22,500 @ £20)		450.0
Less: Material cost	178.8	
Manufacturing cost (22,500 @ £3)	67.5	
Advertising	96	
Fixed costs	40	
Total cost		382.3
Net profit		67.7

Hence the optimum strategy is to sell at £20 per unit using purchase option.

(iii) Expected value = £67,700.

(b) ***Note:*** If the demand is known beforehand, the optimum purchasing policy for each demand at each price can be used. Thus, for a price of £15, the optimum policy for a demand of 36,000 is (iii) giving the minimum cost of £270,000; for a demand of 28,000 it is (iii) giving a cost of £210,000; and for a demand of 18,000 it is (ii) giving a cost of £148,500.

Calculation of profit at different demand rates:

£15 per unit

Demand (000)		*36*		*28*		*18*
Optimal purchase option		*(iii)*		*(iii)*		*(ii)*
	£000	£000	£000	£000	£000	£000
Sales @ £15		540		420		270.0
Material costs	270		210		148.5	
Manufacturing cost @ £3	108		84		54	
Advertising and fixed costs	65		65		65	
		443		359		267.5
Net profit		97		61		2.5

Expected value with perfect information therefore equals:

(97,000 × 0.3) + (61,000 × 0.5) + (2,500 × 0.2) = £60,100

£20 per unit

Demand (000)		*28*		*23*		*13*
Optimal purchase option		*(iii)*		*(ii)*		*(i)*
	£000	£000	£000	£000	£000	£000
Sales @ £20		560		460		260
Material costs	210		174		117	
Manufacturing cost @ £3	84		69		39	
Advertising and fixed costs	136		136		136	
		430		379		292
Net profit		130		81		(32)

Expected value with perfect information therefore equals:

(13,000 × 0.3) + (81,000 × 0.5) + (–32,000 × 0.2) = £73,100

With perfect information, therefore, the company would choose to set the price at £20 and would achieve expected profit of £73,100.

Expected value of information	=	Expected value of best strategy with the information – expected value of best strategy without it.
	=	£(73,1000 – 67,700)
	=	£5,400

This is the maximum that management should be prepared to pay for prior knowledge of demand.

Chapter 8

Objective test questions

Question 1

The correct answer is A.

Question 2

The correct answer is D.

Question 3

The correct answer is B.

For a 90% learning curve the index of learning b = log0.9/log2 = –0.152

The total time for the first 3 units = 3 × 40 × 3 ^–0.152 = 101.55

The total time for the first 2 units = 2 × 40 × 2 ^–0.152 = 72.00

Therefore the time for the third unit = 101.55 – 72.00 = 29.55

Question 4

The correct answer is D.

Question 5

Machine 1 can produce 60/3 × 450 = 9,000 units

Machine 2 can produce 60/5 × 575 = 6,900 units

Machine 3 can produce 60/4.8 × 500 = 6,250 units

The bottleneck resource is therefore machine 3 and the maximum output is 6,250 units.

Question 6

Throughput per unit = £3.80 - £1.40 = £2.40

Time on bottleneck = 4.8/60 = 0.08 of an hour

Return per hour = £2.40/0.08 = £30

Total factory cost = £8,500 + 6,250 × (0.9 + 0.45) = £16,937.50

Cost per hour = £16,937.50/500 =£33.875

Return per hour /Cost per hour = £30/£33.875 = 0.886

TA ratio = 1: 0.886

As the TA ratio is less than 1, action should be taken to increase the throughput or reduce costs.

Exam-type questions

Question 1: Limitation of traditional management accounting

(a) The traditional management accounting techniques for performance measurement are based around budgetary control and standard costing and the associated variances. The budgets are normally prepared annually and the standards are applied to all products of a particular type.

The move towards more flexibility, a readiness to meet customer requirements, smaller batches and continuous improvements results in a wider range of products or 'jobs' geared to customers' specifications with an associated variation in cost, making it difficult to apply a single standard cost. If a single standard were used in this context to calculate variances, these variances would be partly attributable to changes in product specification.

The effect of advanced manufacturing technology is that a greater emphasis is placed on machines and much less emphasis on direct labour. This has two major implications. Firstly the traditional direct labour efficiency variance is of limited use and secondly the method for calculation of unit cost needs to be amended.

The increased emphasis on quality contradicts assumptions made by traditional management accounting, which assumes that products should be made as reliable as is 'cost-effective'. This has been shown to be a short-sighted approach. In the long run, an emphasis on total quality, not only of products but of services to customers and services within the organisation not only increases sales but enormously reduces many costs associated with reworking and correcting errors.

Overall the traditional performance measures may, therefore, be misleading in the new manufacturing environment.

(b) Activity-based costing helps to identify more accurately the activities or 'cost drivers' which are causing costs to be incurred. The advantage of this technique is that not only can standard costs be adapted more quickly to custom-made products or batches made to customers' specifications, but also they can be quickly updated for changes in methods of manufacture, a regular feature of a modern, quality-focused business environment.

If management accountants are to produce meaningful performance reports in the future, they should be concerned not only with comparing results against budgets but also against alternative methods of working. For example, they should be comparing the costs of traditional stock-holding policies against techniques such as 'just-in-time'.

They should also be concerned with non-financial measures of performance, particularly those associated with quality, such as statistical control charts and reject rates.

Ultimately, management accountants are judged by the usefulness of the information that is given to management. They should be aiming to 'own' the information system of a company so that they can present integrated reports involving financial and non-financial factors. In order to do this, they must become very familiar with their firm's technical operations.

Question 2: Learning curve for PQ plc

The company makes 8 batches of 500 toasters, totalling 4,000 toasters. A 90% learning curve applies, so every time output doubles, the average time per unit is 90% of what it was before.

The new machinery would cost £7,000, but the cost of capital is 15%. A simple NPV calculation shows that the investment should not be undertaken.

	Average time per batch	*Total time for batches*
	hours	hours
First batch of 500	500	
First 2 batches of 500 (× 0.9)	450	
First 4 batches of 500 (× 0.9)	648	
First 8 batches of 500 (× 0.9)	583.2	4,665.6

		£
Materials cost	(4,000 × £30)	120,000
Labour cosr	(4,665.6 × £6)	27,994
Extra fixed overheads		25,000
Extra cash spending		172,994
Revenue	(4,000 × £45)	180,000
Cash profit		7,006

Year	*Cash flow*	*Discount factor at 15%*	***Present value***
	£		£
0	(7,000)	1.000	(7,000)
1	7,006	0.870	6,095
NPV			(905)

Question 3: Devon Ltd

Number	*Log value*
0.9	– 0.0458
2	0.3010

b = - 0.0458/0.3010 = - 0.152.

$y = ax^b$ where a = 2 and b = - 0.152.

$x^{-b} = 1/x^b$

So here, $y = 2x^{-0.152}$ or $2/x^{0.152}$

Since the learning effect stops after 50 units, we need to calculate the average unit time for the first 50 units. We also need the average unit time for the first 51 units, because this gives us an average time for the 51st unit. From this we can calculate the time per unit for the 51st unit and all subsequent units.

When x = 50, the average time per unit is 1.1035 days.

When x = 51, the average time per unit is 1.1002 days.

		Total time required
		Days
1st 50 units	(50 × 1.1035)	55.175
1st 51 units	(51 × 1.1002)	56.110
		0.935

Rounding these estimates, we can assume that the first 50 units for each employee require a total of 55 days, and thereafter, each unit takes 1 day.

Each employee in the first year will therefore be able to make 55 + (250 days – 55 days) 240 units.

There are 10 employees available, so total annual production in year 1 will be 2,400 units.

In subsequent years, total annual production will be 2,500 units.

	Year 1	*Years 2 – 4*
	£	£
Materials at £300	720,000	750,000
Labour (2,500 hours at £200)	500,000	500,000
Extra fixed costs	850,000	850,000
	2,070,000	2,100,000
Sales at £2,000	4,800,000	5,000,000
Cash profit	2,730,000	2,900,000

NPV calculation

Year	*Cash flow*	*Discount factor at 10%*	*Present value*
	£000		£000
0	(3,500)	1.000	(3,500)
1	2,730	0.909	2,482
2	2,900	0.826	2,395
3	2,900	0.751	2,178
4	2,900	0.683	1,981
NPV			5,536

On the basis of these estimates, the investment should be undertaken.

Chapter 9

Objective test questions

Question 1

The correct answer is D.

Question 2

The correct answer is C.

Exam-type question

NN Ltd

Part (a)

	Year 1	*Year 2*	*Year 3*	*Whole life*
	£000	£000	£000	£000
Sales	73,000	255,500	191,625	520,125
Research & Development costs	6,000	1,500	0	7,500
Production costs:				
Variable costs	34,675	116,800	87,600	239,075
Variable costs – batch	4,563	12,848	9,636	27,047
Fixed costs	25,000	25,000	25,000	75,000

Marketing costs:				
Variable costs	7,300	26,280	19,710	53,290
Fixed costs	10,000	8,000	8,000	26,000
Distribution costs:				
Variable costs	1,460	5,840	4,380	11,680
Variable cost – batches	701	3,504	3,504	7,709
Fixed costs	6,000	6,000	6,000	18,000
Customer service costs per MDVDC unit	2,920	8,760	6,570	18,250
Operating profit	– 25,620	40,968	21,225	36,572

Part (b)

	Year 1 £000	*Year 2* £000	*Year 3* £000	*Whole life* £000
Sales	83,220	289,080	189,709	562,009
Research & Development costs	6,000	1,500	0	7,500
Production costs:				
Variable costs	41,610	140,160	91,980	273,750
Variable costs – batches	4,563	12,848	8,432	25,842
Fixed costs	25,000	25,000	25,000	75,000
Marketing costs:				
Variable costs	8,760	31,536	20,696	60,992
Fixed costs	10,000	8,000	8,000	26,000
Distribution costs:				
Variable costs	1,752	7,008	4,599	13,359
Variable cost – batches	420	2,102	1,840	4,362
Fixed costs	7,000	7,000	7,000	21,000
Customer service costs	3,504	10,512	6,899	20,915
Operating profit	– 25,389	43,414	15,265	33,289

If the selling price was reduced by £10 per unit in each of the three years of the product's life then the total life cycle profitability of the 'MDVDC' would be reduced by £3,285,430. Thus, the management of NN Ltd should not decrease the selling price unless further economies of scale can be derived.

Part (c)

Life cycle costing attempts to estimate and accumulate costs of a product over the duration of its expected life. This may enable management to ascertain whether the profits earned from its manufacture will cover the total costs incurred during pre and post manufacturing stages. Thus management attention is focused upon the costs that are incurred during the different stages that comprise a product's life cycle. This process aids management understanding and enables the better management of total costs incurred throughout the life cycle. The application of life cycle costing promotes longer-term considerations by management and may assist in the identification of those areas where the application of cost reduction techniques is likely to be most beneficial. Moreover, the taking of a whole life view may also help to identify opportunities for revenue extension. Such opportunities for cost reduction and/or revenue extension are unlikely to be given due consideration if management attention is focused upon the maximisation of profit on a period-by-period basis.

Chapter 10

Objective test questions

Question 1

Total machine hours are 500 × 6 + 2,250 × 8 = 21,000

Total overhead = £226,000

The OAR is therefore £226,000/21,000 = £10.76 per machine hour.

The overhead allocated to product A using an absorption costing system would therefore be 6 × £10.76 = £64.56.

Using ABC, the cost driver rates would be:

Set ups	£118,000/14 = £8,428.57 per production run
Components	£28,000/17 = £1,647.06 per component
Inspections	£80,000/12 = £6,666.67 per inspection

The total overhead allocated to product A would be:

		£
Set ups	10 × £8,428.57	84,285.70
Components	12 × £1,647.06	19,764.72
Inspections	6 × £6,666.67	40,000
		144,050.42

The cost per unit is therefore £288.10, an increase of £223.54.

The correct answer is D.

Question 2

The correct answer is C.

Question 3

The correct answer is B.

Exam-type question

ABC terms

(a) Activity-based costing is a method of costing which is based on the principle that activities cause costs to be incurred, not products. Costs are attributed to activities and the performance of those activities is then linked to products. A cost driver is the factor that causes costs to be incurred (e.g. placing an order or setting up a machine).

(b) (i)

Cost per set-up $\frac{£4,355}{1+6+2+8} = \frac{£4,355}{17} = £256$

Cost per order $\frac{£1,920}{1+4+1+4} = \frac{£1,920}{10} = £192$

Cost per handling of materials $\frac{£7,580}{2+10+3+12} = \frac{£7,580}{27} = £281$

Cost per spare part $\dfrac{£8,600}{2+5+1+4} = \dfrac{£8,600}{12} = £717$

Cost per machine hour (No. of m/c hours = 125 + 1,250 + 600 + 10,500)

$$= \frac{£37,424}{12,475} = £3.00/\text{hr}$$

Costs are then attributed to products using the cost driver rates calculated above, for example:

Product A requires one machine set-up, therefore 1 × £256 = £256

Product B requires six machine set-ups, therefore 6 × £256 = £1,536 and so on.

Product	*A*	*B*	*C*	*D*
	£	£	£	£
Activities:				
Set-ups	256	1,536	512	2,048
Orders	192	768	192	768
Handling	562	2,810	843	3,372
Spare parts	1,434	3,585	717	2,868
Machine time	375	3,750	1,800	31,500
	2,819	12,449	4,064	40,556
No. of units	500	5,000	600	7,000
Cost per unit	£5.64	£2.49	£6.77	£5.79

The costs are then totalled and divided by the number of units to give the cost per unit for each product.

(ii) The activity-based costing approach attributes more costs to products A, B and C and less to product D than the traditional method of accounting for overhead costs. The activity-based costing method gives a more accurate cost by relating it to the resources used to manufacture each product; consequently these costs are more useful for decision-making than those provided by the traditional method.

Chapter 11

Objective test questions

Question 1

The correct answer is B.

After three years, £150,000 has been received, leaving £17,500 still to come. This is reached $\frac{17.5}{70}$ of the way into the fourth year.

Question 2

The correct answer is C.

Year	*Cash flow* £000	*Discount factor*	*Present value* £000
1	40	0.909	36.36
2	50	0.826	41.30
3	60	0.751	45.06
4	70	0.683	47.81
			170.53

After three years £122,720 has been received, leaving £44,780 still to come. This is reached $\frac{44.78}{47.81}$ of the way into the 4th year.

Question 3

The correct answer is B.

170.53 – 167.5 = 3.03, i.e. £3,030

Question 4

The correct answer is B.

By trial and error

Year	*Cash flow* £000	*Discount factor at 11%*	*Present value* £000
0	(167.5)	1	(167.5)
1	40	0.901	36.04
2	50	0.812	40.60
3	60	0.731	43.86
4	70	0.659	46.13
			(0.87)

12% will be further away than 11%.

Exam-type questions

Question 1: Paradis plc

Note: This question requires fairly standard calculation and discussion.

(a) **Payback period for each project**

(Time taken to repay original outlay of £350,000.)

Project A:	£000
Cash in first 3 years	314
Balance required	36
Initial investment	350
Cash in 4th year	112

Payback = 3 years + $\frac{36}{112}$ years = 3.32 years

(assuming cash flows accrue evenly – otherwise 4 years)

Project B:

Cash in first 3 years	£350,000
Payback	3 years

Project C:

Cash in first 2 years	£350,000
Payback	2 years

(b) **Accounting rate of return for each project**

	Project A	*Project B*	*Project C*
	£000	£000	£000
Total cash flow	904	770	630
Less: Total depreciation (no scrap value)	350	350	350
Total accounting profit	554	420	280
Project life (years)	7	5	4
Average profit per year (£000)	79.14	84	70 (1)
Initial capital employed	350	350	350 (2)
Accounting rate of return (1) ÷ (2)	22.6%	24%	20%

(c) **REPORT**

To: Chairman, Paradis plc

From: An Analyst

Date: XX-X-20XX

Report on the choice of capital investment project to be financed by proceeds of recent rights issue

Terms of reference

To provide an independent report on which of three projects, A, B and C, should be preferred by the ordinary shareholders of Paradis plc.

Introduction

This report looks at the strengths and weaknesses of various project appraisal techniques which are in common use, examines how the three projects stand up in the light of each method, and reaches a conclusion as to the best choice of project.

Conclusion

It is recommended that the net present value method of project appraisal be used. On this basis, project A appears to be the best, being marginally better than B. However, it is suggested that further investigations into the uncertainty of cash flow estimates of projects A and C are undertaken.

Traditional appraisal methods

Since you are familiar with both the payback and the accounting rate of return methods, this report deals immediately with their advantages and limitations.

(1) Payback

The payback method is easy both to calculate and to understand. It shows how long investors have to wait before their investment starts to repay the initial outlay. Because no future results are known with certainty, it gives investors an idea of 'how long their money will be at risk', and since uncertainty usually tends to increase the further into the future we look, a short payback period is taken to mean low risk as well as quick returns.

The weakness of using the payback method in isolation is that it does not measure profitability or increase in investor wealth.

For example, refer to the payback period of projects A, B and C. Project C has the shortest payback period and A has the longest. However, the cash flows of A last much longer than those of C, which may make A more profitable in the long run.

(2) Accounting rate of return

This method gives a measure of relative project profitability by comparing the average accounting profit per annum to come from the project with the average capital employed in it. Its advantages are that it is relatively easy to understand, it does measure profitability of returns compared with outlay, and it gives an indication as to whether the firm's target return on capital employed is exceeded.

Its main weaknesses are:

(i) it pays no attention to the **timing** of project returns. Cash received at an early stage is more valuable than the same cash received in a few years time because it can be reinvested to earn interest. For example, project C returns cash very quickly compared with project B, but this effect is lost in the process of averaging profits. Thus B has a higher ARR than C even though its IRR (see later) is lower;

(ii) it is a relative rate of return, rather than an absolute measure of gain in wealth. All rate of return methods ignore the size of the project;

(iii) because it is a percentage measure, there is a tendency to compare the ARR with interest rates, which is totally invalid;

(iv) it uses accounting profits where cash flows may be more appropriate;

(v) there is no objective means of finding a target ARR for a project.

Discounted cash flow methods

Both of the traditional methods are surpassed by discounted cash flow methods. The basic arguments are:

(i) it is better to consider cash rather than profits because cash is how investors will eventually see their rewards (i.e., dividends, sale of shares, interest);

(ii) the timing of the cash flows is important because early cash can be reinvested to earn interest.

The technique of discounting reduces all future cash flows to equivalent values now (present values) by allowing for the interest which could have been earned if the cash had been received immediately.

There are two possible techniques, net present value and internal rate of return.

Net present value

This is simply the net of the present values of the project cash flows after allowing for reinvestment at the company's 'cost of capital' (i.e., the average required return which is set by the market for the company's operations considering the risk of those operations).

Provided that the project is of average risk for the firm and that there is no shortage of capital, the NPV gives a best estimate of the total increase in wealth which accrues to the shareholders if the project is accepted. This should be reflected in an increased market value of the shares.

NPV computations are attached at Appendix A. On this basis, project A gives the greatest increase in shareholder wealth.

Internal rate of return

This is defined as the discount rate which gives the project a net present value of zero. When looking at a single project, the IRR will give the same decision as the NPV (i.e., if the project NPV is greater than zero, its IRR is higher than the cost of capital).

However, the IRR can give an incorrect signal when it is necessary to rank projects in order. Like all rate of return methods, it ignores the size of the project and hence the absolute gain in wealth to come from it. For example, project C has the highest IRR, but although the original outlay is as high as the other two projects, it returns most of that outlay after one year, and thereafter effectively becomes a smaller project with a high rate of return.

The IRR also makes an incorrect assumption about the rate at which cash surpluses can be reinvested: it assumes they are reinvested at the internal rate of return. For example, it assumes that cash from project C can be reinvested at 33%, but cash from A is reinvested at 27.5%. Both of these are wrong: the 20% cost of capital figure is more appropriate. The IRR is therefore unsuitable for comparing projects.

The best appraisal method

Following the arguments above, the best appraisal method is the net present value approach because it takes into account the time value of money in a way which indicates the absolute gain which will be made by shareholders as a result of accepting the project.

On this basis, project A should be accepted, with C just second. However, it should be noted that there are many other factors which affect the decision which have been left out of this report. The most obvious of these is an assessment of project risk. For example, it may be that A is regarded as riskier than C simply because it takes longer to pay back. It can then be argued that A should be discounted at a higher rate than C. This may give it a lower NPV than C.

We must therefore recommend that further analysis is made of the uncertainty attached to the cash flows of projects A and C.

Appendix A: Project net present values

(This assumes that cash flows arise at annual intervals.)

Time	*Disc. factor* 20%	*Project A*	*PV* £000	*Project B*	*PV* £000	*Project C*	*PV* £000
0	1.000	(350)	(350.0)	(350)	(350.0)	(350)	(350.0)
1	0.833	100	83.3	40	33.3	200	166.6
2	0.694	110	76.3	100	69.4	150	104.1
3	0.579	104	60.2	210	121.6	240	139.0
4	0.482	112	54.0	260	125.3	40	19.3
5	0.402	138	55.5	160	64.3		
6	0.335	160	53.6				
7	0.279	180	50.2				
Net present values			83.1		63.9		79.0

Question 2: Khan Ltd

(a) **NPV calculations and IRR estimation**

Note: Two substantial reversals of cash flow are involved in Project 1 and it is therefore sensible to check for multiple solutions to the IRR using trial and error.

Alternative 1

Time	*Cash flow* £	*At 20%* *Discount factor*	*Present value* £
0	(100,000)	1.000	(100,000)
1	255,000	0.833	212,415
2	(157,500)	0.694	(109,305)
	£(2,500)	NPV	£3,110

Alternative 2

Time	*Cash flow* £	*At 20%* *Discount factor*	*Present value* £
0	(50,000)	1.000	(50,000)
1	–	0.833	-
2	42,000	0.694	29,148
3	42,000	0.579	24,318
	£34,000		£3,466

Alternative 1

		At 20%		*At 5%*	
Time	*Cash flow in/out* £	*Discount factor*	*PV of cash flow* £	*Discount factor*	*PV of cash flow* £
0	(100,000)	1.000	(100,000)	1.00	(100,000)
1	255,000	0.833	212,415	1/1.05	242,857*
2	(157,500)	0.694	(109,305)	$1/(1.05)^2$	(142,857)*
	£(2,500)	NPV	£3,110	NPV	£0

		At 30%		*At 50%*	
Time	*Cash flow in/out* £	*Discount factor*	*PV of cash flow* £	*Discount factor*	*PV of cash flow* £
0	(100,000)	1.00	(100,000)	1.00	(100,000)
1	255,000	1/1.3	196,154	1/1.5	170,000
2	(157,500)	$1/(1.3)^2$	(93,195)	$1/(1.5)^2$	(70,000)
	£(2,500)	NPV	£2,959	NPV	£0

****Note:*** Discount factors have not been used at 5% as these lead to a rounding error. You should still be able to draw similar conclusions even if discount tables were employed.

Graph of NPV v cost of capital

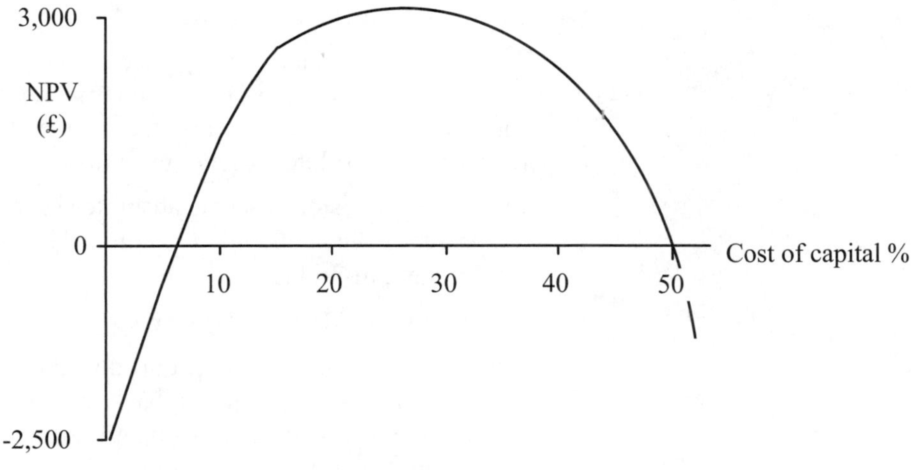

It can be seen from the table and the graph that there are two internal rates of return, 5% and 50%. At any cost of capital between these two limits, this alternative has a positive value.

Alternative 2

Time	Cash flow	At 20% PV	Discount factor	At 25% Present value
	£	£		£
0	(50,000)	(50,000)	1.00	(50,000)
1	–	–	1/1.25	–
2	42,000	29,148	$1/(1.25)^2$	26,880
3	42,000	24,318	$1/(1.25)^3$	21,420
	£34,000	£3,466		£(1,700)

∴ IRR is between 20% and 25%. Interpolating between 20% and 25%:

$$\text{IRR} = 20\% + 5\% \times \left(\frac{3{,}466}{1{,}700 + 3{,}466} \right)$$

~ 23.3%

Summary of results

	Alternative 1	Alternative 2
NPV at 20%	£3,110	£3,466
IRR (approx.)	5%, 50%	23.3%

(b) **Advice to the directors of Khan Ltd**

The two projects, although relating to the same product, have totally different cash flow patterns. It is difficult to see why this should be so. In particular, why does heavy promotion result in no sales in years 2 and 3? Further information would be helpful.

The choice between the two projects should be made on the basis of the net present value. A comparison of internal rates of return is not a valid basis for a decision. This is because the internal rate of return measures only the relative, not absolute, scale of cash flows.

In business decisions it is the absolute size of the surplus, indicated by the net present value, which is important. This is consistent with shareholder wealth maximisation.

(c) **Comments on Mr Court's views**

The views expressed by Mr Court do have some validity and are worthy of serious consideration. The payback method is a very simple means of evaluating projects in terms of the time taken to recover the initial outlay. The method is particularly useful as a quick way of obtaining a view of a project in situations which are subject to rapid change and where the degree of uncertainty in long-term projects may be unacceptable. It may well be that the importing of novelty products is just such a situation.

However, the weakness of payback, as a serious technique, is also clearly illustrated by the examples. Because payback is essentially a simple and crude technique, it is difficult to employ it in situations where the pattern of cash flows is complex, as certainly happens under alternative 1. There is no meaningful way in which patterns of outflows followed by receipts, followed by further outflows, can be evaluated in terms of payback. For this reason it is considered that payback does not provide useful data in this situation.

The second point made by Mr Court concerns the effect of the projects on reported profits. Though this is unrelated to his other point about the payback and does indicate some muddled thinking, nevertheless it is a point that management should consider. It is a major weakness of net present value that it provides only a single measure of a project. No account is taken of the pattern of cash flows and their effect on reported profits over the life of the project. Yet such data is of major concern to a company, both because of the effect on shareholders and on the company's ability to raise finance in the market.

In addition, there is the company's continuing need to finance its operations. Again, it may well be that projects which are attractive in terms of net present value give rise to financing requirements which the company cannot meet. Furthermore, the company's ability to raise external finance will be hampered by any adverse pattern of reported profits.

Finally there is the uncertainty inherent in each of the two projects. No data is available. However, introducing a new product into a market which is very much subject to fashion and crazes must involve a high degree of uncertainty. The evaluation should be extended to consider the probability distribution of both the cost and revenue items, and their correlation to the returns from other activities of the business.

To conclude, while Mr Court's views are expressed in naive terms they nevertheless contain substantial elements of truth which should properly be considered in the evaluation.

Chapter 12

Objective test questions

Question 1

The correct answer is D.

Question 2

The correct answer is D.

Question 3

The correct answer is B.

$\frac{1.06}{1.015}$ = 1.044, implying a real rate of 4.4%

Note: The quick answer of 6 −1.5 = 4.5% is a rough approximation to the real rate, but is not the most accurate answer.

Exam-type questions

Question 1: AB plc

Note: With a product with a three-year life and inflation rates that do not link conveniently to the money cost of capital, the approach to this question is to produce a table showing the cash flows at time 0, 1, 2 and 3. You may wish to state an assumption about the point when cash flows are first subject to inflation. It is worth limiting your calculations to the nearest £000 to save time.

Consider incremental costs and revenues to evaluate whether the new machine is worthwhile. Sales revenue, material cost and overheads are unchanged and therefore are not relevant.

NPV with new machine

Time	*0*	*1*	*2*	*3*
	£m	£m	£m	£m
Labour saving	–	3.36	3.763	4.215
Machine	(5.0)	–	–	–
Net cash flow	(5.0)	3.36	3.763	4.215
15% discount factors	1.0	0.870	0.756	0.658
Present value	(5.0)	2.92	2.84	2.77

NPV = £3,530,000

Recommendation and comment

With a positive NPV of £3.53m, the firm should buy the new machine to develop the products.

- **Reliability of estimates** – using the new machine appears a very safe project but it would be worth checking on how accurate each estimate is felt to be.
- **Hidden costs of new machine** – the suppliers of the new machine have made substantial claims so it is worth obtaining guarantees of its performance and considering whether other costs such as maintenance and higher running costs will be incurred.
- **Installation costs** – no mention has been made of these, including delivery, lost production and possibly extra factory space.
- **Alternative machines** – do these exist? If the product is risky, a cheaper machine providing lower savings might prove to be a preferable option.
- **Effect on other costs** – is there any possible saving of variable overheads of the labour saving and what is the effect on materials cost of using the new machine?
- **True labour savings** – although labour cost per unit will fall, will the firm be able to lay off staff and thereby save costs and will there be any redundancy costs?

Question 2: J plc

(W1) Tax relief

Year	*Bal b/f*	*Tax depr 25%*	*Tax relief 30%*	*Year relief received* 1	2	3	4	5
1	500,000	125,000	37,500	18,750	18,750			
2	375,000	93,750	28,125		14,062	14,063		
3	281,250	70,312	21,094			10,547	10,547	
4	210,938	210,938	63,281				31,640	
Residual value	Nil							31,641
		500,000		18,750	32,812	24,610	42,187	31,641

(Balancing allowance £210,938)

Purchase

Year	*Cash flow*	*Tax relief*	*Net cash flow*	*Discount factor*	*PV*
	£	£	£		£
0	(500,000)		(500,000)	1	(500,000)
1		18,750	18,750	0.926	17,363
2		32,812	32,812	0.857	28,120
3		24,610	24,610	0.794	19,540
4		42,187	42,187	0.735	31,007
5		31,641	31,641	0.681	21,548
Net Present Value			(382,422)		

Leasing

Year	*Payments*	*Tax cash flow*	*Net cash flow*	*Discount factor*	*Present value*
	£	£	£		£
0	(150,000)	22,500	(127,500)	1	(127,500)
1	(150,000)	45,000	(105,000)	0.926	(97,230)
2	(150,000)	45,000	(105,000)	0.857	(89,985)
3	(150,000)	45,000	(105,000)	0.794	(83,370)
4		22,500	22,500	0.735	16,538
		Net Present Value			(381,547)

Therefore leasing is the least cost option by £875 and should be chosen. As the NPVs are so close it may be beneficial to carry out sensitivity analysis to find out by how much the variables would have to change before the decision would change.

Chapter 13

Objective test questions

Question 1

The correct answer is D.

Question 2

The correct answer is D.

Question 3

The correct answer is B.

Exam-type questions

Question 1: NAW Transport Services

Oregon	*Costs*	*DCF @ 9%*	*Present value of cashflows*	*Cumulative discount factor @ 9% p.a.*	*Annual equivalent cost*
	£		£		
Year 0	40,000	1.000	40,000.00		
Year 1	22,500	0.917	20,632.50		
Year 2	27,900	0.842	23,491.80		
Year 3	42,300	0.772	32,655.60		
Year 4	38,700	0.708	27,399.60		
Year 5	44,100	0.650	28,665.00		
			172,844.50	3.890	44,433.03

Santa Fe	*Costs*	*DCF @ 9%*	*Present value of cashflows*		
	£		£		
Year 0	60,000	1.000	60,000.00		
Year 1	18,000	0.917	16,506.00		
Year 2	20,700	0.842	17,429.40		
Year 3	23,400	0.772	18,064.80		
Year 4	26,100	0.708	18,478.80		
Year 5	28,800	0.650	18,720.00		
Year 6	31,500	0.596	18,774.00		
Year 7	34,200	0.547	18,707.40	5.033	37,091.28
			186,680.40		

Management should acquire the 'Sante-Fe' since it has a lower annual equivalent cost than the 'Oregon'.

Question 2: ATZ plc

(a) **Discount over life of machine**

EXE – 12 years.

Item	*Year*	*Cash*	*DF*	*PV*
		£		£
Purchase	0	19,000	1.000	19,000
Overhaul	8	4,000	0.467	1,868
Trade-in	12	(3,000)	0.319	(957)
Annual repair	1–12	2,000	6.814	13,628
				33,539

Divide by annuity factor (12 years, 10%) to obtain annualised equivalent.

Annualised equivalent = £33,539/6.814 = £4,922.

WYE – 6 years

Item	*Year*	*Cash* £	*DF*	*PV* £
Purchase	0	13,000	1.000	13,000
Overhaul	4	2,000	0.683	1,366
Trade-in	6	(3,000)	0.564	(1,692)
Annual repair	1–6	2,600	4.355	11,323
				23,997

Annualised equivalent = £23,997/4.355 = £5,510.

The company should purchase the Exe machine as it has the lowest annualised equivalent cost.

Assumptions:

- cash flows occur at the year end
- the cash flow estimates for each machine have the same level of accuracy
- inflation has been ignored
- both machines have the same level of reliability and both perform to at least the standards required for the job.

(b) The method used in part (a) to compare two machines with unequal lives is to use the annualised equivalent method.

The steps are:

- determine the net present value taking into account all the relevant cash flows over the lifetime of the machines
- divide each net present value by the annuity factor based on the cost of capital and the expected lifetime of the machine; this gives the annualised equivalent
- select the machine with the lowest annualised cost.

Index

KAPLAN PUBLISHING
FOULKS LYNCH

STUDY TEXT REVIEW FORM
Paper P2

Thank you for choosing a Kaplan Publishing Foulks Lynch CIMA Study Text. As we are constantly striving to improve our products, we would be grateful if you could provide us with feedback about how useful you found this Study Text.

Name: ....

Address: ....

....

Email: ....

Why did you decide to purchase this Study Text?

Have used them in the past	☐
Recommended by lecturer	☐
Recommended by friend	☐
Saw advertising	☐
Other (please specify)	☐

Which other Kaplan Publishing Foulks Lynch products have you used?

Exam Kit	☐
Distance Learning Course	☐
Pocket Notes	☐

How do you study?

At a college	☐
On a distance learning course	☐
Home study	☐
Other	☐

Please specify...

Overall opinion of this Study Text

	Excellent	*Adequate*	*Poor*
Introductory pages	☐	☐	☐
Syllabus coverage	☐	☐	☐
Clarity of explanations	☐	☐	☐
Clarity of definitions and key points	☐	☐	☐
Diagrams	☐	☐	☐
Practice/exam-type questions	☐	☐	☐
Self-test questions	☐	☐	☐
Layout	☐	☐	☐
Index	☐	☐	☐

If you have further comments/suggestions or have spotted any errors, please write them on the next page.

Please return this form to: Mirjana Jeremic, Editor, Freepost RRAT-HLYC-5KXA, FTC Foulks Lynch, Unit 2 The Business Centre, Molly Millars Lane, Wokingham, RG41 2QZ

Other comments/suggestions and errors

KAPLAN PUBLISHING
FOULKS LYNCH

CIMA Publications
Student Order Form

Please send your completed order form by post to:
Leeds NDL, West Gate, 6 Grace Street, Leeds LS1 2RP
Tel (UK): 0845 678 0022
Tel (International): + 44 (0) 113 200 6360
Fax: +44 (0) 113 243 0133
Order online: www.kaplanfoulkslynch.com
Email: cimaflexiblelearning@ftckaplan.com

Examination date: Nov 06 ☐		Study Text £28.00 each	Exam Kits £15.00 each	Pocket Notes £10.00 each	Practice 4 Success CDs 100Qs £10.00 300Qs £25.00		Course in a Box (Text, Kit, P/Notes, Tests, CD, Folder) £150.00 each	Total Value
		Quantity	Quantity	Quantity	100Q	300Q	Quantity	
Professional level								
Paper P1	Management Accounting Performance Evaluation	☐	☐	☐	☐	☐	☐	
Paper P2	Management Accounting Decision Making	☐	☐	☐	☐	☐	☐	
Paper P3	Management Accounting Risk and Control Strategy	☐	☐	☐	-	-	☐	
Paper P4	Organisational Management & Information Systems	☐	☐	☐	☐	☐	☐	
Paper P5	Integrated Management	☐	☐	☐	☐	☐	☐	
Paper P6	Management Accounting Business Strategy	☐	☐	☐	-	-	☐	
Paper P7	Financial Accounting and Tax Principles	☐	☐	☐	☐	☐	☐	
Paper P8	Financial Analysis	☐	☐	☐	☐	☐	☐	
Paper P9	Management Accounting Financial Strategy	☐	☐	☐	-	-	☐	
TOPCIMA								
Test of Professional Competence in Management Accounting Study Text		£28.00 ☐		The Knowledge			£28.00 ☐	

SUB TOTAL	**£**
PLUS DELIVERY CHARGE (see chart below)	**£**
TOTAL	**£**

Cardholder Details

Name on card: ………………………………………………………………

Address:

………………………………………………………………

………………………………………………………………

………………………………………………………………

Telephone:

………………………………………………………………

Delivery address (if different from above – a signature will be required)

Name:

………………………………………………………………

Address:

………………………………………………………………

………………………………………………………………

………………………………………………………………

Telephone: ………………………………………………………………

Payment

1 I enclose Cheque/Postal Order/Bankers Draft for £……………………………

Please make cheques payable to '**Kaplan Publishing Foulks Lynch**'.

2 Charge MasterCard/Visa/Switch/Delta no:

Valid from:　　　　Expiry date:

Issue no: (Switch only)　　　　Security Code:

Signature: ……………………………… Date: ……………………

POSTAGE	**Text Books**	**Pocket Notes**	**Course in a Box**
UK	£5 for one book + £2 for each extra	£2 for one book + £1 for each extra	£6 for one package + £4 for each extra
Europe	£7 for one book + £4 for each extra	£3 for one book + £2 for each extra	£12 for one package + £8 for each extra
Rest of World	£22 for one book + £8 for each extra	£8 for one book + £5 for each extra	£30 for one package + £20 for each extra

Please note that all prices on this form are subject to change.

KAPLAN PUBLISHING
FOULKS LYNCH

CIMA Publications

College & Bookshop Order Form

Please send your completed order form by post to:
Kaplan Publishing Foulks Lynch,
Unit 2 The Business Centre,
Molly Millars Lane, Wokingham RG41 2QZ
or by fax to 0118 979 7455

For all queries relating to this order please call 0118 912 3000 or e-mail info@kaplanfoulkslynch.com

ACCOUNT: ____________________

Examination Date: Nov 06 ☐

		Study Text £28.00 each	Exam Kits £15.00 each	Pocket Notes £10.00 each	Practice 4 Success CDs 100Qs £10.00 300Qs £25.00		Course in a Box (Text, Kit, P/Notes, Study Notes, Tests, CD, Folder) £150.00 each	Total Value
Certificate (Current syllabus only)		Quantity	Quantity	Quantity	100Q	300Q	Quantity	
Paper C1	Management Accounting Fundamentals	☐	☐	☐	☐	☐	☐	
Paper C2	Financial Accounting Fundamentals	☐	☐	☐	☐	☐	☐	
Paper C3	Business Mathematics	☐	☐	☐	☐	☐	☐	
Paper C4	Economics for Business	☐	☐	☐	☐	☐	☐	
Paper C5	Business Law	☐	☐	☐	☐	☐	☐	
Professional								
Paper P1	Management Accounting Performance Evaluation	☐	☐	☐	☐	☐	☐	
Paper P2	Management Accounting Decision Making	☐	☐	☐	☐	☐	☐	
Paper P3	Management Accounting Risk and Control Strategy	☐	☐	☐	-	-	☐	
Paper P4	Organisational Management & Information Systems	☐	☐	☐	☐	☐	☐	
Paper P5	Integrated Management	☐	☐	☐	☐	☐	☐	
Paper P6	Management Accounting Business Strategy	☐	☐	☐	-	-	☐	
Paper P7	Financial Accounting and Tax Principles	☐	☐	☐	☐	☐	☐	
Paper P8	Financial Analysis	☐	☐	☐	☐	☐	☐	
Paper P9	Management Accounting Financial Strategy	☐	☐	☐	-	-	☐	

TOPCIMA

Test of Professional Competence in Management Accounting Study Text	£28.00 ☐	The Knowledge	£28.00 ☐	

SUB TOTAL	£
LESS ________% DISCOUNT	£
TOTAL	£

Account details

Contact name: ....

Address: ....

....

....

Telephone: ....

Delivery address (if different to above)

Name: ....

Address: ....

....

....

....

Telephone: ....

Payment

1 Please invoice account ....

under Purchase Order Reference ....

2 I enclose Cheque/Postal Order/Bankers Draft for £..................................

(Please make cheques payable to '**Kaplan Publishing Foulks Lynch**')

3 Charge MasterCard/Visa/Switch/Delta no:

| | | | | | | | | | | | | | | | |

Valid from: | | | | | Expiry date: | | | | |

Issue no: (Switch only) ☐ Security Code: ☐

Signature: .... Date: ....

Please note that all prices on this order form are subject to change